Professor Charles H Gimingham, Muir of Dinnet, Aberdeenshire, August 1993 (D B A Thompson)

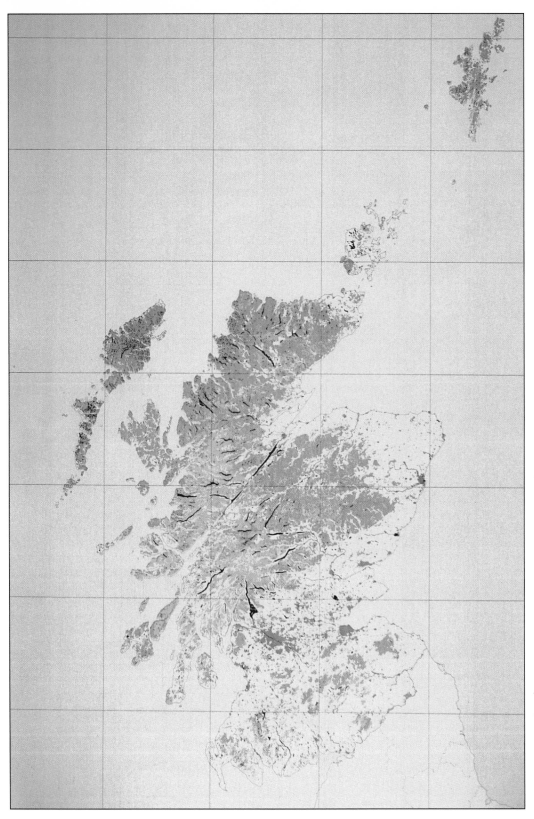

Land cover map of Scotland showing dominant/predominant heather moorland ▓ ,
and moors and heaths where heather is present but not dominant ░ . *Also shown are
water* ■ *and built land* ▒ . *Copyright: Macaulay Land Use Research Institute
(MLURI), The Scottish Office, and Scottish Natural Heritage (SNH).*

HEATHS AND MOORLAND: CULTURAL LANDSCAPES

Edited by
D. B. A. THOMPSON, ALISON J. HESTER and
MICHAEL B. USHER

With a Foreword by
Magnus Magnusson

SCOTTISH
NATURAL
HERITAGE

EDINBURGH: HMSO

Cover photography by D.A. Ratcliffe and D.B.A. Thompson
ISBN 0 11 495180 2

PREFACE

The Research and Advisory Services Directorate of Scottish Natural Heritage (SNH) held its second annual conference in Aberdeen during 25–27 August 1993. The theme 'Heaths and Moorland: Cultural Landscapes' was chosen to commemorate the 70th birthday of Professor Charles H. Gimingham, whose lifelong research in this subject has provided a wealth of valuable insights into the importance, processes and dynamics of heathland ecosystems.

Moorland management has played a major role in shaping the vegetation of the Scottish uplands over the past 300 years. In the north-east of Scotland, where Charles and his students have carried out most of their research, some of the largest expanses of heather-dominated moorland are found. To set the scene for the conference, delegates spent the first day in an area of heath — The Muir of Dinnet — with Charles and some 60 others exploring a wealth of issues, not least the intricacies of the heather cycle and the pros and cons of woodland colonisation. We had spectacular displays of new methods for controlling fires; we should like to thank Jim Parkin and colleagues of SNHs NE Region for their kind hospitality on this National Nature Reserve.

This book is divided into three parts, with the majority of papers about heaths and moorland in Scotland. The first covers the upland heath and moorland resource with a collection of papers on both the drier eastern heath vegetation and the wetter heath and blanket bog habitats generally found in the north and west. Temporal changes in distribution and extent of these different communities are described, together with detailed resumés of climatic factors, associated bird and invertebrate populations, and a broader examination of people's perceptions of moorland.

The second part examines the inherent dynamic processes in moorland, with papers exploring both temporal and spatial scales of change from tens of thousands of years through to annual and seasonal changes — at the plant or animal, patch or community, and landscape scales. The naturally dynamic nature of heaths and the fundamental effects of management are well illustrated, particularly in relation to grazing animals and management by fire. An exposition of the problems facing heather moorland on the European continent provides an enlightening comparison with our own situation in Great Britain. Questions are tackled regarding why the landscape has changed, and the contrasting effects of people and herbivores on this.

Management for the future forms the third part. Here the book examines the effects of management for grouse and red deer, together with wider issues such as peat extraction, protection and change through legislation, the potential effects of such protection on public perceptions, and valuations of heaths and moorland.

The Finale reflects on the main messages of the conference, and exhorts us all to cast our eyes westwards and northwards to the 'wet' heaths that we still know so little about. Here, there are questions about the key issues affecting these landscapes, and what can be gained from our experiences in the drier east of Scotland.

We are grateful to all 70 contributors to this book and to the many anonymous referees who generously gave their time in providing thorough, critical reviews of all the manuscripts presented. We should like to thank all those who helped to plan and run the conference. In particular we thank Marianne Robson for her unflappable support in guiding the organisation of the conference, Marc Duncan for his deskwork in Aberdeen, and our other steering committee members (Dr Bob Aitken, Dr Colin Legg, Mike Matthew, Professor John Miles and Dr Sarah Woodin) for their sage advice and enthusiasm. The University of Aberdeen was a splendid host, and we thank their conference staff for willing assistance. The Lord Provost of Aberdeen generously accorded us a Civic Reception — greatly appreciated by 200 plus participants. Special mention is made of Patrick Gordon-Duff-Pennington (Chairman of the Red Deer Commission), David Laird (Chairman of NE Region, SNH) and Sir John Lister-Kaye (Chairman of NW Region, SNH) — for providing valuable talks, parts of which feature in the Finale rather than as chapters in this book, and for adding spice to a wonderfully enjoyable conference. The staff of HMSO are thanked for their every care and meticulous attention to detail.

Finally, of course, last honours go to Charles Gimingham — who rose to the occasion with characteristic humility and grace.

Alison J. Hester
Des Thompson
Michael B. Usher

CONTENTS

LIST OF CONTRIBUTORS

D S Allen, ADAS Woodthorne, Wergs Road, Wolverhampton, West Midlands WV6 8TQ

H M Armstrong, Scottish Natural Heritage, Research and Advisory Services Directorate, 2 Anderson Place, Edinburgh EH6 5NP

I P Bainbridge, The Royal Society for the Protection of Birds, 17 Regent Terrace, Edinburgh EH7 5BN

R Balharry, Scottish Natural Heritage, Achantoul, Aviemore, Inverness-shire PH22 1QD

R Bardgett, Institute of Grassland and Environmental Research, Plas Gogerddan, Aberystwyth, Dyfed SY23 3EB

L J Bauer, Department of Biological Sciences, University of Durham, Science Laboratories, South Road, Durham DH1 3LE

H J B Birks, Botanical Institute, University of Bergen, Allégaten 41, N-5007 Bergen, Norway

A F Brown, English Nature, Northminster House, Peterborough PE1 1UA

C Bullock, The Macaulay Land Use Research Institute, Craigiebuckler, Aberdeen AB9 2QJ

J E L Butterfield, Department of Biological Sciences, University of Durham, Science Laboratories, South Road, Durham DH1 3LE

A Cameron, Department of Applied Plant Science, Queen's University, Newforge Lane, Belfast BT9 5PX

J C Coulson, Department of Biological Sciences, University of Durham, Science Laboratories, South Road, Durham DH1 3LE

A M Coupar, Scottish Natural Heritage, Main Street, Golspie, Sutherland KW10 6TG

L Cranna, Scottish Natural Heritage, Bridge Road, Portree, Isle of Skye IV51 9ER

G Cumming, Scottish Natural Heritage, Main Street, Golspie, Sutherland KW10 6TG

I Downie, Department of Biological Sciences, University of Durham, Science Laboratories, South Road, Durham DH1 3LE

K J Edwards, Department of Archaeology and Prehistory, The University of Sheffield, Sheffield S10 2TN

C H Gimingham, Department of Plant and Soil Science, Cruickshank Building, University of Aberdeen, St Machar Drive, Aberdeen AB9 2UD

C A Hegarty, Department of Applied Plant Science, Queen's University, Newforge Lane, Belfast BT9 5PX

D J Henderson, The Macaulay Land Use Research Institute, Craigiebuckler, Aberdeen AB9 2QJ

A J Hester, The Macaulay Land Use Research Institute, Craigiebuckler, Aberdeen AB9 2QJ

K R Hirons, School of Geography, The University of Birmingham, Edgbaston, Birmingham B15 2TT

J E Hossell, Environmental Change Unit, University of Oxford, 1a Mansfield Road, Oxford OX1 3TB

D C Howard, Institute of Terrestrial Ecology, Merlewood Research Station, Grange-over-Sands, Cumbria LA11 6JU

P J Hudson, The Game Conservancy Trust, Crubenmore Lodge, Newtonmore, Inverness-shire PH20 1BE

T H Keatinge, Scottish Natural Heritage, Main Street, Golspie, Sutherland KW10 6TG

A H Kirkpatrick, Department of Environmental Science, University of Stirling, Stirling FK9 4LA

S J Langan, The Macaulay Land Use Research Institute, Craigiebuckler, Aberdeen AB9 2QJ

C Legg, Institute of Ecology and Resource Management, The University of Edinburgh, Darwin Building, Mayfield Road, Edinburgh EH9 3JU

A Lily, The Macaulay Land Use Research Institute, Craigiebuckler, Aberdeen AB9 2QJ

A S MacDonald, Scottish Natural Heritage, Research and Advisory Services Directorate, 2 Anderson Place, Edinburgh EH6 5NP

J W Mackay, Scottish Natural Heritage, Research and Advisory Services Directorate, 2 Anderson Place, Edinburgh EH6 5NP

E C Mackey, Scottish Natural Heritage, Research and Advisory Services Directorate, 2 Anderson Place, Edinburgh EH6 5NP

A S MacLennan, Scottish Natural Heritage, South East Region HQ, Battleby, Redgorton, Perth PH1 3EW

S Madden, The Macaulay Land Use Research Institute, Craigiebuckler, Aberdeen AB9 2QJ

M Magnusson, Scottish Natural Heritage, 12 Hope Terrace, Edinburgh EH9 2AS

R H Marrs, Ness Botanic Gardens, University of Liverpool, Environmental and Horticultural Research Station, Ness, Neston, South Wirral L64 4AY

J H Marsden, English Nature, Three Counties Team, Masefield House, Wells Road, Malvern Wells, Worcs WR14 4PA

E M Matthew, Scottish Natural Heritage, North East Region HQ, Wynne Edwards House, 17 Rubislaw Terrace, Aberdeen AB1 1XE

J H McAdam, Agricultural Botany Research Division, Department of Agriculture for Northern Ireland, Newforge Lane, Belfast BT9 5PX

J McConnell, Institute of Ecology and Resource Management, The University of Edinburgh, Darwin Building, Mayfield Road, Edinburgh EH9 3JU

D M McFerran, Department of Applied Plant Science, The Queen's University of Belfast, Newforge Lane, Belfast BT9 5PX

B G Merrell, ADAS Rochester, Otterburn, Northumberland NE19 1SB

J Miles, The Scottish Office, Central Research Unit, New St Andrew's House, Edinburgh EH1 3TG

G R Miller, Gilbank, Schoolhill, Banchory, Kincardineshire AB31 3TP

J A Milne, The Macaulay Land Use Research Institute, Craigiebuckler, Aberdeen AB9 2QJ

W I Montgomery, School of Biology and Biochemistry, The Queen's University of Belfast, Belfast BT9 7BL

F P Mulholland, Agricultural Botany Research Division, Department of Agriculture for Northern Ireland, Newforge Lane, Belfast BT9 5PX

R B Ninnes, 3 Littleton of Airlie, Kirriemuir, Angus DD8 5NS

A J Nolan, The Macaulay Land Use Research Institute, Craigiebuckler, Aberdeen AB9 2QJ

R J Pakeman, Institute of Terrestrial Ecology, Monks Wood, Abbots Ripton, Huntingdon PE17 2LS

J Phillips, The Glebe House, Kippen, Stirlingshire FK8 3DY

E Reid, Scottish Natural Heritage, Research and Advisory Services, 2 Anderson Place, Edinburgh EH6 5NP

A N Rhodes, Department of Geography, University of Newcastle, Newcastle-upon-Tyne NE1 7RU; now at Department of Geography, University of Sheffield, Winter Street, Sheffield S10 2TN

L Scott, Department of Environmental Science, University of Stirling, Stirling FK9 4LA

J T de Smidt, University of Utrecht, Department of Environmental Studies, Faculty of Geographical Sciences, Heidelberglaan 2, PO Box 80.115, 3509 TC Utrecht, The Netherlands

B F L Smith, The Macaulay Land Use Research Institute, Craigiebuckler, Aberdeen AB9 2QJ

C Smith, 7 Malton Way, Clifton, York YO3 6SG

B W Staines, Institute of Terrestrial Ecology, Banchory Research Station, Hill of Brathens, Glassel, Banchory, Kincardineshire AB31 4BY

A C Stevenson, Department of Geography, Daysh Building, University of Newcastle, Newcastle-upon-Tyne NE1 7RU

M J Still, The Macaulay Land Use Research Institute, Craigiebuckler, Aberdeen AB9 2QJ

R A Stillman, Joint Nature Conservation Committee, Monkstone House, City Road, Peterborough PE1 1JY; now at Institute of Terrestrial Ecology, Furzebrook Research Station, Wareham, Dorset BH20 5AS

D B A Thompson, Scottish Natural Heritage, Research and Advisory Services Directorate, 2 Anderson Place, Edinburgh EH6 5NP

P A Todd, Department of Applied Plant Science, The Queen's University of Belfast, Newforge Lane, Belfast BT9 5PX

G Tudor, Scottish Natural Heritage, Research and Advisory Services Directorate, 2 Anderson Place, Edinburgh EH6 5NP

M B Usher, Scottish Natural Heritage, Research and Advisory Services Directorate, 2 Anderson Place, Edinburgh EH6 5NP

S D Ward, Scottish Natural Heritage, Research and Advisory Services Directorate, 2 Anderson Place, Edinburgh EH6 5NP

A Watson, c/o Institute of Terrestrial Ecology, Banchory Research Station, Hill of Brathens, Glassel, Banchory, Kincardineshire AB31 4BY

D Welch, Institute of Terrestrial Ecology, Banchory Research Station, Hill of Brathens, Glassel, Banchory, Kincardineshire AB31 4BY

G Whittington, School of Geography and Geology, University of St Andrews, St Andrews, Fife KY16 9ST

FOREWORD

On behalf of Scottish Natural Heritage, it is my privilege to write this Foreword to *Heaths and Moorland: Cultural Landscapes*. It is also a great personal pleasure because the conference in Aberdeen in 1993, on which this book is based, was dedicated to honouring the life's work of a living legend, Professor Charles Gimingham. Aberdeen is his university; the north east of Scotland is his region (he is a member of the North East Regional Board of Scottish Natural Heritage); and heathland is his domain. So there could be no more appropriate venue for gathering than Aberdeen, where the ancient university has been responsible for pioneer research on heaths and moorland and where, just to the west, some world-famous examples of heather moorland at its best can be found. Scotland, indeed, is an enormously important bastion of surviving heathland in Europe, yet there are significant threats which have to be addressed.

This book stems from the second of the major annual conferences organized under the auspices of the Research and Advisory Services Directorate (RASD) of Scottish Natural Heritage (SNH). In the previous year we met in Inverness to have discourse on 'The Islands of Scotland — Our Marine Heritage' (Baxter and Usher, 1994). In 1993 we were on *terra firma* to discuss the national and international importance of moorland habitats, their changing dynamic ways, their value as 'cultural landscapes' (to use that very 'in' but still rather enigmatic concept), and to think about how best this land should be managed for the future.

There was a rich and varied menu of papers concocted in the kitchens of bodies such as SNH, Institute of Terrestrial Ecology, Macaulay Land Use Research Institute, Red Deer Commission, Game Conservancy Trust, Royal Society for Protection of Birds, and others. They provided a stimulating bill of fare as we sought to give shape and purpose to the future of these unique areas of wild land and beauty.

The beauty of wild land is very much in the eye of the beholder. To a jaundiced observer like David Burt, a Hanoverian officer in General Wade's entourage in the aftermath of the 1715 Rising, the magic of moorland was not apparent. He referred to the

> 'gloomy spaces, different rocks, heath and high and low. To cast one's eye from an eminence toward a group of them, they appear still one above another, fainter and fainter, according to the aerial perspective, and the whole of a dismal gloomy brown, drawing upon a dirty purple, and most of all disagreeable when the heath is in bloom.'

Nor was Daniel Defoe all that much more flattering in his *Tour through the Whole Island of Great Britain* at about the same time: he concluded that heath or heather was the common product of a barren land: 'a foil to the beauty of the rest of England!' Fifty years later, that other quintessential Englishman, Dr Johnson, in his *Journey to the Western Islands of Scotland*, referred to the chaos of the hills as 'matter incapable of form or usefulness: dismissed by nature from her care … quickened only with one sullen power of useless vegetation.'

Within 100 years, however, this 'one sullen power of useless vegetation' had become a source of very useful pleasure to other beholders, as the Victorians applied their single-minded entrepreneurial drive to Scotland's moorlands and began to manage them specifically for the raising and cropping of red grouse — and only red grouse. Early man in Scotland had reduced the original woodland cover by slash and burn; the Victorians only burned — and through controlled burning they transformed chaos into quiltwork, and moorland into mosaic.

Today what was to the Victorians merely a method of practical management to indulge their sporting proclivities is being held up, in some quarters, as the ideal natural heritage for large swathes of Scotland. I know, however, that some people feel a little uncomfortable about exalting such artificial landscapes as proud parts of our natural heritage — especially when we remember the ruthless destruction of other bird species, especially raptors, which was involved in Victorian times. There is, no doubt unworthily, a suspicion abroad that scientists and land managers alike are now conjoined in an unholy alliance to justify the importance of an elite habitat whose method of management emerged less than two centuries ago.

Let me first clarify the parameters of definition within which we are working. Definitions of heath and moorland are commendably loose. Below 250–300 m, land with at least 10 % cover of heather is *lowland* heath. Above this, all areas with prevalent dwarf shrubs are *upland* heaths or moorland, and these tend to coincide with where there is more than 1 m of rainfall in the year, and where the soil is acidic but peat is shallow.

There are two main communities of upland heaths in Great Britain: classic heather moor dominated by ling (*Calluna vulgaris*) found in the more continental parts of Britain, and heather-dominated blanket bog so prevalent in the west and north. The habitat as a whole is found mainly in the UK and Ireland, and only locally along the western seaboard of other north west European countries. In Scotland, 16 % of the land is dominated by heather and 38 % (3 million hectares) has heather present. Clearly, in the chapters of this book we are covering a huge resource.

Our two chief heathland experts in SNH, Michael B. Usher and Des Thompson, have published a paper in *Biological Conservation* (1993) telling us that no less than 15 % of British ground beetle species and 20 % of British spider species are found on the North York Moors, for instance. They attribute this to the myriad of small and large habitat types shaped by burning and grazing and the four-stage development cycle of heather. The authors also show in graphic detail how a broader goal of management for scrub *and* moorland can benefit many more elements of nature.

Des and Michael, and Alison Hester of the Macaulay Land Use Research Institute, and the other researchers and practitioners involved with heather, clearly think that they are on to a particularly good thing, apparently because in Scotland we have open heather communities with *edges*: some rugged, some smooth; some tall, some stunted; some wet, some drier; some on slopes and some on flatter ground. We have heather and other plants varying according to when the torch was last lit, and according to when sheep and deer last grazed, and responding to climate and soils. What we have is a broad array of habitats and microcosms, yielding a gratifying diversity of invertebrates and birds.

Admittedly, the diversity of flowering plants may be actually rather poor, and the overall diversity of wildlife could, possibly, be a lot richer. This surely is our challenge; not to deny the past, but to build for the future. We must try to improve the biodiversity of our heaths, we must encourage scrub and woodland to flourish in some parts, especially where remnants are still present.

Without grouse-moor managers, most of our 'better' moorland areas would perish. Heather — and the very heaths and moors which we now so cherish — would peter away. But we can no longer think in terms of single-issue management. Unless we work towards a goal of managing the hill for red grouse *and* for raptors and waders and other birds *and* for sheep and red deer *and* for the people who eke out a living on the land *and* for the delight of country-lovers all over the world, rather than exclusively for red grouse, grouse moor management will become a dwindlingly attractive course. We need only look at the disastrous start to the 1993 season to recognize what a poor basis red grouse management alone is for sustainability in the management of our natural heritage.

This, I feel, is where 'science' has a huge role to play in its primary meaning of 'knowledge'. Everywhere one can see subtle or dramatic illustrations of man's suppressive impact on the landscape. Where there is little grazing from sheep or red deer, heather seems to thrive; where there is too much, the landscape looks thoroughly beaten. But what really is the state of our moorlands today?

Man's impacts on moorland were put into figures recently in a scientific paper by staff of SNH, English Nature and the Support Unit of the Joint Nature Conservation Committee (Thompson *et al.*, 1995). The paper shows that in England and Wales, since the 1940s, 20 % of what was then upland heather moorland has changed to grassland, bracken or forestry. More starkly, 70 % of what is left is considered to be at risk of change, with at least half of the cover liable to further decline and deterioration under present densities of grazing sheep.

But what of Scotland? In Scotland, we have been garnering statistics on the condition of heaths and moorlands. Obviously, before we go forward we must know as much as possible about the base from which we are launching. In what way has it changed — and is it changing for the worse or for the better? What criteria are we using to make such value-judgements? How does it all fit in to the changing dynamic of our natural heritage?

These were all issues which we had to address in the Cairngorms Working Party. After a series of quite brilliant presentations to us by Michael B. Usher and other members of SNH, when we were initiated into the mysteries of ecotones and other esoteric concepts, we came to the conclusion in 1993 in our final report, *Common Sense and Sustainability: A Partnership for the Cairngorms*, that heather moorland *is*, indeed, uniquely sustainable. We were persuaded that, at least in parts of the central and eastern Highlands, a cycle of good burning practice can maintain a great variety of moorland habitats, and that there need be no conflict between conserving our best moorland areas and the concomitant desire to encourage the regeneration of native Caledonian forests in other areas. Furthermore, it seems that in these moorland areas there has been no net outpouring of nutrients — which seems remarkable, given the acidifying influence on the soils of heather compared with, say, birchwood.

In the western Highlands and Islands I see a different picture. I see lochs with islands abundant with scrub and even some woodland. I see crags with vestiges of former widespread glories. I even see the occasional massive boulder bearing better habitat than the surrounding heavily managed hill! But too little is known about the long-term nature of habitat change or, indeed, about the impacts of sheep, deer and burning on habitats. The conclusion seems inevitable that in the western Highlands and Islands we have upland wet heaths which are not being managed sustainably, and where both the biological and the social fabric of the place are perishing. Is that right? It seems that here in particular we have an urgent need for research, looking both at what was present in the past and what can be sustained into the future through a variety of land-use practices.

I am sure that I do not have to remind readers of the close etymological kinship between the words 'ecology' and 'economics', both derived from the Greek word *oikos* meaning 'house' or 'home' and both embodying the concept of prudent housekeeping of our natural heritage. We have here a wonderful opportunity for bridging the gaps between research and pragmatic management skills on the one hand, and on the other the reasonable need to help the natural heritage to pay for its own keep.

It will not be an easy equation to work out. There are so many imponderables, so many variables, so many different types and sorts and kinds of things to take into account, so many definitions, even. The questions are legion. If some of the answers are out there already, it is surely a task of a book such as this to pull them together and synthesise them. If they are not out there, then we need to take stock of what we do and do not know, what we need to know and how best to find that out.

And who better to start us on that road than the man whom we honoured at the second RASD conference, the man who has already provided a veritable treasury of answers. In Charles Gimingham we have a wonderful embodiment of scholarship and care for the countryside. As a member in his time of both the Nature Conservancy Council (NCC) and the Countryside Commission for Scotland (CCS), he straddled the difficult divide between nature conservation and countryside enjoyment which ended with merger into Scottish Natural Heritage.

He has held academic posts at Aberdeen University since 1945; he has had scores of research students, research assistants and research fellows who can all bear witness to his humanity, wisdom and erudition. He has published two classic textbooks: *Ecology of Heathlands* (1972), followed by *Introduction to Heathland Ecology* (1975). He has just written *The Lowland Heathland Management Handbook*, published by English Nature. Charles Gimingham is now 70 years old. It gave me pleasure to welcome him to the conference in Aberdeen, and it gives me pleasure to pen this Foreword to a book which uniquely celebrates his life's work.

Magnus Magnusson
Chairman, Scottish Natural Heritage

References

Baxter, J. M. and Usher, M. B. (editors) (1994). *The Islands of Scotland: a Living Marine Heritage*. HMSO, Edinburgh.

Thompson, D. B. A., MacDonald, A.J., Marsden, J. H. and Galbraith, C. A. (1995). Upland heather moorland in Great Britain: a review of international importance, vegetation change and some objectives for nature conservation. *Biological Conservation*, **71**, in press

Usher, M. B. and Thompson, D. B. A. (1993). Variation in the upland heathlands of Great Britain: conservation importance. *Biological Conservation*, **66**, 69–81.

PART ONE
HEATHS AND MOORLAND: THE RESOURCE

PART ONE

HEATHS AND MOORLAND: THE RESOURCE

The words 'heath' and 'moor' tend to be used interchangeably, though there is a tendency to use 'heaths' for drier areas and 'moors' where it is wetter. Moorland is used as the umbrella biome. The term 'heath' is applied to a variety of British habitats, ranging from the species-rich grasslands of the English Breckland and the open serpentine grasslands on Fetlar in Shetland, to a variety of heather-dominated communities stretching from Cornwall in the south (where characteristic species may include *Ulex gallii, Erica vagans* and *Agrostis curtisii*), through most of Wales, Northern England and the Scottish uplands, to the Northern Isles of Orkney and Shetland. In all of the northern heaths the heather or ling, *Calluna vulgaris*, is a characteristic plant. However, such are the peculiarities of the English language that many stretches of land classified as 'grouse moor' are in fact 'heaths', and even the majority of the North Yorks Moors National Park is, in fact, a heath!

The term 'moor' is perhaps more difficult to define. When one thinks of moorland there is an immediate picture of expanses of blanket bog juxtaposed with mountains and lochs or lochans of peaty water (cf. Pearsall, 1950). These are complex environments, with peaty soils, and plants such as *Erica tetralix, Juncus* spp. and *Sphagnum* spp. mixed with more scattered plants of *Calluna vulgaris*. It is perhaps preferable to term such habitats as mires (e.g. Rodwell, 1991), though the widespread use of the term 'moorland' will undoubtedly remain in common usage. The peat soil distinguishes them from the podsols and peaty podsols of the heather-dominated heaths. Perhaps the concise Scots Dictionary (Robinson, 1985) comes closest to an all embracing term for heaths and moorland – 'muir', defined as rough, uncultivated, unenclosed heathery land.

Series of heath and mire communities have been recognised in Britain by Rodwell (1991), whose classification of vegetation provides a basis for assessing the geographical spread and variation in British plant communities. However, alternative classifications exist; the CORINE system (Anon., 1991) is widely used on the continent of Europe. Using CORINE, two distinct heath and moorland communities can be recognised. The 'northern Atlantic wet heath with *Erica tetralix*' has a distinctly northern and western distribution (Fig. I.1), though it is scarce on the Northern Isles of Scotland but has an outlier in North Yorkshire, England. Superficially, the distribution of 'dry heath' is similarly predominantly northern and western (Fig. I.2). However, comparison of the two distributions shows dry heath to be more abundant in south-west England, more frequent in eastern Wales, far more widespread in northern England and the Scottish borders, and more

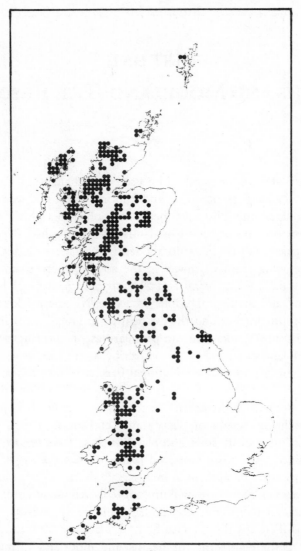

Figure I.1 The GB distribution of northern Atlantic wet heath with *Erica tetralix*. From Tidswell *et al.* (in press).

abundant in the eastern Scottish Highlands, whereas it is infrequent in the Western Isles of Scotland.

These two illustrations set the scene for what is considered to be the 'heaths and moorland' of the British uplands, the subject matter of this book. The heather plant, *Calluna vulgaris*, links these communities, providing a landscape feature and forming the basis of widespread rural economies. Part I therefore focuses on this plant and the other wild species associated with it. Gimingham explains the ecological processes associated with the development of *C. vulgaris*, demonstrating how management by burning maintains this species by preventing other species, usually trees, regenerating in the gaps in *Calluna* stands. The condition of the

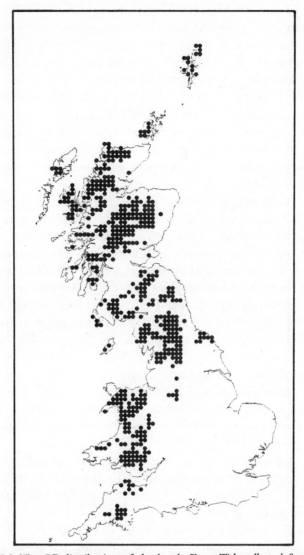

Figure I.2 The GB distribution of dry heath. From Tidswell *et al.* (in press).

C. vulgaris stands is assessed by Bardgett *et al.*, whose model can be used to predict the effects of changes in environmental variables. These ecological interactions provide the habitat for a variety of animals that only occur, or predominantly occur, on moorland.

However, the wetter communities are also widespread, especially in the far north of Scotland (Keatinge *et al.*). The Flow Country of Caithness and Sutherland is essentially an intricate mixture of blanket bog, dry heaths and intermediate communities. Taken as a snapshot, it is possible to estimate areas of all of these communities in Scotland. When two snapshots are taken at different times, it is possible to estimate changes, though it is more difficult to determine the reasons for the changes. Tudor and Mackey show that, over a period of approximately a quarter of a century – since the late 1940s – there was an 18 % reduction in the extent of heath and an 8 % reduction in the extent of bog. The two major land cover types that expanded as a result of these decreases were coniferous plantations and grasslands (both semi-improved and improved).

The invertebrate fauna of these communities can be extremely rich, and is frequently affected by altitude (Coulson *et al.*). It is perhaps an indication of the relative poverty of studies that many species of invertebrates collected are regarded as rare in a national context; will further collecting demonstrate that they have a wider distribution, or that there are indeed many rare species of heath and moorland environments?

One way of exploiting the pollen and nectar production of *C. vulgaris* is by honey bees; MacLennan describes the history of bee keeping in Scotland and the intricate interactions between native plants, rural management practices, one insect species and the resources available to the human communities. This link with human society is further explored by Mackay, who shows that the public appreciate moorland for its open and wild qualities. It is this blend of natural biological communities with their changing colour and texture that provides the fascination of the heathland environment; dark and forbidding in winter, green in spring as the young heather shoots comes through, and purple in summer when the heather is in flower.

This environment is the haunt of a native sub-species of bird, the red grouse *Lagopus lagopus scoticus* (Brown and Bainbridge). Large areas of moorland are managed to encourage this bird, a mainstay of the rural economy in the north and west. Without grouse moors, where the species is annually shot, there would almost certainly have been more change from heath and moorland to coniferous forest and 'improved' grassland. However, there is a delicate balance to be struck between this one species and the other species of birds characteristic of heaths and moorland. The mosaic and gradient structures of many heaths certainly favour a diversity of bird species (Stillman).

This is, then, the setting for the heath and moorland resource. It is widely distributed along the Atlantic coast of the British Isles, but especially widespread in Scotland. Management of grouse moor or deer forest, by regular burning and by grazing, encourages a landscape dominated by dwarf shrubs in which tree regeneration is either drastically reduced or eliminated. These are, therefore, landscapes often created by people for sporting interests, but nevertheless yielding crops of honey, bee's wax, meat from deer, sheep or grouse, and sources of inspiration due to the extensive views and ever-changing colours of heather.

The wildlife and economy of heaths and moorland are ultimately dependent on the well-being of the heather, one of Britain's keystone species (Kapoor-Vijay and Usher, 1993). Its cycle of growth creates the food for many animal species, whilst the patchy structure of its community provides the gaps for the regeneration of other plant species. It is unusual in being able to establish virtual monocultures on these nutrient-poor and acidic soils, but nevertheless it is able to establish huge seed banks which are very long lived, certainly longer than one rotation of a coniferous forest (Benitez-Badillo, 1993). It is this seed bank that might allow heather to be re-established on areas from which it has disappeared as a growing plant due to afforestation or agriculture.

This first section of the book, as indeed the whole of the book, is a tribute to one of the most fascinating species of the British flora – *Calluna vulgaris*, the heather or ling.

References

Anonymous (1991). *CORINE Biotopes.* European Communities, Brussels.

Benitez-Badillo, G. (1993). *The Moorland Seed Bank under Coniferous Forest Plantations on the North York Moors National Park.* M Phil. Thesis, University of York.

Kapoor-Vijay, P. and Usher M. B. (editors) (1993). *Identification of Key Species for Conservation and Socio-economic Development.* Commonwealth Secretariat, London.

Pearsall, W. H. (1950). *Mountains and Moorlands.* Collins, London.

Robinson, M. (editor-in-chief) (1985). *The Concise Scots Dictionary.* Aberdeen University Press, Aberdeen.

Rodwell, J. S. (editor) (1991). *British Plant Communities: Volume 2. Mires and Heaths.* Cambridge University Press, Cambridge.

Tidswell, R., Reid, J. B., Horsfield, D. and Thompson, D. B. A. (in press). The GB distribution of upland and peatland CORINE biotopes. Review Report. Scottish Natural Heritage, Battleby.

1 HEATHS AND MOORLAND: AN OVERVIEW OF ECOLOGICAL CHANGE

C. H. Gimingham

Summary

1. Heaths and moorland are 'cultural landscapes' in the sense that they have been derived, in large part, from former forest by human agency, though the flora and fauna have been established spontaneously.

2. Heather is generally a seral dominant, passing through the familiar set of growth-phases, with the eventual development of canopy gaps. Then further change may take one of three pathways:

    (a) colonization of gaps by shrubs or trees;

    (b) entry of other long-term dominants (e.g. bracken, *Deschampsia flexuosa*, *Molinia caerulea*);

    (c) temporary occupancy by other heathland species followed by return of heather, i.e. a 'cycle'.

3. The cycle occurs only where one of the other trends does not supervene. There is often a natural tendency for heather to be replaced as dominant by other species.

4. Good management keeps heather in the building phase but leads to progressive reduction of floristic diversity. Poor management, especially if it allows the heather to become over-mature, risks the entry of other dominants.

5. Management is essential, otherwise the loss of heather will continue. Traditional management successfully maintains extensive heaths and moors but nature conservation may be better served by a mosaic of stands of different age, structure and composition.

1.1 Introduction

Interest in heaths and moorland goes back to the earliest days of plant ecology in Scotland. In 1902, Smith, one of the first practising ecologists in Scotland, working at the University College of Dundee, wrote a review on 'The origins and development of heather moorland' (Smith, 1902). In this paper he made the case for considering 'that a large proportion of the heather moorland (below 2000 feet) in Scotland has been derived from ancient forest'. This process, he stated, would have been assisted by the removal of timber while 'other causes of conversion are the influence of man through sheep-grazing and drainage, and ... through the favouring of heather and its associates by the regular burning'. Thus, even before the advent of pollen analysis, there was a clear realization that most of our heaths and moors (other than those above the tree limit) are, in the words of our title, 'cultural landscapes'. This term is applied here rather more widely than by some authors, for example Westhoff *et al.*, (1970), who recognize three categories: natural or near-natural; semi-natural (in which the habitat is man-determined, but the flora and fauna are established spontaneously); and cultural (agricultural, afforested and other artificial landscapes). Here we extend the use of the word 'cultural' to include semi-natural systems. Some heaths, like the mossy *Calluna-Vaccinium* 'pine heaths' in the Scottish native pinewood areas, may be 'natural' in the sense that patches of this kind were probably always part of the original pinewood landscape, but even so their continued presence may be a result of human influences.

My own involvement with the ecology of heaths and moorland dates from 1946 when, on taking up a post in Aberdeen, I became quickly aware of the importance of these components of our landscapes in N.E. Scotland and the significance of heather, *Calluna vulgaris*, as the dominant species. It was also evident that heaths and moors here in the north had to be examined in the context of related types in western Europe, extending from southern Scandinavia through the Low Countries to northern Germany, northern and western France and northern Spain, as well as southern England, constituting a broad continuum of variation (Gimingham, 1961). These semi-natural landscapes clearly offered an excellent opportunity to investigate the ecological effects of human influence through the use and management of the vegetation.

There were two main objectives at the outset of my work: first, to investigate the autecology of *Calluna*, and second, to determine some of the ecological consequences of traditional management practices (particularly grazing and burning). It was my view that only in this way could the ecosystem be properly understood and current land uses evaluated, guidelines framed for good management and judgments made between various options for the future. In this opening chapter I shall both look back, selecting for comment some of the conclusions arising from a long series of studies and showing how they have come together in interpreting the processes at work in heaths and moors, and also look forward to the future, considering especially how these studies have led to changes in our outlook and attitudes on a number of issues. In so doing I shall draw heavily on the work of numerous former colleagues and students as well as researchers in many other centres. It is notable that this subject has attracted the attention of many able scientists and remains at the present time a vigorous field of enquiry of strong topical relevance. This is indicated by the interest shown in this conference and in a variety of recent seminars and meetings on heathland ecology, as well as the existence of a thriving European Heathland Workshop and several heathland management initiatives in this country.

During the progress of nearly 50 years of heathland ecology there has been one very major change in perception. At the beginning of this period it seemed that there was little threat to heaths and moors because they were widespread in Britain, but it is now realized that they are fast disappearing throughout the west European heath region, including southern England. While it remains the case that here in the north they are well represented, we are now only too well aware that this is the last region in which this applies, and even here there is evidence of decline. It is against this background of urgency that this paper will consider: (1) some basic research which has led to changes in the interpretation of vegetation dynamics in heaths and moors; (2) the implications of these changes for our approach to management; and (3) some ideas arising from this on the future of upland land uses and of heathland conservation in Scotland. These topics will be discussed in greater detail in later chapters.

1.2 Vegetation Dynamics in Undisturbed Heathland Stands

Watt first published his important ideas on the phased growth and development certain perennial plants, and applied them to the life-history of *Calluna*, in 1947 and 1955. In these works he established the now well-known sequence of phases:

Pioneer.   The colonizing phase, in which young plants may be associated with a variety of other species,

Building.   The phase of maximum growth, the merging of individuals and formation of a dense, even canopy; the most competitive and exclusive phase,

Mature.   The phase in which the canopy begins to become uneven and signs of gaps appear,

Degenerate.   The phase in which plants begin to die back from the centre, opening up obvious gaps.

This sequence (Fig.1.1.) may be observed where heather is undisturbed and is growing in broadly favourable habitats, though not under the special conditions of high altitude, wet, peaty substrata, or certain other environments. The rate of passage through the phases varies considerably according to habitat conditions, but may be completed in average environments in about 30 to 40 years.

Much of our early work in Aberdeen was concerned with analysing and developing knowledge about this concept of phased growth as it applied to *Calluna* (Barclay-Estrup 1970, 1971; Barclay-Estrup and Gimingham, 1969). It has proved, over the years, fundamental for understanding the growth and physiology of the heather plant and the associated changes in microclimate and soil conditions. It has

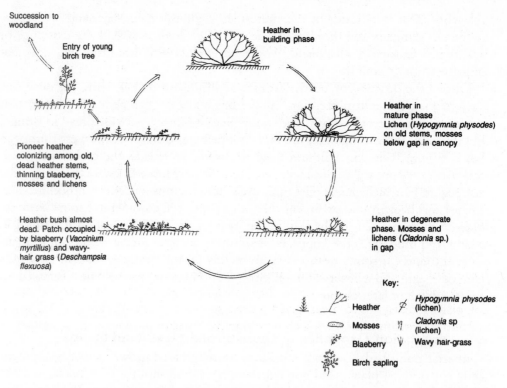

Figure 1.1. Diagram illustrating an example of cyclical change in a heath community, associated with the sequence of growth-phases in heather. Top left — the entry of birch initiates succession towards a woodland community. [Other possible colonists of the gap include bracken (Pteridium aquilinum), purple moor-grass (*Molinia caerulea*)]. From Gimingham (1975).

also proved invaluable in considering the utilization of heather and its responses to various management treatments.

However, Watt (1947, 1955) developed his theory beyond the level of describing a series of growth-phases. He was concerned to understand pattern in vegetation and, working in the rather dry continental conditions of the East Anglian Breckland, he found evidence for a cyclical process which involved the breakdown and dispersal of accumulated humus in the gaps formed in the centres of degenerate heather bushes, and the re-establishment of heather there. He interpreted pattern in the vegetation as created by the presence side-by-side of individuals of heather at all stages in this cycle. He was also familiar with heaths in the north-east of Scotland and suggested that a similar type of cycle would operate here, in which the gap would normally be occupied for a time by other species such as mosses, *Vaccinium* spp., *Empetrum nigrum* or *Arctostaphylos uva-ursi*. After some time the cover created by these plants would, in turn, open up to some extent and admit the re-entry of *Calluna* (Fig. 1.1), but in this case normally by vegetative lateral spread (layering) of stems from neighbouring bushes rather than by the establishment of seedlings.

It has now, however, become apparent that our early ideas on vegetation dynamics in heathland probably made too much of this concept of cycling and regarded it as more universal than it really is (Gimingham, 1988). A cycle implies a steady-state ecosystem, but it has become evident that there are very few heathland ecosystems which show signs of being in a steady state. This may be the case on peaty substrates at rather high altitudes, as for example at Moor House in the Pennines (Forrest, 1971) and perhaps in some rather dry areas of low nutrient status (especially on soils with low phosphorus adsorption capacity) where associated species are few and competition is slight. Elsewhere it seems that heaths, rather than being in a steady state, are potentially dynamic systems, open to various kinds of successional change. While evidence for cyclical changes can certainly be found in undisturbed stands, it seems unlikely that they would often continue indefinitely, and emphasis has shifted to examining other aspects of patch dynamics.

Many features of the biology and autecology of *Calluna* (Gimingham, 1960) indicate that it is essentially a seral, rather than climax, dominant, displaying many of the attributes of *r*-selected, rather than *k*-selected species. It is a relatively rapid colonist of newly bared areas, given a seed source and appropriate conditions of soil and microclimate; it has a high reproductive capacity, producing large quantities of very small, light seeds. Germination is normally spread out over an extended period, while ungerminated seeds stored in the upper layers of the soil may retain viability for many years creating a large seed bank (Mallik *et al.*, 1984; Hester *et al.*, 1991a). However, *Calluna* is perennial and evergreen, and in average habitats the individual has a longer life span than most r-selected species, although in normal circumstances this is limited to 30-40 years. The *Calluna* canopy is at its densest during the building phase and usually little seedling establishment can take place beneath it. But, in the natural undisturbed state, as the bushes become old and degenerate, gaps develop at their centres. The question then arises as to what happens in the gaps.

Colonization of the gaps may follow any one of several pathways, which may be divided into three catgories:

1. Where there is an input of seeds of trees or shrubs (e.g. *Betula* spp., *Pinus sylvestris*, *Quercus* spp., *Juniperus communis*), the gaps offer a regeneration niche (Fig. 1.1). In undisturbed uneven-aged stands of *Calluna* close to seed-parents of birch, our studies have demonstrated a correlation between establishment and survival of birch seedlings and the occurrence of canopy gaps in the stand, whereas invasion is effectively prevented by building phase *Calluna* (Gong, 1984). Observations indicate that this applies equally to pine and oak. In this way succession towards scrub and woodland may be initiated, with *Calluna* in time being shaded out (Hester *et al.*, 1991b).

2. Other possibilities for gap colonization include the entry of certain long-term occupants of the niche which may be able to establish from input of

seed or production of shoots from a rhizome or stolon. Examples include *Deschampsia flexuosa* on dry sites, *Molinia caerulea* in wetter areas, or bracken (*Pteridium aquilinum*) in freely drained situations. The tendency for bracken fronds to appear in gaps but to be excluded by building-phase *Calluna* was demonstrated by Watt in 1955. It is significant, however, that in all these species the competitive balance between them and *Calluna* is shifted in their favour where there is some nutrient enrichment or accumulation.

A community of several species of *Cladonia* lichens may also be a long-term occupant of gaps. There is some evidence (Hobbs, 1985) that such communities produce chemical inhibitors which contribute to the prevention of establishment of *Calluna* and some other species.

3. An additional possibility is that cyclical processes may occur in the gaps. This is a reality where one of the above successional events does not occur. If bare soil is exposed there is a chance that *Calluna* seedlings may establish but this is probably a rather rare occurrence, because other species are generally available to colonize the gaps more quickly. These include mosses, *Erica cinerea, Vaccinium* spp., *Empetrum nigrum, Arctostaphylos uva-ursi*, or certain grasses. Such species, however, are less effective than trees, shrubs, bracken, or the grasses mentioned above, as long-term occupants of the patch. In time their own canopy or turf may be inclined to open sufficiently for re-establishment of *Calluna*, in this case through the adventitious rooting of layered stems from adjacent individuals. (In a transect of 25 contiguous 0.25 m^2 quadrats in an uneven-aged *Calluna* stand at Dinnet Moor, Aberdeenshire, six contained clusters of shoots from layered stems, Scandrett and Gimingham 1989). Thus cycling may occur where other changes do not supervene, and when the various stages of the cycle occur in close proximity *Calluna* may appear to share dominance with another species (such as *Arctostaphylos uva-ursi* on Dinnet Moor, Aberdeenshire) because they are continually, though slowly, changing places as the cycles proceed. This process may continue until such time as the invasion pressure of potential long-term occupants of the patch builds up. However, not enough is known about the successional changes which may take place in heaths and moors if left to themselves without the intervention of any management.

Nonetheless, the conclusion is that, left to itself, *Calluna* may be expected always to give place, sooner or later, to other species. Where heathland survival is at stake it is dangerous to forget this. There is a tendency for some managers of heathland reserves, not observing any immediate signs of vegetational change, to feel that the heath will remain indefinitely and little need be done to maintain it. It is tempting to take this view in the wide treeless expanses of moorland in northern Britain where change, admittedly, is slow. Even here, however, there are almost always scattered trees of birch, pine or rowan (*Sorbus aucuparia*), possibly hidden in a ravine or hollow, producing seed which may in time find regeneration niches in gaps if the heather is allowed to become mature or degenerate.

The foregoing discussion has been concerned with small gaps created by the die-back of degenerate plants. However, larger gaps are quite common, caused by the simultaneous death of relatively old heather bushes over a sizable area. This may be a result, for example, of the effects of an abnormal drought in summer or, accompanied by frost, in late winter, or of an outbreak of heather beetle (*Lochmaea suturalis*) (Berdowski and Zeilinga, 1987) or even, as observed recently in Orkney and in the Cairngorms area, of winter moth (*Operophtera brumata*) or other lepidopteran larvae. Such large gaps cannot be re-colonized vegetatively by *Calluna* except at the edges, and we have shown that they are less favourable for seedling establishment than small ones (de Hullu and Gimingham 1984). They are therefore open to occupancy by other plants, as shown for example by Marrs (1986), in a resurvey of the Breckland sites where Watt first suggested that cyclical processes were at work. Often these have trended to scrub, woodland or bracken following die-back of *Calluna* over quite large areas. While young, building heather is generally less susceptible to the stress caused by these factors, they may be lethal to older plants whether or not they have reached the degenerate phase, and so may cause simultaneous death of bushes over quite large areas.

1.3 Ecological Consequences of Management

In view of the natural tendency for heather to give way to other species if left undisturbed, how is the survival of heaths and moorland to be explained? There is no doubt that the answer is because they have been used and managed. Man was responsible not only for the original forest clearance but also for the maintenance of the open heaths, because they were useful both for grazing animals and for a supply of heather for such purposes as bedding and fodder for animals, for thatch and cladding of the walls of houses, for road foundations, for dyeing wool and for making honey and flavouring beer. The heath landscapes were 'cultural' not only in their origins but also because in time they often became associated with a distinctive way of life for those who lived and worked in them, and with the evolution of special tools and artefacts.

The main components of management were grazing and fire. They depended on the fact that *Calluna* is an efficient sprouter: when the long shoots are topped by grazing, new ones are produced from below, or when most of the above-ground parts are removed by cutting or burning, sprouting takes place from the stem base. Management in these ways also unconsciously exploits the phased growth behaviour of *Calluna*: that is to say it deliberately stops the passage through the sequence of phases at a time when the plants are still in the building phase and at their most productive in terms of edible material. In this phase heather is at its most competitive and exclusive: management prevents it from passing into the mature or degenerate phases when the plants become tall and woody, less palatable and less accessible to grazing animals.

If carefully managed, moderate grazing of building-phase heather has the effect of keeping it in this productive condition over an extended period. But in time there is generally a tendency for the plants to pass into the later phases, and when this happens the stand may be rejuvenated by burning, controlled in such a way as to produce rapid vegetative regeneration, so rapid in fact as virtually to by-pass the pioneer phase with re-establishment of a young building stand in 1-2 growing seasons. Where, however, control is poor, regeneration may be much slower and then a seral stage dominated by other dwarf-shrubs such as *Erica cinerea* on the drier soils, *E. tetralix* on peaty ground, or *Vaccinium myrtillus* may intervene. When efficiently managed, burning (or similarly cutting) brings about uniform regeneration over the whole area treated and produces a uniform, even-aged stand with a smooth dense canopy lacking gaps. This has the consequence of reducing to very few the number of associated species. It has been shown (Hobbs *et al.*, 1984) that the number of species appearing after moor burning is closely dependent on the number present before the fire: normally it is just those already present which regenerate. Periodic burning therefore maintains a species-poor community because it keeps most of the heather on a heath or moor in the building phase in which highly competitive *Calluna* admits the fewest associates.

A further important ecological impact of management concerns the fund of nutrients in the ecosystem. Here there has been another marked change of attitudes in recent years. Between about 1963 and 1970 there was considerable concern in conservation circles that because these traditional management practices would be expected to deplete the system of nutrients, either periodically or continuously, they might be responsible for a progressive decline in the productivity of the uplands, and likewise a decline in their conservation value. What was not fully recognized was that it is precisely because grazing and burning tend to prevent the accumulation of nutrients in the systems that the natural trends in favour of replacement of heather by grasses, trees or bracken have been inhibited, and the continuance of a vegetation adapted to low nutrient status ensured. The consequences of nutrient accumulation (especially increases in nitrogen) have been well documented in the Netherlands where widespread replacement of heath by *Deschampsia flexuosa* or *Molinia caerulea* has occurred (Heil and Diemont, 1983), and the same is now evident in Southeast England where the grasses that take over are *Deschampsia flexuosa, Holcus lanatus* and *Arrhenatherum elatius*.

While all the indications are that management is essential for the perpetuation of heaths and moors, such management must be well planned. Casual or ill-judged management may cause changes opposite to those intended, for the balance between *Calluna* and other vegetation types is extremely sensitive. For example, work on sheep grazing at the former Hill Farming Research Organization (now part of the Macaulay Land Use Research Institute) has shown that if the offtake of edible shoots of *Calluna* in any one year exceeds 30–40 % of the annual production, heather will progressively decline (Grant and Hunter, 1971). Under heavy grazing, especially when accompanied by burning, *Calluna* may be replaced by *Festuca ovina* with *Agrostis* spp., *Nardus stricta, Molinia caerulea, Juncus squarrosus* or *Eriophorum vaginatum* according to soil type and drainage. Grazing intensity has therefore to be constantly monitored and adjusted if the aim is maintenance of heather. It is easy to overgraze and this is a likely cause of much current loss of heather. Where cattle are involved there is even greater risk because of the added effects of trampling, but again with care cattle grazing may in some circumstances prove an effective means of managing heather moor.

However, even the best and most well-adjusted grazing management may require recourse to burning (or in some cases cutting) to rejuvenate heather stands from time to time, but burning too must be carefully judged. Poor burning management, usually when the stand has been allowed to become too old or the fire too hot, leads to slow regeneration and prolonged exposure of bare ground. (This may also result sometimes from burning too frequently.) The effect is similar to that of the creation of large gaps, as already discussed, and a first-class opportunity is provided for colonization by trees and bracken in particular. The highest densities of birch seedlings on heath are found in the pioneer phases of recolonization after severe fires.

It follows that if management is abandoned there will be a trend away from heath and moorland towards other vegetation, but equally this may result from poor management which fails to observe the now well-known rules of good practice. Losses of heath and moorland from these causes add to those due to direct habitat loss from afforestation, conversion to arable land, development for buildings and other purposes.

1.4 Outlook for the Future

Without use and management the vegetation dynamics lead away from heather, whereas with good management we can ensure the continuance of extensive heath and moorland landscapes. The question to be answered is: how far is the continuance of this 'cultural landscape' a desired objective?

Sporting estates and hill sheep farms both have a strong interest in this aim, as do those concerned with the aesthetics of landscape, amenity and informal recreation. This includes the tourist industry which benefits considerably from the beauty of the purple hills and open heather moors. But when the interests of nature conservation are considered the answer may be less straightforward. Recently conservationists in Scotland have tended to align themselves to some extent with the view that it is desirable to protect, at least to some degree, the extensive tracts of moorlands in our uplands. They point on the one hand to their decline elsewhere, and on the other to the requirements of certain species of special importance, for example birds such as the hen harrier or golden plover which benefit from wide areas of open heather-covered country.

The studies of post-fire vegetation dynamics discussed above draw attention, however, to a dilemma. When heather is well-managed and regularly burnt in the dominant building phase, there is inevitably a progressive reduction in floristic diversity. Consequent upon this is a reduction in the diversity of invertebrates (Gimingham, 1985) and other species of interest such as reptiles. For these aspects of nature conservation the maintenance by traditional management of extensive tracts of *Calluna* in the building phase is not ideal.

For this purpose uneven-aged stands would be better, with the *Calluna* completing its cycle of phases and allowing the participation of many associated species, but this would be virtually impossible to maintain unless by extremely labour-intensive hand-control of trees. Experiments are needed to find ways of creating a slightly larger-scale mosaic, perhaps by cutting or burning at varying frequencies, in order to include the species typical both of the early and the later stages of the succession. Systems of integrating patches of scrub and trees in heathland might also offer an attractive scenario for conservation, if practical methods of achieving them could be established.

A further relevant consideration must be the competing proposals for substantial increases in the extent of native woodlands, especially those of pine and birch, in the uplands. In terms of nature conservation this must also be a desirable objective. It will be necessary to weigh up the merits of the following three main approaches to landscape change in the uplands, and to seek an acceptable balance between them.

1. The retention of a substantial element of our cultural, semi-natural heath and moorland,

2. The extension of native woodlands,

3. The creation of areas of patchy heath and moor with a diversity of structure and composition, incorporating elements of scrub and trees (probably the most difficult of the three options to manage).

There should be room for all three types of landscape if the approach is bold enough and applied on a large enough scale. This view has recently been well expressed by Vermeer and Joosten (1992): 'Nature conservation should aim at a *regionalization* of the management. It is easier to preserve or develop natural ecosystems in a landscape-ecological context than in a lot of isolated and scattered 'leftovers' . . . Land use which does not conform with the conservation objectives should be removed from these areas.'

Acknowledgements
It is a pleasure to thank numerous research students and other colleagues whose work, some of which is referred to above, has done so much to advance the subject of heathland ecology. I am also deeply appreciative of the honour I have received in the form of the conference and this volume of papers delivered at it, and for this I gratefully record my thanks to Scottish Natural Heritage and in particular its Research and Advisory Services Directorate, and to Des Thompson and his Steering Committee who organized the meeting. I am also indebted to D.A. Ratcliffe for valuable comments on the manuscript of this paper.

References
Barclay-Estrup, P. (1970). The description and interpretation of cyclical processes in a heath community. II. Changes in biomass and shoot production during the *Calluna* cycle. *Journal of Ecology*, **58**, 243–49.

Barclay-Estrup, P. (1971). The description and interpretation of cyclical processes in a heath community. III. Microclimate in relation to the *Calluna* cycle. *Journal of Ecology*, **59**, 143–66.

Barclay-Estrup, P. and Gimingham, C. H. (1969). The description and interpretation of cyclical processes in a heath community. I. Vegetational change in relation to the *Calluna* cycle. *Journal of Ecology*, **57**, 737–58.

Berdowski, J. J. N. and Zeilinga, R. (1987). Transition from heathland to grassland: damaging effects of the heather beetle. *Journal of Ecology*, **75**, 159–75.

Forrest, G. I. (1971). Structure and production of North Pennine blanket bog vegetation. *Journal of Ecology*, **59**, 453–79.

Gimingham, C. H. (1960). Biological flora of the British Isles. *Calluna vulgaris* (L.) Hull. *Journal of Ecology*, **48**, 455–83.

Gimingham, C. H. (1961). North European heath communities: a network of variation. *Journal of Ecology*, **49**, 655–94.

Gimingham, C. H. (1975). *An Introduction to Heathland Ecology*. Oliver and Boyd, Edinburgh.

Gimingham, C. H. (1985). Age-related interactions between *Calluna vulgaris* and phytophagous insects. *Oikos*, **44**, 12–16.

Gimingham, C. H. (1988). A reappraisal of cyclical processes in *Calluna* heath. *Vegetatio*, **77**, 61–4.

Gong, W. K. (1984). Birch regeneration in heath vegetation. *Proceedings of the Royal Society of Edinburgh*. **85B**, 73–81.

Grant, S. A. and Hunter, R. F. (1971). Interaction of grazing and burning on heather moors. II. Effects on primary production and level of utilization. *Journal of the British Grassland Society*. **26**, 173–81.

Heil, G. W. and Diemont, H. (1983). Raised nutrient levels change heathland into grassland. *Vegetatio*, **53**, 113–120.

Hester, A. J., Miles, J. and Gimingham, C. H. (1991a). Succession from heather moorland to birch woodland. I. Experimental alteration of specific environmental conditions in the field. *Journal of Ecology*, **79**, 303–15.

Hester, A. J., Gimingham, C. H. and Miles, J. (1991b). Succession from heather moorland to birch woodland. III. Seed availability, germination and early growth. *Journal of Ecology*, **79**, 329–44.

Hobbs, R. J. (1985). The persistence of Cladonia patches in closed heathland stands. *Lichenologist*, **17**, 103–9.

Hobbs, R. J., Mallik, A. U. and Gimingham, C. H. (1984). Studies on fire in Scottish heathland communities. III. Vital attributes of the species. *Journal of Ecology*, **72**, 963–76.

Hullu, E de and Gimingham, C. H. (1984). Germination and establishment of seedlings in different phases of the *Calluna* life cycle in a Scottish heathland. *Vegetatio*, **58**, 115–21.

Mallik, A. U., Hobbs, R. J. and Legg, C. J. (1984). Seed dynamics in *Calluna-Arctostaphylos* heath in northeastern Scotland. *Journal of Ecology*, **72**, 855–71.

Marrs, R. H. (1986). The role of catastrophic death of *Calluna* in heathland dynamics. *Vegetatio*, **66**, 109–15.

Scandrett, E and Gimingham, C. H. (1989). Vegetative regeneration by layering in *Calluna vulgaris* (L.) Hull. *Transaction of the Botanical Society of Edinburgh*, **45**, 323–34.

Smith, W. G. (1902). The origin and development of heather moorland. *Scottish Geographical Magazine*, **18**, 587–97.

Vermeer, J. G. and Joosten, J. H. J. (1992). Conservation and management of bog and fen reserves in the Netherlands. In: Verhoeven J. T. A. *Fens and Bogs in the Netherlands* Kluwer Academic Publishers, Dordrecht. pp. 433–78.

Watt, A. S. (1947). Pattern and process in the plant community. *Journal of Ecology*, **35**, 1–22.

Watt, A. S. (1955). Bracken versus heather, a study in plant sociology. *Journal of Ecology*, **43**, 490–506.

Westhoff, V., Bakker, P. A., Leeuwen, C. G. van and Voo, E. E. van der. (1970). *Wilde Planten. Flora en vegetatie in onze naturgebieden. Deel 1: Algemene inleiding duinen, zilte gronden*. Naturmonumenten's Graveland, Netherlands.

2. WET HEATHS IN CAITHNESS AND SUTHERLAND, SCOTLAND

T. H Keatinge, A. M. Coupar and E. Reid

Summary

1. According to the National Vegetation Classification (NVC) (Rodwell, 1991), there are two communities described as wet heath: *Scirpus cespitosus-Erica tetralix* and *Erica tetralix-Sphagnum compactum.*

2. Scottish Natural Heritage (SNH) and its predecessor bodies have, since 1989, located survey teams in Caithness and Sutherland with the aim of surveying the blanket bog resource, in order to assess its importance for nature conservation locally, nationally and internationally.

3. Within this geographical survey area the project team has observed and documented wet heath communities. These are described and some general conclusions are reached about their distribution, physical attributes and community history. The results add to the data presented by Rodwell (1991).

2.1. Introduction

Blanket bogs within Caithness and Sutherland were officially recognised by the United Kingdom Government to be of international importance in an announcement made by the Secretary of State for Scotland in January 1988 (House of Commons Vol 126/80, col 71–73). This announcement suggested that approximately half the un-afforrested peatland (175,000ha) might be protected as Sites of Special Scientific Interest (SSSI). Of this total, 40,000 ha were already notified as SSSI, leaving a further 135,000 ha to notify. In order to proceed with the Secretary of State's intention a Nature Conservancy Council (NCC) project team, based at Golspie, was established in 1989 to survey the quality of the peatlands, and from this, to proceed with the notification programme.

This peatland survey programme has identified, within a general survey regime, communities which can be described, in phytosociological terms, as wet heath. Rodwell (1991) describes this community *Scirpus cespitosus-Erica tetralix* as widely occurring at relatively low altitudes in western and northern Britain, mainly in the western Highlands of Scotland, but also in the uplands of south-west Scotland, Wales the Lake District and south west England (Fig. 2.1). Similar communities have been described in the more oceanic parts of western Europe, particularly Ireland, Normandy and Scandinavia (e.g. Ratcliffe and Thompson, 1988; Averis, 1990). This community was also recorded, and the distribution documented, within selected upland sites throughout Britain by the Nature Conservancy Council (NCC) Upland Survey Team (Fig. 2.2) (Averis *et al.*, in press). The large extent of wet heath throughout the British uplands has been regarded as internationally important and its major occurrence in NW Scotland is regarded as particularly significant (Ratcliffe and Thompson, 1988).

The aim of this chapter is to add to Rodwell's (1991) data on the distribution of wet heath vegetation, detailing the geographical distribution of wet heath, and examining some of the associated site characteristics. An attempt is also made to examine the relationship of this community with those of blanket bog.

2.2 Methods

Detailed vegetation survey was initiated to assess the quality of the blanket bog resource throughout Caithness and Sutherland. This was considered essential in order to assess these results against the recommendations as set out in the

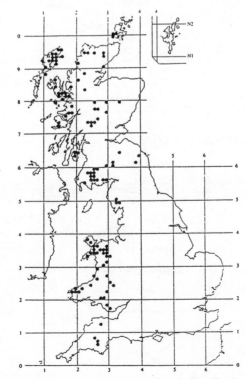

Figure 2.1 *Sirpus cespitosus-Erica tetralix* (M15) wet heath distribution, throughout the British Isles, as described by Rodwell (1991).

Guidelines for the selection of biological SSSI (Nature Conservancy Council, 1989; see also Lindsay *et al.*, 1988).

Survey work was carried out, with the aid of air photography, in survey units measuring 100ha–200ha. Within these units, the vegetgation was assessed, mapped and keyed to a NVC type (the keys and constancy tables are in Rodwell, 1991), and notes were made on community attributes, such as *Sphagnum* cover, pool systems, drainage, burning, and birds. A representative quadrat was taken of the dominant NVC type within the unit using the standard recommended methodology for quadrat recording, as described by Rodwell (1991).

2.3   Results

The distribution of *Scirpus cespitosus-Erica tetralix* wet heath, as recorded by this blanket bog survey, is described in Figure 2.3. This indicates that the community type is present throughout both Districts and is found to be more frequently dominant towards the west.

A comparison is made of this distribution with that of the survey units found to be dominated by two of the more common blanket bog communities i.e. *Scirpus cespitosus-Eriophorum vaginatum* and *Erica tetralix-Sphagnum papillosum* (Fig 2.4.). Like

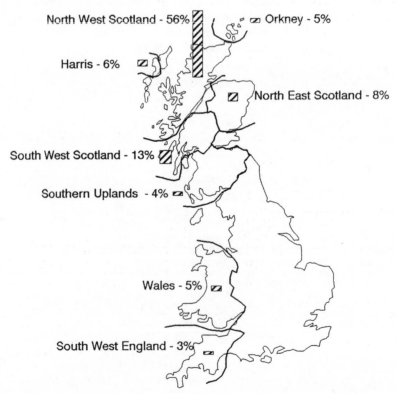

Figure 2.2. The proportion of the Great Britain extent of *Scirpus cespitosus-Erica tetralix* (M15) wet heath as mapped on 292 selected upland sites.

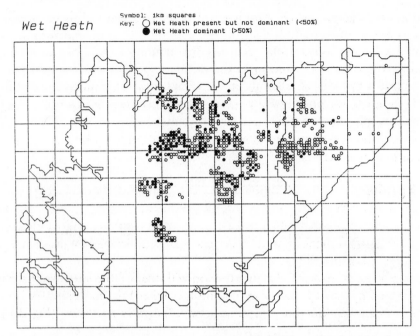

Figure 2.3. The distribution of *Scirpus cespitosus-Erica tetralix* (M15) wet heath within Survey units in Caithness and Sutherland. Filled circles indicate wet heath as the dominant vegetation, open circles as present but not dominant.

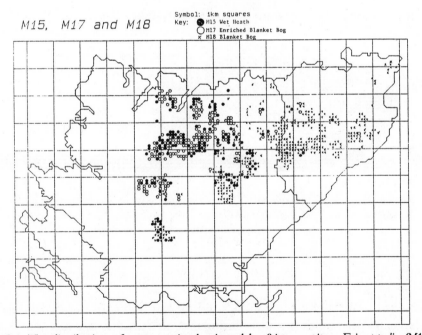

Figure 2.4. The distribution of survey units dominated by *Scirpus cespitosus-Erica tetralix* (M15) wet heath (filled circles), *Scirpus cespitosus-Eriophorum vaginatum* (M17)-enriched blanket bog (open circles) and *Erica tetralix-Sphagnum papillosum* (M18) blanket bog (crosses) in Caithness and Sutherland.

Scirpus cespitosus-Erica tetralix wet heath, *Scirpus cespitosus-Eriophorum vaginatum* is found to have a more westerly distribution, and the two types appear to occur commonly together. In contrast, the recorded distribution of the *Erica tetralix-Sphagnum papillosum* type is more prominent to the east and south of the survey area.

The close geographical relationship of *Scirpus cespitosus-Erica tetralix* wet heath to *Scirpus cespitosus-Eriophorum vaginatum* mire is demonstrated by Figure 2.5. Wet heath is present in approximately 80% of survey units which also record *Scirpus-Eriopho-*

Peatland Survey Units dominated by M17 Enriched Blanket Bog

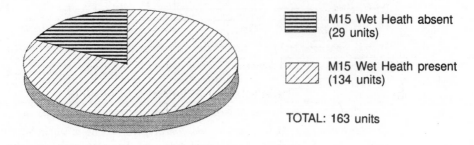

M15 Wet Heath absent
(29 units)

M15 Wet Heath present
(134 units)

TOTAL: 163 units

Peatland Survey Units dominated by M18 Blanket Bog

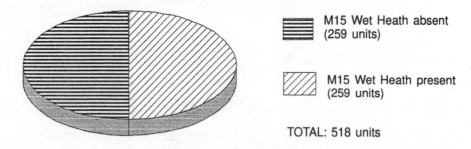

M15 Wet Heath absent
(259 units)

M15 Wet Heath present
(259 units)

TOTAL: 518 units

Figure 2.5. The presence of *Scirpus cespitosus-Erica tetralix* (M15) wet heath in survey units dominated by *Scirpus cespitosus-Eriophorum vaginatum* (M17) and *Erica tetralix-Sphagnum papillosum* (M18) blanket bog communities.

rum vaginatum mire, but occurs less commonly in units dominated by *Erica tetralix-Sphagnum papillosum* mire.

These two blanket bog communities and the wet heath are analysed in relation to the slope and peat depth recorded during the original quadrat collection. A greater proportion of *Scirpus cespitosus-Erica tetralix* wet heath occurs over shallower peats and steeper slopes than for either of the blanket bog communities (Fig. 2.6a, b). Indeed, *Erica tetralix-Sphagnum papillosum* occurs, almost entirely, over deep peat on

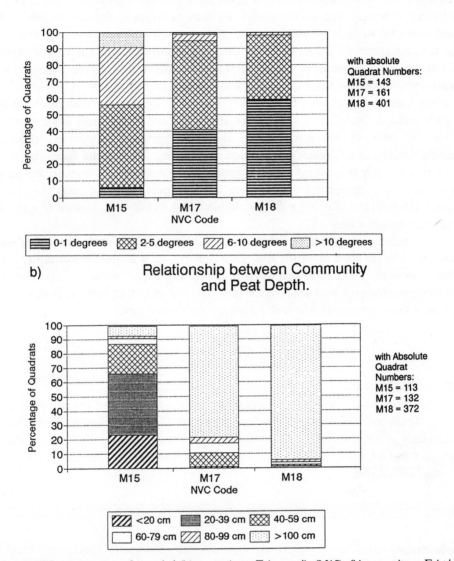

Figure 2.6. The occurrence of sampled *Scirpus cespitosus-Erica tetralix* (M15), *Scirpus cespitosus-Eriophorum vaginatum* (M17) and *Erica tetralix-Sphagnum papillosum* (M18) communities in relation to (a) slope, and (b) peat depth.

gentle slopes, whilst *Scirpus cespitosus-Eriophorum vaginatum* is found mainly over deep peat but is less confined to gentle slopes.

2.4 Discussion

The evidence presented in this paper suggests that though *Scirpus cespitosus-Erica tetralix* wet heath (within the units of survey) has affinities with the more westerly

Scirpus cespitosus-Eriophorum vaginatum blanket bog community in terms of both geography and site characteristics, it occupies a distinct habitat on shallower peats and steeper slopes. The communities are also floristically distinguishable in that there is found to be a greater number and cover of *Sphagnum* species within the blanket bog community than the wet heath community. Indeed, the wet heath community supports a greater cover of herb species and more frequent occurrence of dwarf shrubs such as *Salix repens* and *Salix aurita*.

It has been suggested (e.g. Birse, 1980) that wet heath communities can be derived from woodland. Furthermore, evidence from Rodwell (1991) and Thompson and Miles (this volume) also demonstrates that wet heath can be derived from deep peat communities as a result of drainage or burning. The results from our survey show that wet heath is found more commonly on thinner peats with greater slopes, and is far less commonly found in areas of deep peat. This suggests that the wet heath community, occupying a distinct habitat, is generally not derived from related deep peat communities.

The concluding suggestion, therefore, is that in Caithness and Sutherland *Scirpus cespitosus-Erica tetralix* wet heath may be occurring as a distinct community which could conceivably be a seral precursor to *Scirpus cespitosus-Eriophorum vaginatum* mire. Further investigation and analysis of the palaeoecology, hydrological factors and human influences may confirm the findings of this survey.

Acknowledgements

The data presented here were collected and analysed by members of the Upland Survey Team and the Golspie Peatland Team of NCC, NCCS and SNH. We are particularly grateful to Karen Scott for data processing and production of the figures, and to Drs. David Horsfield, Alison Averis and Des Thompson for reference to unpublished data.

References

Averis, A. (1990). Where are all the Hepatic Mat Liverworts in Scotland? *Botanical Journal of Scotland,* **46** (2), 191–198.

Averis, A., Horsfield, D., and Thompson, D. B. A. (in press). Nature Conservation of the Scottish Uplands: North West Region, Research, Survey and Monitoring Report, Scottish Natural Heritage, Battleby, Scotland, UK.

Birse, E. L. (1980). Plant communities of Scotland. A preliminary Phytocoenonia. Macaulay Institute for Soil Research, Aberdeen, Scotland, UK.

Lindsay, R. A., Charman, D. J., Everingham, F., O'Reilly, R. M., Palmer, M. A., Rowell, T. A., and Stroud, D. A. (1988). The Flow Country. The Peatlands of Caithness and Sutherland. Nature Conservancy Council, Peterborough, UK.

Nature Conservancy Council (1989). *Guidelines for the Selection of Biological Sites of Special Scientific Interest,* NCC, Peterborough.

Ratcliffe, D. A., and Thompson, D. B. A. (1988). The British Uplands: their ecological character and international significance. In M. B. Usher and D. B. A. Thompson (Eds.) *Ecological Change in the Uplands*, Blackwell, Oxford, U.K, pp 9–36.

Rodwell, J. S. (ed.) (1991) *British Plant Communities, Vol. 2: Mires and Heaths*, Cambridge University Press, Cambridge, UK.

Thompson, D. B. A. and Miles, J. (this volume) Heaths and Moorland: some conclusions and questions about environmental change.

3   UPLAND LAND COVER CHANGE IN POST-WAR SCOTLAND

G. J. Tudor and E. C. Mackey

Summary

1. Results describing heather moorland, unimproved grassland and mire from the National Countryside Monitoring Scheme, a sample-based study of land cover change in Scotland from the late 1940s to the early 1970s, are presented.

2. Land cover change from the 1940s to 1970s is characterized by a 12 % reduction in the extent of upland semi-natural land cover types in Scotland, accounted for by an 18 % reduction in the extent of heather moorland, a 9 % reduction in the extent of unimproved grassland and an 8 % reduction in the extent of mire.

3. Sixty two percent of the reduction in the extent of these upland features is attributed to an expansion of coniferous forestry, 20 % to conversion to semi-improved and improved grassland and 18 % is attributed to conversion to a range of other habitat types.

4. Draft results comparing change from the early 1970s to the late 1980s for Central Region provide evidence there of a similar pattern of change extending into the late 1980s.

3.1   Introduction

The passage through Parliament of the Wildlife and Countryside Act 1981 and the debate which this Act engendered, reflected concern about the ways in which the structure and appearance of the countryside had been and may in future be affected by changes in farming, forestry, and other land uses.

In response to this, the National Countryside Monitoring Scheme (NCMS) was established in June 1983 to provide the Nature Conservancy Council (NCC) with data on the extent, change and interchange of land cover in Britain. Since 1986 the project has concentrated on Scotland and is now administered by Scottish Natural Heritage (SNH). NCMS is an important retrospective study of land cover change for the whole of Scotland. Other studies of land cover in Scotland are the 'Land Cover of Scotland' 1988 census (Macaulay Land Use Research Institute, 1993) and the Institute of Terrestrial Ecology's 'Countryside Survey 1990' (Department of the Environment, 1993). These complement the information provided by NCMS in also providing large-scale data on land cover and land cover change in Scotland, at different scales and levels of detail.

A particular value of NCMS is in its quantitative detail, as an aid to countryside management and in providing baseline reference periods for research and monitoring. NCMS results have proved useful to a number of different types of bodies concerned with countryside change in Scotland, such as local authorities and agencies with responsibilities for the rural environment, academics, planners and policy makers. A key objective of the NCMS is to heighten awareness of habitat change in the post-war period and to inform strategies for nature conservation.

Within the NCMS classification are features which are especially characteristic of the uplands of Scotland; these include blanket mire, unimproved grassland, woodland and heather moorland. This chapter primarily describes the extent of, and changes in, the cover of heather moorland in post-war Scotland, in the context of wider land cover change in the uplands and with specific reference to changes also apparent in the land cover of unimproved grassland, mire and woodland. NCMS results for Scotland are presented for the period of the late 1940s and the early 1970s, and additional results for Central Region are also presented for the late 1980s.

3.2 Method

The National Countryside Monitoring Scheme is a sample survey which quantifies the extent of land cover change throughout Scotland between three post-war dates: the late 1940s; the early 1970s (mean dates: 1947 and 1973); and the late 1980s (mean date 1988). At present, results for Central Region only are available for the latter period.

Scotland is characterized by appreciable geographical variation in land cover and so each Administrative Region was stratified into broad land cover classes using Landsat Multi-Spectral Scanner imagery. The resulting strata varied in land cover composition from region to region, but broadly equated to upland, lowland, intermediate and urban classes (where appropriate). A random sample was selected from within each stratum with a sampling rate designed to detect a 10 % change or more in the extent of feature types with 95 % confidence.

When work commenced in Scotland in 1986, the sample was based on 5 km sq sample 'squares', conveniently represented by the coverage of stereo overlap between three adjacent 1:25,000 scale aerial photographs and a single 1:10,000 scale Ordnance Survey map sheet. The statistical design was assessed in 1988 according to the effectiveness of the stratification and sampling techniques in relation to the statistical rigour of the result. As a result, the size of sample squares was reduced to 2.5 x 2.5 km, with a greater number of squares sampled and a minimum of five squares per stratum per district. The final sample coverage of 464 squares represents a 7.5 % sample of Scotland by area.

Land cover, which is classified into 31 areal and 5 linear features (Table 3.1), was interpreted from aerial photography; mapped at 1:10,000 scale; digitized; and processed by geographical information system software specially designed for the project. Field validation was carried out where there was uncertainty in the interpretation. The resulting vector (line-based) data was rasterized (grid-based) to generate data based on 10 m x 10 m pixels, representing 0.01 ha on the ground. Areas and lengths of NCMS classified features were thus calculated and change matrices for areal and linear data between the two study dates were generated. A suite of statistical programs then combined these data with stratification data to produce estimates of extent and change for each region. Regional results were aggregated to provide national estimates, with accuracy indicated by the calculation of standard errors and confidence intervals. Net change figures shown in Table 3.2 have been asterisked where there is a 95 % certainty of a net change in the direction indicated. Note that for the purpose of this chapter the two NCMS mire categories of grass and heather-dominated mire have been amalgamated into a combined blanket mire class, except where differences between the two have been highlighted.

Table 3.1   NCMS feature groups

	Land cover groups	*Feature groups*
1.	Grassland includes all grassland types; semi-natural and artificial	Unimproved Grassland (UG) Semi-improved Grassland (SG) Improved Grassland (G)
2.	Mire includes all areas where vegetation is growing in wet peat	Blanket Mire (heather (BM) and grass (BMG) dominated mire) Lowland Raised Mire (LRM)
3.	Heather Moorland includes all areas of heather other than heather dominated blanket mire	Heather Moorland (HM)
4.	Arable includes all areas under cultivation of crops	Arable (A)
5.	Woodland and scrub includes all areas of trees and scrub as well as areas of recently felled woodland	Broadleaved Woodland (BW) Coniferous Woodland (CW) Scrub, Tall (ST) Scrub, Low (SL) Broadleaved Plantation (BP) Coniferous Plantation (CP) Mixed Woodland (MW)

Table 3.1 (cont'd)   NCMS feature groups

		Young Plantation (YP)
		Felled Woodland (FW)
		Parkland (P)
6.	*Water* includes all areas of open and running water of greater than 10 m in width	Standing Natural Water (SNW) Running Natural Water (RNW) Standing Manmade Water (SMW) Running Canalized Water (RCW)
7.	*Built* includes all built areas, urban and rural as well as surfaced routeways	Built land (B) Transport Corridor (TC)
8.	*Other* semi-natural and artificial feature types which are uncommon and do not fit into any of the above groups	Bracken (BR) Wet Ground (WG) Marginal Inundation (MI) Quarry (Q) Rock cliff (RK) Bare Ground (BG) Recreation (R)
9.	*Linear group*	Feature types Hedgerow without trees (H) Treeline (T) Running Natural Water (RNW) Running Canalized Water (RCW) Unsurfaced Tracks (UT)

Note: All area features refer to discrete areas of 0.1 ha and above

Table 3.2   Area estimates of selected upland land cover features

1940s

Region	Heather moor	Unimproved grassland	Blanket mire	Group total	% of region	Regional area	% of group total for Scotland
Borders	968	1259	209	2436	52	4695	5
Central	361	761	109	1231	45	2716	3
Dumfries and Galloway	755	2375	196	3327	53	6342	7
Fife	15	87	0	101	7	1377	<0.5
Grampian	2682	571	343	3595	41	8686	7
Highland	6010	1054	13 868	20 932	85	24 695	44
Lothian	184	305	25	514	28	1814	1
Strathclyde	1557	3976	2435	7968	55	14435	17

Table 3.2 (cont'd)   Area estimates of selected upland land cover features

Region	Heather moor	Unimproved grassland	Blanket mire	Group total	% of region	Regional area	% of group total for Scotland
Tayside	1610	1413	396	3419	46	7394	7
Orkney	147	122	211	480	43	1115	1
Shetlands	362	298	919	1579	87	1810	3
Western Isles	726	388	1292	2406	85	2847	5
Scotland	15 377	12 608	20 004	47 988	62	77 926	100

1970s

Region	Heather moor	Unimproved grassland	Blanket mire	Group total	% of region	Regional area	% of group total for Scotland
Borders	772	929	60	1760	38	4695	4
Central	316	772	88	1176	43	2716	3
Dumfries and Galloway	279	1868	138	2285	36	6342	5
Fife	5	72	0	76	6	1377	<0.5
Grampian	1978	611	334	2922	34	8686	7
Highland	5303	1256	13 104	19 663	80	24 695	46
Lothian	150	308	19	476	26	1814	1
Strathclyde	1205	3555	1984	6744	47	14 435	16
Tayside	1421	1234	397	3053	41	7394	7
Orkney	122	121	184	428	38	1115	1
Shetlands	339	311	848	1498	83	1810	4
Western Isles	747	378	1201	2325	82	2847	5
Scotland	12 636	11 414	18 356	42 405	54	77 962	100

Net change

Region	Heather moor	Unimproved grassland	Blanket mire	Group total	% of region	Regional area
Borders	−197*	−330*	−149*	−676*	−14	4695
Central	−45	11	−21	−55	−2	2716
Dumfries and Galloway	−476*	−508*	−58	−1041*	−16	6342
Fife	−10*	−15*	0	−25*	−2	1377
Grampian	−704*	40	−9*	−673*	−3	24 695
Highland	−707*	202*	−764*	−1269*	−14	8686
Lothian	−35	3	−6	−38	−2	1814
Strathclyde	−353*	−421*	−451*	−1225*	−9	14 435
Tayside	−189	−179	1	−367*	−5	7394
Orkney	−25	−1	−27*	−52*	−5	1115
Shetlands	−23	14	−71*	−80*	−4	1810
Western Isles	22	−10	−92	−80	−3	2847
Scotland	−2741	−1194	−1648	−5582	−7	77926

Notes All areas given to the nearest square kilometre
    *95% certainty of a net change in direction indicated

*95% certainty of a net change in direction indicated

There are air photo-interpretation difficulties associated with upland land cover mapping. These related mainly to the margins of polygon boundaries where there may for instance be a gradation between heather dominance and grass dominance. Additionally there are problems associated with accurately classifying complex mosaic communities where no one cover type dominates. These are problems common to land cover projects of this nature and decision rules are applied in each method according to the land cover discrimination required. In NCMS for instance, the method provides for a minimum mappable area of 0.1 ha. A detailed account of the NCMS methodology is given in a Technical Report (Scottish Natural Heritage, 1994b).

3.3 The Extent of Upland Land Cover in the 1940s

It was estimated that upland semi-natural land cover types extended over 47 989 km^2 (62 %) of Scotland in the late 1940s (Scottish Natural Heritage, 1994a). Of this 15 377 km^2 was heather moorland, with the remaining area composed of unimproved grassland (12 608 km^2) and blanket mire (20 004 km^2). A summary of the 1940s land cover of Scotland is illustrated in Figure 3.1.

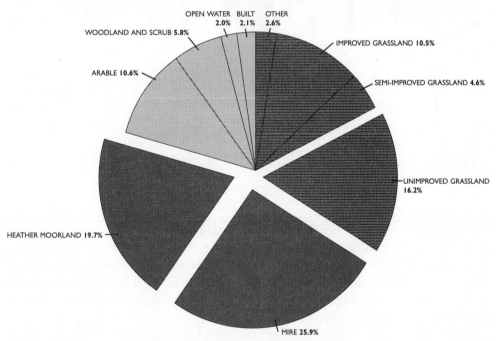

Figure 3.1. Land cover of Scotland (1940s).

3.3.1 Heather moorland

This is defined as areas of heathland shrub communities (*Calluna* and *Erica*) dominated by dense heather, but which can include sub-dominant areas of rough grassland and bilberry (*Vaccinium*) as part of a complex mosaic. The classification includes areas of muirburn if there is sufficient evidence of heather regeneration. The suppression of woodland regeneration means that most heather moorland is semi-natural in character, but some near-natural upland heaths can be found at higher elevations extending above the former tree line and in isolated areas protected from grazing and burning (Rodwell, 1991; Thompson and Brown, 1992).

Heather moorland extended across approximately 20 % of Scotland in the 1940s. Heather moorland cover, found extensively throughout the uplands of Scotland and particularly characteristic of Grampian Region, is illustrated in Figure 3.2. The five regions most extensively covered by heather moorland were Grampian

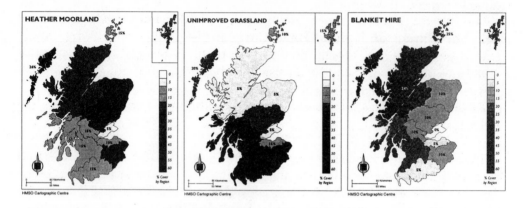

Figure 3.2. Percentage cover of selected upland land cover features in Scotland — 1940s estimates.

(31 %), Western Isles (26 %), Highland (24 %), Borders (21 %) and Shetland (20 %).

Table 3.2 indicates that heather moorland was reduced by 2 741 km^2 (18 %) from the late 1940s to the early 1970s.

3.3.2   Unimproved grassland

This category is characterized by areas of grassland which are not intensively managed and which contain a high proportion of native species, including some invasive species such as bracken and thistle. The category is often associated with areas of low soil fertility, steep slopes and poor drainage. This category also includes areas of former improved or semi-improved grassland which have reverted to a more semi-natural state.

The grassland group (improved, semi-improved and unimproved) was the most widespread land cover in Scotland, representing approximately 31 % (24 349 km^2) of the total land area. 52 % (12 608 km^2) of this was unimproved grassland, itself extending across 16 % of Scotland in the 1940s and particularly characteristic of the central and southern regions. Dumfries and Galloway (37 %), Central (28 %), Strathclyde (28 %) and Borders (28 %) Regions had relatively extensive unimproved grassland cover, illustrated in Figure 3.2.

Table 3.2 shows that unimproved grassland was reduced by 1194 km^2 (9 %) from the 1940s to the 1970s.

3.3.3   Blanket mire

The blanket mire category was defined as areas of vegetation and other surface characteristics indicative of mire which infers a sub-surface peat depth of >0.5 m. This often comprises open treeless bog marked by 'hummock-hollow' morphology, peat hags and an absence of artificial drainage. Vegetation communities are generally dominated by grasses especially cotton grasses (*Eriophorum spp.*) or by heather (*Calluna vulgaris*).

Mire was the largest land cover group after grassland in area terms, and extended over approximately 26 % of Scotland in the late 1940s. The estimation of blanket mire cover, which was particularly characteristic of Highland Region (extending over 56 % of the regional area), Shetland (51 %) and the Western Isles (45 %), is illustrated in Figure 3.2.

Table 3.2 shows that blanket mire was reduced by 1648 km^2 (8 %) between the 1940s and the 1970s.

Together these upland semi-natural features accounted for 54 % of the land cover of Scotland in the early 1970s, representing a 12 % reduction in upland cover from the 1940s. From Table 3.2 it is, however, apparent that while the general tendency was for decline in the three feature types, there were occasional occurrences of Regional gains. This is notable, for instance, of unimproved grassland in Highland Region.

3.4   Interchanges

The dynamics of change become clearer when the interchange of gains and losses between feature types is considered, as illustrated in Figure 3.3. Interchange provides an insight into successional change, where varying levels of grazing intensity and cycles of muirburn on heaths and moorland have been shown to lead to variations in the composition of semi-natural vegetation (Miles, 1985). Figure 3.3 shows, for example, a high degree of interchange between heather moorland and unimproved grassland, with a net change in favour of grassland. Interchange also describes the essentially one-way transition from semi-natural upland features to forestry.

In relation to upland features, some of the main interchanges illustrated in Figure 3.3 are:

1.   Interchange between unimproved grassland, semi-improved grassland and improved grassland, with a tendency to grassland improvement.

2.   There was interchange between heather moorland and unimproved grassland, with a net reduction of heather moorland of 848 km^2 (1 718 km^2–870 km^2) to unimproved grassland and 175 km^2 to semi-improved grassland.

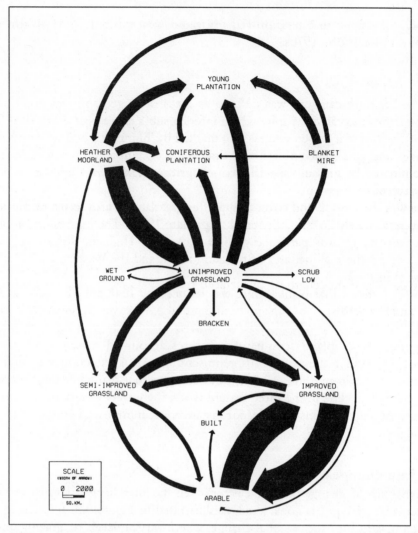

Figure 3.3. Feature interchanges of more than 100 km² between the 1940s and 1970s for Scotland.

3.   There was a reduction in blanket mire to unimproved grassland (448 km²) and to heather moorland (375 km²). This may be explained by the artificial drainage of mire in preparation for forestry, resulting in the mire hydrology being so altered that it no longer qualifies for the mire category in the NCMS classification. Such areas of 'drained mire' are classified as heather moorland or unimproved grassland, according to the remaining vegetation cover. Also, in established forest on former mire, the areas between blocks of trees, such as rides and unsurfaced tracks, are classified according to their current land cover, which is usually grass or heather. There is likely also to be an element of interpretation 'error' associated with the mapping of complex habitats from aerial photography, although there is no reason to suppose that this should affect the interpretation of mire in any systematic way.

4. Conifer plantation became increasingly common in the Scottish landscape between the 1940s and the 1970s, with an estimated increase in mature plantation (planted trees of >3 m in height) of 226 % and a still greater increase in young plantation (planted trees of <3 m in height) of 525 %. Overall, plantation forest is estimated to have expanded from 1 437 km^2 in the 1940s to 6 156 km^2 in the 1970s, a fourfold increase. By the early 1970s, artificially created woodland covered 8 % of Scotland, while the much smaller area of semi-natural woodland cover had declined in extent.

5. Afforestation accounts for 62 % of the total reduction of semi-natural upland features; conversion to semi-improved or improved grassland accounts for a further 20 %; and the remaining 18 % is attributed to 23 further minor land cover changes.

6. Associated with ground preparation for afforestation and agricultural improvement is an increase in the length of running canalized water (drainage ditches) by 26 % and the length of unsurfaced track by 25 %.

7. Overall, the extent of upland semi-natural land cover declined by 5582 km^2 (12 %).

The relative magnitudes of changes from the 1940s to the 1970s in Scotland are summarized in Table 3.3, where gains and losses are estimated with their 95 % confidence intervals. This highlights the expansion of artificially created features on the one hand, notably that of plantation forest, and corresponding reductions in the extent of semi-natural features on the other. Of these, heather moorland has experienced the largest net loss of 2741 km^2.

Table 3.3 A summary of net change of land cover features for Scotland (1940s–1970s)

Feature type	Area estimates			
	Lower	Change	Upper	% Change
Gains				
Young plantation	1819	2584	3349	525
Coniferous plantation	1561	2135	2709	226
Semi-improved grassland	159	454	750	13
Built	334	430	526	42
Recreation	42	75	107	107
Quarry	9	33	57	63
Transport corridor	10	32	54	5
Bare ground	4	21	39	24
Running canalized water	1	1	2	17
No net change				
Improved grassland	−347	248	844	3
Standing manmade water	0	87	174	54
Bracken	−51	64	179	10

Table 3.3 (cont'd)   A summary of net change of land cover features for Scotland (1940s–1970s)

Feature type	Lower	Change	Upper	% Change
Scrub tall	−26	33	92	17
Felled woodland	−17	31	80	97
Broadleaved plantation	−12	8	29	20
Scrub, low	−60	7	74	2
Marginal inundation	−11	5	20	10
Rock/cliff	−1	1	2	<0.5
Running natural water	−8	−3	2	−1
Parkland	−35	−11	13	−14
Standing manmade water	−91	−45	2	−4
Mixed woodland	−111	−49	13	−8
Wet ground	−120	−57	6	−10
Arable	−674	−148	379	−2
Losses				
Coniferious woodland	−172	−96	−20	−51
Broadleaved woodland	−275	−213	−151	−14
Lowland raised nire	−72	−43	−14	−23
Grass dominated blanket mire	−960	−584	−209	−7
Blanket mire	−1516	−1064	−611	−8
Unimproved grassland	−1869	−1194	−519	−10
Heather moorland	−3550	−2741	−1931	−18

Linear estimates

Feature type	Lower	Change	Upper	% Change
Gains				
Running canalised water	8939	14 935	20 930	26
Unsurfaced track	5111	7896	10 681	25
No net change				
Running natural water	−2530	−1176	178	−1
Losses				
Treeline	−2852	−1734	−616	−9
Hedgerows	19 175	−15 946	−12 717	−37

Notes All areas given to the nearest square kilometre
      Lower and Upper refer to the 95% confidence limits.
      There is a 0.95 probability of the true area being between these two limits.

3.5 Evidence of More Recent Change: Central Region Case Study

Preliminary NCMS results for 1988/89, which are available for Central Region, provide an indication of more recent change. Central Region is comprised of a lowland District of Falkirk and Clackmannan, extending across 18 % of the regional area and a less urbanized District of Stirling, extending across 82 % of the regional area (SNH, 1993). Central Region was among regions characterized by moderately high semi-natural land cover at the beginning of the study period (60 % of the region in the 1940s). Table 3.2 shows that the upland semi-natural feature cover in Central Region, estimated to have been 45 % of the regional, area in the 1940s, was reduced to 43 % in the 1970s, representing a reduction of 55 km².

Upland semi-natural land cover for Central Region from the 1940s to the early 1970s, and from the early 1970s to the late 1980s, is summarized in Table 3.4. The underlying interchange results are illustrated in Figure 3.4. These indicate a pattern of change in which:

Table 3.4 Upland land cover change for selected features in central region (2716 km²) between the 1940s, 1970s and 1980s

	Study periods		
	1940s (1947)	1970s (1973)	1980s (1988)
Heather moorland			
Area (km²)	361	316	292
% of region	13	12	11
Net change		−45	−69
% Net change		−13	−19
Annual change (km²)		−2	−2
Unimproved grassland			
Area (km²)	761	772	668
% of region	28	28	25
Net change		11	−93
% Net change		1	−12
Annual change (km²)		−<0.5	−2
Blanket mire			
Area (km²)	109	88	91
% of region	4	3	3
Net change		−21	−18
% Net change		−19	−17
Annual change (km²)		−1	−1
Coniferous plantation			
Area (km²)	44	101	189
% of region	2	4	7
Net change		57	145
% Net change		130	330
Annual change (km²)		2	4

Note. All areas given to the nearest square kilometre

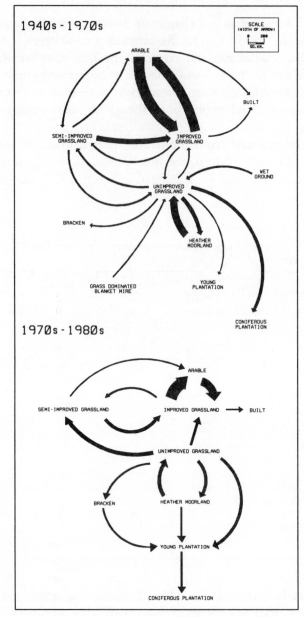

Figure 3.4. Feature interchanges of more than 10.0 km² between the 1940s and 1970s and the 1970s and 1980s for Central Region.

1. Heather moorland, which occurs essentially within Stirling District, extended across 13 % of the regional, area in the 1940s, 12 % in the 1970s and 11 % in the 1980s. The reasons for this reduction were a net conversion to unimproved grassland and afforestation. The net effect was a reduction in the extent of heather moorland at a rate of 2 km² per annum from the 1940s through to the 1980s.

2. Unimproved grassland was the most extensive upland feature type, which accounted for 28 % of the regional area in the 1940s. This remained little changed in the 1970s, with net gains from heather moorland compensated by reductions to coniferous plantation. Other changes largely balanced out, except for an apparent encroachment of bracken. The pattern continued into the 1980s, with a small net conversion of heather moorland to unimproved grassland and continuing afforestation. A further characteristic of the 1970s to the 1980s period was a tendency to grassland improvement.

3. Blanket mire covered 4 % of the regional area in the 1940s, slightly over 3 % in the 1970s and slightly under 3 % in the 1980s. The net annual rate of reduction was 0.8 km^2 from the 1940s to the 1980s.

3.6 Conclusion

The National Countryside Monitoring Scheme for Scotland quantifies land cover change in the post-war period, from the late 1940s to the late 1980s. Results for the late 1940s to the early 1970s indicate reductions in the extent of heather moorland, unimproved grassland and blanket mire, as summarized in Table 3.5.

Table 3.5   Summary of selected upland semi-natural land cover change (km^2)

Feature type	1940s	1970s	Net change	% change
Heather moorland	15 377	12 636	–2741	–17.8
Unimproved grassland	12 608	11 414	–1194	–9.4
Blanket mire	20 004	18 356	–1648	–8.2

Overall, the extent of semi-natural upland features declined by 5583 km^2 (12 %). Afforestation accounted for 62 % of this, and conversion to semi-improved or improved grassland accounted for a further 20 %. The remaining 18 % was attributed to 23 further types of minor land cover interchange.

NCMS results describe considerable geographic variation in land cover and land cover change across Scotland as illustrated by the data presented here. Rates of upland semi-natural land cover reduction were greatest outside of the Highlands and Islands, and especially in regions such as Grampian, Borders and Dumfries and Galloway. Regions with low levels of semi-natural land cover and low levels of change included the agricultural lowland regions of Fife, Lothian and Orkney. NCMS identifieds the expansion of commercial forestry as well as a tendency to grassland improvement as principal changes associated with reductions in upland semi-natural cover. The long-term trend identified by the study is therefore the reduction in important semi-natural features of the uplands especially heather moorland and blanket mire in favour of other land cover types of a lower nature conservation value.

Central Region cannot be regarded as 'typical' of Scotland, but within the region it can be seen that there was a continuing reduction in the extent of upland semi-natural features extending into the late 1980s, similar to changes recorded in the earlier period.

NCMS is currently analysing the land cover of Scotland for the late 1980s from medium-scale aerial photography flown between 1987 and 1989. This phase of the project is subject to the same methodology of data collection, incorporating an improved geographic information system which will enable 1980s estimates to be compared with those of the 1940s and 1970s. The scheduled completion of this work is 1995. Opportunities are also being explored for integrating NCMS results with other land cover studies, notably the Land Cover of Scotland 1988 (Macaulay Land Use Research Institute, 1993).

Acknowledgements

This study is funded by Scottish Natural Heritage. We are especially grateful to the staff of the National Countryside Monitoring Scheme project, and in particular to the current members: K. Loch, G. Gauld, J. Stewart and P. Iles. We would like also to thank Fiona Underwood for her invaluable analytical assistance and statistical advice.

References

Department of the Environment (1993). *Countryside Survey 1990: Main Report.* DOE, London.

Macaulay Land Use Research Institute (1993). *The Land Cover of Scotland 1988: Final Report.* Aberdeen.

Miles, J. (1985). The pedogenic effects of different species and vegetation types and the implications of succession. *Journal of Soil Science,* **36,** 571–84.

Rodwell, J. S. (Ed.) (1992). *British Plant Communities. 2. Mires and Heaths.* Cambridge University Press, Cambridge.

Scottish Natural Heritage (1993). *National Countryside Monitoring Scheme, Scotland: Central.* Scottish Natural Heritage, Perth.

Scottish Natural Heritage (1994a). *The National Countryside Monitoring Scheme the changing face of Scotland 1940s to 1970s Main Report.* Scottish Natural Heritage, Perth.

Scottish Natural Heritage (1994b). *The National Countryside Monitoring Scheme the changing face of Scotland 1940s to 1970s Technical Report).* Scottish Natural Heritage, Perth.

Thompson, D. B. A. and Brown, A. (1992) Biodiversity in montane Britain: Habitat variation, vegetation diversity and some objectives for conservation. *Biodiversity and Conservation.* **1,** 179–208.

4 THE EXTENT AND CONDITION OF HEATHER IN MOORLAND, AND THE POTENTIAL IMPACT OF CLIMATE CHANGE

R. D. Bardgett, J. H. Marsden, D. C. Howard and J. E. Hossell

Summary

1. Based on a ground survey of 1 km squares, estimates of the extent and condition of heather on moorland in England and Wales, and within different biogeographic regions are given.

2. A modelling procedure was then used to predict the impact of global warming on the extent of moorland vegetation in Great Britain.

3. The findings are discussed in relation to other studies and to factors influencing biogeographic variation in the extent and condition of heather.

4.1 Introduction

Heather moorland with mosaics of semi-natural grassland, dwarf-shrub heaths and bogs forms a distinctive habitat, and supports an ecosystem of international importance. In recent years, large areas of heather moorland have been lost to afforestation (Nature Conservancy Council, 1986), agricultural reclamation (Parry *et al.*, 1981), and man-induced change caused by over-grazing by sheep (Felton and Marsden, 1990).

In addition to these pressures, it is likely that the future extent of heather moorland will be influenced by climatic changes associated with the greenhouse effect. There is a growing consensus that increasing amounts of carbon dioxide and other greenhouse gases (e.g. methane and nitrous oxide) in the atmosphere will lead to an incremental increase in average temperature of 3 °C by the year 2100 (Parry *et al.*, 1990). Increasing atmospheric temperatures may influence the future extent of heather-dominated vegetation directly via changes in the productivity of moorland soils and vegetation, and indirectly through increased opportunities for land improvement and cropping, and an extension of the grazing season.

The object of this study was to determine, by ground survey of a stratified sample of 1 km squares, both the present extent and condition of heather-dominated vegetation in the uplands of England and Wales. In addition, a modelling procedure known as the Climatic Land Classification (Hossell, 1992), and based on the Institute of Terrestrial Ecology (ITE) Land Classification (Bunce *et al.*, 1991), was used to provide estimates of the possible impact of climate change on the extent of heather-dominated vegetation.

4.2 Materials and Methods

4.2.1 Definitions

For the purposes of this study, the term 'heather' was used to describe all species of ericaceous dwarf-shrub, including common heather (*Calluna vulgaris*), bell heather (*Erica cinerea*), cross-leaved heather (*Erica tetralix*), bilberry (*Vaccinium myrtillus*), and crowberry (*Empetrum nigrum*). The term 'moorland' describes any unenclosed land in the selected upland land classes.

4.2.2 Survey squares

The survey covered a random sample of 122 one km squares within England and Wales (Figure 4.1). The squares were stratified into eight groups using the ITE Land Classification (Bunce *et al.*, 1991) (upland land classes 17, 18, 19, 20, 22, 23, 24 and 25). A description of the individual ITE land classes is given by Bunce *et al.*, (1991).

4.2.3 Heather condition

Homogenous stands of heather larger than one hectare were mapped on a basis of percentage cover (suppressed <25 %; sub-dominant 25–50 %; dominant >50 %) and height (<15 cm; 15–30 cm; >30 cm). Where *Calluna vulgaris* was present and its growth form suggested heavy-grazing, neglect or inappropriate management, individual stands were assigned to an additional condition category, derived from a classification system of MacDonald and Armstrong (1989).

The area (hectares) of open moorland, blanket bog, heather on moorland, and heather within the categories of cover, height and condition was recorded for each square. Data were converted to values of total extent (±SE), for both England and Wales, and for different biogeographic regions (MacDonald *et al.*, 1990) (Figure 4.1), by calculating the product of the mean coverage per square (±SE) for each land class and the area of that land class within the region, and then summing the land class estimates. The variability of estimates is expressed as the standard error of the mean. Further details of the procedure and the frequency distribution of land classes within each country and biogeographic region are given by Bardgett and Marsden (1992).

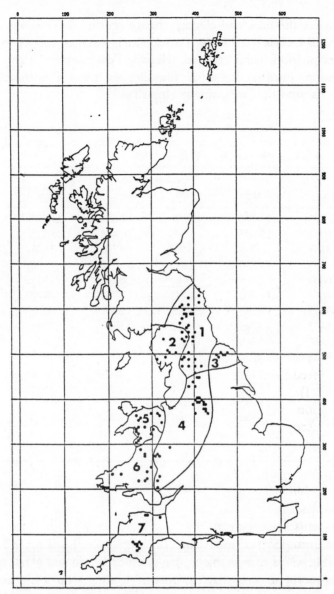

Figure 4.1. Geographical distribution of one km sample squares within England and Wales and the biogeographic regions (from MacDonald *et al.*, 1989). 1. Northeast England, 2. Northwest England, 3. North York Moors, 4. West Midlands, 5. North Wales, 6. South Wales, 7. Southwest England.

4.2.4 Impact of climate change

Using the same procedure as above, estimates of the total extent of moorland (±SE), heather on moorland and blanket bog were produced using different frequency distributions of land classes within Great Britain (as opposed to England and Wales, as above) under a sequence of elevated atmospheric temperatures (0.5 °C, 1.0 °C, 1.5 °C, 2.0 °C and 3.0 °C) derived from Hossell (1992). Areas of the individual ITE land classes under the base and climate change scenarios are shown in Table 4.1. Changes in the land class to which a 1 km square is assigned reflect changes in temperature, precipitation, and related climatic parameters such as potential evapotranspiration. Further details of the Climatic Land Classification modelling procedure and its validation are given by Hossell (1992).

Table 4.1 Area of land classes 17–32 (in km^2) under a base climate and sequence of elevated atmospheric temperatures in Great Britain (from Hossell, 1992)

Land class	Base	Temperature increase (°C)				
		0.5	1.0	1.5	2.0	3.0
17	15 885	15 750	16 290	19 620	23 760	28 665
18	9270	10 485	13 545	18 405	24 435	33 120
19	5175	4995	5400	5760	5085	2115
20	4590	4590	1395	90	0	0
21	6600	6300	5490	3240	1035	0
22	13 815	11 880	12 645	12 330	8910	1710
23	8235	8640	8325	6300	4590	270
24	5400	4545	2835	1530	360	0
25	10 440	9360	16 335	24 120	26 145	12 915
26	9225	8820	10 305	9000	4680	855
27	9405	9540	6615	2700	765	90
28	6570	10 260	6930	3960	1485	45
29	10 530	13 275	14 265	12 060	7875	945
30	3870	5130	945	0	0	0
31	3870	0	0	0	0	0
32	3510	0	0	0	0	0

4.3 Results and Discussion

The estimated area (±SE) of moorland (14 000±800 km^2) in England and Wales in this survey (Table 4.2) is comparable to that given by Felton and Marsden (1990). The results of this survey suggest that the area of heather with less than 25 % cover 11 000±800 km^2) on moorland in England and Wales is approximately 20 % greater than was estimated by Bradbury *et al.*, (1989), using Landsat TM satellite imagery. This discrepancy is likely to be due to the inability of satellite imagery to identify areas of moorland dominated by bilberry (particularly <15 cm tall), which were widely recorded in this survey. Another difference between this survey and that of Bradbury *et al.*, (1989) was in the relative extent of heather on moorland in England and Wales. The results of this survey suggest that 55 % of the total heather was in England (Table 4.2), whereas the Landsat survey (Bradbury *et al.*, 1989) and the 1984 ITE Countryside survey (Barr *et al.*, 1986), estimated 79 % and 83 %, respectively. As above, the inclusion of bilberry-dominated moorland in this survey, is the most likely explanation for the higher estimated area of heather in Wales.

Table 4.2 Estimates of area of moorland, heather moorland and different categories of height, cover and condition and blanket bog for England and Wales. All figures of area and standard errors ± are expressed as thousands of km^2.

Country	Area of moorland	Area of heather	Height			Cover			damaged heather	blanket bog
			<15 cm	15–30cm	>30 cm	<25%	25–50%	>50%		
England	7.79	6.19	2.31	2.01	1.87	2.16	1.15	2.88	1.48	1.88
	±0.47	±0.46	±0.26	±0.25	±0.29	±0.24	±0.17	±0.36	±0.29	±0.35
Wales	6.36	5.25	1.92	1.65	1.68	2.27	1.05	1.94	1.98	1.19
	±0.46	±0.45	±0.29	±0.29	±0.32	±0.33	±0.22	±0.34	±0.29	±0.31
England and Wales	14.15	11.44	4.27	3.66	3.56	4.42	2.20	4.82	3.46	3.07
	±0.81	±0.79	±0.48	±0.48	±0.54	±0.51	±0.35	±0.61	±0.45	±0.56

A large proportion (47 %) of the heather within England was dominant (>50 % cover), and only 24 % showed growth forms associated with heavy-grazing, neglect or inappropriate management (Table 4.2). In Wales, however, a large proportion (43 %) of the heather was suppressed (<25 % cover) and/or showing growth forms associated with heavy-grazing, neglect or inappropriate management (38 %) (Table 4.2). In terms of regional distribution, the majority of the heather was found to be within the west Midlands (3400±300 km square), south Wales (2900±300 km square), and northeast England (2500±300 km square) biogeographic regions (Table 4.3).

Table 4.3 Estimates of area of moorland, heather moorland and different categories of height, cover and condition and blanket bog for biogeographic regions. All figures of area and standard errors ± are expressed as thousands of km^2.

Biogeographic region	Area of moorland	Area of heather	Height			Cover			damaged heather	blanket bog
			<15 cm	15–30cm	>30 cm	<25%	25–50%	>50%		
South West	0.65	0.54	0.20	0.17	0.17	0.24	0.11	0.19	0.21	0.12
	±0.05	±0.05	±0.03	±0.03	±0.04	±0.04	±0.02	±0.04	±0.03	±0.03
South Wales	3.55	2.93	1.07	0.92	0.94	1.27	0.58	1.07	1.11	0.65
	±0.26	±0.25	±0.16	±0.16	±0.18	±0.19	±0.13	±0.19	±0.16	±0.17
North Wales	1.28	1.08	0.39	0.35	0.34	0.44	0.21	0.42	0.39	0.28
	±0.10	±0.09	±0.06	±0.06	±0.06	±0.06	±0.04	±0.07	±0.06	±0.07
North-west	1.18	0.90	0.36	0.29	0.25	0.29	0.16	0.45	0.17	0.31
	±0.09	±0.09	±0.06	±0.05	±0.06	±0.05	±0.04	±0.07	±0.04	±0.08
West Midlands	4.08	3.41	1.24	1.06	1.12	1.26	0.61	1.54	1.01	0.92
	±0.26	±0.26	±0.16	±0.15	±0.18	±0.16	±0.11	±0.21	±0.14	±0.21
North Yorks Moors	0.06	0.05	0.02	0.02	0.02	0.01	0.01	0.03	0.01	0.01
	±0.01	±0.01	±0.00	±0.00	±0.00	±0.00	±0.00	±0.01	±0.00	±0.01
Northeast	3.34	2.54	0.95	0.86	0.72	0.91	0.51	1.12	0.56	0.79
	±0.34	±0.32	±0.16	±0.17	±0.18	±0.14	±0.09	±0.24	±0.10	±0.22

The results of this survey suggest that there is approximately 44 000 km square of suppressed (<25 % cover), and therefore potentially recoverable heather in

England and Wales (Table 4.2). This survey suggests that a large proportion of this heather occurs within south Wales (29 %) and the west Midlands (29 %), where a large proportion of the heather was also damaged by heavy grazing or management neglect (38 % and 30 %, respectively) (Table 4.3). Although less in total extent, a large proportion of the heather in north Wales (36 %) and southwest England (38 %) was damaged by heavy grazing or management neglect (Table 4.3). In contrast, approximately 50 % of the area of heather on moorland in the North York Moors, northeast England and northwest England biogeographic regions was dominant (>50 % cover), while only 15–20 % showed growth forms associated with heavy grazing or management neglect (Table 4.3). The occurrence of large areas of moorland dominated by heather in these regions is likely to be related to the widespread management of moorland for grouse.

The results in Figure 4.2 suggest that the extent of open moorland and heather-dominated moorland is not sensitive to predicted increases in mean atmospheric

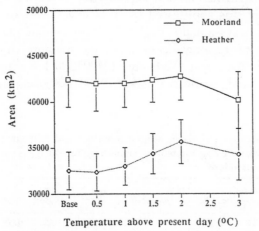

Figure 4.2. Potential impact of elevated atmospheric temperature on the extent (km^2 ± SE) of open moorland and heather on moorland in Great Britain.

temperature up to 3 °C above present day. It is possible, however, that changes in the geographical distribution of heather-dominated vegetation will occur. The model suggests that there is a significant negative linear relationship (r^2=0.82, P<0.01) between increasing atmospheric temperature and the extent of blanket bog in Great Britain, and that increases in the order of 3 °C may result in a reduction of approximately 25 % in its current extent (Figure 4.3). It is likely that the loss in area of blanket bog would be a result of increased evapotranspiration from waterlogged peat soils, resulting in reduced soil wetness and aeration. An increase in the oxidative status of peat soils may in turn enhance microbial decomposition of organic matter, resulting in increased turnover and availability of nutrients for plant growth. These combined factors may produce a shift in vegetation type from blanket bog to more productive dry heath and acid *Nardus* grassland.

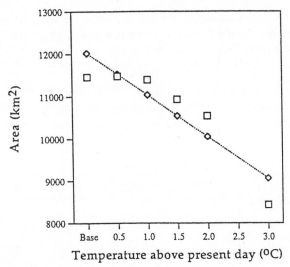

Figure 4.3. Relationship between increasing atmospheric temperature and the extent (km^2) of blanket bog in Great Britain (r^2=0.82, P<0.01).

The lack of effect of climate change on the extent of open moorland is probably because its area is defined by physical features such as walls and fences. Within areas of moorland, however, changes in the species composition of plant communities and soil conditions, are likely to occur. Such changes may exaggerate present losses of heather-dominated vegetation associated with heavy-grazing by sheep, land improvement and afforestation.

Acknowledgements

Part of this work was carried out whilst RDB was working for English Nature. We thank the farmers, landowners and gamekeepers who freely granted access to their land; Paul Evans and Leigh Lock who conducted much of the survey work; and Mark Felton (English Nature) and Chris Pollock (IGER) for their support.

References

Bardgett, R. D. and Marsden, J. H. (1992). *Heather Condition and Management in the Uplands of England and Wales*. English Nature, Peterborough.

Barr, C. J., Benefield, C. B., Bunce, R. G. H., Ridesdale, H. A. and Whittaker, M. (1986). *Landscape Changes in Britain*. Institute of Terrestrial Ecology, Huntingdon.

Bradbury, P., Howard, D. C., Bunce, R. G. H. and Deane, G. C. (1989). Production of maps and estimates of area. In Bunce, R. G. H., *Heather in England and Wales*. HMSO, London, 5–17.

Bunce, R. G. H., Howard, D. C., Clarke, R. T. and Lane, M. (1991). *ITE Land Classification: Classification of all 1 km Squares in Great Britain*. Department of Environment, (unpublished).

Felton, M. and Marsden, J. H. (1990). *Heather Regeneration in England and Wales*. Nature Conservancy Council, Peterborough.

Hossell, J. (1992). *Global Warming and the British Landscape: the Sensitivity of Land Use and Vegetation in Britain to Climatic Change*. (Unpublished PhD thesis, University of Birmingham.)

MacDonald, A. and Armstrong, H. (1989). *Methods for Monitoring Heather Cover*. Nature Conservancy Council, Peterborough.

MacDonald, A., Brown, A. and Thompson, D. B. A. (1990). Heather moorland: nature conservation value and biogeographic variation. In Marsden, J. H. and Felton, M. (Eds), *Heather Regeneration in England and Wales*, Annex 3, Nature Conservancy Council, Peterborough.

Nature Conservancy Council (1986). *Nature Conservation and Afforestation in Britain*. Nature Conservancy Council, Peterborough.

Parry, M., Bruce, A. and Harkness, C. (1981). The plight of British moorlands. *New Scientist*, **28,** 550–1.

Parry, M., Porter, J. H. and Carter, T. R. (1990). Climatic change and its implication for agriculture. *Outlook on Agriculture*, **19,** 9–15.

5 GROUSE MOORS AND UPLAND BREEDING BIRDS

A. F. Brown and I. P. Bainbridge

Summary

1. The international importance of upland breeding bird populations in Great Britain is examined, and the extent of that upland outlined.

2. The extent of grouse moor management, and the value of such management for birds other than grouse, is reviewed. Grouse moors have been instrumental in protecting uplands from forestry and agricultural intensification, but important populations of many upland species are found on moorland managed for other purposes. Very few, if any, species are dependent on grouse moors *per se*.

3. The paucity of quantitative studies of habitat selection, or of the effects of moorland management on species other than red grouse, is noted.

4. Avenues for future research into the relationships between moorland management and upland birds are suggested, and good management practices are outlined.

5.1 The International Importance of Upland Breeding Bird Populations in Britain

The British uplands support internationally important populations of breeding birds: Table 5.1 lists the more important species. Twenty-six British Red Data Birds and 12 candidate Red Data Birds (Batten *et al.*, 1990) are listed. Populations of 7 species are considered to occur in internationally important numbers, 13 species are represented as rare and/or local breeders and 7 species are given 'Special Category' status because the available data do not enable conservationists to have confidence that they will maintain present populations into the near future. Twenty species are listed on Schedule 1 of the Wildlife and Countryside Act 1981 and are thus specially protected under domestic legislation, and 14 species receive special protection under international law as they are listed on Annex 1 of the EC Directive on the Conservation of Wild Birds (EC 79/409).

Table 5.1 Important upland breeding birds in Britain: Red Data Birds, candidate Red Data Birds or those which receive special protection under domestic and/or international law. Italicised species are those most likely to be associated with heather moors.

Species	Red Data Bird (candidate)	Breeds in internationally important numbers	Rare and/or local breeder	Special category	Schedule 1	Annex 1 of EC Birds Directive
red-throated diver	*	*				*	*
black-throated diver	*		*		*	*
slavonian grebe	*		*		*	*
common scoter	*		*		*	
red kite	*		*		*	*
hen harrier	*			*	*	*
buzzard	candidate					
golden eagle	*	*			*	*
merlin	*			*	*	*
peregrine	*	*			*	*
red grouse	*	*				
black grouse	*			*		
dotterel	*			*	*	*
golden plover	*			*		*
lapwing	candidate					
Temminck's stint	*		*		*	
purple sandpiper	*		*		*	
snipe	candidate					
whimbrel	*			*	*	
curlew	*	*				
redshank	candidate					
greenshank	*			*	*	
wood sandpiper	*		*		*	*
red-necked phalarope	*		*		*	*
arctic skua	candidate					
great skua	*	*	*			
snowy owl	*		*		*	*
short-eared owl	candidate					*
shorelark	*		*		*	
dipper	candidate					
whinchat	candidate					
stonechat	candidate					
wheatear	candidate					
ring ouzel	candidate					
raven	candidate					
twite	*	*				
Lapland bunting	*		*		*	
snow bunting	*		*		*	

Species such as red grouse *Lagopus lagopus scoticus*, golden plover *Pluvialis apricaria* and merlin *Falco columbarius* probably nest at higher densities in the British uplands than elsewhere in Europe (Ratcliffe and Thompson, 1988), several arctic breeding species are at the southern edge of their breeding range (whimbrel *Numenius phaeopus*, Temminck's stint *Calidris temminckii*, purple sandpiper *Calidris maritima* and snowy owl *Nyctaea scandiaca*) and some have disjunct world distributions (ptarmigan *Lagopus mutus*, great skua *Stercoraria skua* and twite *Carduelis flavirostris*). Some species even have recognized British races (twite and red grouse). The uplands are also fast becoming a refuge for species such as snipe *Gallinago gallinago*, redshank *Tringa totanus* and whinchat *Saxicola rubetra*, once common birds of the lowlands, but increasingly restricted by habitat destruction to parts of their previous lowland range (Gibbons *et al.*, 1993). Overall, the assemblage consists of a rich mixture of northern arctic-boreal, oceanic, temperate, continental and coastal species.

The extent of British upland habitats has been estimated at 6.6 x 10^6 ha, of which heather-dominated moorlands form a large part, of between 1.4 and 1.7 x 10^6 ha (Ball *et al.*, 1983). A proportion of this heather moorland is actively managed for red grouse, through a combination of activities including burning, predator control and grazing. In this chapter we seek to investigate the contribution that heather moors managed primarily for red grouse make to the importance of the British uplands for birds.

Several authors have compiled lists of 'upland birds' containing between 31 and 75 species (Ratcliffe, 1977; Fuller, 1982; Thompson *et al.*, 1988; Ratcliffe, 1990, 1991; Avery and Leslie, 1990). Ratcliffe (1991) lists 67 species and indicates, by reference to gross habitat associations, that 61 of these are associated with either heaths/grass moors or acid bogs, though it is not possible to determine which species are associated with grouse moors from his data. To narrow our review of the available literature on the importance of grouse moors for birds, we have confined our review to those Red Data Birds and candidate Red Data Birds which Ratcliffe's information suggests are most likely to be associated with heather moorlands. We have not, therefore, included those species with a wide distribution outside the uplands, those which are very rare (<25 breeding pairs in Britain), and those which are mainly associated with trees, woodland, marginal land or open waters (but not also with heaths and grasslands). The 15 species so selected for review are italicized in Table 5.1.

5.2 Current Views on the Ornithological Importance of Grouse Moors

It is frequently stated that heather moors managed for grouse are 'good' for other upland birds and that grouse-moor management and upland bird conservation go hand in hand. Reed (1985) in a paper entitled 'Grouse Moors and Wading Birds' illustrates this: 'good grouse-moor management ... provides an ideal environment for breeding waders and grouse alike'. The RSPB (1991) have also stated: 'management of heather for red grouse ... provides habitat for other birds such as golden plover and curlew *Numenius arquata*. The RSPB recognizes this contribution to the conservation of upland birds by the owners and managers of grouse moors'. The Moorland Gamekeepers' Association has claimed that 'many of the upland breeding species which are of international importance are dependent upon the habitat produced by management practices funded solely by grouse shooting'. The prevalence of this thinking has resulted in what is at times an uneasy alliance between those whose primary aim is to manage heather moorlands for grouse, those who seek to conserve the wild bird populations in the British uplands and those who wish to use upland grouse moors for recreation.

We offer the observation that in the 1970s and 1980s, the rapid and continual increase in upland afforestation, especially in the north of Britain, may have forced conservationists into thinking that the decline of grouse moors there would inevitably result in the spread of conifer afforestation, with the consequent loss of almost all of the upland bird species that they were seeking to conserve (e.g. NCC, 1986). Faced with a simple choice of grouse moor or Sitka spruce, conservationists in the north became advocates of the grouse moor. In some English moorland areas the pressures on moorland were rather different. In the Peak District, the conflict was, and still is, between grouse and sheep, rather than grouse and trees. Anderson and Yalden (1981) have shown a trebling of sheep numbers in the area between 1950 and 1980, coupled with the considerable loss of heather moor, and studies on birds in these areas have reported declines in golden plover and dunlin, (Yalden, 1974), black grouse (Lovenbury *et al.*, 1978; Yalden, 1986) and red grouse (Yalden, 1972). Again, in these circumstances the conservationists' choice was for the management of grouse moor rather than its degradation by overgrazing.

Changes in policies and fiscal support for forestry have radically altered this balance since 1988, especially in England and Wales. It is no longer straightforward to predict the land-use changes which might follow the closure of a managed grouse shoot (Ratcliffe, 1993; Turner, 1993). Changes in support for agriculture have been smaller thus far, but continuing changes in the Common Agricultural Policy may make prediction of land-use change even more difficult in the near future. In some areas, especially Scotland, afforestation may follow, of native pine or broadleaves, or more usually of non-native conifers; there may be a deliberate increase in sheep grazing, or deer populations may increase; recreational access might be encouraged, or the moorland could be left unmanaged, leading to the development of rank heather, and in lightly-grazed areas, of scrub and native woodland. Grouse-moor interests might argue this to be detrimental; those concerned for upland bird conservation should examine the consequences of the changes carefully before deciding whether to adopt or espouse grouse moor management practices over wide areas.

In this context, three important questions need to be addressed: (1) Are grouse moors beneficial for upland breeding birds? (2) Are any upland birds dependent upon habitat or other management for red grouse? (3) Would cessation of grouse-moor management lead to a decline in the abundance or importance of our upland breeding bird assemblages? If any of these is true, we may predict that moors managed for red grouse will support other breeding birds of some considerable nature conservation interest. They may be expected to hold more species, hold some species in numbers or densities greater than on unmanaged moors or those species should have better breeding success on grouse moors. At the extreme, some species may also be confined to grouse moors. Cessation of management for grouse should lead to a decline in population productivity, numbers and perhaps range of key upland species. Unfortunately, no single study has tackled these problems in a satisfactory manner.

5.3 Evidence on the Value of Grouse Moor Management to Upland Birds

5.3.1 *The extent of grouse moors and their management*

It would, of course, be incorrect to equate all upland with grouse moor. However, there is debate as to the extent of moorland managed for grouse, and thus the contribution grouse-moor management makes to upland bird conservation. Bunce and Barr (1988) estimated from the ITE Merlewood Classification system that some 6.5 % (0.5 x 10^6 ha) of the British uplands is used mainly as grouse moor. Based on the size of sporting estates, Hudson (1992) estimated that almost three times this area (1.7 x 10^6 ha) was used principally as grouse moor. Hudson (1992) suggests that the former is an underestimate of the extent of grouse moor, and acknowledges that his estimate includes ground that is not heather-dominated moorland. However, even Hudson's estimates do not suggest that the uplands are dominated by grouse-moor management, rather that only some 5–15 % of the upland area is subjected to the range of practices associated with grouse management.

Evidence that grouse-moor management which includes burning is practised over only a relatively small area of upland Scotland is also provided by Bayley *et al.* (1991), whose remote-sensing studies found that only 6 % of the area of Scotland with greater than 25 % heather cover showed visible evidence of management by burning. A study by Hester and Sydes (1992) in the Borders and Grampian Regions (which they considered to have more intensive grouse-moor management than much of Scotland) found that the proportion of heather moorland burned annually was around 1–2 %. Only 10.2 % of the Borders' and 6.8 % of Grampian's heather moors showed recent evidence of burning (estimated by Hester and Sydes to be in the previous 11 years). Together, these studies suggest that at least 90 % of the uplands are not subject to grouse-moor burning regimes, especially in Scotland where many of the important upland breeding bird populations are found.

These estimates of the extent of burning of grouse moors should not be interpreted as the full picture of grouse-moor management. There are many unburnt areas where other grouse-moor management practices, such as legal predator control or controlled grazing occurs. These practices may have a beneficial effect on some breeding birds (e.g. Parr, 1980), but we cannot suggest a means of estimating their extent or level of their application without experimentation.

5.3.2 *Direct observations, associations and multivariate studies*

Some grouse moors support important breeding bird populations. Survey data held by English Nature, RSPB and others clearly demonstrates the rich diversity and high densities found, for example, on some north Pennine grouse moors (Shepherd, 1990). These same data also demonstrate that not all grouse moors hold good populations of upland breeding birds. In addition, many non-grouse moors (those in Shetland for example) support outstanding upland breeding bird populations (Rothwell *et al.*, 1988).

Avery and Leslie (1990) investigated the association between birds and heather using information in the BTO Breeding Bird Atlas at the 10 km square scale (Sharrock, 1976). An analysis of the 31 species whose distribution showed a 50 %+ coincidence with heather moorland led to the production of 'species richness' and 'conservation' indices for 40 randomly selected heather moorland 10 km squares throughout Britain. These show the areas of highest diversity and conservation value to be in the north and west of mainland Scotland, down into Strathspey. The distribution of British Red Data Birds shows a similar pattern, with the richest areas towards the north and west (Gibbons *et al.*, 1993). Hudson (1988) undertook a similar analysis, again based on the atlas but using a coarser scale (25 10 km squares) for 48 moorland bird species identified by Fuller (1982), excluding those associated with water or montane plateaux. He noted far less distinct trends, with slightly fewer species in Wales than in England and Scotland. We know of no data which show the distribution of moorlands burnt and managed for grouse, but much of the upland in the wetter north and western parts of Scotland is not associated with intensive grouse-moor management. Hudson's (1992) review of grouse shooting intensities suggests that much of these areas falls into the poorer grouse ground, with far fewer birds shot per km^2 than in south and east Scotland and the Pennines, areas which score lower on the indices of both Avery and Leslie (1990) and Hudson (1988). Hudson (1988, 1992) does suggest a weak positive association between breeding densities of golden plover (from Ratcliffe, 1976) and the grouse bag, but from these studies it is difficult to concur with the view that intensive grouse-moor management is vital for the survival of many of our internationally important upland species.

Multivariate studies of the distribution and abundance of upland breeding birds at a more regional scale are available for the south Pennines (Haworth and Thompson, 1990; Stillman and Brown, 1994) and the eastern highlands of Scotland (Brown and Stillman, 1993), both areas containing moorland managed primarily for grouse. Not surprisingly, there was a highly significant positive association between the numbers of red grouse and the area of heather in both study areas, as was shown by Miller *et al.* (1966). Interestingly though, of the other species included in the analyses, only skylark *Alauda arvensis* in Scotland and merlin, ring ouzel *Turdus torquatus*, twite and meadow pipit *Anthus pratensis* in the Pennines showed a positive association with the area of *Calluna* moor available in the sampling units. Dunlin *Calidris alpina* strongly avoided *Calluna*-dominated moors in the south Pennines. Other species showed no significant associations with or apparent aversion to *Calluna*-dominated moor. Indeed, none of the species studied in the south Pennines had habitat preferences and aversions similar to or the same as those of red grouse.

These studies also indicated that the more important factors related to distribution and abundance were geographical location (Avery and Leslie, 1990) and topography, particularly altitude and slope. Clearly then, within moorland habitats, many of the important factors in upland bird distribution and abundance are not amenable to management. This is not to say that features which are amenable to management are unimportant, but that there is no simple, straightforward association of management for grouse and overall ornithological importance. Data are not currently available which allow a strict quantitative comparison between managed and unmanaged moors in the same area and it is thus very difficult to compare like with like at this scale.

5.3.3 Single species studies

Several of the species selected for review occur well outside the main grouse moor areas. Whimbrel are found principally on the serpentine heaths and some of the blanket bogs of Shetland (Richardson, 1990), greenshank *Tringa nebularia* breed in submontane wet moorland dominated by exposed bedrock or in areas of pool complexes in north and west Scotland (Thompson *et al.*, 1986; Thompson and Thompson, 1992) and both great skuas and arctic skuas *Stercorarius parasiticus* are found largely on northern maritime heaths, generally in Shetland but also in north and west mainland Scotland (Furness, 1987; Ewins *et al.*, 1988) where some nest on grouse moors with a low intensity of management. Dotterel *Charadrius morinellus* nest on montane plateaux (Thompson and Whitfield, 1993) and strongly avoid *Calluna* and *Empetrum* bog and dwarf *Calluna* heaths for feeding, though the transition between bog and *Racomitrium* heath is a favoured habitat (Galbraith *et al.*, 1993). Snow buntings *Plectrophenax nivalis* nest in boulder fields and feed in snowbed grasslands and *Juncus* heaths (Thompson and Whitfield, 1993). Red kites *Milvus milvus* require upland woodlands for nesting and woodlands and sheepwalk for hunting (Newton *et al.*, 1981). Although they will hunt over heather moors they show no strong association with them and they are not dependent on them. They were also formerly lowland birds: persecution has caused the range contraction to the uplands. Similarly, peregrines *Falco peregrinus* occur in a wide range of habitats, including grouse moors, urban areas and sea coasts, with the requirement of a ledge on a cliff or other tall structure as a nest site as a common factor.

The remaining nine species all clearly have some association with grouse moors. Golden eagles *Aquila chrysaetos* are associated with a variety of upland habitats, perhaps because of their very large home ranges, and in many areas they do take red grouse as an important part of their diet (Brown and Watson, 1964; Watson *et al.*, 1987; Watson *et al.*, 1993). In many areas, for example in north-east Scotland, heather moorland forms an important element of their hunting range (Watson *et al.*, 1987). Most eagle nests (96 %) are on cliffs (Watson and Dennis, in press) with the remaining 4 % in trees near to the moorland edge, generally in areas where cliffs are scarce or unavailable. Although Brown and Watson (1964) found no clear association between nesting densities and available prey or carrion, later studies indicate that nesting density is related to the amount of carrion available in winter. Breeding densities are thus highest in the western Highlands. Harding *et al.*, (1994), in re-examining the work of Watson *et al.*, (1992), found both carrion densities and eagle densities to be lower in areas with high numbers of grouse moors. Breeding success, though, appears to be better where live prey is most abundant, in the eastern Highlands, where grouse moors comprise much of the upland area (Watson *et al.*, 1992).

Bibby and Etheridge (1993) found that practically all hen harrier *Circus cyaneus* nests located in Britain during the 1988/1989 national survey were in heather and all nests located by Picozzi (1978) were in long, rank heather, generally near a stream. However, harriers nesting on grouse moors face additional problems compared with those nesting elsewhere. Bibby and Etheridge (1993) estimated that harrier breeding success in 1988 and 1989 was lower on grouse moors than in other habitats. Etheridge and Summers (in press), analysing data from almost 1000 nests over a six-year period, found a survival rate of nests to fledging of 23 % on grouse moors, 72 % on other heather moors and 55 % on afforested ground, and productivity per pair of 0.8, 2.4 and 1.7 chicks on those three habitats respectively. Illegal killing of adults and destruction of nests and young appeared to be responsible. Bibby and Etheridge (1993) concluded that 'grouse moors are not just suppressing breeding production but acting as a drain on the adult population'; this conclusion appears to be further reinforced by the continuing studies.

Of all the upland bird species, merlins are perhaps most closely associated with heather moors. For example, Rebecca (1993) found grouse moor to be the major habitat within a 1 km radius of 86 % of 101 merlin nests in 1991 in his eastern Highland study area. Similarly, Nattrass *et al.* (1993) also record that of 280 merlin nests located in England in 1992, 87 % were on the ground on heather moors with 87 % of these on moors primarily managed for red grouse. This close association with heather has been found in all merlin studies (Newton *et al.*, 1978, 1986; Newton *et al.*, 1981; Meek, 1988; Bibby, 1986; Haworth and Fielding, 1988; Ellis and Okill, 1990; Parr, 1991; Rebecca *et al.*, 1992). Merlins nest in moderate to tall heather, often on moderately sloping ground. The short-eared owl *Asio flammeus*, another bird often associated with grouse moors, nests in a range of habitats, including upland heather moors, submontane grasslands and coastal marshes (Glue, 1977).

Red Grouse are heather dependent and well studied (see Lance and Lawton, 1990 for a review). Black grouse *Tetrao tetrix* appear to require a range of habitats during the year. Parr and Watson (1988) found that they used tall heather for roosting, that most nests found were in tall heather and that heather was eaten at certain times of the year. Picozzi (1986) also found strong selection for heather by nesting black grouse and those with broods used wet moorland areas and grasslands but avoided dry moorland. In contrast, Cayford *et al.* (1989) found that Welsh birds selected dry moorland, though those with chicks avoided the open moor. Heather was a staple food throughout the year, but it seems likely from his study that at least some of this came from heather in the understorey of nearby forest.

Golden plover nest in a wide variety of upland habitats (Ratcliffe, 1976). They appear to associate strongly with short vegetation. On one north-east Scottish heather moor the mean height of preferred vegetation was about 10 cm and territories were separated in some cases by 'expanses of long heather not used by the birds' (Parr, 1980). Adults with young strongly favoured grass patches within the moor, even where these were less than 1 % of the moor by area. Interestingly, Crick (1992) found that golden plovers on grass moors nested on average 11 days later than those on heather moors or bog in the same region, and tended to have a smaller clutch size. Failure rates for nests on grass in the 1980s were treble that of nests on heather or bog at the same time, and were double the failure rate experienced in the previous decade. Most of the difference was caused by far higher nest failures in north-west England and in Wales in the 1980s. There has been no thorough study of habitat usage or habitat selection by golden plover in this country.

A recent study of twite by Brown *et al.* (in press) found that although their distribution was not significantly associated with the area of *Calluna*, birds had a much higher proportion of second broods on heather moor than on grass or unspecified moor, and nests on heath suffered far fewer losses (35 %) during the nesting phase compared with those on grass (60 %) or unspecified moor (51 %). Ring ouzels usually nest on the ground in tall vegetation, often heather but in a wide variety of other vegetation or structures. They are usually near to some irregularity in otherwise uniform habitat (Flegg and Glue, 1975; Poxton, 1986).

Together, these studies give interesting descriptions of habitat use and suggest ways in which moorlands might be managed for each species. The most notable feature of them, however, is the almost total lack of quantitative studies of habitat selection.

5.4 Conclusions

Moorlands managed for grouse are not necessarily of a high nature conservation interest for other bird species. Many upland habitats other than grouse moors support important upland bird populations. Traditional grouse-moor management including burning is currently practised only over a small proportion of the uplands and these tend to be away from the more important areas for upland birds. There is scant evidence concerning the associations of upland birds with heather moors, even less for those managed as grouse moors. No other species appear to share the same habitat preferences and aversions as do red grouse. Given the limited data, we conclude that grouse-moor management is not a prerequisite for the maintenance of internationally important upland bird populations in Britain.

Grouse moors may, however, provide suitable breeding habitat for certain raptors. Bibby and Nattrass (1986) found higher densities of merlins on grouse moors than on other habitats and it may be that over half of the British merlin population nests on grouse moors. Many hen harriers also nest on grouse moors (Bibby and Etheridge (1993) estimated 29 %) and there can be no doubt too, that with a cessation of persecution of the latter, they could be of even greater importance. Golden eagles also appear to breed more successfully in areas containing large areas of heather moorland. Red grouse and black grouse both select heather for food throughout, or at certain times of, the year and can thus be regarded as being heather-dependent. Black grouse, though, can obtain heather from native woodland understorey and the importance of open heather moorland is not clear. The remaining species occur in a wide variety of upland habitats. In several cases the larger fraction of their population occurs outwith grouse moors or they breed at higher densities in other habitats. Interestingly, the few studies of breeding success involving comparisons between heather moors and other uplands give differing results: golden plover and twite appear to have better breeding success on heather moors than in other habitats, whereas for breeding raptors it is lower.

At least two explanations might account for the variations in the observed relationships between grouse-moor management and bird conservation interest. The moorland manager may indeed provide features valuable to other upland breeding birds during the course of his management for grouse that would otherwise not have been present. The manager is clearly not influencing some of the more important features, such as slope, elevation, aspect and underlying soil chemistry. He could, however, prevent the total loss of heather through overgrazing, create a short sward by burning on the flatter ground and remove the predators of ground-nesting birds. Such moors may be rich in grouse and in other species. Grouse moors low in bird conservation interest may simply not be managed well and this may well now be the prevalent type of grouse moor in Britain. For example, on an unburnt moor where predator control is not practised, the heather might be too tall and the predation pressure too high to allow waders to breed successfully. In contrast, in an area subject to chronic overgrazing, the area of old heather favoured by nesting raptors might be too small and the raptors might be eliminated. The reintroduction of traditional grouse-moor management practices, perhaps following heather regeneration, may restore the important bird populations to such areas.

Alternatively, the fact that species of conservation interest breed on grouse moors might merely reflect their catholic choice of breeding habitats. The presence of a rich upland breeding bird community on a managed grouse moor might be coincidence. Moors where features which are critical to the survival of a species are present naturally, and are not removed or damaged by management for grouse, may be of particular conservation importance. In the absence of grouse moor management, the important bird populations might well have been there anyway. For example, we know that golden plover breed at a very high density on one area of limestone grassland. Might the important factor be a short sward, irrespective of the upland vegetation type? That merlins nest in the taller heather of grouse moors is not so surprising when there is potentially little alternative for them to adopt on heather moorlands. Merlins do nest in forest edge, copses, isolated trees and bracken, and if these were available at higher densities on, say, grassland areas, then merlins might be more abundant there, and they might enjoy greater breeding success as found for tree-nesting merlins in Northumberland (Newton *et al.*, 1986). It is interesting to note that hen harriers are most numerous in Europe in the rolling, heather-free countryside of France.

Information is not available to allow convincing discrimination between these two explanations. This reflects the observed great variability in the interest of different moors, an almost complete lack of quantitative studies of habitat selection by key species and no published information at all on the impacts of traditional management practices of grouse moors on upland bird populations other than red grouse. We suggest that the belief of some grouse moor owners, their keepers, grouse shooters, conservationists and ramblers, that grouse-moor management maintains the internationally important upland breeding bird interests of Britain, may be misplaced. Grouse-moor management may well be compatible with a number of wider bird conservation interests but those interests do not appear to depend upon such management; other moorland may be of equal or even higher value. We urge that until more evidence is available, assertions about the nature conservation benefits of grouse-moor management should be made with caution.

5.5 Future Research and Future Management

It should be possible to obtain further evidence on the value of grouse moors and traditional management practices to birds other than grouse. One of the problems of assessing the effects of management on upland birds is that of separating the effects of different factors. The principal management activities in the uplands are burning, grazing and predator control, and it will be necessary to test their effects in different ways.

To investigate the effects of burning management, we suggest experimental manipulation of burning on a series of paired moorland areas with similar physical and geographical features and predator control. The distributions and densities of breeding birds, and their breeding success should be monitored for a number of years, to allow tests of appropriate hypotheses covering the benefits of burning management. Such experiments would have to be carried out over a very long time period: Hester and Sydes (1992) state that the effects of burning are still visible for at least 11 years, so any such experiment would have to be long-term. Experiments examining changes in bird populations after the introduction of a burning regime would only investigate part of the question.

Experiments into the effects of heavy grazing pressures on moorland might be conducted in a similar way, with the key being the location of pairs of moors, one well managed as a grouse moor, the other overgrazed, but with similar geology, altitude and keepering. Again the results of experimental manipulation would take a considerable time to emerge.

A study of the effects of legal predator control (of foxes and crows) may be more suited to experimental manipulations, as predator control is not linked intrinsically to vegetation change. If paired areas of suitable size, with and without predator control but similar in all other respects, could be located, crossover experiments similar to those done on Salisbury Plain (Tapper *et al.*, 1991) could be carried out, ceasing predator control on some areas, commencing it on others and maintaining it on controls. Data on the breeding success of key moorland species are of particular importance, as predator control measures may have little effect on the numbers and distribution of birds settling on the moor to breed.

It may be possible to investigate other effects by similar means: we present a number of possible factors and manipulations (these are, in fact, management prescriptions for heather moorlands) in Table 5.2. Such studies could lead to a better understanding of the value of different management practices on moorland areas.

Table 5.2   Prescriptions for grouse-moor management which may benefit upland breeding birds

- Allow heather burning in September as well as spring.

  There appear to be few, if any objections on ornithological grounds to this, whereas late spring burning may destroy early nests of moorland birds.

- Leave heather to grow very long on steep slopes, in gullies and narrow cloughs and at the moorland edge, retain the development of scrub and retain bracken.

- Consider fencing such areas to encourage natural regeneration by exclosing grazing sheep and deer.

- Reduce herbivore levels on grouse moors to ensure heather retention and encourage scrub growth in gullies.

- In areas with intensive burning, lengthen burning rotation on some parts of the steeper sloping terrain to allow some heather to grow taller.

  These prescriptions will help to provide nesting sites for merlin and twite and possibly for short-eared owl and hen harrier; song posts, foraging perches and nest sites for passerines such as whinchat, stonechat, tree pipit, ring ouzel and twite and, when overhangs and rocks are also present in cloughs, it will provide nesting sites for ring ouzel. They may also afford cover for grouse in hard weather or for avoiding predators.

- Use a short burning rotation on flat or gently sloping (<15 °) ground.

- Maintain a light summer grazing regime.

  These provide a short sward on the flatter ground which may benefit breeding waders in both the heather and the grassy areas on managed heath. These are favoured by nesting golden plover and other waders especially in the period when they have young chicks.

- Do not burn heather where it is already prostrate through natural causes, such as in the montane zone or ridge tops.

  This should be unnecessary, growth is very slow and these are important areas for ground nesting waders.

- Do not burn in areas with pools on wet heath and blanket bog where these are on ridge tops or hill summits.

- Do not drain bog pools.

  Both of these prescriptions ensure that wet areas are retained for use by nesting and feeding dunlin and by feeding wader adults and chicks; draining and burning both destroy hydrology. Heather will regenerate here anyway and rank growth is minimal.

- Do not drain the moor.

  This achieves little in terms of heather or grouse production and any drying will only be detrimental to feeding waders and grouse chicks.

Table 5.2 (cont'd)   Prescriptions for grouse-moor management which may benefit upland breeding birds

---

- Block existing drains.

  This should create relatively nutrient-rich sphagnum pools, providing foraging areas for wader and grouse chicks alike.

- Retain wet flushed areas.

  These are used as wader and grouse feeding places. Wader chicks may be moved many hundreds of metres, in some instances over a kilometre, to feed in such areas so they must be important to them.

- Control ground predators and crows.

  Legal predator control may benefit a range of upland breeding birds, but data to demonstrate this are not available at present.

- Do not destroy raptors.

  We hesitate to include this in the list of prescriptions — it should go without saying, and is of course illegal. However, this still occurs and should be recognized as unnecessary, bad and illegal practice.

These investigations need not be costly, at least to moorland owners. Many of the practices we suggest as being beneficial to upland birds are already carried out on many moors. The adoption of some of these practices on other grouse moors, along experimental lines and linked with bird population monitoring, would appear to be the least costly approach. Such a move would also be welcomed by conservation organisations. Detailed studies of population productivity, habitat use and selection and overall population ecology, involving the use of individually marked birds, should be integral to the study. We suggest that key species include merlin, golden plover, curlew, twite and ring ouzel.

Some of the prescriptions outlined above are similar to those recommended for conservation of upland plants and invertebrates (e.g. Usher and Thompson, 1993). Such compatibility probably relates to the desire to increase heterogeneity of vegetation type, form and structure at a variety of scales. We might expect that an increase in the diversity of invertebrate prey for both grouse chicks and the other bird species would result in an increase in the diversity and abundance of other bird species on the moor; this in turn would provide raptors with increased food alternatives to grouse.

These prescriptions could thus lead to an enhancement of the nature conservation interest of grouse moors, without necessarily incurring an economic cost. If demonstrated to be effective in this way, they may also form the basis for the development of a system of incentive-driven positive management prescriptions, designed to provide for the good management of the open uplands of Britain, and counter the continuing degradation and loss, through farming intensification and forestry, of one of the country's most valuable and important habitats.

Acknowledgements

We are grateful for the comments received from Rhys Green, Mark Avery, Gwyn Williams and Jayne Manley on an early draft of this paper, and for the helpful comments of the referees.

References

Anderson, P. and Yalden, D. W. (1981). Increased sheep numbers and the loss of heather moorland in the Peak District, England. *Biological Conservation*, **20**, 195–213.

Avery, M. and Leslie, R. (1990). *Birds and Forestry.* T. and A. D. Poyser, London.

Ball, D. F., Radford, G. L. and Williams, W. M. (1983). *A Land Characteristic Databank for Great Britain.* I.T.E. Occasional Paper No. 13. I.T.E., Bangor.

Batten, L. A., Bibby, C. J., Clement, P., Elliot, G. D. and Porter, R. F. (1990). *Red Data Birds in Britain.* T. and A. D. Poyser, London.

Bayley, A. A., Burnhill, P. M., Dowie, P. J., Ewington, H. and Hotson, J. McG. (1991). *Distribution of Heather and Agricultural Activity in Britain.* Project report to DoE, June 1991. ESRC Research Laboratory for Scotland, Edinburgh.

Bibby, C. J. (1986). Merlins in Wales: site occupancy and breeding in relation to vegetation. *Journal of Applied Ecology*, **23**, 1–12.

Bibby, C. J. and Etheridge, B. (1993). Status of the hen harrier *Circus cyaneus* in Scotland in 1988–89. *Bird Study*, **40**, 1–11.

Bibby, C. J. and Nattrass, M. (1986). Breeding status of the merlin in Britain. *British Birds*, **79**, 170–85.

Brown, A. F., Crick, H. Q. P. and Stillman, R. A. (in press) The distribution, numbers and breeding ecology of Twite *Acanthis flavirostris* in the south Pennines. *Bird Study.*

Brown, A. F. and Stillman, R. A. (1993). Bird-habitat associations in the eastern Highlands of Scotland. *Journal of Applied Ecology*, **30**, 31–42.

Brown, L. H. and Watson, A. (1964). The Golden eagle in relation to its food supply. *Ibis*, **106**, 78–100.

Bunce, R. G. H. and Barr, C. J. (1988). The extent of land under different management regimes in the uplands and the potential for change. In Usher, M. B. and Thompson, D. B. A. (Eds). *Ecological Change in the Uplands.* Blackwell Scientific Publications, Oxford, 415–426.

Cayford, J. T., Tyler, G. and Macintosh-Williams, L. (1989). *The Ecology and Management of Black Grouse in Conifer Forests in Wales.* RSPB research report, Sandy.

Crick, H. Q. P. (1992). *Trends in the Breeding Performance of Golden Plover in Britain.* Joint Nature Conservation Committee Report Number 23. JNCC, Peterborough.

Ellis, P. M. and Okill, J. D. (1990). Breeding ecology of the merlin *Falco columbarius* in Shetland. *Bird Study*, **37**, 101–10.

Etheridge, B. and Summers, R. W. (In press). Nest survival and productivity of hen harriers (*Circus cyaneus*) breeding in different habitats. In *Proceedings of the Symposium on the Ecology and Conservation of Harriers, Canterbury 1993.* Hawk and Owl Trust, Kent.

Ewins, P. J., Ellis, P. M., Bird, D. B. and Prior, A. (1988). The distribution and status of arctic and great skuas in Shetland 1985/86. *Scottish Birds*, **15**, 9–20.

Flegg, J. J. M. and Glue, D. E. (1975). The nesting of the ring ousel. *Bird Study*, **22**, 1–8.

Fuller, R. J. (1982). *Bird Habitats in Britain.* T. and A. D. Poyser, Calton.

Galbraith, H., Murray, S., Duncan, K., Smith, R., Whitfield, D. P. and Thompson, D. B. A. (1993). Diet and habitat use of the dotterel *Charadrius morinellus* in Scotland. *Ibis*, **135**, 148–55.

Gensbol, B. (1984). *Collins Guide to the Birds of Prey.* Collins, London.

Gibbons, D. W., Reid, J. B. and Chapman, R. A. (1993). *The New Atlas of Breeding Birds in Britain and Ireland: 1988–1991.* T. and A. D. Poyser, London.

Glue, D. E. (1977). Feeding ecology of the short-eared owl in Britain and Ireland. *Bird Study*, **24**, 70–8.

Harding, N. J., Green, R. E. and Summers, R. W. (1994). *The Effects of Future Changes in Land Use on Upland Birds in Britain*. RSPB Research report, Edinburgh.

Haworth, P. F. and Fielding, A. H. (1988). Conservation and management implications of habitat selection in the merlin *Falco columbarius* in the south Pennines. *Biological Conservation*, **46**, 247–60.

Haworth, P. F. and Thompson, D. B. A. (1990). Factors associated with the breeding distribution of upland birds in the south Pennines, England. *Journal of Applied Ecology*, **27**, 562–77.

Hester, A. J. and Sydes, C. (1992). Changes in burning of Scottish heather moorland since the 1940s from aerial photographs. *Biological Conservation*, **60**, 25–30.

Hudson, P. J. (1988). Spatial variations, patterns and management options in upland bird communities. In Usher, M. B. and Thompson, D. B. A. (Eds), *Ecological Change in the Uplands*. Blackwell Scientific Publications, Oxford, 381–397.

Hudson, P. J. (1992). *Grouse in Space and Time. The Population Biology of a Managed Gamebird*. Game Conservancy Ltd., Fordingbridge.

Lance, A. N. and Lawton, J. H. (Eds) (1990). *Red Grouse Population Processes*. Proceedings of a workshop convened by the British Ecological Society and the Royal Society for the Protection of Birds, Sandy.

Lovenbury, G. A., Waterhouse, M. and Yalden, D. W. (1978). The status of black grouse in the Peak District. *The Naturalist*, **103**, 3–14.

Meek, E. R. (1988). The breeding ecology and decline of the merlin *Falco columbarius* in Orkney. *Bird Study*, **35**, 209–18.

Miller, G. R., Jenkins, D. and Watson, A. (1966). Heather performance and red grouse populations. I. Visual estimates of heather performance. *Journal of Applied Ecology*, **3**, 313–26.

Nattrass, M., Clement, P. and Brown, A. (1993). *The Status of the Merlin and the Hen Harrier in England in 1992*. English Nature, Peterborough.

NCC (1986). *Nature Conservation and Afforestation in Britain*. Nature Conservancy Council, Peterborough.

Newton, I., Davies, P. E. and Moss, D. (1981). Distribution and breeding of red kites in relation to land use in Wales. *Journal of Applied Ecology*, **18**, 173–86.

Newton, I., Meek, E. and Little, B. (1978). Breeding ecology of the merlin in Northumberland. *British Birds*, **71**, 376–98.

Newton, I., Meek, E. and Little, B. (1986). Population and breeding of Northumbrian merlins. *British Birds*, **79**, 155–70.

Newton, I., Robson, J. E. and Yalden, D. W. (1981). Decline of the merlin in the Peak District. *Bird Study*, **28**, 225–34.

Parr, R. (1980). Population study of golden plover *Pluvialis apricaria*, using marked birds. *Ornis Scandinavica*, **11**, 179–89.

Parr, R. and Watson, A. (1988). Habitat preferences of black grouse on moorland-dominated ground in north-east Scotland. *Ardea*, **76**, 175–80.

Parr, S. J. (1991). Occupation of new conifer plantations by merlins in Wales. *Bird Study*, **38**, 103–11.

Picozzi, N. (1978). Dispersion, breeding and prey of the hen harrier *Circus cyaneus* in Glen Dye, Kincardineshire. *Ibis*, **120**, 498–509.

Picozzi, N. (1986). *Black Grouse Research in North-east Scotland*. Report to World Pheasant Association. Institute of Terrestrial Ecology, Banchory.

Poxton, I. R. (1986). Breeding ring ouzels in the Pentland Hills. *Scottish Birds*, **14**, 44–8.

Ratcliffe, D. A. (1976). Observations on the breeding of the golden plover in Britain. *British Birds*, **23**, 63–116.

Ratcliffe, D. A. (1977). *A Nature Conservation Review*. Cambridge University Press, Cambridge.

Ratcliffe, D. A. (1990). *Birdlife of Mountain and Upland*. Cambridge University Press, Cambridge.

Ratcliffe, D. A. (1991). Upland birds and their conservation. *British Wildlife*, **2**, 1–12.

Ratcliffe, D. A. (1993). Nature Conservation and afforestation policy. *Ecos*, **14**, 19–22.

Ratcliffe, D. A. and Thompson, D. B. A. (1988). The British uplands: their ecological character and international significance. In Usher, M. B. and Thompson, D. B. A. (Eds), *Ecological Change in the Uplands*. Blackwell Scientific Publications, Oxford, 9–36.

Rebecca, G. (1993). The importance of the breeding population of the merlin (*Falco columbarius*) in north-east Scotland. In Nicholls, M. K. and Clarke, R. (Eds), *Biology and Conservation of Small Falcons*. Hawk and Owl Trust, London, 39–41.

Reed, T. M. (1985). Grouse Moors and Wading Birds. *The Game Conservancy Annual Review*, **16**, 57–60.

Richardson, M. G. (1990). The distribution and status of whimbrel *Numenius p. phaeopus* in Shetland and Britain. *Bird Study*, **37**, 61–8.

Rothwell, A., Stroud, D. A. and Shepherd, K. B. (1988). *Shetland Moorland Bird Surveys*. CSD Report 775. Nature Conservancy Council, Peterborough.

RSPB (1991). Species and Habitat Action Plans. *RSPB Conservation Review*, **5**, 40.

Sharrock, J. T. R. (1976). *The Atlas of Breeding Birds in Britain and Ireland*. British Trust for Ornithology and Irish Wild Bird Conservancy, Tring.

Shepherd, K. B. (1990). *An Inventory of NCC Moorland Bird Surveys in the North Pennines*. CSD Report 1169. Nature Conservancy Council, Peterborough.

Stillman, R. A. and Brown, A. F. (1994). Population sizes and habitat associations of upland breeding birds in the south Pennines, England. *Biological Conservation* **69**, 307-314.

Tapper, S., Brockless, M. and Potts, G. R. (1991). The Salisbury Plain Predation Experiment: the conclusion. *The Game Conservancy Annual Review*, **22**, 87–91.

Thompson, D. B. A., Thompson, P. S. and Nethersole-Thompson, D. (1986). Timing of breeding and breeding performance in a population of greenshanks (*Tringa nebularia*). *Journal of Animal Ecology*, **55**, 181–99.

Thompson, D. B. A., Stroud, D. A. and Pienkowski, M. W. (1988). Afforestation and upland birds: consequences for population ecology. In Usher, M. B. and Thompson, D. B. A. (Eds), *Ecological Change in the Uplands*. Blackwell Scientific Publications, Oxford, 237–59.

Thompson, D. B. A. and Whitfield, D. P. (1993). Research on mountain birds and their habitats. *Scottish Birds*, **17**, 1–8.

Thompson, P. S. and Thompson, D. B. A. (1992). Greenshanks *Tringa nebularia* and long-term studies of breeding waders. *Ibis*, **133** suppl I, 99–112.

Turner, R. M. (1993). Britain's Forests – An Age of Enlightenment? *Ecos*, **14**, 14–18.

Usher, M. B. and Thompson, D. B. A. (1993). Variation in the upland heathlands of Great Britain: conservation importance. *Biological Conservation*, **66**, 69–81.

Watson, A. (1965). A population study of Ptarmigan (*Lagopus mutus*) in Scotland. *Journal of Animal Ecology*, **34**, 135–72.

Watson, A., Payne, S. and Rae, S. R. (1989). Golden eagles *Aquila chrysaetos*: land use and food in northeast Scotland. *Ibis*, **131**, 336–48.

Watson, J. and Dennis, R. H. (in press). Nest site selection by golden eagles (*Aquila chrysaetos*) in Scotland. *British Birds*.

Watson, J., Langslow, D. R. and Rae, S. R. (1987). *The Impact of Land Use Changes on Golden Eagles in the Scottish Highlands*. Nature Conservancy Council Chief Scientists' Directorate, Research Report Number 720, Peterborough.

Watson, J., Leitch, A. F. and Rae, S. R. (1993). The diet of golden eagles *Aquila chrysaetos* in Scotland. *Ibis*, **135**, 387–93.

Watson, J., Rae, S. R. and Stillman, R. (1992). Nesting density and breeding success of golden eagles in relation to food supply in Scotland. *Journal of Animal Ecology*, **61**, 543–50.

Yalden, D. W. (1972). The Red Grouse (*Lagopus lagopus scoticus* (Lath.)) in the Peak District. *The Naturalist*, **922**, 89–102.

Yalden, D. W. (1974). The status of the golden plover *Pluvialis apricaria* and dunlin *Calidris alpina* in the Peak District. *The Naturalist*, **930**, 81–91.

Yalden, D. W. (1986). The further decline of the black grouse in the Peak District, 1975–1985. *The Naturalist*, **111**, 3–8.

6   BIRD ASSOCIATIONS WITH HEATHER MOORLAND IN THE SCOTTISH AND ENGLISH UPLANDS

R. A. Stillman

Summary

1. The results of two surveys of upland breeding birds in the eastern Highlands of Scotland and the south Pennines of England are used to show the range of associations found between bird species and dwarf shrub moorland dominated by *Calluna vulgaris* (L.) Hull.

2. Red Grouse (*Lagopus lagopus* L.), Merlin (*Falco columbarius* L.) and Meadow Pipit (*Anthus pratensis* L.) were positively associated with heather moor cover in one or both areas, whilst Dunlin (*Caladris alpina* L.) and Skylark (*Alauda arvensis* L.) showed negative associations and the remaining species studied showed no significant associations. In both areas the major environmental features associated with bird distribution were altitude, and vegetation gradients from grassland to heather moorland.

3. As the bird species studied showed a range of habitat associations, a higher species diversity would be expected in areas with a mosaic of different habitat types than in areas of pure heather moorland.

6.1   Introduction

The uplands of Britain provide breeding habitat for several rare and endangered bird species (Ratcliffe, 1990; Ratcliffe and Thompson, 1988; Stroud *et al.*, 1990). Due to the extent of the uplands and the dispersed nature of many upland bird populations, conservation of these species depends largely on the maintenance of suitable breeding habitats across large areas, rather than simply within a few protected sites. Knowledge of basic habitat associations is an important aspect in recommending management leading to suitable breeding habitats for a range of upland bird species.

In recent years a large number of upland bird surveys have been conducted throughout much of Britain (see Brown, 1991 for a review). The preliminary aim of many of these surveys has been to identify areas of particular importance for upland breeding birds. However, when habitat features are recorded in addition to bird numbers these surveys can be used to identify general associations between birds and their habitats. Brown and Stillman (1993) and Brown *et al.* (1992) have shown how the results of such surveys can be used to identify the habitat associations of a suite of upland breeding birds in the eastern Highlands of Scotland and the south Pennines of England. In this chapter the range of habitat associations found in these two studies are compared with particular emphasis on bird associations with dwarf shrub moorland dominated by *Calluna vulgaris.*

6.2 Methods

Brown and Stillman (1993) studied habitat associations using survey data collected from a stratified random sample of 71 km squares (based on the national grid) located in the uplands of Grampian, Tayside and Central regions. A complete survey of the uplands of these regions was not feasible due their extent (over 10 000 km^2) and remoteness. The survey data used by Brown *et al.*, (1992) were collected from all unenclosed moorland in the Pennines to the south of Skipton in Yorkshire and comprised 402 complete km squares.

A constant search effort for birds was maintained throughout each study area. Each area was surveyed twice for breeding birds during the season, once between April and May and once between May and June. Population estimates for each square were taken as the maximum count recorded on either of the two visits. For the purpose of comparing the two studies only those bird species occurring at relatively high population densities in either of the study areas have been considered (Table 6.1). The habitat associations of Dunlin and Merlin were not studied in the eastern Highlands due to their rarity in this area.

Table 6.1   Bird species recorded in the eastern Highlands and southern Pennines surveys.

Merlin*	*Falco columbarius* (L.)
Red Grouse	*Lagopus lagopus* (L.)
Golden Plover	*Pluvialis apricaria* (L.)
Dunlin*	*Caladris alpina* (L.)
Curlew	*Numenius arquata* (L.)
Snipe	*Gallinago gallinago* (L.)
Skylark	*Alauda arvensis* (L.)
Meadow Pipit	*Anthus pratensis* (L.)
Whinchat	*Saxicola rubetra* (L.)
Wheatear	*Oenanthe oenanthe* (L.)

*Habitat associations not studied in the eastern Highlands.

Vegetation composition was recorded in both areas as the percentage cover of each of the habitat types listed in Table 6.2. The main aim of both surveys was to estimate breeding bird abundance rather than to make detailed recording of the habitat and so the habitat types were necessarily broad. In addition, each square surveyed was described in terms of its location (easting and northing), altitude and slope. Further details of the survey methods may be obtained from the original reports.

Table 6.2   Vegetation features recorded in the eastern Highlands and south Pennines surveys. The codes given in the descriptions refer to Phase 1 classes (Nature Conservancy Council 1990).

Name	*Description*
Heather moorland	Dry heath (D1) in both areas and occasionally montane heath (D4) in the eastern Highlands. In both areas *Calluna vulgaris* (L.) Hull was the most frequently dominant species, with *Vaccinium myrtillus* L. occasionally dominant. Co-occurring species in both areas were *Vaccinium vitis-idea* L. and *Empetrum nigrum* L.
Grass moorland	Unimproved or semi-improved acid grassland (B1) dominated by *Agrostis* spp., *Festuca* spp., or *Nardus stricta* L.. Improved grassland (B4) was not included in either survey.
Bog	Wet heath (D2) or bog (E1). In both areas *Eriophorum* spp. were dominant, whilst *Sphagnum* spp. were frequent in the eastern Highlands but rare in the south Pennines.
Wet flush	Wet flush (E2) or marshy grass (B5) dominated by *Juncus* spp and *Carex spp.*
Bracken	Areas dominated by *Pteridium aquilinium* (L.) Kuhn. (C1).

6.3   Results

6.3.1   *Bird associations with heather moorland*

Pearson correlation was used to study the associations between the abundance of each bird species (log transformed) and heather moorland cover. As the analysis involved 17 separate statistical tests only correlations significant at the 1 % level are considered. With the exception of Meadow Pipit, bird species tended to show similar associations with heather moorland in the two areas. Red Grouse was the only species to show significant positive associations in both study areas. Merlin was only studied in the south Pennines, but also showed a positive association. Meadow Pipit were positively associated with heather in the Pennines, but showed no significant association in the Highlands. Skylark were negatively associated with heather moor in both study areas, and dunlin showed a similar association in the Pennines (but were not studied in the Highlands). No other species showed any significant associations in either of the study areas.

6.3.2 Bird associations with other habitat features

In order to study the associations of bird species with a range of habitat features principal components analysis was used in both studies to produce a set of independent habitat gradients. This approach was required due to the high degree of correlation between many of the habitat variables. Redundancy analyses (Ter Braak, 1987) were then used to produce ordinations of the bird data, whilst constraining each axis of the ordination to be directly related to the habitat gradients. Figure 6.1 shows the first two axes of redundancy analyses between bird numbers and the major habitat gradients associated with bird distribution. In the figure the distance between two species represents similarly in their distributions and the

(a) Eastern Highlands

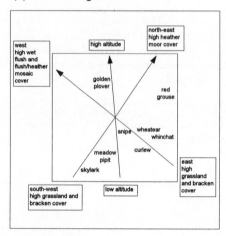

(b) South Pennines

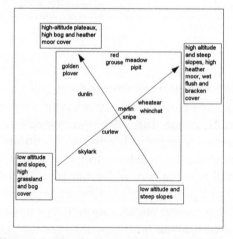

Figure 6.1. Species coefficients for the first two axes of redundancy analyses between bird species abundance (log transformed) and habitat features in the eastern Highlands (a) and south Pennines (b). The arrows show the directions of the major habitat gradients associated with bird distribution. Redrawn from Brown and Stillman (1993) and Brown *et al.*, (1992)

arrows show the directions of the habitat features most strongly linked with bird distribution. The habitat associations of individual species are shown by their location along these arrows. The ordinations for account for 27 % of the variation in bird numbers in the Highlands and 9 % in the Pennines, and 86 % of the bird-habitat relationship in the Highlands and 69 % in the Pennines. Full details of the composition of the habitat gradients and methods of analysis are contained in the original reports.

Altitude is associated with bird distribution in both study areas. In the eastern Highlands one of the three habitat gradients most strongly linked to bird distribution represents a simple transition from low to high altitude. Similarly, in the south Pennines both of the major habitat gradients associated with bird distribution represent transitions in altitude. Golden Plover and Red Grouse are associated with high altitude in both areas, and Dunlin and Meadow Pipit in the south Pennines. Curlew and Skylark are related to low altitude in both areas, and Meadow Pipit in the eastern Highlands. With the exception of Meadow Pipit species show the same associations with altitude in both areas. The vegetation gradients associated with bird distribution contain a number of vegetation types, but generally represent transitions from grassland to heather moorland. Skylark and Curlew are associated with the grassland extreme of this gradient and Red Grouse with the heather moor extreme in both areas. Meadow Pipit is linked to grassland in the eastern Highlands, but to heather moor in the south Pennines.

6.4 Discussion

6.4.1 Comparison of bird-habitat associations

The eastern Highlands and south Pennines study areas differed markedly in their topography. Altitude was generally higher in the eastern Highlands study sites, and varied to a far greater extent between sites. Sites also tended to be more steeply sloping in the eastern Highlands. Considering these differences and the different geographical locations of the study areas, it is perhaps surprising that bird species showed such similar habitat associations. In both areas altitude and vegetation gradients from grassland to heather moorland were particularly associated with bird distribution. The consistency of these associations suggests that they represent real patterns and are likely to be repeated in other upland areas.

Three species, Red Grouse, Merlin and Meadow Pipit, showed positive correlations with the cover of heather moorland, while Dunlin and Skylark showed negative correlations and the remaining species no significant associations. These associations with heather moorland are in general agreement with those of previous studies. The strong association of Red Grouse with heather moor is not surprising as it would be expected from the ecology of this species (Hudson, 1986). Bibby (1986) showed site occupancy of Merlins in Wales to be positively associated with heather cover, and Haworth and Thompson (1990) showed a similar association in a moorland to the north of the south Pennines study area. Meadow Pipit have previously been shown to be associated with heather moorland elsewhere (Stroud *et al.*, 1987; Tyler, 1987), and so the lack of association with heather in the Highlands is in contrast to previous studies. Few studies have found positive associations of other species with heather moorland. Stroud *et al.*, (1987) found that breeding waders in Caithness and Sutherland tended to avoid dry heather, and in extensive review of previous studies Brown and Bainbridge (this volume) have found no evidence that upland bird species show any dependence on heather moorland managed for Red Grouse. The fact that few species show strong positive associations with heather moorland suggests that other factors are more important in determining their distributions.

6.4.2 Upland bird species diversity

The bird-habitat associations found in the eastern Highlands and south Pennines may be used to indicate the likely relationships between vegetation composition and bird species diversity. The bird species studied tended to show a range of habitat associations, and no one vegetation type was positively related to the abundance of more than a few species. It therefore follows that areas suitable for one species will not necessarily be as suitable for others, and that upland areas with a low range of habitat types will be likely to have a lower bird species diversity. Similarly, Bignal *et al.*, (1988) have suggested that the large range of habitat types found on Islay is responsible for its diverse range of breeding and wintering bird species. In particular, the results from the eastern Highlands and Pennines do not give any evidence that bird diversity on heather moorland should be any greater than that on other vegetation types. The highest diversity of upland breeding birds should be expected to occur in areas with a mosaic of different habitat types.

Acknowledgements

The surveys were organized by Andy Brown and Kevin Shepherd, and conducted by David Allen, Mark Bates, Jeremy Bishop, Mike Carr, Paul Gill, James Harvey, Stuart Marsden, John McLoughlin, Robert Pilcher, Mike Smedley, Jeff Stenning, Roland and Penny Stevens, Jonathan Stirling and Richard Winspear. Additional merlin data for the south Pennines were supplied by the local raptor monitoring groups. I am grateful for the efforts of all those involved in the field surveys, and to the landowners, gamekeepers and tenants who allowed surveys to be conducted on their land. I have had much valued discussion with Andy Brown on the survey results.

References

Bibby, C. J. (1986). Merlins in Wales: site occupancy and breeding in relation to vegetation, *Journal of Applied Ecology*, **23**, 1–12.

Bignal, E. M., Curtis, D. J. and Matthews, J. (1988). *Islay: Land Types, Bird Habitats and Nature Conservation. Part 1: Land Use and Birds on Islay*, Nature Conservancy Council Chief Scientist Directorate Report No. 809, Peterborough.

Brown, A. F. (1991). *An Annotated Bibliography of Moorland Breeding Bird and Breeding Wader Surveys, 1970–1990*, Joint Nature Conservation Committee Report No. 8, Peterborough.

Brown, A. F., Stillman, R. A. and Shepherd, K. B. (1992). *Bird-Habitat associations in the South Pennines of England,* Joint Nature Conservation Committee Report No. 102, Peterborough.

Brown, A. F. and Stillman, R. A. (1993). Bird-habitat associations in the eastern Highlands of Scotland, *Journal of Applied Ecology,* **30,** 31–42.

Haworth, P. F. and Thompson, D. B. A. (1990). Factors associated with the distribution of upland birds in the south Pennines, England, *Journal of Applied Ecology,* **27,** 562–77.

Hudson, P. J. (1986). *Red Grouse: The Biology and Management of a Wild Gamebird,* The Game Conservancy Trust, Fordingbridge.

Nature Conservancy Council (1990). *Handbook for Phase 1 Habitat Survey: A Technique for Environmental Audit,* Nature Conservancy Council, Peterborough.

Ratcliffe, D. A. (1990). *Birdlife of Mountain and Upland,* Cambridge University Press, Cambridge,

Ratcliffe, D. A. and Thompson, D. B. A. (1988). The British Uplands: their ecological character and international significance. In Usher, M. B. and Thompson, D. B. A. (Eds), *Ecological Change in the Uplands,* Blackwell Scientific Publications, Oxford, 9–36.

Stroud, D. A., Reed, T. M., Pienkowski, M. W. and Lindsay, R. A. (1987). *Birds, Bogs and Forestry: The Peatlands of Caithness and Sutherland,* Nature Conservancy Council, Peterborough.

Stroud, D. A., Mudge, G. P. and Pienkowski, M. W. (1990). *Protecting Internationally Important Bird Sites,* Nature Conservancy Council, Peterborough

Ter Braak, C. J. F. (1987). *CANOCO – a FORTRAN Program for Canonical Community Ordination by [partial] [detrended] [canonical] Correspondence Analysis, Principal Components Analysis and Redundancy Analysis (Version 2.1),* Agriculture Mathematics Group, Wageningen.

Tyler, S. J. (1988). Birds and bracken in Wales. In Nature Conservancy Council *Birds in Wales,* Bangor, 56–62.

7 THE INVERTEBRATES OF THE NORTHERN SCOTTISH FLOWS, AND A COMPARISON WITH OTHER PEATLAND HABITATS

J. Coulson, L. Bauer, J. Butterfield, I. Downie, L. Cranna and C. Smith

Summary

1. A study was made of the invertebrates caught by pitfall trapping at eight sites in the Scottish Flows between April and October 1990. Several rare invertebrates were recorded.

2. The species composition has been compared with those obtained in an intensive study of peatland and upland grassland sites in the north of England. Using indicator species from the latter study, the invertebrate fauna of the Flows shows affinities with both lowland mires and upland blanket bog, a combination not previously recorded.

3. Analysis of the community structure of three taxa whose species are mainly or totally predatory showed that they all had a very strong relationship with altitude and it is suggested that this represents a temperature effect.

4. Both the staphylinid and spider faunas differed from those on peatlands in the north of England and they probably represent distinct communities. In contrast, the carabid community on the Flows was typical of blanket bog in the north of England.

5. The Flows did not exhibit the marked spring emergence of insects typical of upland blanket bog and the emergence period was longer. There was also an indication that the overall biomass of invertebrates was lower on the Flows than on upland blanket bog.

6. It is concluded that the lower altitudes, and hence less cold ambient temperatures, of the Flows are primarily responsible for differences in the invertebrate fauna from that on upland bogs.

7.1 Introduction

The Flows of Caithness and Sutherland, Scotland, are extensive areas of deep blanket peat near sea-level. The area has been described in detail by Ratcliffe and Oswald (1988). The average temperature is consistently higher than on the areas of blanket peat in upland Britain because of the low altitude, and the mean annual temperature at Wick is 3°C higher than at Moor House at 550 m in the northern Pennines (30-year annual averages of 8°C and 5°C, respectively). In other respects, the Flows and upland blanket bog are similar and in both cases the deep peat has a high organic content and water table. The low nutrient levels in both areas lead to the vegetation being dominated by *Calluna vulgaris* and *Eriophorum vaginatum*. They do, however, differ in the gradient. Typically, the peat surface in the Flows forms a gradient of less than 1° while that on blanket bog often exceeds 7°. As a result, the run-off from the Flows is much slower and this reinforces the high rainfall in maintaining a high water table.

The similarity of substrate in upland blanket bog and in the peatlands of Caithness and Sutherland suggested a 'natural' experiment in which an assessment of the main environmental factors influencing the invertebrate communities could be made. In this chapter we attempt to evaluate whether vegetation, organic content of the soil, high water table or temperature is the most important factor determining the composition of the invertebrate fauna.

Little is known of the invertebrate fauna of the Caithness and Sutherland Flows peatlands. In distribution maps of invertebrates within Britain, many common species are not represented on the Flows, but this is primarily because the area has not been studied rather than an indication of their absence. For example, we have found 49 species of spiders not previously listed for the Flows or even for Caithness as a whole.

Coulson and Whittaker (1978) stressed the importance of the peatland invertebrate fauna and their reasons are summarized as follows:

1. There are many species. In any one area there are probably over 30 invertebrate species to each vertebrate species.

2. The biomass of invertebrates is at least an order of magnitude greater than that of vertebrates. In the northern Pennines, for every sheep there is between 5–10 times the biomass of invertebrates in the soil. Thus, the invertebrates play an important role in influencing the selective decomposition of plant remains and determining the amount of primary production transferred to peat.

3. Invertebrates concentrate nutrients, usually having ten times the concentrations of nitrogen and phosphorus in their bodies in comparison to the vegetation. As a result, they are crucially important in concentrating and recycling nutrients to the primary producers on the nutrient poor peatlands.

4. Finally, invertebrates are the food of many of the bird and other vertebrate species of peatlands. In the Flows, where there has been so much concern over

well-being of the breeding bird populations, the food supply for these birds is obviously a factor that needs to be evaluated

Unfortunately food for birds is still often the only reason for studying invertebrates in peatlands. It is time we recognized the importance of invertebrates in their own right (Coulson, 1988, 1992).

The invertebrate fauna of high altitude blanket peat has strong northern affinities, showing a close link with the fauna of northern Scandinavia and Iceland (Coulson and Whittaker, 1978). This contrasts with the invertebrate community of upland grasslands, which is primarily an impoverished, lowland grassland community with affinities with the fauna of central Europe, rather than more northern areas (Coulson and Butterfield, 1985).

The invertebrate faunas of northern heath (shallow peat over a poor mineral soil dominated by *Calluna*) and blanket bog (deep peat dominated by *Calluna-Eriophorum*) differ. Northern heath, which is prevented from reaching a tree dominated climax by burning and grazing and is therefore primarily a man-made habitat, tends to lack the northern element in its fauna and is relatively species poor. Blanket bog areas represent a natural, tree-free community, although their extent in Britain has varied due to climatic change and by the intensity of grazing (Coulson, 1992).

In this study, the communities of three major invertebrate groups, the Araneae (spiders), Carabidae (ground beetles) and Staphylinidae (rove beetles) found in the Flows are compared with those from other peatlands investigated in northern England and an attempt is made to examine the question as to whether the Flows have an unique invertebrate fauna, perhaps caused by the combination of low altitude, relatively high temperatures and virtually no drainage gradients over much of the area.

This study was initiated as a joint pilot investigation by LC and JCC to answer basic questions about the invertebrate fauna of the Flows.

7.2 Methods

In 1990, we trapped terrestrial invertebrates on eight sites in the Flows (Table 7.1). Ten pitfall traps with a 45 mm diameter mouth were placed in a line 2 m apart at each site (except at HT where five traps were used). The traps were in position from April until mid-October 1990 and the captures were collected at monthly intervals. Each trap contained about 3 cm of a 2 % formalin in water mixture plus a few drops of detergent to assist in reducing the surface tension and to encourage captured invertebrates to sink into the preservative. The traps and method were the same as that used in our other studies (Coulson and Butterfield, 1981; 1985). The captures were divided in to major groups and the majority identified to species, although certain groups of Diptera, e.g. Chironomidae and Phoridae were not identified. The Staphylinidae and Carabidae formed almost all of the beetles captured and beetles belonging to minor groups have not been named. The weevil *Strophosomus sus*, which we had previously found to be an indicator species of heath in northern England (Coulson and Butterfield, 1985), was searched for in the captures but was not found. Lepidoptera were not considered because pitfall trapping is an inappropriate method for sampling them.

Table 7.1   The sites used in the Scottish Flows survey. The National Vegetation Classification (NVC) codes (Rodwell, 1991) are given. More detailed vegetation accounts are in Coulson (1991).

Site	Soil	Symbol	National Grid Reference	Altitude (m)	NVC
Canisbay	deep peat	C	ND 344708	60	M18
Dunbeath	deep peat	DP	ND 157359	160	M18
Dunbeath	shallow peat over mineral	DM	ND 161360	180	M15
Halsary	deep peat + ditch and trees	HT	ND 179496	90	M19
Halsary	deep peat	H	ND 193496	90	M18
Killimster	deep peat	K	ND 306557	20	M19
Ruthermire	deep peat	R	ND 305633	40	M18
Strathy	deep peat	S	NC 794559	130	M18

7.2.1   *Database*

Extensive information now exists on the invertebrate fauna of upland blanket bog. In particular, there have been intensive studies centred on the Moor House National Nature Reserve in Cumbria, at about 550 m (Coulson and Whittaker, 1978) and a survey of the invertebrates of peatland and upland grasslands in northern England (Butterfield and Coulson, 1983; Coulson and Butterfield, 1981, 1985, 1986) which contribute to a detailed database. We have used information from 56 peat and upland sites in the north of England for comparison with the data obtained in the Flows. Most of the data are available in Coulson and Buterfield (1981, 1985), but more recent information from the Pennine plateau has been obtained by Downie *et al.* (1994) and data from two sites on blanket bog at Gunnerside, in North Yorkshire have also been included. There are also data available for other peat sites in Scotland (e.g. Curtis, 1979, 1985; Curtis and Stinglhammer, 1983) but in most cases, the data cover only part of the year or the numbers of each species captured are not given. They have not been included in the quantitative comparisons made in this paper.

7.3   **Results**

In all, 270 invertebrate species were identified from the eight sites in the Flows (Coulson, 1991) and a maximum of 134 species were found at any one site, indicating considerable inter-site differences. Many of the species were represented by a few specimens only and in some cases by one individual. Clearly many more species are still to be recorded, even at the sites we studied, but most of the numerous and therefore important species for characterizing the sites are likely to have been found.

7.3.1   Use of indicator species

In the assessment of sites over the whole of northern England, 19 invertebrate species could be used to characterize different communities of lowland mires, blanket bog or northern heath, and these were designated as indicators (Coulson and Butterfield, 1981, 1985).

Table 7.2 shows the occurrence of these indicator species at the eight sites examined on the Flows and a comparison with their presence on the study sites in northern England. All three species which were indicators of lowland mires in northern England were present on at least three sites on the Flows, with the small cranefly *Molophilus occultus* present at six sites. Similarly, all five species which we had previously associated with (upland) blanket bog were present, although the bug *Cicadula quadrinotata* was found at but one site. However the flightless cranefly, *Molophilus ater*, was found on all sites. In contrast, only five of the 11 indicator species of northern heath were recorded and three of these were represented at only one or two sites and in small numbers. Apart from the harvestman *Lacinius ephippiatus*, which occurred at six sites, typical northern heath species were absent or infrequent. Thus the flow sites appeared to have a combination of the indicator species for both lowland mires and blanket bog. This combination has not been recorded previously but recognises the physical nature of the sites; low-lying and dominated by blanket bog.

Table 7.2   The distribution of invertebrate indicator species, identified as typical of upland blanket bog, northern heath and lowland mires (Coulson and Butterfield, 1982), found in the Scottish Flows. The number of sites (out of 8) where each species was found in the Flows are shown with the status (+=presence, –=absence, (+)=occasional) in peatland types in northern England.

Species	Taxa	Flows (8 sites)	Lowland mires	Northern heaths	Blanket Bog
Lowland mires					
Dolichopus atratus	Diptera	3	+	–	–
Molophilus occultus	Diptera	6	+	–	–
Agonum ericeti	Coleoptera	5	+	–	(+)
Blanket bog					
Ormosia pseudosimilis	Diptera	3	–	–	+
Tipula subnodicornis	Diptera	5	(+)	–	+
Molophilus ater	Diptera	8	–	–	+
Agonum fuliginosum	Coleoptera	6	–	–	+
Cicadula quadrinotata	Hemiptera	1	+	–	+
Northern heath					
Bradycellus ruficollis	Coleoptera	4	–	+	–
Bradycellus collaris	Coleoptera	–	–	+	–

Table 7.2 (cont'd)   The distribution of invertebrate indicator species, identified as typical of upland blanket bog, northern heath and lowland mires (Coulson and Butterfield, 1982), found in the Scottish Flows. The number of sites (out of 8) where each species was found in the Flows are shown with the status (+=presence, –=absence, (+)=occasional) in peatland types in northern England.

Species	Taxa	Flows (8 sites)	Lowland mires	Northern heaths	Blanket Bog
Olisthopus rotundatus	Coleoptera	1	–	+	–
Pterostichus madidus	Coleoptera	–	(+)	+	–
Tapinocyba praecox	Araneae	–	–	+	–
Strophosomus sus	Coleoptera	–	–	+	–
Lacinius ephippiatus	Opiliones	6	–	+	–
Trichocellus cognatus	Coleoptera	2	–	+	–
Dyschirius globbosus	Coleoptera	2	(+)	+	–
Xanotholinus linearis	Coleoptera	–	–	+	–
Othius myrmecophilus	Coleoptera	–	–	+	–

7.3.2   Multivariate analysis

In a previous study, (Coulson, 1988), the difference in the distribution of predatory and herbivorous species on upland grasslands and peatlands was investigated. Many invertebrate herbivore species rarely occurred on both grasslands and peatlands whereas the predatory species showed considerable overlap. This difference can be attributed to the tendency of herbivores to show associations with specific plants or plant groups while the predators have no such affinities. The difference in plant communities between grassland and bog effected a major change in the invertebrate herbivore species distribution. The predators were less influenced by the plant species and their distributions were more influenced by the physical characteristics of their environment, including the architecture of the vegetation, rather than its species composition. Accordingly, we have put the emphasis on the predatory groups in trying to relate the fauna of the Flows to upland and peatland areas since the herbivores closely follow any vegetational changes.

We have examined three well-represented groups in detail (Carabidae (ground beetles), Staphylinidae (rove beetles) and the Araneae (spiders)), using Detrended Corresponence Analysis (DCA) (Ter Braak, 1988) as a means of examining the community differences between a range of upland and peatland sites and relating these to the invertebrate fauna of the Flows. We used log-transformed numbers of captures of each species and downweighting of rare species as a balance between considering differences in abundance and not giving excessive importance to the few, dominant species. The eigenvalues (Table 7.3) are a measure of the separation of the species' distributions along the ordination axis.

Table 7.3   The eigen values for three invertebrate groups derived from DCA scores. Those which explain more than 15 % of the sum of squares are printed in bold type.

Taxa	Axis 1	Axis 2	Axis 3	Axis 4
Araneae	**0.431**	**0.161**	0.128	0.086
Carabidae	**0.381**	**0.289**	**0.182**	0.113
Staphylinidae	**0.442**	**0.237**	0.145	0.104

Plots of axis 2 against axis 1 for the Carabidae, Araneae and Staphylinidae are shown in Figures 7.1 to 7.3, respectively. In all three groups, the positioning of sites in relation to axis 1 is similar. The correlation coefficients (r) of axis 1 site scores for pairs of the taxa considered all exceeded 0.80, strongly suggesting that

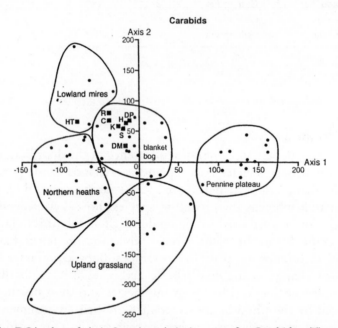

Figure 7.1. The DCA plot of Axis 2 against Axis 1 scores for Carabidae. The circles represent sites in northern England and the squares and initials the eight Flow sites. Previously recognized communities are enclosed. Note that the Flows' sites fall within the blanket bog community.

axis 1 is measuring the same environmental factor in all three cases. Axis 1 scores are closely and linearly correlated with altitude (spiders r=0.87, carabids r=0.83, staphylinids r=0.90, d.f.62, p<0.001 in all cases). There is a very close relationship between altitude and temperature in the same general area and it is likely that the effective environmental factor is annual ambient temperature rather than altitude (The average difference of approximately 7 °C between the sites near sea-level and those at about 900 m must be a critical factor in the development of an ectothermic animal.) This relationship with axis 1, suggests that a major component of peatland/upland invertebrate communities (or at least of predators) changes progressively with altitude.

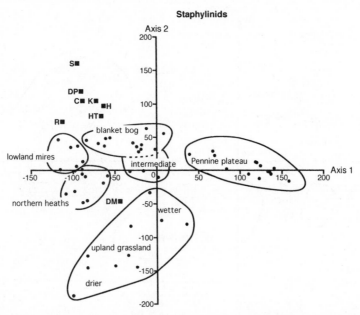

Figure 7.2. The DCA plot of Axis 2 against Axis 1 scores for Staphylinidae. The circles represent sites in northern England and the squares and initials the eight Flow sites. Previously recognized communities are enclosed. Note that the Flows sites do not fall within existing community boundaries.

In contrast to axis 1, axis 2 does not appear to be measuring the same parameters in the three taxa. For the two beetle taxa, the peat sites have positive scores while the better drained upland grasslands, which are on mineral soils, are given negative scores. It is likely that the water content of the soils, rather than rainfall, is an important variable producing the sequence of grassland – northern heaths – blanket bog (with lowland mires) in the carabid and staphylinid communities. For the spiders, the scores for lowland mires tend to lie close to the northern heaths but separated from the blanket bog. It appears that the high water table in the lowland mires is not playing a positive part in determining the community structure of the spiders. As the lowland mires were comparatively small areas surrounded by dry ground this may have been due to the influence of these drier areas.

For both beetle taxa, the axis 3 scores of the Flow sites fall within the range of the upland sites and this axis does not indicate differences between the Flows and other sites. For the spiders however, the plot of axis 3 against axis 1 separates the Flow sites from the blanket peat and northern heath sites (although both have similar scores on axis 2) and they are within, or adjacent to, the lowland mires grouping (Figure 7.4).

It is appropriate to give special consideration to the two pairs of Flow sites at Halsary (HT and H) and at Dunbeath (DM and DP) because the pairing involved a typical deep peat site adjacent to an atypical area. At HT, deep drainage ditches have been cut in the peat within the past five years and conifers planted (although

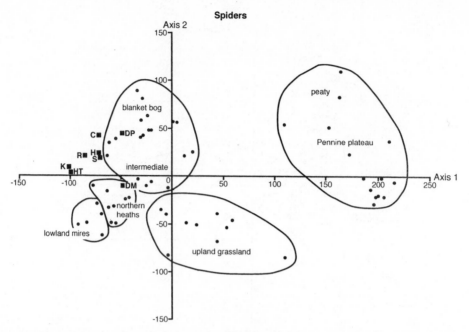

Figure 7.3. The DCA plot of Axis 2 against Axis 1 scores for spiders (Araneae). The circles represent sites in northern England and the squares and initials the eight Flow sites. Previously recognized communities are enclosed. Note that the Flows sites do not fall within the existing community boundaries (see Figure 7.4).

the trees are still too small to have any influence on the site). Otherwise the site is similar to H. The site scores for the spiders show that HT, compared with H, has moved away from the blanket bog clustering; while for the carabids it moves out of the blanket bog grouping into the lowland mires. There is, however, little difference between the two sites for the staphylinids. At Dunbeath, DP is a typical blanket bog site and DM is on a mineral outcrop producing a slightly raised site with shallow peaty soil with an appreciable mineral content. Compared with DP, which lies within the Flows cluster, the site scores for the staphylinids place DM on the other side of the blanket bog group and close to the upland grassland and northern heath sites. The spiders indicate a change from the blanket bog to the border between blanket bog and northern heath, while for the carabids there is little change from DP and DM remains clearly within the blanket bog cluster. It is evident that the response of the different taxa to changes in the habitat vary considerably.

Our preliminary conclusions based on indicator species, that the Flows have close links with lowland mires and blanket bog, were not fully confirmed by the DCA analyses. In the case of the carabids, the plots of axis 2 against 1 show the Flows sites falling well within the blanket bog cluster and approaching the lowland mires grouping. The carabid communities of the Flows are similar to those on many blanket bog areas and are not unique, although three species found on the Flows, *Notiophilus palustris*, *Trechus rivularis* and *Cymindis vaporariorum*, were not recorded from the peatlands we surveyed in northern England.

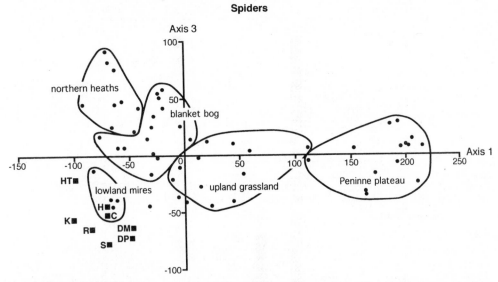

Figure 7.4. The DCA plot of Axis 3 against Axis 1 scores for spiders. The circles represent sites in northern England and the squares and initials the eight Flow sites. Previously recognized communities are enclosed.

In contrast, axis 2 against axis 1 plots for spiders and staphylinids both show the Flows sites discretely grouped and separate from the other sites. For the staphylinids the Flow sites lie higher on axis 2 than any of the other sites, indicating the presence of unique components in the community. They lie equally close to the blanket bog and lowland mire groups, indicating affinities with both. On the basis of the spider fauna, the Flows sites are placed to the left of the blanket bog sites, suggesting an altitude/temperature induced difference in the community structure. The unique nature of the spider fauna of the Flows is also indicated on axis 3 where again the Flows sites are remote from the other sites.

Eight spider species were recorded in the Flows but not in the survey of peatlands in the north of England. These species are *Xysticus erraticus, Pholcomma gibbum, Tibellus maritimus, Hypsosinga pygmaea, Micragus apertus, Satilatlas britteni, Diplocephalus latifrons* and *Aphileta misera.*

However, the separation of the Flows sites in the spider and staphylinid ordinations is not produced by the presence or absence of these rare species, since deletion of these from the data set makes little difference to the axes scores. The differences arise mainly from the relative abundances of the common species, even though these have been considered on a logarithmic scale.

7.3.3 Seasonal abundance of invertebrates

Pitfall traps give an acceptable indication of the seasonal abundance of invertebrates, particularly short-lived species such as craneflies (Tipulidae). Figure 7.5 shows a comparison of the captures in pitfall traps in the same year on the Flows and at Chapel Fell, an area of blanket bog at 615 m in Co. Durham sampled in the

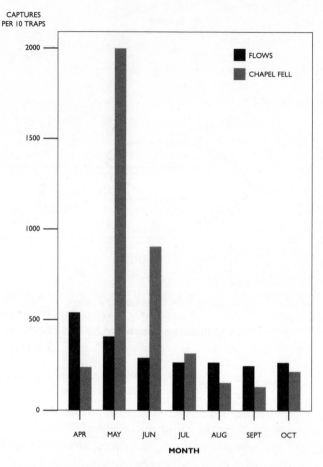

Figure 7.5. The numbers of invertebrates caught each month in 10 pitfall traps on an upland blanket bog site (Chapel Fell 615 m) and in the Flows in 1990.

same year. Chapel Fell shows the typical blanket bog spring peak of emergence in May and early June which is many times greater than in the flows. On the other hand, April captures and those later in the year are higher on the Flows, but the total captures during the year are appreciably lower on the flows. This type of difference has also been found between upland blanket bog and lowland mires in the north of England (Coulson and Butterfield, 1981).

7.3.4   Rare species

The status of many of the invertebrates of the Flows is poorly known. This particularly applied to the Staphylinidae and it is clear that Caithness and Sutherland have been poorly collected, otherwise we would not have found 49 species of spiders new to Caithness and nine for Sutherland (based on Locket *et al.*, 1974).

Trechus rivularis (Carabidae) is a Red Data Book Grade 1 species. This appears to be the first Scottish record, but it has recently been found in localities in England, Wales and Northern Ireland (Luff and Wardle, 1991). The spiders *Satilatlas britteni* and *Hilaira pervicax* are rare, while *H. frigida* has not been previously recorded near sea level in Britain. The fungus gnat *Brevicornu kingi* (Mycetophylidae, Diptera) is only known from a few high altitude sites in Scotland and has not been found near sea level before. In the Staphylinidae, *Acidota crenata*, *Lathrobium fovulum* and *Mycetoporus baudueri* have been rarely recorded elsewhere in Britain. Throughout almost all of its worldwide distribution, *Lonchoptera furcata* (Lonchopteridae, Diptera) is known only as females. A male taken in the Flows is the first Scottish example, although several have been taken in England (Coulson and Butterfield, 1982). No rare Tipulidae (Diptera) Opiliones (harvestmen) or plant bugs (Hemiptera) were recorded but it is of interest that the harvestman *Mitopus ericaeus*, (a closely related species to *M. morio*) which is widespread on most upland blanket bog sites in northern England (Jennings, 1982), was not recorded from the Flows.

7.4   Discussion

The invertebrate fauna of the Flows has unique features. The use of previously determined indicator species suggested that the Flows fauna has characteristics of both the lowland mires and upland blanket bog. However, different taxa show different affinities. There is virtually nothing which can be considered as unique in the carabid community of the Flows; it is typically that of blanket bog. However the staphylinid and spider communities, although similar to those in northern England, are distinct communities in their own right. These communities may prove to be unique since they have not (so far) been found elsewhere in Britain and are unlikely to be found in the same form on the continent of Europe because of the much greater number of species there.

Coulson and Butterfield (1981, 1985) identified a series of characteristics for the upland blanket peat invertebrate communities: Earthworms are virtually absent and there is a vast synchronized spring peak of emergence of terrestrial insects in spring, the peak being dominated by flies, particularly craneflies. This peak is more pronounced at higher altitudes (Coulson, 1988) and heralds a major return of nutrients to the soil and the plants. Both predatory vertebrates and invertebrates take advantage of this short period of superabundant food and breeding in upland birds is typically synchronized with the insect emergence.

The shallow peats of northern heaths, which are the main grouse moors of eastern Britain, are usually below 500 m and often extend virtually to sea level in Scotland. They are characterized by a burning cycle which results in an almost total dominance of *Calluna* during the growth and mature phases, bare ground following burning and a more varied flora if allowed to reach the degenerative phase. These areas are prevented from reaching the woodland climax by burning and grazing. They do not have the marked spring emergence of insects and, do not, typically, have species associated with more northern areas. They also lack earthworms. In contrast, lowland mires have a high water table and combine many aspects of the vegetation of upland bogs. The lowland mires have several characteristics of the Flows in that the mires have virtually no gradient and water drainage is, accordingly, minimal. Both have a high water table throughout the year, have a relatively high mean annual temperature and have a much lower biomass of invertebrates compared with that found on high altitude blanket bog.

The carabid fauna of the Flows is typical of blanket bog in northern England, while the spiders and staphylinid beetles faunas, although similar to those of blanket bog and lowland mires, are unique as far as our knowledge exists. From the conservation viewpoint, we think it is important to note that drainage of a site for less than five years has already changed the carabid fauna and modified the spider community, although it has had little effect on the staphylinids. The presence of an increased ground gradient at DM, which has, presumably, been responsible for preventing bog formation, has a different invertebrate community. Apart from earthworms being present in some numbers, the staphylinids show a marked difference in species, moving close to a grassland community, while the spiders have a community closely associated with northern heath. The carabid fauna differed little from that on the neighbouring blanket bog.

The Flows do not have the marked spring peak of insect emergence which is so spectacular on upland blanket bog. In part only, this is caused by the longer growth and activity period and earlier spring, with the species which contribute to the spring peak in the uplands each having a different emergence time in the Flows. This is well illustrated in three craneflies. *Tricyphona immaculata* emerges at least a month earlier in the Flows than at Moor House, Cumbria (550 m), but the emergence of *Tipula subnodicornis* is advanced probably by only a week and that of *Molophilus ater* seems little changed. These differences appear to arise from each species starting their physiological response to the spring rise in temperature on different dates in milder areas (Coulson *et al.*, 1976). The differences are suppressed in the uplands by the cold temperatures in March and April which retard development of all three species. Eventually, when the spring rise in temperature occurs, the three species respond together with the result that they emerge at almost the same time.

The lack of a marked spring peak in emergence on the Flows is also a result of low population densities of the key spring emerging species. Whilst the year of study could have been one with exceptionally low densities in the Flows, such low densities are not unexpected since first instar larvae are particularly sensitive to dehydration (Coulson, 1962) which occurs more frequently at lower altitudes where rainfall tends to be lower and the evaporation potentials higher. Coulson (1988) has shown that abundance of *Tipula subnodicornis* is altitude related on blanket bog and presumably the Flows form an extension of this relationship.

The consequence of these findings is that it seems unlikely that it will be possible to explain the exceptional avifauna of the Flows in terms of exceptionally high densities of insect food. Obviously there are adequate numbers of insects to allow the wading birds to breed successfully in most years, but it may be necessary to look to other factors, such as low predation rates to explain richness in bird species.

The answer to the question posed in the Introduction is that both altitude and soil characteristics influence the invertebrate fauna. The lowland blanket bog invertebrate fauna is modified by being at higher temperatures and evidence for this was found in all three taxa considered, where axis 1 scores of the DCA analysis were closely correlated with temperature. Nevertheless, the lowland blanket bog of the Flows possesses many species characteristic of upland blanket bog, although often not in the same abundance. There are relatively few invertebrate species in the Flows associated with other habitats, the exception being lowland mires, which have similar flora, temperatures and peat accumulations.

Acknowledgements

We are indebted to Shirley Goodyer for overseeing the sorting of the pitfall catches, identifying the Homoptera and some of the Diptera; to Julie Mayes for sorting most of the samples and to Eric Henderson for identifying the Harvestmen.

We are grateful to the Nature Conservancy Council for financial support, and particularly to Iona Finlay for coordinating the collection of the traps throughout the study and sending them to Durham, for information on the sites, and for many kindnesses. Iona was ably assisted by Ian Mitchell on several occasions. Malcolm Cameron collected the traps at Dunbeath and David Duncan did the same at Strathy.

We are grateful for support and permission to sample given by Ackergill Tower, Barrock Estate, Dunbeath Estate, The Forestry Commission, Fountain Forestry, Trustees of Sir George Duff Dunbar, C. S. Georgeson, G. Gunn and A. Hall. We are also grateful to two anonymous referees for constructive comments.

Appendix 7.1 The species and numbers of specimens recorded on each study site 1990. [+]indicate new record for Caithness; *new record for Sutherland

					Sites			
Araneae spiders	C	DP	DM	H	HT	K	R	S
Drassodes cupreus								3*
[+]*Haplodrassus signifer*		3	1	1		1	1	
Clubiona trivialis	1	12					4	2
[+]*Agroeca proxima*	7	2	2	14		30	29	16
[+]*Scotina gracilipes*						1		
Xysticus cristatus	1	7	1				3	
[+]*Xysticus erraticus*							1	
[+]*Oxyptila trux*	6	1	3	2	1	2	1	
[+]*Tibellus maritimus*	1						1	
[+]*Neon reticulatus*						1	1	
Pardosa nigriceps	6			6	8	40	12	1
Pardosa pullata	147	290	1172	178	70	149	151	184
[+]*Alopecosa accentuata*		2		1				
[+]*Alopecosa pulverulenta*		3	40	28	6			3
[+]*Trochosa terricola*	8	28	90	8	10	13	5	5
[+]*Trochosa ruricola*						1		
Pirata piraticus	42	252	52	76	1	66	102	82
[+]*Antistea elegans*	4	35		11	9	9	9	77*
Ero furcata	1							
Robertus lividus	5	2	3	3	3	5	3	
Pholcomma gibbum		1				1	1	

Appendix 7.1 (cont'd)   The species and numbers of specimens recorded on each study site 1990. +indicate new record for Caithness; *new record for Sutherland

				Sites				
	C	DP	DM	H	HT	K	R	S
+*Theonoe minutissima*	1						2	
Pachygnatha clercki	2		38			5	2	
Pachygnatha degeeri			63					
+*Hypsosinga pygmaea*	1					1		
+*Ceratinella brevis*		3		2		4	10	1*
Ceratinella brevipes	22	20	5	7	1	36	1	4
Walckenaeria acuminata	9	5	7	2	6	5	3	
Walckenaeria nudipalpis	5	5	5	4			7	3
+*Walckenaeria clavicornis*	12	47	4	7		2	11	3*
+*Walckenaeria vigilax*			2	3				1*
Walckenaeria antica		1	5				2	
+*Walckenaeria kochi*		1	1	1		5		
+*Dicymbium brevisetosum*		1	7				1	
+*Dicymbium tibiale*			1					
Dismodicus bifrons	22							
Hypomma bituberculatum	4	12				3	3	
Metopobactrus prominulus		2	2				1	
Gonatium rubens		6		3	7	1		
Peponocranium ludicrum				2		2		1
Pocadicnemis pumila			2			4		
+*Pocadicnemis juncea*						1		
+*Hypselistes jacksoni*	1	1	1			1		3*
+*Oedothorax gibbosus/tub*	1	1	4					
Oedothorax fuscus		2						
+*Oedothorax tuberosus*						1	1	
+*Oedothorax agrestis*		1						
Trichopterna thorelli								2*
+*Silometopus elegans*		3	9	1			1	5
Cnephalocotes obscurus	1	1						1
+*Microlinyphia pusilla*	4	1		1			1	
+*Tapinocyba pallens*		1			4			
Satilatlas britteni		5					1	
Monocephalus fuscipes	2		10	1		1		
+*Lophomma punctatum*		3				8	1	
Gongylidiellum vivum						1		
+*Micrargus apertus*	11	9		5	2	9	8	
Erigonella hiemalis	1		18			1		
Savignya frontata				1				
Diplocephalus permixtus	1	4	1					
+*Diplocephalus latifrons*			1					
Araeoncus crassiceps	5	1		2		1		3*
+*Scotinotylus evansi*		7	1	2				
Erigone atra	2		1			1		
Erigone promiscua	1		3					
+*Latithorax faustus*		17						
Drepanotylus uncatus								1*
+*Leptothrix hardyi*				1				
+*Hilaira pervicax*		2	1			16		
+*Hilaira frigida*		5						
+*Aphileta misera*		1						
Agyneta decora	12	24	12	21	2	21	26	23
+*Agyneta cauta*		2		4			1	
+*Meioneta rurestris*				1				
+*Meioneta saxatilis*	7			3		1	9	

Appendix 7.1 (cont'd) The species and numbers of specimens recorded on each study site 1990. [+]indicate new record for Caithness; *new record for Sutherland

				Sites				
	C	DP	DM	H	HT	K	R	S
[+]*Centromerus dilutus*				1	1	2	1	
Centromerita concinna	21	58	22	24	6	4	2	6
[+]*Saaristoa abnormis*	7	1		4		4	3	1
[+]*Bathyphantes setiger*		1						
[+]*Bathyphantes parvulus*	19	5	2	5	19	60	8	
Bathyphantes gracilis							1	
Stemonyphantes lineatus	11	1	1		1		2	
Tapinopa longidens				1		1		
Bolyphantes alticeps	1	1	7			3	4	
Bolyphantes luteolus		4	2	3	1	3	3	1
[+]*Lepthyphantes pallidus*					1			
Lepthyphantes ericaeus	7	10	10	11	10	15	21	2
Lepthyphantes mengei	14	3	10	7	5	7	15	3
Lepthyphantes zimmermanni	14	3	1	4	31	24	6	
[+]*Lepthyphantes cristatus*					1			
Lepthyphantes tenuis					1		1	
Allomengea scopigera			1			1		

Summary

	C	DP	DM	H	HT	K	R	S
Non-Linyphiidae species	14	13	11	12	10	15	15	9
Linyphiidae species	27	41	32	30	17	32	31	18
Total species	41	54	43	42	27	47	46	27
% Linyphiidae	66	76	74	71	63	68	67	67
Overall % Linyphiidae				69%				

Opiliones harvestmen

	C	DP	DM	H	HT	K	R	S
Mitopus morio	96	36	323	7	76	150	26	15
Rilaena triangularis	25	90	8	3	12	16	4	
Nemastoma bimaculatum	26	9	4	1	11	33	12	
Oligolophus tridens	23	11	5	5	2	7	3	1
Paroligolophus agrestis	9	25	46	9	2	7	6	2
Lacinius ephippiatus	2	1	9	1		25	2	
Lophopilio palpinalis	34	30	14	22	6	25	14	
Total species	7	7	7	7	6	7	7	3

Hemiptera bugs

Heteroptera

	C	DP	DM	H	HT	K	R	S
Salda morio	37	94	2	18		1	83	14
Salda saltatoria		4	2					1

Homoptera

	C	DP	DM	H	HT	K	R	S
Philaenus spumarius					8	1		
Neophilaenus lineatus	1	19	3	16		6	4	5
Ulopa reticulata	13	12	2	14		6	12	
Aphrodes bifasciatus	11	3	4		10	4	12	8
Palus panzeri				1			5	
Jassargus pseudocellus			62					
Streptanus marginatus			20					
Streptanus sordidus			26					
Macustus grisescens	42	3		3	8	16	14	3
Cicadula quadrinotata			1					
Macrosteles sp.			1					
Dicranoneura citrinella			1					

Appendix 7.1 (cont'd) The species and numbers of specimens recorded on each study site 1990. +indicate new record for Caithness; *new record for Sutherland

				Sites				
	C	DP	DM	H	HT	K	R	S
Kelisia vittipennis								2
Javesella discolor			1					
Delphacodes distincta	3	3		2		2	1	4
Sorhoanus xanthoneurus								1
Aphididae		3	6	3	60*			
Coccoidea	4			4		2		
Total species	6	7	12	6	3	7	7	8

*Note: aphids associated with the trees

Diptera flies
Nematocera
Tipulidae

	C	DP	DM	H	HT	K	R	S
Tipula subnodicornis	13	26				2	5	5
Tipula paludosa			7					
Tipula marmorata				1				
Limonia dilutior					3			
Limonia autumnalis	1	1	1					
Pedicia rivosa	6	3	3				5	
Tricyphona immaculata	11	1	10	6	3	5	16	11
Pilaria nemoralis						1		
Limnophila meigeni							1	1
Erioptera trivialis			2					
Erioptera diuturna	1	5	3	11			8	16
Ormosia pseudosimilis			5		23	1		
Molophilus ater	23	18	7	13	1	19	8	5
Molophilus occultus	3	21	8	13		7	4	2
Total species	7	7	9	5	4	6	7	6

Mycetophilidae

	C	DP	DM	H	HT	K	R	S
Macrocera parva				1				
Neuratelia nemoralis				1				
Anatella unguigera	1							
Exechia nigroscutellata				1				
Exechia pseudofestiva				1				
Exechia spinuligera						1		
Rhymosia armata						1		
Brevicornu sericoma	3							
Brevicornu kingi	1							
Brevivornu sp.	2	1	3			1		
Mycetophila luctuosa				1				
Mycetophila marginata group					2			
Boletina gripha	1	27	5	7	2	1	6	
Total species	5	2	2	6	2	4	1	0

Bibionidae

	C	DP	DM	H	HT	K	R	S
Bibio lepidus	2		2					
Dilophus febrilis			1	3	5	3	2	

	C	DP	DM	H	HT	K	R	S
Sciaridae	13	69	117	32	90	51	15	10
Scatopsidae						1		
Other Nematocera (Chironomidae)	314	105	235	181	3	241	112	110

Appendix 7.1 (cont'd)   The species and numbers of specimens recorded on each study site 1990. [+]indicate new record for Caithness; *new record for Sutherland

	C	DP	DM	H	HT	K	R	S
					Sites			
Brachychera Empididae								
Tachypeza nubila			4		3			
Platypalpus longicornis			1					
Platypalpus nigritarsus		1	2		3	3	1	
Hybos femoratus							3	
Bicellaria subpilosa					1			
Rhamphomyia hybotina					2			
Empis veralli	1							
Dolichocephala guttata	5		1	4		1		
Total species	2	1	4	1	4	2	2	
Dolichopodidae								
Dolichopus atratus	1	1		1				
Dolichopus brevipennis					1			
Dolichopus plumipes			2					
Dolichopus rupestris					4			
Hydrophorus nebulosus		6	1	7	1			2
Argyra elongata			1					
Campsicnemus loripes	1	9	34	5	1	3	3	2
Campsicnemus alpinus	3	38	17	33	4	1	15	8
Micromorphus albipes			2					
Total species	3	4	5	5	5	2	2	3
Lonchopteridae								
Lonchoptera furcata	1		1					
Lonchoptera lutea	2		2		6	1		
Phoridae	51	16	96	15	21	26	12	6
Acalyptratae								
Sepsidae								
Sepsis orthocnemis			1					
Sphaeroceridae								
Copromyza nitida	1	1	30	1	13	3	1	
Copromyza similis						1		
Copromyza stercoraria			2	2	1			
Leptocera fontinalis	1	1	2		2	3	4	
Leptocera breviceps			7					
Leptocera fenestralis								1
Leptocera coxata			1					
Leptocera clunipes			3	1			1	1
Leptocera nana	2	2	8	1			1	
Leptocera rufilabris					1	3		
Leptocera vitripennis			18		2	7	1	
Spelobia pseudosetaria						2		
Other Acalyptratae	2	3	78	4	4	10	3	1
Calyptratae								
Scathophagidae								
Scathophaga furcata	2	3	1			2	1	
Scathophaga stercoraria	2	2	2			19	2	
Other Calyptratae	4	3	19			3	2	
Total Diptera species	20	17	33	26	20	19	20	11

Appendix 7.1 (cont'd) The species and numbers of specimens recorded on each study site 1990. +indicate new record for Caithness; *new record for Sutherland

	Sites							
	C	DP	DM	H	HT	K	R	S
Coleoptera beetles								
Carabidae								
Cychrus caraboides			1			2	1	
Carabus glabratus	6		1		3		1	
Carabus problematicus	45	105	61	46	31	45	30	36
Carabus violaceus			5					
Leistus rufescens	2				1	1		
Nebria salina	2	1	21	1			1	
Notiophilus aquaticus	9	6	1	6		3	2	
Notiophilus biguttatus			1					
Notiophilus germinyi			3	1				
Notiophilus palustris				1				
Loricera pilicornis		3	2	2		3		
Dyschirius globosus		13	2					6
Patrobus assimilis		15	15		3		3	2
Patrobus atrorufus							1	
Trechus obtusus			2			1		
Trechus quadristriatus						1		
Trechus rivularis				1				
Pterostichus adstrictus			2					
Pterostichus diligens	1	16	4	9	1		11	1
Pterostichus niger	19		22		2	12	9	
Pterostichus nigrita*	122	91	67	73		15	115	10
Olisthopus rotundatus	1							
Agonum ericeti	1	11	2	9			4	
Agonum fuliginosum	7	8		5	1	14	2	
Agonum muelleri		1						
Amara lunicollis			3					
Trichocellus cognatus				1	17			
Bradycellus harpalinus					3			
Bradycellus ruficollis				1	17	2	1	
Cymindis vaporariorum					1			
Number of species	11	11	18	13	11	10	13	5
* *P. nigrita* not separated								
from *P. rhaeticus*								
Staphylinidae								
Acidota crenata	1				1			
Aloconota gregaria	1		1			1		
Amischa analis			6	1				
Anotylus rugosus				1				
Anotylus sculpturatus			1					
Anthobium unicolor				1	101	2		1
Astilbus canaliculata	4	3	2	39		3		7
Atheta alpestris						1		
Atheta arctica		3		8				
Atheta atramentaria						3		1
Atheta elongatula			6					1
Atheta excellens		1			1			
Atheta exigua		1		1				
Atheta fungi	1				1			
Atheta gagantina				1				
Atheta hypnorum					1			
Atheta oblongiuscula		1						

Appendix 7.1 (cont'd)   The species and numbers of specimens recorded on each study site 1990. ⁺indicate new record for Caithness; *new record for Sutherland

	Sites							
	C	DP	DM	H	HT	K	R	S
Atheta occulta			9					
Caldocera aethiops					1	1		
Cypha laeviuscula		1	11			4		2
Erichsonius cinerascens	4							
Euaesthetus laeviusculus								2
Eusphalerum minutum			1					3
Gabrius trossulus				3				
Gymnusa brevicollis		4		1		8	8	1
Lathrobium brunnipes		1		2	1		2	
Lathorbium fovulum	1	9		3			5	4
Lathrobium fulvipenne		1						
Lesteva heeri	10	16				5		2
Lesteva longoelytrata	1			1				
Liogluta nitidula					3	1		
Mycetoporus baudueri					4	1		
Mycetoporus clavicornis	2			1			1	
Mycetoporus longulus			1					
Mycetoporus rufescens					1			
Mycetoporus splendidus			2		10	4	2	
Ocalea picata			1					
Ocyusa hibernica					1			
Olophorum piceum	29	1	10	1	26	2	30	
Othius myrmecophilus				1				
Othius punctulatus	3	3	1	3	1	1	1	
Oxypoda umbrata				1				
Quedius boops	1	2	1	1			2	1
Quedius curtipennis			6					
Quedius molochinus	6	1	5	2	1	3	5	
Quedius nitipennis		2	2					
Quedius umbrinus			1					
Sipalia circellaris					3			
Staphylinus aeneocephalus			20					
Staphylinus erythropterus								1
Stenus brevipennis	1		4	3		1	2	
Stenus geniculatus	1	1				2	1	
Stenus impressus	1				2	3	2	
Stenus nitidiusculus						2		
Tachinus elongatus					1			
Tachinus marginellus							1	
Tachinus signatus					1			
Tachyporus chrysomelinus						2	1	
Tachyporus hypnorum	2	1				7	10	
Xantholinus linearis							3	
Total species	17	18	20	20	19	21	16	12

References

Butterfield, J. E. L. and Coulson J. C. (1983). The carabid communities on peat and upland grasslands in northern England. *Holarctic Ecology*, **6**, 163–174.

Coulson, J. C. (1962). The biology of *Tipula subnodicornis* Zetterstedt with comparative observations on *Tipula paludosa* Meigen, *Journal of Animal Ecology*, **31**, 1–21

Coulson J. C. (1988). The structure and importance of invertebrate communities on peatlands and moorlands, and effects of environmental and management changes. In Usher, M. B. and Thompson, D. B. A.

(Eds.) *Ecological Change in the Uplands* Special publication of the British Ecological Society, Blackwell Press, Oxford. 365–80.

Coulson J. C. (1991). *A preliminary investigation of the invertebrates of the Flows of northern Scotland.* Report to the Nature Conservancy Council, Peterborough, 1–24.

Coulson J. C. (1992). The influence of Man on the fauna of peatlands Bragg, O. M. (Ed.) Hulme, P. D., Ingram, H. A. P. and Robertson, R. A. In *Peatland Ecosystems and Man: An Impact Assessment.* International Peat Society, Jyväskylä, Finland, and Department of Biological Sciences, University of Dundee, 297–308.

Coulson J. C. and Butterfield J. E. L. (1981) *The geographical characterization of moorland using invertebrates.* Report to the Nature Conservancy Council, Peterborough, 1–116 + appendix.

Coulson J. C. and Butterfield, J. E. L. (1982). The distribution and biology of Lonchopteridae (Diptera) in upland regions of northern England. *Ecological Entomology,* **7,** 31–8.

Coulson J. C. and Butterfield J. E. L. (1985). The invertebrate communities of peatlands and upland grasslands in the north of England and some conservation implications. *Biological Conservation,* **34,** 197–225.

Coulson J. C. and Butterfield J. E. L. (1986). The spider communities on peat and upland grasslands in northern England. *Holarctic Ecology,* **9,** 229–39.

Coulson J. C., Horobin, J. C., Butterfield, J. and Smith, G. R. J. (1976). The maintenance of annual life-cycles in two species of Tipulidae (Diptera); a field study relating to development, temperature and altitude. *Journal of Animal Ecology,* **45,** 215–33.

Coulson J. C. and Whittaker J. B. (1978). The ecology of moorland animals. In Heal, O. W. and Perkins, D. F. (Eds), *The Ecology of Some British Moors and Montane Grasslands* Springer-Verlag, Berlin, 52–93.

Curtis D. J. (1979). *Upland spiders – sampling studies in winter 1978–79.* Report to the Nature Conservancy Council, South-west Scotland Region, Balloch, 1–20.

Curtis D. J. (1985). Scottish wetland spiders. 1 – peat bogs in Strathclyde. *Scottish Naturalist,* 45–65.

Curtis D. J. and Stinglhammer H. R. G. (1983). *Araneida and Opiliones recorded on Silver Flowe 1981–1983.* Report to the Nature Conservancy Council, Edinburgh.

Downie, I. S., Coulson J. C., Bauer, L. J., Butterfield, J. E. L., Davies, L. and Goodyer, S. A. (1994). The invertebrates of Cross Fell and Dun Fell summits, Cumbria. *Vasculum,* **79,** 48–62.

Jennings A. L. (1982). A new species of harvestman of the genus *Mitopus* in Britain. *Journal of Zoology, London,* **198,** 1–14.

Locket, G. H., Millidge, A. F. and Merrett, P. (1974). *British Spiders Vol III.* Ray Soc., London, 1–315.

Luff, M. L. and Wardle J. (1991). *Trechus rivularis* Gyll. (Col. Carabidae) in Northumberland. *Entomologist's Monthly Magazine,* **126,** 42.

Ratcliffe, D. A. and Oswald, P. H. (Ed.) (1988). *The Flow country: The peatlands of Caithness and Sutherland.* Nature Conservancy Council, Peterborough.

Rodwell J. S. (Ed). (1991). *British Plant Communities, Vol 2. Mires and Heaths.* Cambridge University Press, Cambridge.

Ter Braak C. J. F. (1988). CANOCO – a FORTRAN Program for *canonical community ordination* by [partial] [detrended] [canonical] Correspondence Analysis, Principle Components Analysis and Redundancy Analysis (Version 2.1). Agricultural Mathematics Group, Wageningen, Netherlands.

8 HONEY PRODUCTION FROM HEATHER MOOR IN SCOTLAND

A. S. MacLennan

Summary

1. A brief history of beekeeping in Scotland is given, and the role which heather moor has played in this.

2. Recent changes in land use affecting heather moor and beekeeping potential are described.

3. An indication is given of the management of beehives on the moors and the potential value of crops which may be obtained.

4. The main requirements for heather honey production on heather moors are briefly discussed.

5. Consideration is made of some of the issues relating to honey production and moorland conservation and management.

8.1 Introduction

The keeping of bees for honey and wax production has taken place in Scotland for perhaps as long as 2000 years. While management techniques and distribution of production have evolved over the years, these are conditioned by fairly standard basic principles determined by the needs and capabilities of the bees themselves.

Honey in Northwest Europe is obtained from the honey bee (*Apis mellifera*) — a specialized colonial insect which in peak of summer may have up to 60 000 workers in a colony. To overcome seasonal scarcity or the winter close season the bees store pollen and nectar, the latter in the altered form of honey, obtained mainly from flowering plants. These materials are stored in specially built wax combs, often in large quantity (>100 kg), depending on the richness of the locality in which the colony is located and the weather pertaining during the main honey and pollen production season. It is this storage capacity which is managed by beekeepers to produce a crop of honey, wax and other products.

For honey bees to survive and produce a surplus of honey in any area they need certain conditions. First, the locality must support adequate pollen bearing flowers

to feed young bees and adequate nectar to feed adult bees. These must be in sufficient quantity to allow storage of surplus to maintain the colony over any close
season(s) and be available in reasonable sequence throughout the Spring to
Autumn period to allow build-up of the colony. While bees will range over 4 km to
collect nectar and pollen, ideally these would be within 2 km of the colony to allow
efficient collection. Bees also require suitably warm, dry weather to enable the bees
to fly freely and work their food sources. They become inactive and stay in the
shelter of the colony cluster below around 11° C and need around 13°–14° C
minimum temperature to work satisfactorily. Heavy or prolonged rain prevents
flight and also may render vegetation unworkable.

8.2 History of Bee Management in Scotland

Following the disappearance of the ice after the last glaciation, as conditions improved so dwarf shrub, scrub and woodland cover re-established in Scotland, till
by the beginning of the present climate period (c.3500 BP) we have the vegetation
pattern outlined by McVean and Ratcliffe (1962). This shows that the bulk of
north Scotland at this time was covered by relatively thick forest of birch-pine on
dry acid areas, oak-birch on richer soils and alder-willow along the straths, while the
South had extensive cover of oak — ash woodland again with alder and willow on
the wetter ground. Main non-wooded areas were near the sea (salting, dune grassland); along river flood plains and loch margins, and land above the tree line.

The severe climatic conditions and lack of flowering plant cover would have prevented honey bees from occurring naturally during glacial and immediate post
glacial episodes. It is most unlikely that they would have been present even at the
beginning of the present climatic period since almost all the trees which dominated
the landscape at this time with the exception of the willows, holly, cherries and
rowans, are not of any significant value to bees, though some may provide pollen,
(hazel, for example). Open areas would have been too limited and those by the sea
and above the tree line too exposed to be available to honey bees. Even though
suitable nectar and pollen bearing flowering plants may have been present in the
ground flora of the woods, these areas would also be unsuitable for honey bees
which will not work within shade. Fire probably maintained a certain amount of
open ground within the woodland zone but the location of this would be unpredictable, and honey bee colonies are insufficiently mobile to exploit these.
Conditions which allowed honey bees to prosper within Scotland required the
influence of man. The natural environment of Scotland began to be increasingly
affected and modified by man from Mesolithic times onward. The clearance of
forest, the use of fire, and with the advent of agriculture, the effects of stock grazing and eventually cultivation all resulted in increasing modification of the natural
vegetation and the creation of open ground. New plants, many of which were
suitable for bees, were introduced both by design and accident.

It is difficult to surmise at what point in this expansion of heath, grassland and
woodland edge that an adequate resource of flowering plants would have been
created to provide conditions for bees to survive and prosper. This would have

Dry heaths

(Above) Evening sun on a dry heath, Strathnaver, Sutherland (M B Usher)

(Left) The typical purple flowers of Calluna vulgaris (ling) at Cluniemore, Pitlochry (M B Usher)

(Right)
The white flowered form of ling, on Lhiattee ny Beinnee, Isle of Man (M B Usher)

(Above) Bothy by Loch Stack,
with wet heath and Arkle in background,
Sutherland
(L Gill)

(Left) Narthecium ossifragrum
(bog asphodel), at Acheilidh,
Sutherland (M B Usher)

(Below) Scirpus cespitosus (deer-sedge), at
Brimham, North Yorkshire (M B Usher)

probably varied according to locality. Analysis of pollen deposits found in pottery on Rum and in Caithness and Fife has led archaeologists to postulate that honey was being used around 4000 BP as the basis for production of fermented brews. While at least one of these interpretations would appear to be feasible other explanations are more probable. For example, it is quite possible that the honey could have been imported, and it is much more likely that it was not until the late Bronze Age (c.2700 BP) that sufficient modification of the landscape had taken place to allow bees to be kept in more climatically favoured eastern areas such as Fife, the Lothians, Tayside or the Moray Firth lowlands. From the point when conditions became suitable for the introduction of bees, numbers would have increased and spread steadily as agriculture and population expanded till by the Middle Ages beekeeping appears to have been a significant cottage industry.

Land use in the lowlands from Iron Age through to late Mediaeval times evolved into an admixture of cultivation, pasturage, common and wood, with the latter increasingly being depleted as greater edge and open space were created. The variety of niches for flowering plants productive for bees within the 3–4 km foraging range would have meant that many cottagers could have kept bees, the honey obtained being an admixture of a range of arable 'weeds' such as charlock, *Sinapis arvensis* woodland edge plants such as willow herb, *Epilobium angustifolium* bramble, *Rubus fruticosus* and heaths such as *Erica cinerea* and especially *Calluna vulgaris*. Bees in this period were kept in 'Skeps' woven mainly from straw, rushes or wicker. These colonies would have been largely static, held on the land of the cottager, probably close to the house for security reasons, since the honey and wax were valuable resources, all too easily stolen. From the 17th century some of the more substantial cottages, farm houses or garden walls began to incorporate spaces for bee skeps, often with locking devices to prevent their theft. The success of beekeeping throughout Scotland still depended greatly upon the quality of the summers, (as it still does) and in indifferent years mortality of stocks would have been great. An example of such a period in the late 18th century is provided by Henderson (1815)

'About 20 years ago every farmer on the South east coast of Sutherland had two or three beehives which generally answered very well, but of late years they have not thriven and many have given them up as they say that the seasons have been for many years so very indifferent that bees will not prosper in this district.'

The major land use changes from the 17th century onwards, and particularly those of the 18th and 19th century gradually began to separate out the settlement and agricultural lands from the heaths in many places, making heather no longer so widely accessible to beekeepers although production from other sources was maintained. The development of sporting estates in the late 19th century however resulted in management of moors for young quality heather which incidentally was ideal for large-scale honey production, wherever the bees had access to these areas. The development in the USA of the modern movable frame hive by Langstroth in 1851 and its gradual introduction to Scotland in the last three decades of the 19th century provided the capacity to manage bee stocks scientifically and commercially. A more professional approach to the management of bees and the preparation and marketing of bee products had begun in Scotland as early as the first half of the 18th century. This was now able to be expanded to include the recognition of the advantages of transporting hives to tap geographically restricted but seasonally rich resources such as fruit crops or heather moors. This was considerably helped by the advent of more efficient transport which meant that numbers of hives could be moved economically over more substantial distances.

By the 1930s large numbers of beekeepers were moving bees to the heather in late summer, often using ingenious devices such as mobile bee houses. The provision of a sugar allowance to beekeepers during World War II gave a major boost to beekeeping as a cottage industry and further encouraged the cropping of heather. This period, ending in the early 1950s probably represented a peak in terms of beekeeping numbers and in the practice of moving hives to the heather. The free availability of sugar once rationing had ceased gradually thinned out the numbers of temporary enthusiasts while major changes in agricultural practices (particularly the widespread use of herbicides and insecticides) had already begun to erode the productivity of agricultural land for bees by the late 1940s (Deans, 1948) and this trend became even more pronounced in the following decades. These changes coupled with several indifferent seasons in the 1970s and mid-1980s further reduced the numbers keeping bees by the late 1980s to perhaps the lowest levels in centuries.

Much traditional heather ground became unavailable to bees in the 1930–90 period, some as a result of the removal of traditional management allowing rank heather, scrub or trees to develop; some was reclaimed for agriculture or the heather lost through overgrazing or lime application. The great majority was lost to forestry, in particular the lower ground moors most productive for heather were also the best suited for timber production. Now in many areas where traditional heather moor was abundant there is a real shortage of extensive quality heather for bees. In addition, many moors which have been partially planted now receive little or no burning over parts adjacent to these plantations leading to rank, poor quality heather becoming the norm there.

Despite this there has recently been an increase in the numbers engaged in the activity. This partly reflects a revival in interest in this traditional craft, but also the rewards of recent changes in land use, such as the advent of new, highly productive honey and pollen crops like oil seed rape or the greater planting of clover leys in 'set aside' areas (though this has now been curtailed). Several reasonable beekeeping summers in the late 1980s and early 1990s have also helped by providing the necessary weather conditions for honey collection. Heather moor continues to be sought out whenever suitable and in 1993, hives could be seen at remaining suitable locations throughout Scotland indicating that heather honey is still a highly valued commodity and that present day beekeepers are still interested in continuing the cropping of this resource.

8.3 Productivity of Heather Moor for Bees

The carrying capacity of a heather moor for bees varies according to the age, exposure and aspect of the moor and condition of the heather, the soil conditions, and preceding weather. Highest returns will be from young, dense heather on dry morainic soils on south facing slopes at low altitudes in a season where adequate warmth and moisture has encouraged free production of nectar and bees can operate more effectively. Where these conditions become less optimal for example on peat soils, with increasing altitude or north facing slopes and in excessively wet, cold or dry summers the nectar production will be reduced. The density of hives is thus a matter of judgement for the beekeeper taking these elements into account. On well-managed dense heather moor one hive per 2 ha could be possibly considered, with a 100 ha block supporting 50 hives. The number of hives would have to be reduced where density and age of heather was less favourable. Cumming and Logan (1950) suggest that 100 hives per square mile is a reasonable density which is one hive per 2.6 ha.

While ideally the hives might be evenly placed across the moor, other factors such as access, shelter, security and public safety will dictate their disposition. In terms of their ability to exploit the resource this is not a problem since the bees will effectively forage up to 3 km and thus a wide area of moor will be exploited by a group of hives. Where the bees are moved to the heather they will only be on the moor for a period of 6–10 weeks. If bell heather (*Erica cinerea*) is a significant part of the crop the hives will be put in place at the end of June and kept on site till the end of the *Calluna* crop (early September). If only a *Calluna* crop is obtained the hives will be moved on site some time in the last week in July or first week in August.

It is difficult to generalize as to the economic returns which may be derived from heather honey production since this will vary considerably according to local circumstances and the position of the individual producer. One can, however consider the value of the produce and the potential gross productivity of such areas. Heather honey is able to command prices considerably in excess of other honey types and, depending on the form of packaging can command over £3 per pound (say £7 per kg) especially where retailed in the comb. While the weather conditions during the heather flowering period is a major control and in some years no surplus is obtained, an average year may result in 9 kg surplus per hive while a top quality hive in an exceptional year may provide as much as 50 kg. At £3 per lb. (450 g) the average value of the production of a hive is thus £63.

On a top quality moor where one hive per 2 ha may be deployed, the productivity of the moor may be calculated as £31.5 per ha in an average year, potentially rising to as much as £175 per hectare in an exceptional one if 50 kg per hive is obtained. Even on a lower quality moor where the density is one hive per 3 or 4 ha, returns will be from £16–£21 per ha in an average year with up to £88–£117 per ha in an exceptional one. While clearly these relatively crude figures need to be set against production costs, there is nevertheless sufficient to indicate that these heather moors are able to supply a valuable product hitherto given little consideration by moorland managers, a product which can have added value when employed in local hotels, guest houses and tea shops.

8.4   Management of Heather Moor to Benefit Bees

To effectively produce honey from heather moor needs only a few basic requirements, many of which are already met in the best managed localities.

1.   It is important that low- and medium-altitude moorland is retained as far as
     possible since only the lower, sheltered moors have a microclimate in which
     honey bees can effectively operate. The higher the moor, the more exposed
     and marginal it becomes for honey production.

2.   As large a proportion of the moor as possible should be of *Calluna vulgaris*
     or *Erica cinerea* which is young and flowering freely. Management to ensure
     maximum cover of these and regular rejuvenation should be ensured by
     appropriate grazing intensity and regular cutting or burning. In practice
     intensive grouse moor management is very satisfactory. It is also important
     that moor is not broken into blocks by trees thereby preventing or inhibiting
     burning.

3.   Suitable access is required to allow hives to be placed on or as close as
     possible to the moor, but controlled to discourage theft.

4.   The hives require a sheltered stance, preferably south facing, in a secure area,
     stock fenced if necessary and out of sight from potential vandals or thieves.
     The location needs to be far enough away (>100m) from any public routes
     to avoid any problems from stinging. (The foraging bees present no
     problems to either recreational interests or other land users in the moor.)

8.5   Honey Production as a factor in Heather Moor Conservation

The utilization of heather moorland for honey production has ancient roots which
evolved over the last century into a highly organised annual mass transportation of
hives to and from the moors to exploit the brief productive flowering season. This
was able to happen on such a scale because of the intensive management of these
areas for sport and pasturage as well as the extent of the resource in Scotland. The
major land use changes of the last 50 years and particularly those of the past two
decades have dramatically reduced the availability of extensive low altitude good
quality heather moor. While locally beekeepers have lamented the loss of large
parts of favoured areas, many of these changes occurred at a time when beekeeping was in decline and unable to influence such land use decisions to any significant
degree.

Cumming and Logan (1950) considered that with appropriate cooperative management beekeeping in Scotland could be developed into an important and
profitable rural industry, capitalizing on its Scottish image and particularly on the
production of heather honey as a specialism. While they could not have anticipated
the major post war changes in land use which affected beekeeping, the disparity between their vision and present conditions may indicate a missed opportunity. Much
of the most productive heather moor resource has gone, but extensive areas still
remain where the production of honey from *Erica cinerea* or *Calluna* can still be one

of a set of objectives in management, provided that the value of the activity is recognized as such and built into the decision making process.

The utilization of heather moor for honey production provides virtually no income for the manager of the land unless he or she is also the beekeeper. Nominal rentals may be obtained, but given that bees will forage up to 4 km, the placement of hives rent free adjacent to a moor can ensure its exploitation without any cost to the beekeeper. It may be, however that more of a formal link between manager, landowner and beekeeper would be mutually beneficial and this should be explored. Irrespective of the potential for directing economic benefits to the landowner, the opportunity also exists to publicize the value of moorland management for honey production. The addition of a further objective of management for such areas (particularly one which complements the existing set) should be welcomed, since it increases the justification for the retention and management of heather moor and gives a potentially wider public support base for such management. Heather honey is seen by the public as an acceptable, desirable product in contrast say to the more elite image of grouse. The widening of general public support can only have benefits in justifying any public expenditure to maintain and manage moorland. It is recommended that a more formal recognition of this product as an objective of heather moor management should be given where appropriate.

While it may now be impossible to create the framework outline by Cumming and Logan (1950) of a widespread beekeeping cottage industry actively marketing a quality Scottish product, there may still be potential for some of that vision to be realised in those localities where the resources still remain, provided that provision can be made for their survival and management.

Bibliography

Burtt, C. E. (1971). *The Weather and Honey Production*, Central Association of Beekeepers; Edinburgh.

Clark, G. (1942). Bees in antiquity *Antiquity*, **16**, No. 63, 208–15.

Crane, E. (1983). *The Archaeology of Beekeeping*, Duckworth, London.

Cumming, A. R. and Logan, M. (1950). *Beekeeping Craft and Hobby*, Oliver and Boyd, Edinburgh.

Deans, A. S. C. (1948). The production of Heather Honey, *The Scottish Beekeeper's Handbook*, Edinburgh.

Dickson, J. (1978). Bronze age mead, *Antiquity*, **52**, 108–113.

Foster, A. M. (1988). *Bee Boles and Bee Houses*, Shire Publications, Aylesbury.

Fraser, H. M. (1958). *A History of Beekeeping in Britain*, Bee Research Association, London.

Henderson, J. (1815). *A General View of Agriculture in the County of Sutherland*, Macmillan, London.

Highland Regional Council. (undated) The Achavanich Cist Burial, *HRC Libraries and Leisure Services Leaflet*, Inverness.

Howes, F. N. (1979). *Plants and Beekeeping*, Faber and Faber, London.

McVean, D. N. and Ratcliffe, D. A. (1962). *Plant Communities of the Scottish Highlands*, HMSO, London.

Robertson, J. (1808). *A General View of Agriculture in the County of Inverness*, Phillips, London.

Scottish Beekeepers Association. (1971). Survey of heather areas in Scotland, *Scottish Beekeeper*, **26**(9), 180–2.

Whitehead, S. B. (1954). *Bees To The Heather*. Faber, London.

Wickham-Jones, C. (1990). *Rhum — Mesolithic and Later Sites at Kinloch. Excavations 1984–86*, Society of Antiquaries of Scotland Monograph 7. 126–7.

9 PEOPLE, PERCEPTIONS AND MOORLAND

J. W. Mackay

Summary

1. Existing (and very limited) survey evidence on public appreciation of moorland and on recreation trips to moorland in Scotland is reviewed.

2. Data are presented from an *ad hoc* interview survey to elicit from the public their images of moorland landscapes.

3. Public valuation of the wild and open qualities of moorland landscapes and its role in developing the argument for conserving moorland in Scotland are also discussed.

9.1 Introduction

This chapter is about enjoyment of moorland by the general public — a theme which touches on aesthetics, public perceptions and participation in open-air recreation. Scientists and moorland managers have an informed understanding of moorland environments, but these are minority views. It is the perceptions of moorland held by the general public (perhaps less tutored but no less valid) that are explored here.

Moorland in Scotland is a landscape under pressure, not least from continued afforestation. Understanding how the public value moorland is important in considering how best to conserve these landscapes. This is particularly so given the high recreational value placed by the public on fine countryside — indeed, recreational interest groups have long led the argument to conserve the best of our landscapes.

9.2 The Meaning of Moorland

A first difficulty in this kind of social science inquiry lies in the interpretation of seemingly simple words like moor and moorland. Perhaps this has always been true. A 1809 quotation from the *Farmers' Magazine* (cited in the Scottish National Dictionary, Vol. VI, p. 355) states: 'In every quarter of the country moors occur . . . They are composed of various kinds of soils; for the term moor is extremely vague'. Refined systems of classifying vegetation can help to resolve that definitional problem for the specialist. Uncertainty about the common-place use of the word moor may, however, still exist and this is understandable, given the varied circumstances in which moorland-type vegetation is found in Scotland. Whatever the present scientific view, it would then be prudent to anticipate that the general public will have a very broad view of moorland, encompassing some habitats which are not very natural and even some which are more montane in character.

It is not clear then whether the public view moorland mainly as an upland landform of low relief; or as any open land covered by certain kinds of rough vegetation; or as land that occurs in certain geographic settings because it is above the cultivated limit or providing the foreground to higher hills. An exploratory question 'What is moorland?' was put to a group of hillwalkers (see Appendix 9.1) and, from their responses, moorland appears to range across these three possibilities. For this group of people (to select out the main themes) moorland was heather-clad, uncultivated, boggy, treeless and flat or undulating land. There was no consistent view on the matter.

It is worth recording that moor was once much closer to where most people lived. Muirend, Muirton and Burghmuir are all place-names within the existing built-up area of Perth. The burghmuir was the common land or muir attached to the town, and all these place-names are frequently to be found in Central Scotland, along with other combinations such as Muirhead, Muiredge, Muirhouse and all the others with geographic labels attached to muir, like Stenhousemuir or Stockiemuir. In the distribution of these names we can see the imprint of a previous lower boundary between the cultivated in-bye and unimproved land.

This diversion into place names is a reminder that moor is also a word of changed meaning. Indeed its use in some parts of Scotland (certainly as moor rather than muir) may be a more recent import, possibly influenced by mapmakers and also by the incoming of field sports as a land use in the uplands. It is probably unwise to seek a precise definition of the word moorland in Scotland, given the range of physical and bioclimatic settings in which moorland-type vegetation or landforms exist, from grassy heaths on lowland hills to extensive blanket bog in the north. As a starting point, no more can be said from a non-scientific stance than to define moorland as open land above the cultivated limit, but not including the higher hills.

9.3 Do People Enjoy Moorland?

There is no strong evidence that moorland in Scotland is a prime destination for open-air recreation compared with popularly visited places at the coast or loch-edge. In a survey of walkers and walking by System 3 Scotland (Scottish Natural Heritage, 1993), details were obtained of about 1350 recent walks, of which 9 % were described by respondents as being located in 'a mountain or moorland' setting. However, many of these walks will not have been taken on moorland *per se* but close to the hills or on the mountains. Perhaps the most convincing evidence of limited use of moorland for recreation is that the respondents to this survey were also asked to provide a word description of the place of this last walk. Only seven

seven of these descriptions or place names includes the word 'moor' and all are close to towns in Central Scotland. Inspection of the lists suggests that a small proportion (between 2–3 %) were in moorland settings, such as the Pentlands. So there is no indication from this survey, or from general knowledge of where people go for trips out, that moorland in itself is a main destination for open air recreation by the general public.

Where does moorland fit in the broad sweep of public perception of Scotland's landscapes? Again the evidence is thin and confined to a single market research question about public perception of scenery from an unpublished survey (1987) for the former Countryside Commission for Scotland. In this question, respondents were asked to indicate their first and second preferences from a list of characteristic Scottish landscape types (Table 9.1). This is not a complete list of landscape types: indeed, it rather reflects the stereotypes of Scottish countryside and it is mainly upland in its choices. The outcome was that while the category 'open moorland and heather hills' was not the least preferred, it did not emerge as widely popular, with only 10 % of the sample choosing it as either first or second preference. One point of note is of an increasing preference for 'open moorland and heather hills' from the AB to the DE social groups, and also with increasing age class (not shown in the table). Little weight can be placed on this single piece of evidence.

Table 9.1   Preferred Scottish Scenery (Total respondents 1011).

	First choice (in %)	Second choice (in %)
Open moorland and heather hills	10	12
Lowland farmland with small woods and trees	4	6
High and rocky mountain scenery	15	17
Glens with farms and forests	12	13
Rocky coast with cliffs	6	10
Lochs surrounded by hills	35	22
Views at the coast to islands	17	17
Don't know	2	4

9.4   But What Does Moorland Evoke?

The words moor or moorland may evoke a range of images for the general public. To help explore these images, a small sample of residents of Perth were asked in an on-street interview survey which words they would immediately associate with the terms 'moor' and 'moorland' (see Appendix 9.1). From 46 valid interviews, some 216 words were offered, which can be categorized (Table 9.2) into three broad groupings: first, those which describe the physical elements of moorland; second, those which involve a degree of evaluation of the character of moorland; and third, the residue, including words which are more personal or interpretative in their meaning. Each of these groups is subdivided into a further three groupings to give nine categories, although these subdivisions are somewhat arbitrary. All the words are set out in Table 9.2 and they can be collapsed for a simpler analysis (Table 9.3) by amalgamating words which are synonyms or close equivalents.

Table 9.2   Words associated with moor and moorland: Perth survey.

Physical — Descriptive of place

Natural elements (58)	*Spatial Elements* (27)	*Sensory Experience* (31)
Heather (15)	Open (3) Openness	Springiness underfoot
Shrubs	Space (3) Spacious	Quiet (9) Quietness
Gorse (2)	Open space (3)	Peace and quiet
Whin	Wide open spaces	Silent Silence
Grass	Wide Wideness	Noise of birds
No trees	Goes into space	Smell of heath
Bracken	Vast landscape	Colour (2)
Heath (2)	No end to the views	Green (2) Greenery
Lichen	Nothing to stop you	Brown
Wildlife (5) Nature	Isolated (3)	Cold (4)
Birds (2)	Remote (3) Remoteness	Damp (3)
Eagles	Away from everything	Nice cool place
Grouse (4)	Flat	Extreme weather
Partridge		
Pheasant		
Wild game		
Deer		
Bogs (4) Boggy (3) Marshy		
Peat (2)		
Rough		
Craggy		
Fresh air (2)		
Foggy misty		

Character — Evaluative of place

Benign Features (30)	*Neutral Features* (13)	*Averse Features* (25)
Freedom (3) Free	Wild (2) In the wilds	Bleak (6)
Free to run	Wildness (2) Wilderness	Barren (3)
Peaceful (11) Peace	Solitude	Desolate
Away from it all	Empty	Dreich
Tranquillity Calm/Serenity	Awesome	Lonely (5) Loneliness
Relaxed (2) Relaxing	Challenging	Deserted (2)
Secluded	Mysterious	Arduous
In tune with nature	Timeless	Hostile
Interesting	Nothing going on	Windswept
Wonderful		Nondescript (sometimes)
Nice		
Romantic		

Table 9.2 (cont'd)   Words associated with moor and moorland: Perth survey.

Interpretive of Place		
Emotion (14)	*Utility* (12)	*Location* (6)
Fear	Shooting (2)	Fennick
Don't like open spaces	Shooters/beaters	Rannoch
Wouldn't like to be there	Poor ground	Wuthering Heights
Fearful alone	Sheep	English
Need companion	Public use	Very Scottish
Leads to inner thoughts	Exercise	Scotland
Meditation	Walking	
Spiritual	Environment (2)	
Closer/nearer to God	Conservation	
Nice to be there		
Boring		
No worries		
Like to know it is there		

Table 9.3   Words associated with moor and moorland — Summary Perth Survey.

Physical — descriptive of place		
Natural elements	*Spatial elements*	*Sensory experience*
Plants and animals (42)	Openness (18)	Quiet/silence (13)
Bogs/peat (10)	Remoteness/isolation (8)	Colour (6)
Physical elements (6)	Others (1)	Weather related (9)
Other		Others (3)

Character — evaluative of place		
Benign features	*Neutral*	*Averse features*
Freedom (5)	Wild/empty (8)	Bleak/desolation (13)
Peaceful (16)	Others (5)	Lonely (8)
Relaxing (3)		Others (4)
Others (6)		

Interpretive of place		
Emotion	*Utility*	*Location*
Fearful (13)	Land use (6)	Various (6)
Spiritual (5)	Recreation (3)	
Others (4)	Conservation (3)	

The output from this kind of inquiry needs to be handled with great care. Pilot interviews suggested that some prompting was needed for a brief, on-street interview, and the nature and extent of prompts can readily influence the outcome. So we should take this evidence as no more than a ranging-shot across difficult survey terrain and therefore no detailed analysis is attempted here. Some interesting pointers do emerge.

- First is the relative richness of he wordlist with a wide range of response types, from the emotive to the relatively non-comprehending.

- Second, although the 'natural elements' heading in Table 9.2 has most words, the responses here are the least sophisticated: grouse and heather take away about 20 items and, from the others, there is no indication of a deep understanding of the natural history of moorland. Indeed, of the four birds named, two (partridge and pheasant) are not moorland species, although the connotation here is probably more with the use of moors for game shooting.

- The lack of significant socio-cultural responses (apart from a few references to shooting) is of interest: it is possible to put together a kaleidoscope of word images which link with past and present human use of moorland, from standing stones to field patterns, sheilings, crofting, peat-cutting, Sheriffmuir, Culloden, Covenanters, butts, and afforestation. Little of this emerges. Again, like natural history, it requires a more tutored understanding of the land, not held or not in the surface consciousness of the general public.

- The evocation of the spatial, the abstract and the emotive in moorland is strong: moorland on this evidence is open, remote, quiet, wet, having freedom, peaceful, wild, bleak and lonely. We must be careful here not to ascribe any preferences to these words — bleak and lonely can either be a frightening or a stimulating element of the recreational experience.

- The associations in the words given by individual respondents signal that moorland has qualities that can be placed along a scale from very high aesthetic value to strong distaste — a vision of moor as blasted heath. The balance of opinion lies towards the positive end of the scale, but a more sophisticated survey model is needed to explore beyond this point.

Using a self-completion questionnaire, the members of a Perthshire hill-walking club were asked to write down the words they most closely associated with moor or moorland. From 37 valid responses, 222 words were classified in the same way and the outcome shows close accord with the interview survey. The hill-walkers could offer a longer and more informed list of words descriptive of the natural history of moorland, and there are more socio-cultural references, which might be expected from a sample with more experience of visiting moorland. The aesthetic response is less rich, but this is probably a signal that the prompts used in the on-street survey did influence the responses.

There is some parallel here with an earlier word association study by Shimwell (1982) with a small group of ecologists and land managers. The prime images within this sample were of moorland as windy, desolate, remote, wild and invigorating — although direct comparison between the present and this earlier survey is not possible because of different methods.

9.5   Where Do These Images Come From?

It is easy at a personal level to identify with the emotive images of moorland reported above. However, the fragmentary evidence mentioned earlier on recreation trips suggests that moorland is more of a minority taste. If most people do not recreate much on moorland why do they still espouse a good aesthetic appreciation of such places? One conventional explanation lies in the way in which late 18th and early 19th century literature led fashion in celebrating the wild and picturesque in landscape, a trend led in Scotland by Sir Walter Scott.

So the roots of our current landscape preferences were influenced — it is argued — by what intrigued the educated classes at the turn of the previous century. It is difficult to relate all this to contemporary visits. Scott created the tourist trail to the Trossachs through his narrative poem 'The Lady of the Lake', but very few visitors today will make the connection between their trip and Scott's poem. Moorland has its own champions in literature through the authorship of Hardy and the Brontes. Again it is difficult to make the direct connection to contemporary taste in Scotland, except that the lady in Perth who immediately responded to the words 'moor' or 'moorland' with 'Wuthering Heights and England' might be reflecting a view that moorland in its purest form is something that exists south of the Border: or perhaps she had just seen the recent television presentation of the book.

Part of the explanation of present day appreciation of moorland is the likelihood (but we cannot be entirely certain) that the Scottish public's images of moor merge with images of other elements of our wild and natural landscapes — that is, a strong sense of upland Scotland generally being wild, open and challenging terrain, a theme returned to later.

So it is difficult to evade a conclusion that moorland in Scotland is too diverse and often too closely associated with hill and mountain country to evoke any single image. There is a very wide spectrum of moorland settings, from the mainly grassy heaths of the Campsies and other uplands in central Scotland, to the more classic, dry — and in season purple — heather moors of the eastern Grampians, and onwards to the black, wet moors of the north — moorland as blasted heath, but often in these areas acting as the foreground to fine mountains.

In recreational uses and values we can also see diversity: the uplands in central Scotland are conveniently located for short outings to viewpoint hills, for walks, picnics and other family outings — but only when weather permits. The more extensive heather moors and the blasted-heath, black moor are landscapes mainly for looking at, in the main not welcoming or easily penetrated by the general public. For those engaging in active open-air recreation, moorland of this kind is sometimes part of the long walk in, providing for some the anticipation to, although not the high point, of the recreational experience.

So moorland in itself does not offer explicit targets or goals for most visitors. Perhaps this range of recreational opportunity on moorland goes some way to explain the diverse survey responses set out above. Moorland visited for informal recreation on fine days can have a positive image of peace, space and openness;

moorland tramped through as approach to the hills can be wearisome; moorland of the wet, black category can be awesome or unwelcoming.

9.6   The Role of Recreation in Protecting Moorland Landscapes

The moorlands of the English and Welsh upland landscapes have been given high conservation value through the selection and designation process for the main National Parks and also some of the Areas of Outstanding Natural Beauty. This has been carried through into statutory obligations on the National Park Authorities to map moorland in their areas and to give it special protection. Marion Shoard describes this process in a useful article in which she analyses the value of moorland as recreational space for the urban populations of England.

In this way, public policy south of the Border has set in place a strong framework to protect the recreational value of moorland, and even if all the areas proposed as National Park have not reached that status (such as the northern Pennines), there are other safeguards against adverse land use change in these areas, not least the end to afforestation there.

Attitudes, however, to the protection of moorland landscapes are still ambivalent in Scotland. The focus of landscape conservation has lain more with the higher hills. The selection of National Scenic Areas reflects this emphasis, inheriting much of the stimulus of W.H. Murray's survey for the National Trust for Scotland (1962). In both these appraisals, Rannoch Moor was seen as the moor to protect, but in large part the justification seems to rest mainly on it being a moor readily enjoyed from above, as seen from the hills of Achallader, the Black Mount and eastern Glen Coe, while the Moor in turn provides the foreground for the same high hills. Recent recreational literature for upland Scotland has often been dismissive of moorland, leaning much more on the drama of the mountains. Indeed in the above survey, Murray noted that 'the big Scottish moors will soon be forested; this on the whole is good and to be desired'.

If there is a difference in the higher valuation given to moorland for public enjoyment south of the Border, compared with Scotland, it may simply be a matter of the supply of different kinds of landscape for enjoyment of the wild and open; and the accessibility of these places to urban populations. Scottish moorlands close to cities, say the Campsies or the Pentlands, have their own supporters and affection: in Stevenson's words — 'the hills of home'. But in Scotland the recreational eye has always been drawn onwards to more enticing, more dramatic and higher destinations. For the populations in the northern English cities, Pennine moorland is an end point in the continuum of change outwards from the urban scene: in Scotland moorland is often an intermediate destination or transition zone leading onwards to the higher hills.

Perhaps there is a need to be bolder in promoting the recreational values of wildness, openness, solitude, and hazard, which attach to the best of our upland landscapes, whether moor or mountain. These recreational values have been implicit in landscape designation, and they have underlain much of our concern to conserve the uplands. The acquisition by the National Trust for Scotland of its important mountain properties began the process in Scotland, and this was initially funded by mountaineers.

If there is an opportunity to create some redress for care of moorland, it might come from new thinking about how we might better protect the wildland qualities of upland Scotland. The idea of wildness as a prime recreational value is not new, but it has mainly been promoted through the protection of territorially limited areas of mountain country, say, Glen Coe or the Black Cuillin. Jewels these places may be, but if there is to be effective action to halt attrition to their qualities, then they may need to be placed in wider settings — a more extensive approach, in which adjacent moors could provide the frame for the grander landscapes. As the high hills become busier it could be that some areas of moorland might acquire greater status as sanctuary, a reservoir for solitude, although this will always be a minority taste.

9.7 Conclusion

The openness of Scotland's uplands creates a sense of space and scale and their bareness and harshness contribute to a sense of drama and hazard. But much of this is not a preferred ecological condition, being the end point of continued grazing, or management action such as burning. If a more ecologically based approach to management were to encourage more woody vegetation, would future hill-goers resent natural scrub as they head upwards, just as they resent skirts of Sitka spruce round the hills? Perhaps: but there are mitigating factors in that any change to natural woodland and scrub on hill ground will be long in the accomplishment, compared to the short time-scale of recent afforestation; and time is a major healer in adjustment of public perception. Ecological change of this kind will be less homogenous in its effect; it will look better than conifer plantations, and the value of open land for economic uses and other ecological aims will ensure that openness remains a characteristic of the Scottish uplands. And we can hope for, indeed work for, a commonality of interest between recreational value and ecological health.

Appendix 9.1   Survey Methods

Fifty people were interviewed on-street in Perth, Scotland on 14 August 1993 and asked to state the words which they most closely associated with moor or moorland. In the survey, two prompts were used consistently. The first asked respondents: 'If you were on moorland how would that feel?' The second prompt asked the respondent: 'Think about walking across moorland — would that create any other ideas?' The sample was constructed by quota sampling, by age–class, and gender. Although data on social class were not collected, the sample appeared to be generally representative of the population, but perhaps lightly sampled at each end of the social-class spectrum. Four interviews were discarded in the analysis, either because of limited comprehension of the question by the respondent or because undue prompting was needed to elicit responses.

Thirty-nine members of a Perthshire hill-walking club were given a short self-completion questionnaire when out on a club outing on 5 September. The main question asked respondents to write down the words that they most closely associated with moor or moorland. Two incomplete responses were discarded in the analysis.

References

Murray, W. H. (1962). *Highland Landscape: A Survey.* National Trust for Scotland. Edinburgh, 80 pp.

Shimwell, D. W. (1982). Images of moorland, amenity and wildlife. In Hearn, K. (Ed.) *Recreation Ecology Research Group Report 8.* Recreation Ecology Research Group, Ashford. 66–84.

Shoard, M. (1982). The lure of the moors. In Gold, J. and Burgess, J. (Eds.) *Valued Environments.* Allen and Unwin, London, 55–73.

System 3 Scotland. (1987). *Report of a Survey of Attitudes to Conservation of the Countryside.* Unpublished report to the Countryside Commission for Scotland, Battleby.

System 3 Scotland (1993). *Report of a Survey of Walking in the Scottish Countryside.* Research, Survey and Monitoring Series, No. 3, Scottish Natural Heritage, Battleby.

Snapshots of change

(Right)
*Aerial photograph of the Ochil Hills, Stirling,
taken on 10 June 1988. Note the "fence line".*
(Scottish Development Department,
Crown Copyright)

(Below)
*Close view of a "fence line" grazing effect, here
showing a slope of Glenfintaig,
Spean Bridge* (D J Henderson)

*(Below) Regeneration of pinewood and heather
(at left) in Abernethy Forest, Cairngorms, following
the erection of a deer-exclusion fence* (M B Usher)

Birds of heath and moor

(Left)
Golden plover (Pluvialis apricaria)
chick (A F Brown)

(Above)Merlin male (Falco columbarius)
(Laurie Campbell)

(Above) Greenshank male (Tringa nebularia)
(D B A Thompson)

(Right) Whinchat male(Saxicola rubetra)
(Laurie Campbell).

PART TWO
DYNAMIC PROCESSES: LANDSCAPE AND ENVIRONMENTAL CHANGE

PART TWO

DYNAMIC PROCESSES: LANDSCAPE AND ENVIRONMENTAL CHANGE

Heaths and moorland are dynamic systems, undergoing continuous processes of change at many spatial and temporal scales. At least this is how they have been perceived by ecologists over the last 40 or so years (e.g. Watt, 1955; Ratcliffe, 1959; Miles, 1985; Usher and Thompson, 1993), though many people beholding bleak, barren earthy brown expanses of heather in winter might refute this!

Below the tree-line probably all but the wettest blanket bog would naturally succeed to trees in the absence of interference through burning or heavy grazing. The first paper, by Colin Legg, sets the scene with an appraisal of the effects of scale on our perception of the patterns and processes of change in heathland vegetation. Seed banks are but one factor affecting change (Cumming and Legg), influencing not only the likelihood of regeneration of heather but of succession through to scrub or woodland. Hester and Miller explain how such successions are now fundamentally affected by grazing in the Scottish uplands, and it is this factor which urgently needs to be addressed if woodland and scrub regeneration is to be encouraged. New information on altitudinal zonations of trees and moorland gives a fascinating insight into factors affecting these 'climatically-controlled' vegetation boundaries (McConnell and Legg).

Grazing preferences of herbivores and the resilience of different plant species together affect the rates and patterns of vegetation change caused by grazing. Armstrong and Milne describe a model which can be used to predict the consequences of changes in stocking rates of sheep on their consumption of different types of heathland vegetation. Some applications of these questions to wetter heaths are described by Nolan and Henderson. Much less data exist for red deer (Staines *et al*, Part III), although the MLURI are currently researching and developing a similar model for these herbivores.

Invasion of heathland by other species, such as bracken, can be extremely difficult to control (Marrs and Pakeman; Ninnes), and it is suggested that climatic warming may further exacerbate this problem by increasing the potential range and vigour of this species in many parts of Britain. This can have fundamental consequences for nature conservation, wildlife (Allen) and recreation.

The effects of nutrient changes on heathlands are examined in the context of their sensitivity to soil acidification in Scotland (Langan *et al*.) and their sensitivity to severe heather beetle attack under conditions of high atmospheric nitrogen inputs in the Netherlands (de Smidt). Both studies indicate the vulnerability of heathland communities to change. Such changes are put into a historical perspective by Stevenson and Birks, with a resumé of changes in heather pollen counts in Britain over the last 10,000 years, again highlighting the prime importance of burning and grazing in affecting heathland dynamics. A case history from the Outer Hebrides indicates that even where trees and scrub were naturally infrequent, fire still played a major role in the maintenance and spread of heather moorland (Edwards *et al.*). Palaeoecological reconstructions of burning histories from mor-humus soils can often bridge the gap between more conventional palaeoecological studies and more recent information gleaned from aerial photographs and satellite imagery (Rhodes).

This part ends with a discussion of patch dynamics of heaths. Patchiness affects both plants and animals in many different ways, some of which are explored with examples from the North York Moors (Usher). This leaves the question of the wider implications of patchiness and scale in moorland vegetation; both present a serious challenge for the successful management of heath, both for a range and for a diversity of wildlife and vegetation.

Levin's (1992) important review of ecological scale and pattern might have had heaths and moorlands at its core — the patterns one sees at a distance are not necessarily those that influence the major dynamic processes!

References

Levin, S. A. (1992). The problem of pattern and scale in ecology. *Ecology*, **73,**1943–1967.

Miles, J. (1985). The pedogenic effects of different species and vegetation types and the implications of succession. *Journal of Soil Science*, **36,**571–584.

Ratcliffe, D. A. (1959). The vegetation of the Carneddau, North Wales. 1. Grasslands, heaths and bogs. *Journal of Ecology*, **47,**371–413.

Usher, M. B. and Thompson, D. B. A. (1993). Variation in the upland heathlands of Great Britain: conservation importance. *Biological Conservation*, **66,**69–81.

Watt, A. J. (1955). Bracken versus heather: a study in plant sociology. *Journal of Ecology*, **43,**490–506.

10 HEATHLAND DYNAMICS: A MATTER OF SCALE

C. Legg

Summary

1. Heath vegetation may be seen as homogeneous stands of fairly uniform structure and composition. Alternatively, it can be considered as either a small-scale mosaic of individual plants and shoots, or a landscape-scale mosaic of different plant communities.

2. Similarly, the vegetation may appear relatively stable in time with few changes in essential structure or composition. Or, it can be considered as dynamic with frequent replacements of individuals as plants age and die, or again, as a seral stage in succession towards woodland vegetation.

3. The patterns and the processes observed depend on the scale of observation and the viewpoint of the observer. Choosing the correct scale for observation and experimental work is crucial in interpreting and understanding the mechanisms which determine patterns and processes in vegetation.

4. It is argued that the large-scale and long-term processes that play a major role in shaping the ecological landscape are not always predictable from small-scale observations.

5. The importance of understanding scale is discussed in relation to the regeneration of *Calluna vulgaris* and *Betula* species in heathland, the long-term effects of fire and disturbance on erosion, and the monitoring of vegetation change.

10.1 Heathlands as dynamic systems

All vegetation is dynamic in nature. Individual shoots and plants mature and die and are replaced by others. Those that replace them may or may not be the same species. Vegetation can therefore be considered as a shifting mosaic of plants and shoots, each of which is developing, growing, dying and being replaced. The inter-relationships between these components of the plant community in both space and time has become known as 'Watt's cyclical regeneration model' (Marrs, 1988) after the description of the relationship between pattern and process in vegetation by Watt in his influential Presidential Address to the British Ecological Society (Watt, 1947). Heath vegetation provided Watt with one of his main examples (Watt, 1947; 1955) where the heather plant passes through several developmental phases (pioneer, building, mature and degenerate) before dying and being replaced.

Viewed over a longer period of time, however, the vegetation may appear rather static. In many situations there are few changes in structure and appearance of the vegetation from one generation of plants to the next and the present heath vegetation in many areas has retained much of the essential character that it had 100 years ago.

Heathlands, however, do not necessarily regenerate themselves. The vegetation which replaces old heather plants may not be the same as that formerly present. Heaths below the natural treeline have been derived mostly from woodland vegetation following anthropogenic disturbance and alteration of the environment through grazing and burning (Gimingham, 1972). In some regions of Scotland, however, large areas that were formerly heather-dominated have now changed to grass-dominated systems or woodland vegetation (Hester and Sydes, 1993).

The management practices which created the heathland community are relatively recent (100 to 200 years) in some areas and in others they are ancient, as in the New Forest (Webb, 1986), Breckland (Godwin, 1944) and probably also in such anciently inhabited areas as the Muir of Dinnet, Aberdeenshire and Shetland. The traditional management systems, however, can no longer be maintained. The consequence of this is that secondary succession will always be tending to change the vegetation in some direction — typically towards woodland (Figure 10.1). Countering the effects of succession is the effect of management through grazing,

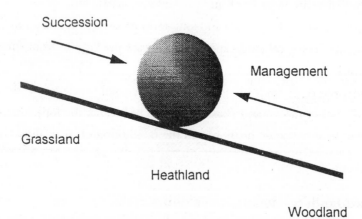

Figure 10.1. Heath vegetation can be considered as a seral stage in the succession from grassland to woodland on nutrient-poor, acid soils. While successional forces tend to drive this change in one direction towards scrub and woodland, management by grazing and burning tends to reverse the trend. Excessive burning or grazing may change heath vegetation into grassland.

controlled burning and turf cutting. If the management is too severe then grassland may result; too little management and trees might be expected to colonize and
scrub woodland develop.

On the geological time-scale there is increasing evidence that heath vegetation
types found during the main interglacial periods of the Quaternary were of rather
different composition to the present (Holocene) vegetation dominated by *Calluna
vulgaris* (L.) Hull (referred to henceforth as *Calluna*) (Stevenson and Birks, this volume). The present community type is relatively recent in origin.

Whether vegetation is seen as a continually shifting mosaic of individuals, or as
a relatively constant vegetation type, or as one seral stage in a succession, or as a
temporary association of species on the geological stage is very much a matter of
the scale of observation. The importance of scale in some of the main processes
of vegetation dynamics in heathland is therefore considered further.

10.2   Scale in vegetation dynamics

There has been a plethora of papers published recently discussing the importance
of both spatial and temporal scale in ecology (e.g. Jarvis and McNaughton, 1986;
van der Maarel, 1988; Falinski, 1988; Allen and Hoekstra, 1990; Grace, 1991;
Fahrig, 1992; Levin, 1992). As Levin pointed out: 'The observer imposes a
perceptual bias, a filter through which the system is viewed'. An appreciation of
our own perceptual bias, and the realization that our own bias may be different to
that of other people, is an essential part of understanding the mechanisms which
drive the dynamic processes in vegetation.

A corollary of this is that '. . . every organism is an "observer" of the environment, and life history adaptations such as dispersal and dormancy alter the
perceptual scales of the species . . .' (Levin, 1992). This also is of considerable importance when trying to understand the mechanisms underlying the ecology of
different species and, indeed, of the different life-stages within each species. Thus
the environment with which a *Calluna* seed interacts during germination will be
that within a few millimetres of the seed, and the whole germination process may
take place in a time window of a few weeks. The ecology of a pine woodland community, on the other hand, operates on a minimum area of several hectares and a
time-scale of several centuries.

What is the appropriate level for ecological research? The human 'perceptual
bias' or 'filter' tends to be imposed by what you can easily see and walk over —
dimensions from a metre to a kilometre — and changes which can be observed
over no more than a few decades — time scales which are convenient relative to
human memory and working life. The mechanisms which determine the patterns
mostly operate at a scale below that at which the patterns are observed (Levin,
1992); those studied are commonly limited by the three-year research project.

There have been several attempts to identify 'natural' levels of integration in
vegetation. For example, van der Maarel (1988) recognized six spatial scales (defined by the spatial dimensions of the individual, patch, population, community,
landscape and region) and related these to eight different processes in vegetation

dynamics operating at a range of temporal scales (Figure 10.2). In addition, there are the 'conventional' levels of organization in ecology defined by the cell, organism, population, community, ecosystem, landscape, biome and biosphere (Allen

	Individual	Patch	Population	Community	Landscape	Region
Fluctuations	X	XX	XX			
Gap dynamics	X	XX	XX			
Patch dynamics	X	X	X			
Cyclic succession		X	XX	X		
Regeneration succession		XX	XX	XX		
Secondary succession		X	XX	XX	XX	
Primary succession			XX	XX	XX	
Secular succession				X	X	X

Figure 10.2. The relationship between spatial and temporal scales in vegetation dynamics. *X* indicates the spatial scales at which each process operates (after van der Maarel, 1988).

and Hoekstra, 1990), or the levels of integration as used in classification of the individual, the species and the vegetation unit (Weigleb, 1989). Levels of organization are largely independent of spatial and temporal scales as illustrated by Allen and Hoekstra who describe an entire ecosystem of decomposers contained within a rotting log (part of an individual organism); the upper surface of the log forms a landscape occupied by a population of mosses. These levels of organization also need to be considered critically.

It is clear that there is no single 'correct' level of integration for observation; each process involves mechanisms which are operating at several different spatial scales. Different problems require different solutions. Choosing the wrong timescale may result (and often has resulted) in false conclusions. Equally, failing to appreciate the scale limitations of other people's work may result (and frequently has resulted) in the misapplication of their conclusions.

10.3 The Watt Model

Most studies of vegetation dynamics in British heathlands have concentrated on the dominant species, *Calluna vulgaris*. The life cycle of this plant spans some 30 to 40 years passing through the four growth phases (pioneer, building, mature and degenerate) lasting from 3 to 10 years each as described by Watt (1955). These changes in growth form are driven by mechanisms that operate within the human scale and can be observed within a three-year research project. Thus the work of Barclay-Estrup (Barclay-Estrup and Gimingham, 1969; Barclay-Estrup, 1970) has provided a semi-quantitative confirmation of the process originally described by Watt (1955). The resulting model of the *Calluna* cycle, where correctly applied, has proved extremely valuable for describing and understanding the dynamics of heathlands and has provided a basic framework for heathland research since (e.g. Gimingham, 1972, 1987; Hobbs and Gimingham, 1987; de Hullu and Gimingham, 1984).

Only in the last decade, where research has moved away from the objectives of grouse-moor management and the 10- to 15-year burn cycle towards issues related to the long-term processes of succession and to conservation has the Watt model been found wanting (Gimingham, 1988; Marrs, 1988). There are four particular difficulties with the model which relate to problems of scale.

First, there is the layering of *Calluna* stems. In many areas the majority of the heather stems fall prostrate and, where covered in litter and moss, produce adventitious roots (Beijerinck, 1940). This can establish a perpetual 'even-aged' stand of shoots which are physiologically in the building phase. Stems more than 12–15 years old die off at the base as new adventitious roots are produced above (A. MacDonald, personal communication 1993.). In these sites only a relatively small proportion of plants may enter a distinct degenerate phase. The model, which was originally developed by Watt from observations on East Anglian Breckland, may be less appropriate when applied elsewhere in the geographical range or habitat range of the species. Beijerinck pointed out in 1940 that layering, which is common in peaty areas, is not observed in dry sandy regions. It is a common but dangerous assumption in ecology that the properties of a species described from a restricted geographical locality, or from one habitat type, can be applied equally well elsewhere.

Second, there is catastrophic death. Marrs (1986) has distinguished between death of heather plants caused by the ageing process (endogenous initiation) and death caused by external factors (exogenous initiation) such as severe weather and attack by the heather beetle (*Lochmaea suturalis* Thomson) (Berdowski and Zeilinga, 1987). These exogenous factors often affect all of the plants within a large area causing the simultaneous death of whole stands. Where exogenous factors predominate, which appears to be the case in many lowland heaths, few heather plants will survive long enough for the degenerate phase to be reached. Marrs (1986) demonstrated that the distinction between endogenous and exogenous disturbance is largely one of scale. For example, competitive interactions between neighbours will be seen as endogenous if the whole community is under consideration, but exogenous from the point of view of the individual plant. Equally, the susceptibility of an even-aged stand of *Calluna* to an exogenous factor, such as beetle attack, is partly a function of the age of the plants. The relative importance of endogenous and exogenous disturbance depends on the frequency, or return time, of the catastrophic disturbance viewed on the time scale of the life-span of *Calluna*. Some sites are more susceptible to exogenous disturbances than others and the distinction is important for management planning. For example, stands more than 16 years old at Cavenham Heath became particularly susceptible to exogenous disturbances, while the threshold age in The Netherlands is only 10 years at some sites (Marrs, 1986).

Third, absence of seed regeneration may pose difficulties. Although Beijerinck (1940) remarks that '*Calluna* germinates excellently on the humus formed from its own refuse' and that 'generation may succeed generation without a decline in the vegetation being perceptible', heather seedlings have, in Scotland, only rarely been observed to establish in the centre of degenerate plants (Miles, 1981), perhaps because of the prevalence of bryophytes and peaty surface layers. The alternative route for the reinitiation of the cycle through vegetative lateral spread of shoots from neighbouring plants (Watt, 1955) would seem to be the norm in most parts of the country (A. MacDonald personal communication, 1993.). The litter layer must first be eroded away from the centre of the plant to expose humic or mineral soils before seedlings will establish. This again may be a more common phenomenon in the more continental climate observed by Beijerinck or in the dry, sandy heaths of East Anglia described by Watt where there is relatively little accumulation of litter and bryophytes than in the wetter climate and more peaty soils of the north and west of Britain.

Finally, there may be invasion by other species. Heather plants in the pioneer and degenerate phases offer reduced competitive resistance to invasion from other species and the system may eventually break down completely through invasion of birch (*Betula pendula* Roth. and *B. pubescens* Ehrh.), pine (*Pinus sylvestris* L.), bracken (*Pteridium aquilinum* (L.) Kuhn.) or other species (Gong, 1984; Marrs and Hicks, 1986; Marrs *et al.*, 1986). The probability that an invasion will occur depends primarily on the availability of propagules and the distribution in space and time of suitable microsites for germination and establishment.

There are perhaps several reasons why the Watt model has been so successful despite these difficulties. The majority of research, in upland Britain at least, has been constrained to managed vegetation where burning is designed to prevent the vegetation from progressing beyond the building phase; there has therefore been relatively little interest in the ecology and biology of mature- and degenerate-phase plants. Further, the model was originally developed to describe processes operating at the level of the individual plant in an uneven-aged stand; application of the model, however, has often been at the level of the stand where the average properties of the managed, even-aged population is the object of study, rather than the precise details of behaviour of individuals. Stands are assigned to a particular phase on the basis of the canopy structure, or the age of individual stems at ground level, rather than the age of the stand. Layering stands can therefore be assigned to the building or mature phase without reference to their true age and 'pioneer phase' plants may be derived either from seed, or from the layering of slender shoots from neighbouring plants.

10.4 Dispersal and migration

The seeds and seed-retaining flowers of heather, and the fruits of birch and pine are all wind dispersed. The dispersal distances often quoted in the literature (e.g. 50–100 m for *Betula* spp. (Atkinson, 1992); up to 810 m for *Pinus sylvestris* (Smith, 1900); and 100 m in wind speeds of 10 ms^{-1} or 250 m in wind speeds of

30–40 ms^{-1} for *Calluna* (Nordhagen, 1937; Beijerinck, 1940)) mean very little in the absence of quantitative information on the density of seed rain. The conclusion generally reached is that the vast majority of seeds fall within a radius twice the height of seed release. This means a couple of metres for heather, and 40–50 m for the trees. Indeed, the vast majority of heather seeds fall less than 1 m from the point of release (Figure 10.3). This relationship is very important for foresters who are looking for good regeneration of forest cover in small-scale clearings, conser-

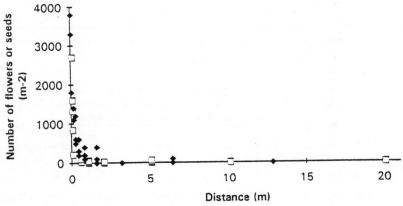

Figure 10.3. Density of seed rain (◆) and deposition of wind-dispersed *Calluna* flowers (□) (which may retain some seeds) plotted against distance from the edge of a source area of building-phase *Calluna*. The linear axes demonstrate that the majority of seeds are deposited very close to the source (based on Legg *et al.*, 1992).

vationists who are trying to restore ancient birch woods and heathland managers who are looking for colonization of patches in a small-scale heathland mosaic.

There is another process involved at a different scale. The distribution of the seed density in wind-dispersed species is generally assumed to follow a log–log relationship with distance from source (Gregory, 1973). Plotted on a log–log scale (Figure 10.4) it is clear that a small number of seeds may travel much greater distances. Thus Miller has shown significant levels of regeneration of pine to over 3 km from the nearest seed source (Welch *et al.*, 1990). Significant, that is, for those interested in the migration of species, or in the retention of a treeless wilderness. But the numbers involved would not be considered 'significant' by the forester interested in good forest regeneration. The forester imposes a different 'perceptual bias' on the scale at which the pattern is observed to that of the heathland ecologist. Species dispersed by birds or large mammals may be even more widely dispersed (Welch *et al.*, 1990).

The dispersal of the majority of seeds to within a short distance of the parent plant and migration by the long-distance transport of occasional seeds are clearly extremes of the same process viewed at two different scales. It may help, however, to consider them as two separate processes: the first is the creation of a dense seed rain from which a new stand or population can be established to replace the

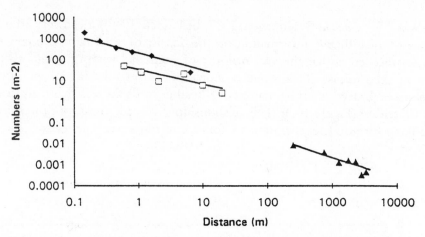

Figure 10.4. Density of seed rain (◆) and deposition of flowers (□) plotted against distance from the edge of a source area of building-phase *Calluna* on log-log axes (based on data in Legg *et al.*, 1992). The data for *Pinus* (▲) are the density of seedling and saplings established over a period of some 10–20 years from seeds dispersed from the edge of a pine forest on the northern slopes of the Cairngorms (from Welch *et al.*, 1990). The points plotted represent the means of several observations.

present generation; the second is the migration of isolated plants to new geographical locations from which new populations can establish in subsequent generations. The absence of seed sources has been postulated as an important factor in the stability of the more remote heathlands in Scotland (Miles, 1973, 1981; Rodwell, 1991b), but this information would suggest that colonization could occur at low density even in the more remote areas given suitable microsites and conditions for establishment.

In terms of scale, then, the ecology of establishment in birch can be viewed as ranging upwards from factors determining the germination of seeds at the scale of a few centimetres over a period of weeks (Figure 10.5). The critical phase of establishment, escaping the grazing animals, requires plants to reach a certain size and may take several years, while the regeneration of a population of birch to create a stand or a birch woodland is a phenomenon operating over decades and hectares. The majority of seed dispersal occurs over tens of metres and is repeated every year, but the occasional long-range dispersal may involve tens of kilometres and be a relatively rare event.

The seeds of *Calluna* are small (about 0.2 mm x 0.3 mm x 0.5 mm) and can, under certain circumstances, be carried considerable distances (Beijerinck, 1940). They are produced in vast numbers (between 10^5 and 10^6 per m², Legg *et al.*, 1992) and a seed bank of 10^5 to 8×10^5 seeds per m² may develop. How is it that, with so may germinable seeds available, the plant is still unable to regenerate from seed in the gaps created by degenerate plants? The Watt model would only require one or two seedlings to successfully establish over the five-or ten-year period that plants remain in the degenerate phase for seed regeneration to be equal in importance to regeneration from layering.

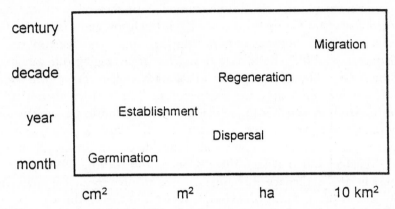

Figure 10.5. The temporal and spatial scales of various processes in the ecology of establishment of *Betula* spp. in heathlands.

Being so small, the seedling has very precise requirements for a safe site. Though many seeds may germinate (de Hullu and Gimingham, 1984) relatively few survive long enough for roots to penetrate the litter and establish an independent access to reliable soil moisture. Germination is affected by the presence of litter and mosses (Mallik *et al.*, 1984; Hobbs and Gimingham, 1987; Equihua and Usher, 1993) and lichens (Hobbs, 1985; Legg *et al.*, 1992). The conclusion is that heather is quite unable to regenerate from seed in the type of environment created by the parent plant. Good regeneration, it seems, will only occur on exposed mineral or consolidated, bare peat soils following decomposition and erosion of the litter and mor humus (Watt, 1955). One might predict that regeneration in mature heath vegetation would be far higher for a plant producing a smaller number of larger seeds. Instead of producing up to a million tiny seeds per square metre every year, why not produce a few large seeds which would provide the seedling with sufficient resources to have a good chance of establishment through a litter and moss carpet? There are many different aspects of this question; for example the risk of seed predation may be one important factor (Harper, 1977). The main ecological function of the seed bank of *Calluna* is not the routine maintenance of the population which, in many situations, can be achieved by layering, but for the capture of new microsites created by unpredictable disturbance events.

Calluna behaves as a pioneer species. It is common in acid woodland where, though not tolerating the deepest shade, it is an early colonizer of gaps created by fallen trees or natural fire. The seeds may remain dormant in the soil for up to 150 years (Cumming and Legg, this volume). This enables the plant to transcend the barrier of time and to reoccupy sites as soon as suitable conditions are created. The decay of seeds in the seed bank is likely to be approximately exponential (Harper, 1977). A consequence of this is that the longevity of the seed bank is a function of the initial size of the seed bank: the more seeds present the more likely that some seeds will survive to the next perturbation event. This provides a considerable selection pressure for the production of a large number of small seeds. The association between seed size, dormancy and unpredictability of the habitat has been noted elsewhere (Thompson *et al.*, 1993; Hodgson and Grime, 1990).

There is a trade-off between dispersal through space and dispersal through time (Klinkhamer *et al.*, 1987); both have the effect of averaging out variability in the environment, or enabling the species to take advantage of the infrequent occurrence of suitable microsites for regeneration. The relative merits of the two strategies depend on whether the regeneration sites tend to become available on a spatially-predictable pattern (i.e. recurring at the same location) but at unpredictable time intervals, or are commonly available but in a spatially unpredictable fashion (Venable and Lawlor, 1980; Cohen and Levin, 1991; Fahrig, 1992). Patchyness in time and space are here measured relative to the life-span and dispersal ability of the plant. Thus, while birch invests in dispersal through space, heather invests in dispersal through time (Figure 10.6). As a consequence of this there will often be an ample seed bank for restoration of heathland vegetation on sites of former (recent) dominance by heather (Miller and Cummins, 1987), though the

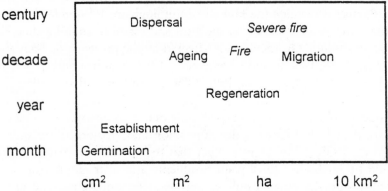

Figure 10.6. The spatial and temporal scales of various processes in the ecology of establishment of *Calluna*.

creation of heathland vegetation in new locations will require the introduction of seed if anything more than a few isolated plants is required. Birch, on the other hand, can effectively invade new areas from a seed source at some considerable distance though the species retains no dormant seed bank beyond one or two years (Atkinson, 1992). Normal management fire provides frequent and spatially predictable microsites for seedling establishment and the regeneration of *Calluna*, either from stem bases or from seed, is normally very good.

10.5 The long-term effects of fire and burning management

In very general terms it has been assumed that the nutrients which are lost as smoke, wind-blown ash and subsequent leaching during and following a fire are replaced within a relatively short period by inputs from rainfall and particulate matter derived from fires in adjacent patches of vegetation (Figure 10.7a). The data to support this type of model have mostly been based on small-scale, short-term laboratory-based experiments and observations of single fires (e.g. Allen, 1964; Chapman, 1967; de Jong and Klinkhamer, 1983). Repeated management fires are therefore assumed to have no significant long-term effects on the nutrient status of the system (Figure 10.7b).

There is, however, a temporal heterogeneity which should be considered. A fire in younger heather causes reduced nutrient losses because of the reduced density of fuel, and the more rapid recovery of the vegetation (Figure 10.7c). Fires in older heather, however, cause more damage and recovery is slower (Hobbs and Gimingham, 1984; Hobbs and Legg, 1983; Berdowski and Siepel, 1988).

Under these circumstances it is not difficult to see that there may be a gradual long-term trend in nutrient status. In phosphorus this could be a downward trend, while in nitrogen, at least in the sites at greater risk from atmospheric pollution, the trend may be upwards. This points to the need for long-term investigations, or some other means of getting access to long-term processes. The process-orientated models of Chapman *et al.*, (1989) on the nutrient status of soils in dune heaths begin to aim towards this objective.

There may be other aspects of heathland systems which are subject to slow, but progressive change resulting from management. These include the changes in hydrology resulting from burning over peaty soils, the gradual drying and shrinkage of the organic horizons and exposure to slow oxidation. Where peat has developed under one vegetation type, the changes in vegetation caused by management might be expected to result in reduced stability of the substrate itself.

The problem becomes more significant when the effects of occasional severe fire are considered. Ignition of the peat and subsequent erosion may cause major losses of soil organic matter and nutrients (Figure 10.7d). Recovery of vegetation is very slow (Maltby *et al.*, 1990; Legg *et al.*, 1992). If ignition of the peat destroys either the seed bank or the fibrous root-mat which provides surface stability after a normal fire, then regeneration will be very poor and progressive erosion may lead to a complete breakdown of ecosystem structure and functioning. In this case regeneration is dependent on the occasional long-distance migration of heather from neighbouring stands and the establishment of a closed sward may be delayed for many years.

There is now increasing evidence that some of the major peatland erosion in the Pennines may have been initiated by similar unusual, but severe events. Tallis (1987) has demonstrated that the onset of widespread erosion at Holme Moss in the southern Pennines appears to be associated with one or more severe fires in the 18th century which resulted in the loss of the surface horizons of peat. Tallis also suggests that some of the marginal erosion of blanket peat in the southern Pennines may be linked with a severe rainstorm which is reported to have occurred in 1777. He concludes that the analysis of current environmental stresses 'offers few clues to the causes of peat erosion'. Clearly, events which occur only very infrequently on the human time-scale may be major factors in shaping the landscape. Any long-term view of heathland management must therefore include an assessment of the risk associated both with these relatively rare events which can have

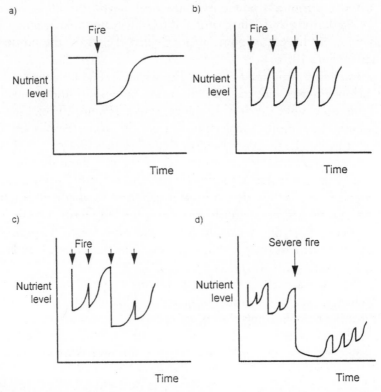

Figure 10.7. A simple representation of the effects of management fire on the nutrient status of heath vegetation. (a) A simple model based on short-term observations and small-scale experiments; (b) extrapolation of the simple model to a repeated fire cycle; (c) extension of the simple model to include variable time intervals between fires; (d) extension of the simple model to include occasional severe fire.

major long-term consequences, and the slow and almost imperceptible but insidious changes in habitat quality.

10.6 Levels of organization

In addition to temporal and spatial scale, it is also necessary to recognize the correct organizational scale with which to study vegetation. Three levels are proposed by Weigleb (1989): the individual; the species and the vegetation unit. All three organizational levels have been used in the descriptions of vegetation dynamics in heathlands. For example, the Watt model of the heather cycle is based on structure imposed by ageing processes at the level of the individual; the descriptions of heath vegetation dynamics using vital attributes (Hobbs *et al.*, 1984) applying the methods of Nobel and Slatyer (1980) operate at the level of the species, while the transition diagrams of Miles (1985) or the transition matrix models of Legg (1980) and Hobbs and Legg (1983) represent the interrelationships between vegetation units at large and small spatial scales respectively.

The concept of the individual is easily understood and accepted by most ecologists even though there will be frequent practical difficulties of definition in the field. Equally, few would question that the species forms a distinct natural unit. Although difficulties occur in many taxonomic groups when considered on a national or world-wide scale, there are few difficulties in assigning the majority of plants to discrete taxa at the species level in more local-scale ecological surveys. Of the three levels, the vegetation unit is the least well-defined and needs most consideration.

The National Vegetation Classification (NVC) will provide the first reasonably comprehensive classification of British vegetation (Rodwell, 1991a, and 1b; 1992) though the plant communities of the Scottish Uplands have been described in some detail by McVean and Ratcliffe (1962) and Birse (1980). The NVC now provides the first choice for any work which requires the classification or description of vegetation units. It is important to remember, however, that any classification of vegetation is to a large extent an artificial classification. It will always be possible to split some community types into sub-communities or to fuse communities together where the differences seem insufficiently distinct. Few stands will be exactly represented by the type and intermediate stands which cannot easily be accommodated in the standard classification will always be found. Although there is broad agreement between the different classifications, the differences show that there is a considerable degree of arbitrariness in the definition of plant communities.

This provides new problems of scale which must not be overlooked. For example, although the NVC gives a framework for describing successional relationships of different heath vegetation types (Rodwell, 1991b), it may not always be adequate to give the detail required in particular circumstances. Thus a patch of *Calluna vulgaris* — *Vaccinium myrtilus* heath, *Calluna vulgaris* sub-community (NVC community H12a) which contains 5–10 % cover of *Pteridium aquilinum* fronds will need to be managed in a quite different way to nearby stand of H12a containing 5–10 % cover of *Nardus stricta* L. or a scattering of *Betula* seedlings. The successional pathway following fire may be quite different in each case.

There are two ways of changing scale in classification. The first would be to use higher or lower levels in a hierarchical classification. Curtis *et al.*, (1990) look at different levels of division in a TWINSPAN analysis of vegetation and habitat types and show that a classification of higher status than that equivalent to the NVC community would not contain sufficient information for the effective conservation management of habitats and land use. To split the communities into ever smaller sub-communities in order to get more precise definitions of the ecological properties of the vegetation would largely defeat the object of using a classification in the first place.

The second way of changing scale would be to recognize that mosaic in vegetation can be observed at a range of spatial scales. The NVC is based on the notion of the structurally and floristically homogeneous stand. This is not defined precisely but might be expected to occupy from a minimum of several square metres to a hectare or so; vegetation is sampled typically using a 4 m^2 quadrat. Samples are grouped into communities on the basis of their component species. But heath vegetation can equally be considered as a mosaic of shoots and individual plants on a much smaller scale and a classification of patches on a scale of 10 cm x 10 cm has been used for modelling post-fire succession by transition matrices (Legg, 1980; Hobbs and Legg, 1983). These studies effectively recognised that the dynamic properties of a patch are determined by the structure and attributes of the locally dominant species.

Conversely, Brown *et al.*, (1993b) provided a regional biogeographical classification of Scottish upland vegetation at a scale of several square kilometres, approximately equivalent to the topographic unit. Topographic units are grouped together in the classification on the basis of the similarity of their component vegetation units (NVC communities or equivalent). This approach not only gives a useful context in which to understand the distributions of vegetation types, but may reveal unexpected patterns such as the exclusion of geology as a discriminating factor in the classification outside the Breadalbane range (Brown *et al.*, 1993a).

One final concept that links scale to vegetation dynamics is that of the 'biological minimum area' described by Barkman (1989). The biological minimum area can be defined either as the smallest stand area sufficient for the community to be well developed and devoid of edge effects, or as the smallest stand that is big enough for the complete rejuvenation of the community. The fragmentation of heathland sites in the New Forest was examined in the classic study by Moore (1962) who demonstrated a loss of obligate heathland species as fragment size decreased and isolation increased. As heath fragments become smaller so the total number of species present in the community increases (Webb and Hopkins, 1984), but this is due to an increase in the number of primarily agricultural species invading from outside the area (Webb *et al.*, 1984) which more than compensates for a decline in the number of species restricted to the heathland habitat. The analysis of the relationship between fragment size and diversity by Webb and Vermaat (1990) provides an interesting example of one means of estimating the minimum size of fragment to retain its biological integrity, but little is known about the biological minimum area required to contain the dynamic processes of disturbance by fire and subsequent succession for long-term persistence. Further studies on the importance of scale in the dynamics of fragmented systems is clearly needed.

10.7 Conclusion

There is a need to consider a wide range of spatial, temporal and organization scales when tackling any particular problem is heathland ecology. Extrapolations from one scale to another require great care, especially when trying to apply models constructed by other people.

When planning surveys or experiments it is necessary to define the statistical 'population' or 'sampling universe' (Kenkel *et al.*, 1989) about which you intend to make inferences. Replication with an appropriate sampling design should ensure that the sample is representative of a specified geographical range and specified range of vegetation types. This then permits valid inferences to be made about other sites and situations. There are often pragmatic difficulties in sampling a wide range of sites, but the tendency in the past to gather data on one specific instance which cannot then be applied with confidence to other situations should be avoided wherever possible.

Long-term experiments are not usually possible, but many of the processes of greatest concern to ecologists and land managers are long-term processes. For example, climate change due to the greenhouse effect of atmospheric pollutants, if, or when, it happens, will be a large-scale influence on vegetation. Changes will occur on the regional scale over a period of 50–100 years. It may be dangerous to make predictions through extrapolation from small-scale experiments and observations where what may actually happen is that a slight change in the competitive balance between keystone species results in a complete change in ecosystem structure and function. This is what appears to be happening with increases in atmospheric nitrogen deposition in heathlands in the Netherlands where an increase in the palatability of *Calluna* to the heather beetle, *Lochmaea suturalis*, and a slight change in the competitive balance between *Calluna* and *Deschampsia flexuosa* (L.) Trin. has resulted in heathlands being replaced by grassland (Heil and Diemont, 1983; de Smidt, this volume). That rapid changes in the distribution and dominance of species can occur has been demonstrated by the evidence of very rapid, short-term expansion and contraction in the range of *Pinus sylvestris* in the pollen record for Caithness and Sutherland (Gear and Huntley, 1991) Some climate predictions suggest that one of the more important consequences of climate change will be an increased variability of the climate. Prediction of vegetation response will be even more difficult if many of the main changes occur as a response to the occasional severe climatic events (Mearns, *et al.*, 1989).

The challenge, therefore, is to devise new and ingenious ways of observing and investigating long-term processes which will permit valid predictions when 'scaling up' from the small-scale, short-term experiments and observations.

References

Allen, S. E. (1964). Chemical aspects of heather burning, *Journal of Applied Ecology*, **1**, 347–67.

Allen, T. F. H. and Hoekstra, T. W. (1990). The confusion between scale-defined levels and conventional levels of organisation in ecology. *Journal of Vegetation Science*, **1**, 5–12.

Atkinson, M. D. (1992). *Betula pendula* Roth (*B. verrucosa* Ehrh.) and *B. pubescens* Ehrh. Biological flora of the British Isles, *Journal of Ecology*, **80**, 837–70.

Barclay-Estrup, P. (1970). The description and interpretation of cyclical processes in a heath community. II. Changes in biomass and shoot production during the *Calluna* cycle, *Journal of Ecology*, **58**, 243–9.

Barclay-Estrup, P. and Gimingham, C. H. (1969). The description and interpretation of cyclical processes in a heath community. I Vegetational change in relation to the *Calluna* cycle, *Journal of Ecology*, **57**, 737–58.

Barkman, J. J. (1989). A critical evaluation of minimum area concepts, *Vegetatio*, **85**, 89–104.

Beijerinck, W. (1940). *Calluna*. A monograph on the Scottish heather. *Verhandelingen der Koninklijke Nederlandsche Akademie van Wetenschappen, Amsterdam*, **38**, 1–180.

Berdowski, J. J. M. and Siepel, H. (1988). Vegetative regeneration of *Calluna vulgaris* at different ages and fertilizer levels, *Biological Conservation*, **46**, 85–93.

Berdowski, J. J. M. and Zeilinga, R. (1987). Transition from heathland to grassland: Damaging effects of the heather bettle, *Journal of Ecology*, **75**, 159–75.

Birse, E. L. (1980). *Plant Communities of Scotland. A Preliminary Phytocoenonia.* Soil Survey of Scotland No. 4, Macaulay Institute for Soil Research, Aberdeen.

Brown, A., Birks, H. J. B. and Thompson, D. B. A. (1993a). A new biogeographical classification of the Scottish uplands. II. Vegetation — environment relationships, *Journal of Ecology*, **81**, 231–51.

Brown, A., Horsfield, D. and Thompson, D. B. A. (1993b). A new biogeographical classification of the Scottish Uplands. I. Descriptions of vegetation blocks and their spatial variation, *Journal of Ecology*, **81**, 207–30.

Chapman, S. B. (1967). Nutrient budgets for a dry heath ecosystem in the south of England, *Journal of Ecology*, **55**, 677–89.

Chapman, S. B., Rose, R. J. and Clarke, R. T. (1989). A model of the phosphorus dynamics of *Calluna* heathland, *Journal of Ecology*, **77**, 35–48.

Cohen, D. and Levin, S. A. (1991). Dispersal in patchy environments: the effects of temporal and spatial structure, *Theoretical Population Biology*, **39**, 63–99.

Cumming, G. and Legg, C. J. (this volume). Longevity of the *Calluna* seed bank determined from a history of lead smelting at Leadhills and Wanlockhead.

Curtis, D. J., Bignal, E. M. and Moos, C. H. (1990). *The importance of adequately detailed habitat classification in relation to land-use and wildlife conservation*, CSD Commissioned Research Report No. 1012, Nature Conservancy Council, Peterborough.

Equihua, M. and Usher, M. B. (1993). Impact of carpets of the invasive moss *Campylopus introflexus* on *Calluna vulgaris* regeneration, *Journal of Ecology*, **81**, 359–65.

Fahrig, L. (1992). Relative importance of spatial and temporal scales in a patchy environment, *Theoretical Population Biology*, **41**, 300–14.

Falinski, J. B. (1988). Succession, regeneration and fluctuations in the Bialowieza Forest, Vegetatio, **77**, 115–28.

Gear, A. J. and Huntley, B. (1991). Rapid changes in the range limits of Scots pine 4000 years ago, *Science*, **251**, 544–7.

Gimingham, C. H. (1972). *Ecology of Heathlands* Chapman and Hall, London.

Gimingham, C. H. (1987). Harnessing the winds of change: heathland ecology in retrospect and prospect, *Journal of Ecology*, **75**, 895–914.

Gimingham, C. H. (1988). A reappraisal of the cyclical processes in *Calluna* heath, Vegetatio, **77**, 61–4.

Godwin, H. (1944). Age and origins of the 'Breckland' heaths of East Anglia, *Nature*, **154**, 6–7.

Gong, W. K. (1984). Birch regeneration in heath vegetation, *Proceedings of the Royal Society of Edinburgh*, **85B**, 73–81.

Grace, J. (1991). Physical and ecological evaluation of heterogeneity, *Functional Ecology*, **5**, 192–201.

Gregory, P. H. (1973). *The Microbiology of the Atmosphere* Aylesbury, Leonard Hill.

Harper, J. L. (1977). *Population Biology of Plants* Academic Press, London.

Heil, G. W. and Diemont, W. H. (1983). Raised nutrient levels change heathlands into grassland, *Vegetatio*, **53**, 213–20.

Hester, A. J. and Sydes, C. (1993). Changes in burning of Scottish heather moorland since the 1940s from aerial photographs, *Biological Conservation*, **60**, 25–30.

Hobbs, R. J. (1985). The persistence of *Cladonia* patches in closed heathland stands, *Lichenologist*, **17**, 103–10.

Hobbs, R. J. and Gimingham, C. H. (1984). Studies in fire on Scottish heathland communities II. Post-fire vegetation development, *Journal of Ecology*, **72**, 585–610.

Hobbs, R. J. and Gimingham, C. H. (1987). Vegetation, fire and herbivore interactions in heathland, *Advances in Ecological Research*, **16**, 87–173.

Hobbs, R. J. and Legg, C. J. (1983). Markov models and initial floristic composition in heathland vegetation dynamics, *Vegetatio*, **56**, 31–43.

Hobbs, R. J., Mallik, A. U. and Gimingham, C. H. (1984). Studies on fire in Scottish heathland communities. III Vital attributes of the species, *Journal of Ecology*, **72**, 963–76.

Hodgson, J. G. and Grime, J. P. (1990). The role of dispersal mechanisms, regenerative strategies and seed banks in vegetation dynamics of the British landscape. In R. G. H. Bunce and D. C. Howard,

(Eds), *Species Dispersal in Agricultural Habitats*, Belhaven Press and Institute of Terrestrial Ecology, London, 65–81.

Hullu, E. de and Gimingham, C. H. (1984). Germination and establishment of seedlings in different phases of the *Calluna* life cycle in a Scottish heathland, *Vegetatio*, **58**, 115–21.

Jarvis, P. G. and McNaughton, K. G. (1986). Stomatal control of transpiration: scaling up from leaf to region, *Advances in Ecological Research*, **15**, 1–49.

Jong, T. J. de and Klinkhamer, P. G. L. (1983). A simulation model for the effects of burning on the phosphorus and nitrogen cycle of a heathland system, *Ecological Modelling*, **19**, 263–84.

Kenkel, N. C., Juhasz-Nagy, P. and Podani, J. (1989). On sampling procedures in population and community ecology, *Vegetatio*, **83**, 195–207.

Klinkhamer, P. G. L., de Jong, T. J., Metz, J. A. J. and Val, J. (1987). Life history tactics of annual organisms: the joint effects of dispersal and delayed germination, *Theoretical Population Biology*, **32**, 127–56.

Legg, C. J. (1980). A Markovian approach to the study of heath vegetation dynamics, *Bulletin d'Ecologie*, **11**, 393–404.

Legg, C. J., Maltby, E. and Proctor, M. C. F. (1992). The ecology of severe moorland fire on the North York Moors: seed distribution and seedling establishment of *Calluna vulgaris*, *Journal of Ecology*, **80**, 737–52.

Levin, S. A. (1992). The problem of pattern and scale in ecology, *Ecology*, **73**, 1943–67.

Mallik, A. U., Hobbs, R. J. and Legg, C. J. (1984). Seed dynamics in *Calluna — Arctostaphylos* heath in north eastern Scotland, *Journal of Ecology*, **72**, 855–71.

Maltby, E., Legg, C. J. and Proctor, M. C. F. (1990). The ecology of severe moorland fires on the North York Moors. Effects of the 1976 fires, and subsequent surface and vegetation development, *Journal of Ecology*, **78**, 490–518.

Marrs, R. H. (1986). The role of catastrophic death of *Calluna* in heathland dynamics, *Vegetatio*, **66**, 109–15.

Marrs, R. H. (1988). Vegetation change on lowland heaths and its relevance for conservation management, *Journal of Environmental Management*, **26**, 127–49.

Marrs, R. H. and Hicks, M. J. (1986). Study of vegetation change at Lakenheath Warren: a re-examination of A. S. Watt's theories of bracken dynamics in relation to succession and vegetation management, *Journal of Applied Ecology*, **23**, 1029–46.

Marrs, R. H., Hicks, M. J. and Fuller, R. M. (1986). Losses of lowland heath through succession at four sites in Breckland, East Anglia, England, *Biological Conservation*, **36**, 19–38.

McVean, D. N. and Ratcliffe, D. A. (1962). *Plant Communities of the Scottish Highlands* HMSO, London.

Mearns, L. O., Schneider, S. H., Thompson, S. L. and McDaniel, L. R. (1989). Climate variability statistics from general circulation models as applied to climate change analysis. In G. P. Malanson (Ed), *Natural Areas Facing Climate Change*, SPB Academic Publishing, The Hague, 51–73.

Miles, J. (1973). Natural recolonization of experimentally bared soil in a Callunetum in northeast Scotland, *Journal of Ecology*, **61**, 399–412.

Miles, J. (1981). Problems in heathland and grassland dynamics, *Vegetatio*, **46**, 61–74.

Miles, J. (1985). The pedogenic effects of different species and vegetation types and the implications of succession, *Journal of Soil Science*, **36**, 571–84.

Miller, G. R. and Cummins, R. P. (1987). Role of buried viable seeds in the recolonization of disturbed ground by heather (*Calluna vulgaris* (L.) Hull) in the Cairngorm Mountains, Scotland, UK, *Arctic and Alpine Research*, **19**, 396–401.

Moore, N. W. (1962). The heaths of Dorset and their conservation, *Journal of Ecology*, **50**, 369–91.

Noble, I. R. and Slatyer, R. O. (1980). The use of vital attributes to predict successional changes in plant communities subject to recurrent disturbance, *Vegetatio*, **43**, 5–21.

Nordhagen, R. (1937). Studien über die monotypische Gattung *Calluna* Salisb., *Bergens Mus. Arb., naturvid. rekke*, **4**, 1–55.

Rodwell, J. S. (1991a). *British Plant Communities, Vol. 1 Woodlands and Scrub*. Cambridge University Press, Cambridge.

Rodwell, J. S. (1991b). *British Plant Communities. Vol. 2 Mires and Heaths*. Cambridge University Press, Cambridge.

Rodwell, J. S. (1992). *British Plant Communities. Vol. 3 Grassland and Montane Communities*. Cambridge University Press, Cambridge.

Smidt, J. T. de (this volume). The imminent destruction of Northwest European heaths due to atmospheric nitrogen deposition.

Smith, R. (1900). On the seed dispersal of *Pinus sylvestris* and *Betula alba, Annals of Scottish Natural History,* **33,** 43–6.

Stevenson, A. C. and Birks, H. J. B. (this volume). Heathlands: long-term ecological changes and interactions with climate and people.

Tallis, J. H. (1987). Fire and flood at Holme Moss: erosion processes in an upland blanket mire, *Journal of Ecology,* **75,** 1099–129.

Thompson, K., Band, S. R. and Hodgson, J. G. (1993). Seed size and shape predict persistence in soil, *Functional Ecology,* **7,** 236–41.

van der Maarel, E. (1988). Vegetation dynamics: patterns in space and time, *Vegetatio,* **77,** 7–19.

Venable, D. L. and Lawlor, L. (1980). Delayed germination and dispersal in desert annuals: escape in space and time, *Oecologia,* **46,** 272–82.

Watt, A. S. (1947). Pattern and process in the plant community, *Journal of Ecology,* **35,** 1–22.

Watt, A. S. (1955). Bracken versus heather, a study in plant sociology, *Journal of Ecology,* **43,** 490–506.

Webb, N. R. (1986). *Heathlands, The New Naturalist,* Collins, London.

Webb, N. R., Clarke, R. T. and Nicholas, J. T. (1984). Invertebrate diversity on fragmented *Calluna*-heathland: effects of surrounding vegetation, *Journal of Biogeography,* **11,** 41–6.

Webb, N. R. and Hopkins, P. J. (1984). Invertebrate diversity on fragmented *Calluna*-heathland, *Journal of Applied Ecology,* **21,** 921–33.

Webb, N. R. and Vermaat, A. H. (1990). Changes in vegetational diversity on remnant heathland fragments, *Biological Conservation,* **53,** 253–64.

Weigleb, G. (1989). Explanation and prediction in vegetation science, *Vegetatio,* **83,** 17–34.

Welch, D., Miller, G. R. and Legg, C. J. (1990). Plant dispersal in moorlands and heathlands in Britain. In R. G. Bunce and D. C. Howard, (Eds), *Species Dispersal in Agricultural Habitats,* Belhaven Press, London. 117–132.

11 LONGEVITY OF THE *CALLUNA VULGARIS* SEED BANK DETERMINED FROM A HISTORY OF LEAD SMELTING AT LEADHILLS AND WANLOCKHEAD, SCOTLAND

G. Cumming and C. Legg

Summary

1. *Calluna vulgaris* produces a large seed bank in peaty moorland soils which may retain viability for many years. Assuming that the peat is undisturbed, the depth of burial gives an indication of the age of the seeds.

2. The vertical profile of viable seeds and the distribution of lead in the top 20 cm of peat from Wanlockhead in the Southern Uplands were compared with the known history of lead smelting in the area.

3. It was concluded that the deepest germinable seeds may be about 150 years old.

11.1 Introduction

There have been several reports published suggesting that *Calluna vulgaris* (L.) Hull (referred to hereafter as *Calluna*) may have long-lived seed banks (reviewed in Legg *et al.*, 1992). The half-life for seed survival in Scotland has been estimated as from 0.5 to 5 years depending on soil type and altitude (Miller and Cummins, 1987). Thus with a typical seed bank it could take over 100 years to deplete the stock. In Sweden, *Calluna* seed banks have been observed in soils under plantations of 73-year old *Picea abies* (L.) Karsten, however these findings give 'no hint of the upper limit of longevity' (Granström, 1988).

This project assessed the upper limit of longevity of the *Calluna* seed bank in a moorland blanket peat by correlating the vertical distribution of germinable seeds with the lead concentration in the peat profile and a well-documented history of lead smelting at a nearby site.

11.2 Methods

Eight pairs of peat cores were collected from an area of blanket peat four miles north-east of Wanlockhead in the Southern Uplands, Scotland. Four pairs were taken from a site still dominated by *Calluna* (Grid Ref. NS 921 178, 450 m a.s.l.), while the other four were from a site where, from aerial photographic evidence, the *Calluna* had been replaced by *Molinia caerulea* (L.) Moench. (referred to as *Molinia* hereafter) as the dominant between 1950 and 1974 (Grid Ref. NS 924 176, 430 m a.s.l.). Details of soil horizons were recorded. One core of each pair was prepared to look at the germinable *Calluna* seed bank, while its partner was analysed to show the distribution of pollen types, the lead contamination and other properties of the peat.

The seed-bank cores (6.5 cm diameter x 15 cm deep) were cut into 1 cm slices and the outer material discarded to remove possible contamination from other horizons. Samples were incubated at 30°C, for seven days before being sieved and spread 2–3 mm deep over capillary matting. These were then positioned randomly under mist-irrigation in a heated glasshouse on the 23 December 1992. Germinating *Calluna* seeds were counted from 29 January until 10 May 1993.

The second core of each pair were sliced at 0.5-cm intervals. The outer material was removed from each disc to avoid vertical contamination and a 1-cm^3 sample taken for pollen analysis. To estimate lead concentration the samples were ashed at 420°C and digested in nitric acid before analysis using an atomic absorption spectrophotometer (Allen *et al.*, 1974). Bulk density and loss on ignition were also estimated. Chronological correspondence between the two cores of each pair were assessed from the profile descriptions and horizon boundaries.

Information about the history of lead smelting at the site was obtained from records held by the Allan Ramsay Library at Leadhills and the Museum of Lead Mining at Wanlockhead, and from Porteus (1876) and Sinclair (1792). The chronology of the peat profiles was established by matching markers in the lead profile with the history of lead smelting in the area.

11.3 Results

Lead ore has been mined at Wanlockhead and Leadhills for many centuries but on-site smelting commenced at Wanlockhead in 1683. Production increased steadily until 1843 when a new smelt mill was installed (Figure 11.1). Although processing a greater quantity of material, the new mill reduced emissions of lead pollution from 20 % of yield to just 8 %. However, the increases in production, to a maximum of about 1310 tonnes yr^{-1} by 1910, soon outweighed the effects of improvements in technology. Production ceased in the early 1920s. Though the accuracy of the production figures published in official records can be questioned, the trends in production and the dates of commencement and cessation of smelting, and of installation of the new smelt mill are reliable.

From the cores taken in *Calluna*-dominated vegetation the mean germinable Calluna seed bank was 67 000 seeds m–2 (S.E. 9000), compared with 12 000 seeds m–2 (S.E. 5500) for the *Molinia* site cores. At both sites the majority of seeds were

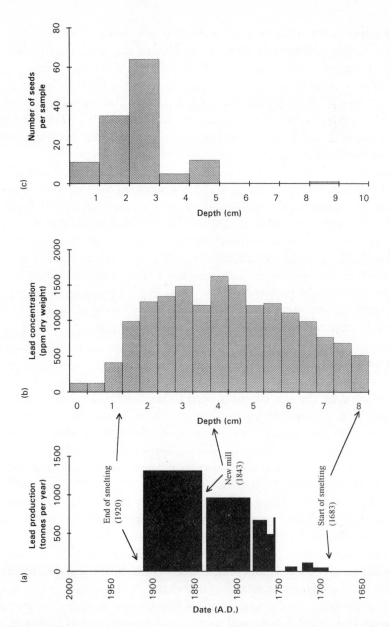

Figure 11.1. Bar graphs comparing the history of lead smelting at Wanlockhead (a) with the contaminant lead (b) and seed distribution of a single heathland peat core. Depth scales have been adjusted to allow for differences between the horizons in the seed and lead cores.

found in the top 6 cm (Figure 11.1) though very few seeds occurred near the surface at the *Molinia* site. Isolated seeds found below 7 cm were attributed to contamination.

Bulk density and loss on ignition showed no significant changes with depth below the litter layer, indicating that the net rate of peat accumulation had remained about constant. Pollen analysis also showed no indication of change in vegetation type at the *Calluna*-dominated sites, though there was a marked increase in the Graminae: Ericaceae ratio near the surface of the *Molinia*-dominated sites. Lead concentrations ranged from 50 to 1700 ppm dry weight for the *Calluna* dominated site and 100 to 650 ppm dry weight for the *Molinia* dominated site. These values contrast with the 2–20 ppm found in normal soil (Allen *et al.*, 1974). The lead concentration showed two peaks at about 3 cm and 4–5 cm. but declined to low concentrations near the top and bottom of the profiles (Figure 11.1).

For evaluation of the age of the seed bank the distribution of lead contamination in the peat profile was compared with the smelting history. As an example, the results for one core from the *Calluna* site are presented in Figure 11.1; similar patterns were obtained in the other cores. The dip in lead contamination at a depth of 3.5 to 4 cm is assumed to correspond to the installation of the new smelt mill at Wanlockhead. The second contamination peak at a depth of 3.0 cm corresponds with the peak in the smelting industry around 1910. After accounting for horizon differences between the pair of cores, the dip in lead concentration attributed to the installation of the new smelt mill in 1843 approximately coincides with the lower limit of germinable *Calluna* seeds in each of the cores.

11.4 Discussion

The small numbers of seeds germinating from near the surface of the *Molinia* site can be explained by the absence of a seed influx over the last few decades. Seeds germinating from below this represent the seed bank surviving from the former heathy vegetation type. Assuming that the seed influx was similar at the two sites before the transition from *Calluna* to *Molinia* dominance, the difference in numbers of seeds in the 3–5 cm horizons between the two sites would suggest a lower survival rate for seeds in the grassland soils.

An assumption of the dating system used here is that neither the seeds, nor the pollutant lead are migrating vertically through the peat profile. Although the mobility of lead in the peat profile has been questioned (Mannion, 1989), evidence produced by other authors (e.g. Livett *et al.*, 1979) suggests that the mobility of lead in peat is extremely low and less than that of other heavy metals such as copper and zinc. With the high concentrations found and the proximity of the source it is unlikely that the shape of the lead profile will have been modified by leaching. The abrupt peaks and troughs in several of the lead contamination and seed distribution graphs for the *Calluna*-dominated cores support the view that there is little or no vertical mixing at this site. The grassland cores, however, show lower concentrations of lead, and the vertical distribution is less distinct than at the heath site making dating more difficult. While this may be partly due to the higher bulk density and ash content of the peat at this site, there is also a much greater biomass from *Molinia* roots which are deep-rooting compared with the relatively shallow and fibrous roots of the main heathland species. This indicates greater soil activity at the grassland site which may, in turn, indicate a higher probability of vertical movement of the contaminant through the profile and a smearing of the lead signal. The root biomass may also be contributing significant quantities of organic matter with relatively low lead concentrations at this horizon.

The dating method used here further assumes a relatively constant rate of peat accumulation; the absence of trends in the bulk density and loss on ignition data below the surface litter support this assumption.

The results of this study have important implications for the restoration of heath vegetation in upland peaty habitats. It is likely that a persistent viable seed bank of *Calluna* may remain in the peaty soils for up to 150 years following the loss of plants from the above-ground vegetation. Where heath vegetation has been replaced by grassland, as happens due to intensive grazing or poor burning management, it may be possible to restore cover of *Calluna* by providing suitable microsites for germination and establishment from the seed bank. This would require a reduction in the dominance of the grass species and some disturbance of the top 2–3 cm of soil to bring seeds to the surface.

11.5 Conclusions

Using this simple method the longevity of the *Calluna* seed bank would appear to be about 150 years at this site. The absence of germinating seeds from the lower part of the profile, despite the abundance of *Calluna* pollen, indicates that the viability of seeds does not exceed 150 years. The usefulness of this method is affected by distance from a source of pollution, the quality of historical information, and the vegetation type.

Acknowledgements

The authors would like to thank the staff of the Wanlockhead Museum Trust and technical staff of the Institute of Ecology and Resource Management for their assistance with this project. Also Philip Simpson, Stuart Taylor, and especially Jennifer McConnell for practical support.

References

Allen, S. E., Grimshaw, H. M. Parkinson, J. A. and Quarmby, C. (1974). *Chemical analysis of ecological materials*, Blackwell Scientific Publications, Oxford.

Granström, A. (1988). Seed banks at six open and afforested heathland sites in southern Sweden, *Journal of Applied Ecology*, **25**, 297–306.

Legg, C. J., Maltby, E. and Proctor, M. C. F. (1992). The ecology of severe moorland fire on the North York Moors: seed distribution and seedling establishment of *Calluna vulgaris*, *Journal of Ecology*, **80**, 737–52.

Livett, E. A., Lee, J. A. and Tallis, J. H. (1979). Lead, zinc and copper analysis of British blanket peats, *Journal of Ecology*, **67**, 865–91.

Mannion, A. M. (1989). Palaeoecological evidence for environmental change during the last 200 years. II. Chemical data, *Proceedings in Physical Geography*, **13**, 192–215.

Miller, G. R. and Cummins, R. P. (1987). Role of buried viable seeds in the recolonisation of disturbed ground by heather (*Calluna vulgaris* [L.] Hull.) in the Cairngorms UK, *Arctic and Alpine Research*, **19**, 396–401.

Porteus, J. (1876). *God's Treasure House in Scotland*, Simpin, Marshall and Co., London. pp. 302.

Sinclair, J. (1792). *The Statistical Account of Scotland*, William Creech, Edinburgh. pp. 579.

12 SCRUB AND WOODLAND REGENERATION: PROSPECTS FOR THE FUTURE

A. J. Hester and G. R. Miller

Summary

1. This paper describes the factors affecting tree regeneration in upland Britain and how they have shaped the current nature and distribution of woodland and scrub.

2. Grazing animals are perhaps the most fundamental determinants of the speed and extent of succession to scrub and woodland in the uplands.

3. We explore the future prospects for woodland regeneration, both under current management regimes and in the event of future changes in government policies affecting upland land use.

12.1 Introduction

By all accounts, semi-natural woodland and scrub were once much more widely distributed in Britain than they are today (Poore and McVean, 1957; Spence, 1960; McVean and Ratcliffe, 1962; Ratcliffe, 1981; Bennett, 1989). Most decline has occurred since the arrival of early man and rates of disappearance have varied enormously both at different times and in different parts of the country (well reviewed by Birks, 1988). There is rather less information available on the regeneration of scrub and woodland in Britain. This paper focuses primarily on Scotland, with an emphasis on the uplands, where scrub and woodland regeneration is an issue of particular concern. Woodland and scrub cover only a tiny proportion of the land area of Scotland, and much of what remains is now species-poor and highly fragmented. Area estimates vary from 1340 km^2 of semi-natural woodland (Roberts *et al.*, 1992; Forestry Commission, 1983) to 2634 km^2 of semi-natural woodland and scrub (National Countryside Monitoring Scheme, 1993 f), i.e. between 1.7 and 3.4 % of the land area. By comparison there are approximately 13 000 km^2 of heather (*Calluna vulgaris*) moorland in Scotland (National Countryside Monitoring Scheme, 1993 f; Macaulay Land Use Research Institute, 1993).

The widespread losses of woodland and scrub have almost certainly been caused by many years of felling, burning and grazing over much of the British uplands (Fraser, 1933; Chard, 1953; Miles and Kinnaird, 1979b; Emberlin and Baillie, 1980; Chapman and Crawford, 1981; Miller, Kinnaird and Cummins, 1982; Mitchell, 1990). Initial losses were primarily through felling and burning, with grazing and burning further restricting subsequent regeneration in many areas. This is reflected in the current poor condition and restricted, often inaccessible locations of much of the woodland remaining in the British uplands. Selective felling, browsing or grazing will also have had differential effects on the species diversity of the remaining areas of woodland and scrub. Climatic change also appears to have played a part in the contraction of tree cover (Lewis, 1911; Pearsall, 1950; Keatinge and Dickson, 1979; Wilkins, 1984; Birks, 1988; Bennett, 1989) but seemingly to a much lesser extent than have the effects of man.

12.2   Rates and Extent of Regeneration

Relatively little information exists on the rates and extent of scrub and woodland regeneration in different parts of Scotland. Roberts *et al.*, (1992) calculated that 445 km^2 of the existing semi-natural woodland in Scotland has developed since the mid-19th century; the National Countryside Monitoring Scheme (NCMS) estimates for regeneration of semi-natural woodland and scrub in Scotland between the 1940s and 1970s are given in Table 12.1. The table focuses on regeneration alone for the purposes of this chapter, but it is important to note that there were actually net *losses* of woodland (but not scrub) in most regions; in Highland Region, for example, the total area of broadleaved woodland declined from 529 km^2 in the 1940s to 477 km^2 by 1988, whereas scrub cover increased from 75 km^2 in the 1940s to 127 km^2 in 1988. From Table 12.1 some 39 % of semi-natural woodland and scrub present in the 1970s had regenerated since the 1940s. Of this, about 60 % was scrub, presumably comprising: (a) young trees which would be developing into woodland and (b) species such as gorse (*Ulex europaeus*) and broom (*Cytisus scoparius*), which have lifespans of well under 30 years.

Figure 12.1 shows the proportions of scrub and woodland which colonized different vegetation types in Scotland between the 1940s and 1970s. Proportional areas of grass/arable, heather and scrub in the 1940s were 41 %, 19 % and 0.8 % respectively. Comparisons of these figures give an indication of the relative likelihood of change from a particular community to woodland and scrub. For example, 20 % of broadleaved woodland developed on areas which were previously scrub, whereas scrub only covered 0.8 % of the land area in the 1940s; i.e. broadleaved woodland was more than 20 times as likely to develop from scrub than from areas which were previously grass/arable or heather (as one would expect through natural succession).

Table 12.1   Estimates of areas (km^2) of semi-natural* woodland and scrub that have regenerated in Scotland between the 1940s and 1970s by Region (NCMS 1988–1993f).
Classes: BW: broadleaved woodland, CW: coniferous, MW: mixed, ST: tall scrub (3–5m high, closed canopy), SL: low scrub <3m, no clear canopy).

Class:	BW	CW	MW	ST	SL	Total	Land area
Borders	15.5	0.0	12.4	9.1	19.7	56.7	4695
Central	25.9	0.0	8.4	16.4	13.7	64.4	2716
Dumfries and Galloway	19.0	1.7	15.0	15.2	21.8	72.7	6341
Fife	9.4	0.0	2.5	5.3	10.8	28.0	1377
Grampian	51.6	2.2	30.3	37.2	123.6	244.9	8686
Highland	59.3	3.9	28.7	47.6	55.2	194.7	24 695
Lothian	14.6	0.4	5.2	9.7	12.3	42.2	1814
Strathclyde	58.6	5.2	42.6	25.7	51.8	183.9	14 435
Tayside	30.2	2.4	47.0	18.0	45.6	143.2	7394
Total increase	284.1	15.8	192.1	184.2	354.5	976.7	
Total area of class in 1970s	1312	91	532	227	472	2634	

*Mixed woodland class contains mixed plantations as well as semi-natural stands.

12.3   Factors affecting Regeneration

Regeneration is affected by a complex of interrelated factors which may be of varying importance at different sites. We have divided them into four main categories here and outline some important aspects of each.

12.3.1   Seed availability

Scarcity of seeds can restrict native tree regeneration due to the fragmented nature of much of the woodland and scrub in upland Scotland and the large expanses of treeless ground. Isolation of dioecious species, such as willows (*Salix* spp), juniper (*Juniperus communis*) and aspen (*Populus tremula*), can also greatly reduce seed production in some areas, thus greatly reducing the likelihood of regeneration of these species in parts of Scotland (Mardon, 1991). For wind-dispersed tree species, most seeds fall within a distance of about twice the height of the parent tree (Sarvas 1948; Harper 1977; Legg, this volume). Therefore, the probability (both temporal and spatial) of seeds falling far from parent trees is generally small (Legg, this volume). If regeneration niches are more abundant (such as in sparse vegetation), a scarcity of seeds will, of course, be less of a problem for regeneration than where regeneration niches are scarce. Miller and Cummins (1982), for example, found successful regeneration of pine (*Pinus sylvestris*) at an upper altitudinal tree limit at Creag Fhiaclach despite a relatively sparse seed rain.

CHANGES TO SCRUB/WOODLAND (ALL CATEGORIES)

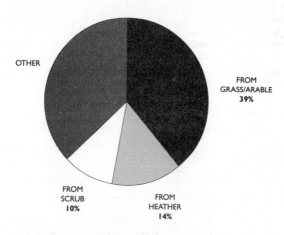

CHANGES TO BROADLEAVED WOODLAND

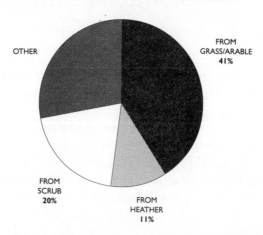

Figure 12.1. Proportions of scrub/woodland present in the 1970s which had colonized grass/arable, heather, scrub and other vegetation types since the 1940s (data from NCMS, 1988–1993f). Less than 10 % of woodland/scrub colonized any other vegetation types, so these types are combined in the 'other' category. (a) all 'semi-natural' woodland and scrub; (b) broadleaved woodland.

Grazing animals can have both negative and positive effects on seed production and dispersal. Heavy browsing can keep saplings under severe check and thus prevent or restrict seed production, but consumption of seeds and dispersal in dung can be an important mechanism of spread for some species, such as rowan and juniper (Livingston, 1972; Gilbert, 1980; Kullman, 1986). Little systematic work has been done on the effectiveness of bird dispersal of seeds from trees and shrubs.

12.3.2 Climate

There are natural climatic limits for all tree species, but climatic factors can also *differentially* affect the likelihood of germination, establishment, reproduction and survival of any one species, due to differences in climatic requirements at different stages of their growth. Climatic fluctuations can strongly affect the success of species which are already close to their climatic limits and the presence of adults does not necessarily indicate an immediate suitability of a site for further regeneration. Kullman (1979), for example, found evidence that existing tree-line birch (*Betula* spp) scrub in central Sweden had only established during a series of warm summers. Subsequent climatic deterioration apparently prevented further colonization by birch, but the already established saplings were able to survive. More recent work on pine has indicated that temperature variations in late winter or spring (particularly extremes, however short in duration) are probably more important than summer temperatures in controlling expansion or contraction of the altitudinal limits of the tree-line (Barclay and Crawford, 1982, 1984; Kullman, 1988; Grace, 1990). Other climatic extremes, such as severe winds, can also have major effects on woodland regeneration. Goodier and Bunce (1977) suggested that infrequent, extreme winds (e.g. the great storms in Scotland in 1953 and in England in 1987) may periodically cause windthrow of trees, allowing new flushes of regeneration on the exposed soil.

12.3.3 Seed bed

Many species, particularly small-seeded light-demanding species such as pine and birch, require gaps in the vegetation to germinate and establish (Livingstone, 1972; Miles, 1973a and b; Kinnaird, 1974; Prach, 1985). The presence of animals may in this sense be beneficial for regeneration; it is widely stated, although little researched, that grazing and trampling can both reduce competition from established vegetation and create microsites suitable for germination and establishment of tree species (Buttenshøn and Buttenshøn, 1985; Mitchell and Kirby, 1991).

Some plant communities are naturally more resistant to invasion than others, primarily due to their structure. For example, a dense and vigorous stand of heather or bracken (*Pteridium aquilinum*) (Cavers and Harper, 1967; Kinnaird, 1971; Miles, 1974; Gong and Gimingham, 1984) can resist invasion by tree species. The resistance of such communities may be reduced by the presence of grazing animals; alternatively, species may only invade after the established vegetation starts to senesce (e.g. Gong and Gimingham, 1984).

12.3.4 Burning and grazing

Sporadic fires are thought to have been a natural feature of boreal forests even before the arrival of man (Zackrisson, 1977). There is also widespread evidence for man's use of fire as a means of managing vegetation (Gimingham, 1972; Birks, 1988). Burning can both aid and hinder tree and scrub regeneration; a single fire can create favourable ground conditions for post-fire germination, but rotational burning destroys established seedlings and saplings, preventing succession to scrub and woodland (Wormell, 1970; Sykes and Horrill, 1981; Gong and Gimingham, 1984). Regular use of fire in Britain is generally associated with the management of heathland (Gimingham, 1972), but there is evidence for the use of fire limiting high altitude scrub regeneration both in England (Mesolithic burning, see Tallis and Switsur, 1990) and Scotland (medieval times, see Pears, 1967).

In many parts of the uplands, high densities of grazing animals probably represent the greatest hindrance to tree and scrub establishment (Miller, 1971; Miles and Kinnaird, 1979a and b; Miller *et al.*, 1982; Mitchell and Kirby, 1991). Currently there are about 9 400 000 sheep (Agricultural Census data) and 300 000 red deer in Scotland (Clutton-Brock and Albon, 1989) and their effects on the vegetation can be dramatic (see also Staines *et al.*, this volume; Armstrong and Milne, this volume). Almost all the red deer in Scotland are confined to the uplands (Clutton-Brock and Albon, 1989), but only about 25 % of the sheep (SOAFD, 1993a). Animal densities vary widely, both regionally and locally; Grampian, for example, had 799 552 sheep censused in 1990, whereas in the Borders Region (just over half the size of Grampian) there were 1 479 718. Comparison with the scrub and woodland regeneration figures in Table 12.1 suggests a negative relationship between sheep densities and tree regeneration in these two regions, as one might predict. However, such gross relationships do not hold for many of the other regions because of the overriding importance of the local distribution of sheep within a region (which is very difficult to obtain data on) and differences in numbers of other herbivores present such as red deer. Highland Region, for example, has relatively low sheep numbers but high red deer numbers (Staines *et al.*, this volume) and relatively poor scrub and woodland regeneration rates (Table 12.1). It is difficult, therefore, to make generalized predictions about the effects of different stocking rates because the readily available information on herbivore densities is generally at too coarse a scale to be a useful indicator of the likely effects on the vegetation. Staines *et al.* (this volume) draws tentative conclusions about the effects of different deer densities on tree regeneration in Scotland, from the limited information available. Much of this information, however, suffers from a lack of data on densities of other herbivores using the same area.

Information on herbivore densities alone is also of limited value because of the variety of factors affecting both the spatial and temporal distribution of browsing damage by different herbivores. The browsing of saplings can be considered from two perspectives: that of the grazing animal or that of the plant. Selection by the animal is primarily affected by: (a) the palatability and digestibility of the different woody species, (b) the surrounding vegetation (both in terms of food availability, digestibility and concealment of saplings); and (c) season, which affects both (a) and (b). Sapling responses to browsing are affected by: (a) the severity of damage; (b) the resilience of each species to damage; (c) competition from the surrounding vegetation; and (d) season, which affects (a), (b) and (c).

Red deer (and roe deer, *Capreolus capreolus*) will browse most tree and scrub species found in the Scottish uplands (Holloway, 1967; Miller, 1971; Mitchell, *et al.*, 1977; Cummins and Miller, 1982; Miller *et al.*, 1982; Mitchell, *et al.*, 1982; Mitchell, 1991). Examinations of species preferences have sometimes yielded contradictory results due to the wide variability in other factors. In general, however, the most preferred species are willows, rowan and aspen, with birch less preferred and pine and juniper least preferred, except in winter, when the latter two species may be taken in preference to the deciduous species. Cummins and Miller (1982) give a good example of the effects of both surrounding vegetation and time of year; pine at Beinn Eighe National Nature Reserve was found to be heavily browsed through-out the year where saplings of deciduous (i.e. preferred) species were sparse, but where they were more abundant, pine was browsed mainly in winter when the other saplings were leafless. Less work has been done on the browsing preferences of sheep (Fitter and Jennings, 1975; Buttenshøn and Buttenshøn, 1985; Young and Gordon, 1991), but it is generally thought that they may be similar to those for deer. For sheep, which are grazers rather than browsers, the herbaceous component of the surrounding vegetation may have more of an effect on their choice of browse than is the case with deer. Very little is known about such relationships. The species composition of the surrounding vegetation will also affect sapling visibility. Visibility of saplings in heather, for example, will change little seasonally and will depend mainly on their height above the heather canopy. On the other hand, sap-lings among bracken or *Molinia caerulea* will be much more visible in winter than in summer.

Tolerance of different tree species to browsing damage varies widely (Mitchell, 1991; Miller *et al.*, 1982). In general, pine seems the least tolerant of damage, and damage outside the growing season tends to result in the poorest recovery of most species. The effects of differential defoliation on competition between saplings and the surrounding herbaceous vegetation are little understood, yet are likely to be im-portant (Mitchell, 1991). For instance, heavy grazing of the vegetation surrounding a sapling may reduce competition (certainly above and perhaps below ground) and therefore the sapling may grow faster.

Other animal species, such as the mountain hare (*Lepus timidus*), various rodents and invertebrates, can also have important effects on tree regeneration (McVean, 1966; Fitter and Jennings, 1975; Hewson, 1977; Miles and Kinnaird, 1979a and b; Gilbert, 1980; Miller *et al.*, 1982; Pulliainen and Tunkkari, 1987). However, little is known about the interactions between animal species. For example, in the absence of large herbivores, tall grass growth is likely to favour population increases of small mammals which in turn could affect the nature and degree of damage to any regenerating tree species.

12.4 Prospects for the Future

Looking to the future, many parts of upland Scotland could benefit from the re-establishment of woodland and scrub as an integral part of a mosaic of natural upland habitats; the consequent increase in structural complexity of the vegetation would enhance both plant and animal species diversity and provide shelter for both wild and domestic animals. Open ground is also important, for example, as habitat for certain upland birds, or because it supports other vegetation of high conserva-tion or landscape value such as heather moorland, upland bogs or herb-rich grasslands. However, given the current levels of grazing in the uplands, the retention of open ground is rarely a problem, even below the tree-line. It is difficult to address the question of exactly how much more scrub and woodland should be encouraged and where; this is strongly dependant on the perceived purpose of the regeneration, which encompasses aims as wide ranging as landscape and habitat enhancement, wildlife and soil benefits, and the preservation/recreation of both genetic and structural diversity.

12.4.1 Grazing/browsing

The high densities of grazing animals in much of the uplands mean that some sort of grazing control is usually necessary if woodland regeneration is to be successful. Current management recommendations almost invariably include the total or partial exclusion of grazers by fencing, either against stock or deer or, less frequently, rabbits. This gives instant control over these grazing animals, and has been particularly successful in areas where saplings were already present in the vegetation but previously kept in check by browsing. Where tree seed sources and regeneration niches are also present, new regeneration can also occur. However, several problems are associated with fencing. First, it is costly; second, it is impractical in many areas, both aesthetically and logistically due to inaccessibility, cost and snow damage, for example. Third, fencing without reducing herbivore numbers in the surrounding area simply increases grazing pressure on the vegetation outside the fence (Staines *et al.*, this volume). Finally, as previously discussed, the exclusion of grazing animals also removes the beneficial effects of gap creation and reduction of competition from other vegetation within the fence. In many areas fenced to encourage tree regeneration, little new regeneration has occurred after an initial establishment phase immediately after the removal of herbivores (e.g. Rassal Ashwood National Nature Reserve in north-west Scotland). In such situations the introduction of controlled grazing, either annually at specific times of year or after several years without grazing, could provide microsites for continued seedling establishment. Much more information is required on the precise effects of different numbers and species of grazing animals, timing of access and other related factors (Mitchell and Kirby, 1991; Young and Gordon, 1991). Successful management of woodland and scrub needs to incorporate herbivore use, as already happens in parts of Europe (e.g. Adams, 1975).

Herbivore densities can alternatively be reduced by culling or capture. Desirable animal densities will vary according to the species of animal, availability of other forage (e.g. nutrient-rich herbaceous species), and the numbers (and species) of woody seedlings and saplings present (Staines *et al.*, this volume). This is a crucial area for further work, as no clear relationships have yet been established between herbivore: sapling ratios and the relative success of different scrub or woodland species under a range of conditions.

Attempts to reduce numbers of red deer by culling/capture rather than by fencing are now being made in some areas, such as at Creag Meagaidh National Nature Reserve and Abernethy Forest (RSPB Reserve). In both areas, numbers of deer were sufficiently high to severely restrict the regeneration of scrub and woodland. Since the initiation of culling/capture of deer, both areas have shown considerable growth of saplings which were already established but previously held in check by browsing (see Staines *et al.*, this volume).

Browsing damage may also be reduced by providing diversionary feeding at locations distant from woody seedlings and saplings. Alternatively, sowing or fertilizing grass areas close to the regenerating woodland can provide more attractive grazing. However, this can exacerbate browsing problems by attracting herbivores from far afield. In some areas such approaches have been successful (Konig 1970; Miles and Kinnaird 1979b), but in others they have tended to encourage animals to spend more time in the general area than they did before provision of additional feeding (Clutton-Brock and Albon 1989).

Finally, persistent human disturbance can discourage the activity of animals such as red deer and so accelerate woodland regeneration where there is a ready source of seeds. The extensive pine regeneration in parts of Rothiemurchus forest may be at least partly due to the popularity of the area with tourists over the last 50 years or so. More recently, pine saplings have spread upwards into red deer wintering ground in the northern corries of Cairn Gorm from the old forest margin at about 500 m (Miller, 1986). Examination of the age structure of the sapling population over an area of some 1200 ha revealed a sudden surge of colonization after 1960, when the newly completed ski road and chairlift provided easy human access to the area (Fig 12.2). Presumably the increase in tourist activity had caused the overwintering deer population to avoid the area.

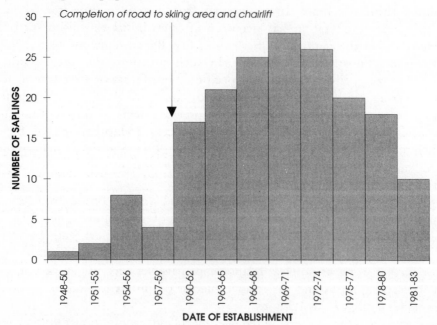

Figure 12.2. Numbers of pines established per year in the northern corries, Cairn Gorm, Scotland (data from Miller, 1986).

12.4.2 *Planting/sowing/ground preparation*

Several organizations (e.g., the Forest Authority, Scottish Natural Heritage, Reforesting Scotland, RSPB, Loch Garry Tree Group) are actively involved in different ways in promoting tree regeneration in Scotland. In many areas the lack of remaining seed sources means that direct sowing or planting is considered necessary for the rapid creation of woodland or scrub; in other areas where seed sources are present but ground conditions are not considered favourable, burning, disturbance or removal of the Ao horizon and other ground treatments have been explored. Much work has been done on methods for establishing native trees and shrubs (McVean, 1966; Wormell, 1968; Ball, 1975; Soutar and Peterken, 1989; Soutar and Spencer, 1991; Reforesting Scotland, 1993) and current knowledge is sufficiently advanced to enable the successful planting of appropriate species within many different types of vegetation, even on exposed ground. Possibilities for developing markets for commercial timber from our native species are also being explored (e.g. Lorraine-Smith and Worrell, 1991). Little work has focused specifically on the establishment of montane scrub species such as the willows (Mardon, 1991); this is particularly crucial in view of the current rarity of high altitude scrub in Scotland. When sowing or planting trees or scrub the use of local provenances where possible should be encouraged, for the preservation of remaining genetic diversity (Soutar and Spencer, 1991); in the Forest Authority native pinewood grant scheme this is tightly controlled. Regeneration from plantations of different origin, however, raises problems for genetic integrity which are difficult to control.

12.4.3 *Policy changes*

The need to reduce numbers of sheep and deer in Scotland has been widely and strongly argued for many years, yet in practice little has been done on a large scale. Reduction of sheep numbers would require changes in current government policies on upland grazing, in particular the system of headage payments for stock within Less Favoured Areas. The present system is thought to have had widespread detrimental effects on regeneration of woody species by indirectly encouraging overgrazing (Nature Conservancy Council, NCC, 1990). As part of the new EC Agri-Environment Regulations, additional payments linked with reductions in sheep numbers are available within the Environmentally Sensitive Areas, and extensions of this type of payment are now being considered, for example within the proposed Heather Moorland Scheme (SOAFD, 1993b). If such payment systems are extended and widely taken up by farmers (currently the Agri-Environment measures are voluntary) this could ultimately increase the likelihood of upland tree and scrub regeneration, although complete removal of headage-based payments and replacement with environmentally-linked payments would probably be more effective (NCC, 1990; Crabtree and Chalmers, in press).

Reducing sheep stocks will not in itself be effective in promoting widespread tree and scrub regeneration. Red deer are equally destructive where densities are high, as is the case in some ESAs where sheep have been fenced out (Nolan *et al.*, 1993), and there is a risk that they may expand their range to occupy any ground vacated by sheep (Clutton-Brock and Albon, 1992). Therefore deer numbers also need to be controlled to ensure regeneration. Until recently, estate owners have generally been under-culling the ever-increasing deer stocks (Callander and MacKenzie, 1991; Staines *et al.*, this volume). However, the Red Deer Commission has now produced agreement to aim to reduce red deer stocks by 100 000 over the next couple of years. Even this is unlikely to result in widespread regeneration; a reduced Scottish population of 200 000 red deer will still be greater than that recorded in the mid-1960s, when there was already thought to be a serious deer problem!

There are also proposals within the Agri-Environment Regulations (e.g. SOAFD, 1993b) to directly promote establishment of woodland and scrub through incentives additional to those in the existing Farm Woodland Premium scheme; it is not yet clear what final form these proposals will take (see Ward *et al.*, this volume).

12.4.4 Research

The central theme of this paper is the fundamental need to develop land management regimes that will promote the successful re-establishment of scrub and woodland as an integral part of a mosaic of upland plant communities, yet our current knowledge is inadequate to do this. Research needs can be divided into two main areas. First, we need to know more about the ecology of individual plant species: the effects of climatic and edaphic factors and, crucially, of grazing on growth, reproduction, seed dispersal and establishment. Our understanding of montane scrub species is particularly deficient in these respects. Second, we need to develop a better understanding of habitat use by different animal species and the relative importance of woodland and scrub species for grazing and shelter. The consolidation of such information should facilitate predictions about the likely effects of reducing grazing pressure in terms of changes in habitat use, reductions in browsing damage, and the nature and course of plant succession. Integration of such knowledge with landscape, wildlife and conservation aims should provide a sound basis upon which to implement rational and sustainable upland land use.

Acknowledgements

We are grateful to Rick Worrell, Keith Kirby and John Milne for their comments on the manuscript.

References

Adams, S. N. (1975). Sheep and cattle grazing in forests: a review, *Journal of Applied Ecology*, **12**, 143–52.

Armstrong, H. M. and Milne, J. A. (this volume). The effects of grazing on vegetation species composition.

Ball, M. E. (1975). The nursery production of native Scottish trees and shrubs, *Scottish Forestry*, **29**, 102–10.

Barclay, A. M. and Crawford, R. M. M. (1982). Winter desiccation stress and resting bud viability in relation to high altitude survival in *Sorbus aucuparia* L., *Flora.*, **172**, 21–34.

Barclay, A. M. and Crawford, R. M. M. (1984). Seedling emergence in the rowan (*Sorbus aucuparia*) from an altitudinal gradient, *Journal of Ecology*, **72**, 627–36.

Bennett, K. D. (1989). A provisional map of forest types for the British Isles 5000 years ago, *Journal of Quaternary Science*, **4**, 141–4.

Birks, H. J. B. (1988). Long-term ecological change in the British uplands. In Usher, M. B. and Thompson, D. B. A. (eds), *Ecological Change in the Uplands*, Blackwell Scientific Publications, Oxford, 37–56.

Buttenshøn, J. and Buttenshøn, R. M. (1985). Grazing experiments with cattle and sheep on nutrient poor acidic grassland and heath. IV. Establishment of woody species, *Natura Jutlandica*, **21**, 117–40.

Callander, R. F. and MacKenzie, N. A. (1991). *The Management of Wild Red Deer in Scotland*. Rural Forum Scotland, Perth.

Cavers, P. B. and Harper, J. L. (1967). Studies in the dynamics of plant populations I. The fate of seeds and transplants introduced into various habitats, *Journal of Ecology*, **55**, 59–71.

Chapman, H. and Crawford, R. M. M. (1981). Growth and regeneration in Britain's most northerly natural woodland, *Transactions of the Botanical Society of Edinburgh*, **43**, 327–35.

Chard, J. S. R. (1953). Highland birch, *Scottish Forestry*, **7**, 125–28.

Clutton-Brock, T. H. and Albon, S. D. (1989). *Red Deer in the Highlands*. BSP Professional Books, Oxford.

Clutton-Brock, T. H. and Albon, S. D. (1992). Trial and error in the Highlands, *Nature*, **358**, 11–12.

Crabtree, J. J. and Chalmers, N. A. (1994). Economic evaluation of standard payments and capital grants as conservation instruments, *Land Use Policy*, **11**, 94-106.

Cummins, R. P. and Miller, G. R. (1982). Damage by red deer (*Cervus elaphus*) enclosed in planted woodland, *Scottish Forestry*, **36**, 1–8.

Emberlin, J. C. and Baillie, I. C. (1980). Aspects of birch regeneration in two woods at Inverpolly National Nature Reserve, Wester Ross, *Scottish Forestry*, **34**, 13–34.

Fitter, A. H. and Jennings, R. D. (1975). The effects of sheep grazing on the growth and survival of seedling junipers (*Juniperus communis* L.), *Journal of Applied Ecology*, **12**, 637–42.

Forestry Commission (1983). *Census of Woodlands and Trees 1979–82*. HMSO, Edinburgh.

Fraser, G. K. (1933). Studies of certain Scottish moorlands in relation to tree growth, *Forestry Commission Bulletin No. 15*, HMSO, Edinburgh.

Gilbert, O. L. (1980). Juniper in upper Teesdale, *Journal of Ecology*, **68**, 1013–24.

Gimingham, C. H. (1972). *Ecology of Heathlands*. Chapman and Hall, London.

Goodier, R. and Bunce, R. G. H. (1977). The native pinewoods of Scotland: the current state of the resource. In Bunce, R. G. H. and Jeffers, J. N. R. (eds), *Native Pinewoods of Scotland*, ITE, Cambridge, 78–87.

Gong, W. K. and Gimingham, C. H. (1984). Birch regeneration in heathland vegetation, *Proceedings of the Royal Society of Edinburgh*, **85B**, 73–81.

Grace, J. (1990). Cuticular water loss unlikely to explain tree-line in Scotland, *Oecologia*, **84**, 64–8.

Harper, J. L. (1977). *Population Biology of Plants*. Academic Press, London.

Hewson, R. (1977). Browsing by mountain hares *Lepus timidus* on trees and shrubs in northeast Scotland, Notes from the Mammal Society, **34**, 168–71.

Holloway, C. W. (1967). '*The effect of red deer and other animals on naturally regenerated Scots pine*' (Unpublished PhD thesis, University of Aberdeen).

Keatinge, T. H. and Dickson, J. H. (1979). Mid-Flandrian changes in vegetation on mainland Orkney, *New Phytologist*, **82**, 585–612.

Kinnaird, J. W. (1971). Birch regeneration in relation to site characteristics, *Nature Conservancy Research in Scotland, 1968–1970*, 31–32.

Kinnaird, J. W. (1974). Effect of site conditions on the regeneration of birch (*Betula pendula* Roth. and *B. pubescens* Ehrh.), *Journal of Ecology*, **62**, 467–72.

Konig, E. (1970). Effects of fresh food on the prevention of peeling damage by red deer, *Proceedings of the International Congress of Game Biology*, **9**, 176–81.

Kullman, L. (1979). Change and stability in the altitude of the birch tree-limit in the southern Swedish Scandes 1915–1975, *Acta Phytogeographica Suecica*, **65**, 1–121.

Kullman, L. (1986). Temporal and spatial aspects of subalpine populations of *Sorbus aucuparia* in Sweden, *Annales Botanika Fennici*, **23**, 267–75.

Kullman, L. (1988). Short-term dynamic approach to tree limit and thermal climate: evidence from *Pinus sylvestris* in the Swedish Scandes, *Annales Botanika Fennici*, **25**, 219–27.

Legg, C. (this volume) Heathland dynamics: a matter of scale.

Lewis, F. J. (1911). The plant remains in the Scottish peat mosses, *Transactions of the Royal Society of Edinburgh*, **41**, 45–70.

Livingston, R. B. (1972). Influence of birds, stones and soil on the establishment of pasture juniper, *Juniperus communis* and red cedar, *J. virginiana*, in New England pastures, *Ecology*, **53**, 1141–47.

Lorraine-Smith, R. and Worrell, R. (1991). *The Commercial Potential of Birch in Scotland*. Forestry Industry of Great Britain, London.

Macaulay Land Use Research Institute (1993). *The Land Cover of Scotland 1988 (LCS88)*. Executive Report, Macaulay Land Use Research Institute, Aberdeen.

McVean, D. N. (1966). Establishment of native trees and shrubs on Scottish nature reserves by direct seed sowing, *Scottish Forestry*, **20**, 26–36.

McVean, D. N. and Ratcliffe, D. A. (1962). *Plant Communities of the Scottish Highlands*. Monographs of the Nature Conservancy No. 1, HMSO, London.

Mardon, D. K. (1991). Conservation of montane willow scrub in Scotland, *Transactions of the Botanical Society of Edinburgh*, **45**, 427–36.

Miles, J. (1973a). Early mortality and survival of self-sown seedlings in Glenfeshie, Invernesshire, *Journal of Ecology*, **61**, 93–8.

Miles, J. (1973b). Natural recolonization of experimentally bared soil in Callunetum in north-east Scotland, *Journal of Ecology*, **61**, 399–412.

Miles, J. (1974). Experimental establishment of new species from seed in Callunetum in North-East Scotland, *Journal of Ecology*, **62**, 537–51.

Miles, J. and Kinnaird, J. W. (1979a). The establishment and regeneration of birch, juniper and Scots pine in the Scottish Highlands, *Scottish Forestry*, **33**, 102–19.

Miles, J. and Kinnaird, J. W. (1979b). Grazing: with particular reference to birch, juniper and Scots pine in the Scottish Highlands, *Scottish Forestry*, **33**, 280–9.

Miller, G. R. (1971). Grazing and the regeneration of shrubs and trees. *Range Ecology Research, First Progress Report*, Nature Conservancy, Edinburgh, 27–40.

Miller, G. R. (1986). *Development of Subalpine Scrub at Northern Corries, Cairngorms SSSI: Preliminary Report*. Institute of Terrestrial Ecology, Banchory.

Miller, G. R. and Cummins, R. P. (1982). Regeneration of Scots pine *Pinus sylvestris* at a natural tree-line in the Cairngorm mountains, Scotland. *Holarctic Ecology*, **5**, 27–34.

Miller, G. R., Kinnaird, J. W. and Cummins, R. P. (1982). Liability of saplings to browsing on a red deer range in the Scottish Highlands, *Journal of Applied Ecology*, **19**, 941–51.

Mitchell, B., McGowan, D. and Willcox, N. A. (1982). Effects of deer in a woodland restoration enclosure, *Scottish Forestry*, **36**, 102–12.

Mitchell, B., Staines, B. W. and Welch, D. (1977). *Ecology of Red Deer. A Research Review Relevant to their Management in Scotland*. Institute of Terrestrial Ecology, Cambridge.

Mitchell, F. J. G. (1990). The impact of grazing and human disturbance on the dynamics of woodland in SW Ireland, *Journal of Vegetation Science*, **1**, 245–54.

Mitchell, F. J. G. (1991). Grazing in Upland Woods (NCC/MLURI contract report). Macaulay Land Use Research Institute, Aberdeen.

Mitchell, F. J. G. and Kirby, K. J. (1991). The impact of large herbivores on the conservation of semi-natural woods in the British uplands, *Forestry*, **63**, 333–53.

NCC (1990). Nature Conservation and Agricultural Change. *Focus on Nature Conservation*, **25**, 1–44.

Natural Countryside Monitoring Scheme (1988). *Scotland, Grampian*. Nature Conservancy Council, Peterborough and Countryside Commission for Scotland, Battleby.

Natural Countryside Monitoring Scheme (1991a). *Scotland, Borders*. Nature Conservancy Council, Peterborough and Countryside Commission for Scotland, Battleby.

Natural Countryside Monitoring Scheme (1991b). *Scotland, Lothian*. Nature Conservancy Council, Peterborough and Countryside Commission for Scotland, Battleby.

Natural Countryside Monitoring Scheme (1992). *Scotland, Dumfries and Galloway*, Scottish Natural Heritage, Battleby.

Natural Countryside Monitoring Scheme (1993a). *Scotland, Central*. Scottish Natural Heritage, Battleby.

Natural Countryside Monitoring Scheme (1993b). *Scotland, Fife.* Scottish Natural Heritage, Battleby.

Natural Countryside Monitoring Scheme (1993c). *Scotland, Highlands.* Scottish Natural Heritage, Battleby.

Natural Countryside Monitoring Scheme (1993d). *Scotland, Strathclyde.* Scottish Natural Heritage, Battleby.

Natural Countryside Monitoring Scheme (1993e). *Scotland, Tayside.* Scottish Natural Heritage, Battleby.

Natural Countryside Monitoring Scheme (1993f). NCMS Phase I (1940s–1970s). Summary Report for Scotland. Scottish Natural Heritage, Battleby.

Nolan, A. J., Still, M. J., Bell, J. S. and Gauld, J. H. (1993). *The Environmentally Sensitive Areas Designated in Scotland. Breadalbane ESA Biological Monitoring Report, Year 3, 1991.* Macaulay Land Use Research Institute, Aberdeen.

Pears, N. V. (1967). Present tree-lines of the Cairngorm mountains, Scotland, *Journal of Ecology,* **55,** 815–30.

Pearsall, W. H. (1950). *Mountains and Moorlands.* Collins, London.

Poore, M. E. D. and McVean, D. N. (1957). A new approach to Scottish mountain vegetation, *Journal of Ecology,* **45,** 401–39.

Prach, K. (1985). Succession of vegetation in abandoned fields in Finland, *Annales Botanika Fennici,* **22,** 307–14.

Pulliainen, E. and Tunkkari, P. S. (1987). Winter diet, habitat selection and fluctuation of a mountain hare *Lepus timidus* population in Finnish Forest Lapland, Holarctic Ecology, 10, 261–67.

Ratcliffe, D. A. (1981). The vegetation. In Nethersole-Thompson, D. and Watson, A. (Eds), *The Cairngorms,* Melven Press, Perth, 42–76.

Reforesting Scotland, (1993). *Reforesting Scotland, Volume 8.* Reforesting Scotland, Scourie, Sutherland.

Roberts, A. J., Russell, C., Walker, G. J. and Kirby, K. J. (1992). Regional variation in the origin, extent and composition of Scottish Woodland, *Botanical Journal of Scotland,* **46,** 167–89.

Sarvas, R. (1948). A research on the regeneration of birch in south Finland, *Communications Instituto Quaestionum Forestalium Finlandiae,* **35,** 1–91.

SOAFD (1993a). *Agriculture in Scotland Report for 1992,* CM 2320. HMSO, Edinburgh.

SOAFD (1993b). *Scotland's Agriculture and Environment. Implementing the EC Agri-Environment Regulation* (EC 2078/92). SOAFD, Edinburgh.

Soutar, R. G. and Peterken, G. F. (1989). Regional lists of native trees and shrubs for use in afforestation schemes, *Arboricultural Journal,* **13,** 33–43.

Soutar, R. G. and Spencer, J. W. (1991). The conservation of genetic variation in Britain's native trees, *Forestry,* **64,** 1–12.

Spence, D. H. N. (1960). Studies on the vegetation of Shetland. III. Scrub in Shetland and in South Uist, Outer Hebrides, *Journal of Ecology,* **48,** 73–95.

Staines, B. W., Balharry, R. and Welch, D. (this volume) Moorland management and impacts of red deer.

Sykes, J. M. and Horrill, A. D. (1981). Recovery of vegetation in a Caledonian pinewood after fire, *Transactions of the Botanical Society of Edinburgh,* **43,** 317–25.

Tallis, J. H. and Switsur, V. R. (1990). Forest and moorland in the south Pennine uplands in the mid-Flandrian period. II. The hillslope forests, *Journal of Ecology,* **78,** 857–83.

Ward, S. D., MacDonald, A. J. and Matthew, E. M. (this volume) Scottish heaths and moorland: how should conservation be taken forward?

Wilkins, D. A. (1984). The Flandrian woods of Lewis, *Journal of Ecology,* **72,** 251–58.

Wormell, P. (1968). Establishing woodland on the Isle of Rhum, *Scottish Forestry,* **22,** 207–20.

Wormell, P. (1970). The recovery of plantations after fire on the Isle of Rhum, *Scottish Forestry,* **24,** 93–100.

Young, J. B. and Gordon, I. J. (1991). *The Potential for Domestic Stock Grazing for Wildlife Conservation in Forests* (Research Review). Forestry Commission, Edinburgh.

Zackrisson, O. (1977). Influence of forest fires on the northern Swedish boreal forest, *Oikos,* **29,** 22–32.

13 ARE THE UPLAND HEATHS IN THE CAIRNGORMS PINING FOR CLIMATE CHANGE?

J. McConnell and C. Legg

Summary

1. This project investigated possible fluctuations in the altitudinal zonation between forest and heath vegetation as a response to climate.

2. Pollen profiles from above and below the *Pinus sylestris* L. treeline at Creag Fhiaclach in the Cairngorms are presented. Data were collected from replicated cores. Variation between cores emphasises the spatial heterogeneity of pollen accumulation and hence the need for replication.

3. Although the treeline has remained relatively stable at about 648 m (2000 ft) a.s.l., results show a dynamic interface between the heath and forest systems. There is some evidence that the southern, and less exposed, end of the treeline was at a higher elevation in the past.

13.1 Introduction

Positions of treelines throughout the current post-glacial have been correlated with climatic maxima and minima. During the climatic maximum of the Boreal-Atlantic transition forest cover reached its highest post glacial elevation in Britain (Birks, 1988). *Pinus sylvestris* stumps from the Cairngorms dating back to this period show that there was extensive forest cover up to at least 790 m a.s.l. (Pears, 1968). A second post-glacial re-advance during the sub-Boreal occurred to a lesser height of 701 m (Pears, 1968). The extension of forest cover during the Boreal-Atlantic transition to 720 m around Lochan nan Cat on Tayside was determined by Donner (1963) from the ratio of arboreal pollen to non-arboreal pollen (AP/NAP). Using variation in the representation of *Pinus sylvestris* pollen to detect former treelines has been suggested by Ward *et al.*, (1987).

At 648 m a.s.l. the treeline at Creag Fhiaclach is thought to be the best natural *Pinus sylvestris* treeline in the U.K. (Watt and Jones, 1948). As the gross stratigraphy is of a thin layer of blanket peat over block scree, macrofossils do not occur above the current treeline. Previous treelines are investigated at this site using microfossil analysis.

Nomenclature follows Clapham *et al.*, (1987) for vascular plants and Moore *et al.*, (1991) for palyomorphs. To avoid unnecessary repetition *Pinus sylvestris* and *Calluna vulgaris* (L.) Hull are referred to by generic name only.

13.2 Methods

A nested analysis of variance of modern pollen data from Creag Fhiaclach demonstrated that the treeline could be detected from a highly significant (P = 0.0001) change in the *Pinus* pollen percentage (Figure 13.1).

Five replicate peat cores were taken at six altitudes ranging from 606 m to 758 m, spanning the treeline at 648 m. Replicates were 30 m apart along the

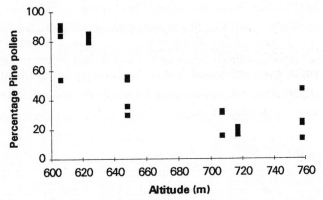

Figure 13.1. Changes in representation of *Pinus* from contemporary pollen trapped on moss polsters. The percentage of *Pinus* pollen in the spectrum drops rapidly above the treeline which is at 648 m a.s.l.

contour. Cores were sub-sampled at 5 mm intervals. Alternate samples were used for pollen preparation. Preparation consisted of peat matrix disaggregation with 10 % KOH and a 'Whirlimix' stirrer, followed by standard Erdtman (1960) acetolysis and mounting in glycerol jelly. A total of 482 counts were made with a mean pollen sum of 398 total land pollen.

Data reduction was achieved using principal components analysis (PCA) on pollen percentages of all taxa. Pollen percentage data are commonly analysed using covariation matrix (Bennett, *et al.*, 1992). The first axis from a PCA on the covariance matrix was dominated by *Pinus* with a loading on the eigenvector of –17.11 and Calluna with a loading of 18.12. The first axis was then a *Pinus–Calluna* gradient which explained 82 % of the variance. However, the plots of the pollen data were distorted by a small number of extreme values. Using a correlation matrix has the effect of giving greater weight to rare taxa. A PCA on the pollen correlation matrix gave a similar first axis to the covariance matrix. The lowest eigenvector loading was –0.804 for *Pinus* and 0.787 for *Calluna*. Here the first axis accounts for

18 % of the variance reflecting the reduced dominance of the *Pinus–Calluna* ratio. Even with this weighting a PCA on a correlation matrix still demonstrates the clear boundary between the *Pinus* and *Calluna* communities at the treeline. As the correlation matrix reduces the distortion of high *Pinus* and *Calluna* pollen ratios in the plots of the PCA, it was the results from the correlation matrix which were used to produce Figure 13.2.

13.3   Results

The principal component is then a transition of *Pinus* to *Calluna*. Negative values indicate forest pollen assemblages while positive values are characteristic of heath vegetation. Forest pollen assemblages were typical at all depths in the cores from the lowest two altitudes (Figures 13.2a and b). The highest altitude (Figure 13.2f) was consistently of heathland pollen assemblages.

At the treeline there was some fluctuation between forest and heath assemblages in all five cores (Figure 13.2c). These fluctuations showed no synchrony with depth. At 707 m (Figure 13.2d) all samples were *Calluna* dominated down to − 3.25 cm. The two most southerly replicates, 4 and 5, had forest pollen assemblages below this depth. Replicates 2 and 4 had some forest pollen assemblages at 717 m (Figure 13.2e). These were consistent between −1.25 cm and −8.25 cm for replicate 2, but were erratic for replicate 4.

13.4   Discussion

Pinus and *Calluna* can produce copious quantities of pollen estimated at 18 000 and 158 000 grains per flower respectively (Pohl, 1937). *Pinus* pollen is released high into the air stream and tends to travel long distances. High levels of *Pinus* pollen have been collected from a trawler 12 miles off the Finnish coast (Lanner, 1966). On Shetland, pollen traps have recorded up to 30 grains $m^{-2}d^{-1}$ (Tyldesley, 1973) and peat deposits have contained up to 10 % *Pinus* pollen (Hawksworth, 1969). As *Pinus* pollen forms consistently high background levels it is unlikely that over the small spatial scale of this study the absolute numbers of *Pinus* grains changed significantly. Change in the proportion of *Pinus* in the pollen spectrum was more probably due to the abrupt change in the absolute numbers of *Calluna* pollen grains (which are more locally deposited).

On this site, *Calluna* flowering is at its maximum ($57 \times 10^4 \pm 5 \times 10^4$ m^{-2} unpublished data) at the treeline where conditions are sheltered. As the altitude increases the number of flowers produced per unit area begins to decrease. Miller and Watson (1978) also found a strong negative correlation between *Calluna* flower production and altitude. Below the treeline shade from the forest canopy effects the abundance and vigour of *Calluna* itself and flower production (Iason and Hester, 1993). At this site, the number of flowers dropped to $2 \times 10^4 \pm 0.7 \times 10^4$ m^{-2} (unpublished data). *Calluna* is replaced by *Vaccinium myrtillus* L. and, to a lesser extent, *Vaccinium vitis-idaea* L. Distribution of *Calluna* flowers explains the change in *Pinus* pollen representation in the fossil pollen assemblage.

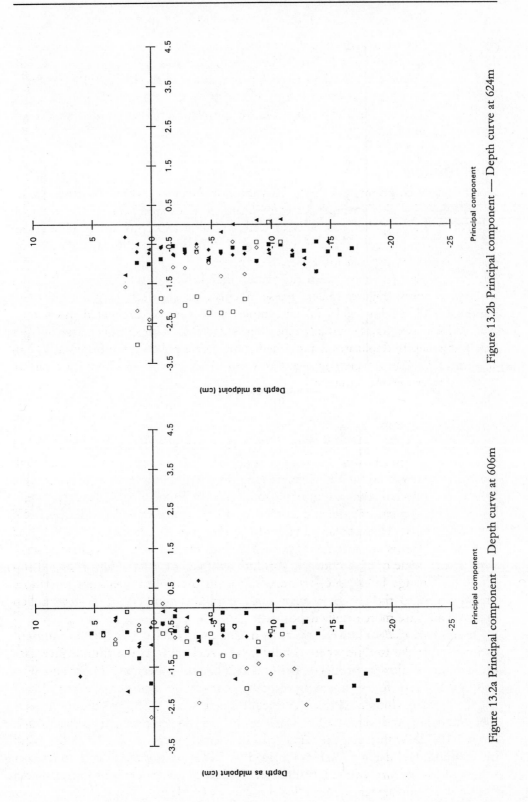

Figure 13.2b Principal component — Depth curve at 624m

Figure 13.2a Principal component — Depth curve at 606m

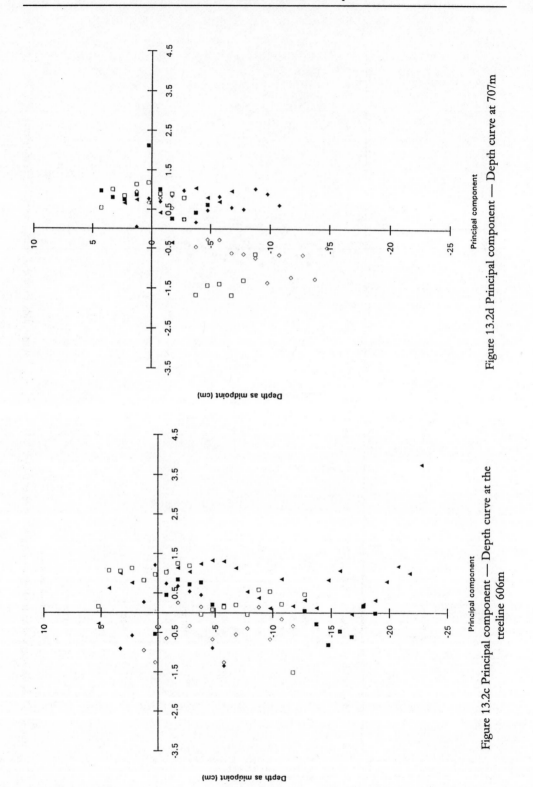

Figure 13.2d Principal component — Depth curve at 707m

Figure 13.2c Principal component — Depth curve at the treeline 606m

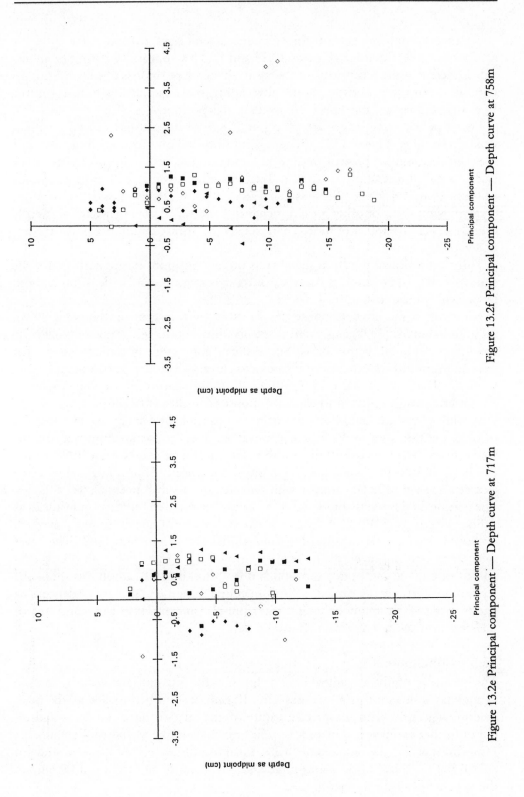

Figure 13.2f Principal component — Depth curve at 758m

Figure 13.2e Principal component — Depth curve at 717m

There is some evidence of forest pollen assemblages reaching 707 m at the southern end of the ridge (Figures 13.2e and f). This appears to represent an elevated treeline in the recent past in the more sheltered positions. The southernmost core at the present treeline shows alternating forest and heath pollen spectra. Forest cover may not have been complete in this position.

Forest pollen assemblages are found at 717 m on the more exposed northern end of the ridge (Figure 13.2b). There is no evidence of forest cover at any time between here and the present treeline so these could represent an isolated group of trees formally present at this altitude. Treelines often advance with isolated groups of trees establishing first (Stevens and Fox, 1991). Alternatively, a dense patch of *Juniperus communis* L. or other local dominants in the vegetation, may have artificially created pollen assemblages more characteristic of forest by limiting local *Calluna* pollen deposition.

This treeline is and has been stable at its present position, except perhaps for the southern end. Is, however, the treeline at its maximum potential elevation allowed by present climatic conditions?

Migration is the usual response of plants to climatic change, (Huntley, 1991). Gear and Huntley (1992) suggested that *Pinus* distribution was sensitive to climatic conditions on a latitudinal basis. Successional computer simulations show that treeline responses are even more sensitive to climate change than to latitudinal distribution (Davis and Botkin, 1985). Besides a more rapid response, the amplitude of climatic change required to elicit a response is smaller at treelines.

Stability of the treeline as inferred from this palynological study suggests that the modern treeline is below its potential elevation. Support for a suppressed treeline comes from a study of annual ring width at this site. Grace and Norton (1990) found that the narrowest rings occurred 150 m below the treeline. Annual ring widths at the treeline also showed less correlation with climatic variables than trees at lower altitudes. The treeline on this site is composed of a narrow band of Krummholtz individuals, as defined by Griggs (1946). Pinus occurs above the treeline as numerous saplings which decrease in frequency with increasing altitude (Miller and Cummins, 1982). The lower stature and resultant higher tissue temperatures of the Krummholtz individuals adequately explain the unexpected variation in ring widths. But, the carbon balance of the Krummholtz trees at the treeline is far from critical from the ring width evidence. The narrow band of Krummholtz trees could represent only the lower altitudinal limit of this tree form and not its maximum elevation.

13.5 Conclusions

The constancy of the altitudinal limit to forest at this site indicates that the treeline is not simply determined by temperature. If climate is to be invoked as the main determining factor then the precise nature of the relationship is complex and requires further evaluation. The precise role of climate in the altitudinal limitation of *Pinus* forest at this site requires further evaluation. A more comprehensive study of annual rings and late wood maximum density in Krummholtz trees and saplings at the treeline may help to resolve this.

Acknowledgements

This research was supported by the Department of Education for Northern Ireland. We thank Professor J. Grace for helpful comments on the paper and SNH for permission to use the site at Creag Fhiaclach.

References

Bennett, K. D., Boreham, M. J., Sharpe, M. J. and Switsur, V. R. (1992). Holocene history of environment, vegetation and human settlement on Catta Ness, Lunnasting, Shetland, *Journal of Ecology*, **80**, 241–73.

Birks, H. J. B. (1988). Long-term ecological change in the British uplands, in Usher, M. B. and Thompson, D. B. A. (Eds) *Ecological Change in the Uplands*, Blackwell, Oxford, 37–56.

Clapham, A. R., Tutin, T. G. and Moore, D. M. (1987). *Flora of the British Isles*, Cambridge University Press, Cambridge.

Davis, M. B. and Botkin, D. B. (1985). Sensitivity of cool-temperate forests and their fossil pollen record to rapid temperature change, *Quaternary Research* **23**, 327–40.

Donner, J. J. (1963). On the post-glacial history of the Grampian Highlands of Scotland, *Societas Scientiarum Fennica*, **24**, 5–29.

Erdtman, G. (1960). The acetolysis method, *Svensk Botanisk Tidsskrift*, **54**, 561–4.

Gear, A. and Huntley, B. (1992). Rapid changes in the range limits of Scots pine 4000 years ago, *Science*, **251**, 544–6.

Grace, J. and Norton, D. A. (1990). Climate and growth of Pinus sylvestris at its upper altitudinal limit in Scotland: Evidence from tree growth-rings, *Journal of Ecology*, **78**, 601–10.

Griggs, R. F. (1946). The timberlines of Northern America and their interpretation, *Ecology*, **27**, 275–89.

Hawksworth, D. L. (1969). Studies on the peat deposits of the Island of Foula, Shetland, *Transactions of the Botanical Society of Edinburgh*, **40**, 576–91.

Huntley, B. (1991). How plants respond to climate change: migration rates, invidualisum and the consequences for plant communities, *Annals of Botany*, **67**, (supplement), 15–22.

Iason, G. R. and Hester, A. J. (1993). The response of heather (*Calluna vulgaris*) to shade and nutrients — predictions of the carbon-nutrient balance hypothesis, *Journal of Ecology*, **81**, 75–80.

Lanner, R. M. (1966). Needed: a new approach to the study of pollen dispersion, *Silvae Genetica*, **15**, 50–2.

Miller, G. R. and Cummins, R. P. (1982). Regeneration of Scots pine *Pinus sylvestris* at a natural tree-line in the Cairngorm Mountains, Scotland, *Holarctic Ecology*, **5**, 27–34.

Miller, G. R. and Watson, A. (1978). Heather production and its relevance to the regulation of red grouse populations. In Heal, O. W. and Perkins, D. F. (Eds). *Production Ecology of British Moorlands and Montane Grasslands*, Springer-Verlag, Berlin, 277–85.

Moore, P. D., Webb, J. A. and Collinson, M. E. (1991). *An Illustrated Guide to Pollen Analysis*, Hodder and Stoughton, London.

Pears, N. V. (1968). Post-glacial treelines of the Cairngorm Mountains, Scotland, *Transactions of the Botanical Society of Edinburgh*, **40**, 361–94.

Pohl, F. (1937). Die Pollenerzeugung der Windbluter, *Botanisch Centralblatt*, **56A**, 365–470.

Stevens, G. C. and Fox, J. F. (1991). The causes of treeline, *Annual Review of Ecology and Systematics*, **22**, 177–91.

Tyldesley, J. B. (1973). Long-range transmission of tree pollen to Shetland. I. Sampling and trajectories, *New Phytologist*, **72**, 175–81.

Ward, R. G. W., Haggart, B. A. and Bridge, M. C. (1987). Dendrochronological studies of bog pine from the Rannoch Moor area, western Scotland. In Ward, R. G. W. (Ed), *Applications of tree ring studies*, British Archaeological Reports, International Series, **333**, 215–225.

Watt, A. S. and Jones, E. W. (1948). The ecology of the Cairngorms. I. The environment and the altitudinal zonation of the vegetation. *Journal of Ecology*. **36**, 283–304.

14 THE EFFECTS OF GRAZING ON VEGETATION SPECIES COMPOSITION

H. M. Armstrong and J. A. Milne

Summary

1. The foraging and ingestive behaviour of large herbivores is an important determinant of preferences for particular plant species and communities, and therefore of the extent of defoliation of individual plants.

2. The extent to which moorland and heath plant species can withstand or avoid defoliation, and the effect of defoliation on their competitive ability, are also central to understanding the effects of grazing on plant species composition.

3. Current understanding of these factors is used to predict the consequences of changes in stocking rate on the grazing pressure to which individual vegetation types in a hill grazing system are likely to be subject.

4. An approach to the prediction of the effects of a given grazing pressure on vegetation species composition is described, and the relationship between grazing pressure and species diversity is outlined.

14.1 Introduction

The species composition of heaths and moorlands affects their nature conservation, agricultural, landscape and amenity value and is determined by a large number of factors most of which are outwith the control of land managers. Grazing and burning are, however, two important factors over which land managers usually have some control. Sheep and cattle grazing systems are usually managed with income generation as the primary objective but there is now increasing public pressure for the effects on flora, fauna and landscape to be given greater consideration and, in some instances, for grazing to be managed to maintain or enhance specific habitat types. The prescription of suitable stocking systems at a given site requires that the effects of different stocking systems on vegetation species composition can be predicted. This is complex not only because of the variety of management practices and large herbivore species found on heaths and moorlands but also because of the complexity of their grazing behaviour, the wide variety of plant responses to being grazed and the numerous interactions of these with environmental factors. This chapter presents a two-part approach to predicting the effects of grazing at a site on any vegetation type. The first part describes a means of predicting the degree of utilization likely on different vegetation types at different times of the year at a site and the second part describes an approach to predicting the effects of this on vegetation species composition.

14.2 Translating from Stocking regime to Utilization Rate

Hill-grazing systems are generally made up of a mosaic of different vegetation types over which herbivores are able to range freely. Since grazing animals have seasonal preferences for different types, and these are affected by a number of factors, annual stocking rates do not usually represent a good measure of the grazing pressure exerted on any vegetation type. The first step in predicting the effects of a given grazing management regime on the vegetation is, therefore, to predict the degree of utilization of each vegetation type during a typical year. Figure 14.1 shows the structure of a simulation model which has been designed to meet this objective for hill vegetation grazed by sheep in the UK (Armstrong and Sibbald, 1992). The model predicts daily biomass production of a range of common hill vegetation types. It then uses a simple foraging model to predict the amount eaten by the whole sheep flock (offtake) from each vegetation type. Standing biomasses are updated each day, taking into account senescence and litterfall of grasses and offtake by sheep. In late winter, before the start of the next growing season, the proportion of the annual production grazed by sheep (the utilization rate) is calculated for each vegetation type.

In the model, the daily amount eaten by a sheep from each vegetation type on any day (intake) is obtained by relating the potential daily intake of digestible material possible from the vegetation type and its area to the potential daily intakes possible from all the vegetation types and their areas. It is therefore related not only to the nutrient intake possible from that vegetation type but also to what can be obtained elsewhere. Although this results in the sheep eating most from the most nutritionally rewarding vegetation type, it also results in them sampling all others as well. The three attributes of the vegetation which determine the potential intake of digestible material are, first, the digestibility of live and dead material of grass species or of the current year's growth of heather shoots (Figure 14.2), second, the proportion of live to dead material in grass swards and, third, the biomass available to sheep. Thus a sward with a high proportion of live material but with a low biomass may be less preferred than a sward with more dead material but a higher biomass. Sheep alter their choice between vegetation types as these attributes change during the year.

14.2.1 Seasonal distribution of intake between vegetation types

Figure 14.3a shows how intake by sheep is predicted to be distributed between a range of vegetation types in each month of the year on a hill farm with a low stocking rate of 0.62 ewes ha^{-1}. Each ewe is assumed to produce one lamb. The proportion of the total area made up of each vegetation type was set as follows: heather, 0.52; reseeded grassland, 0.01; *Agrostis/Festuca*, 0.05; *Festuca/Agrostis*, 0.37; *Molinia*, 0.05. In May, the order of preference between vegetation types is *Agrostis/Festuca*, *Festuca/Agrostis*, *Molinia* then

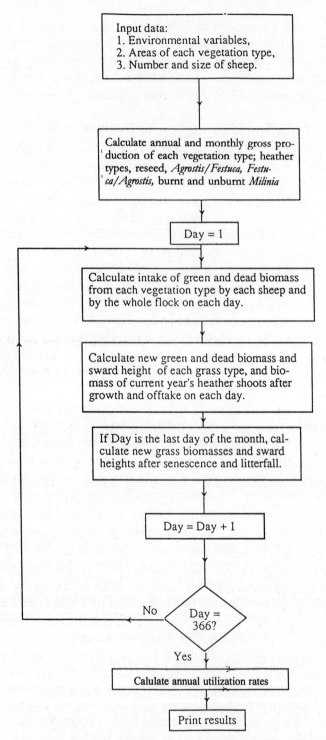

Figure 14.1. Structure of the model to predict the degree of utilization of upland vegetation types by sheep as described by Armstrong and Sibbald (1992).

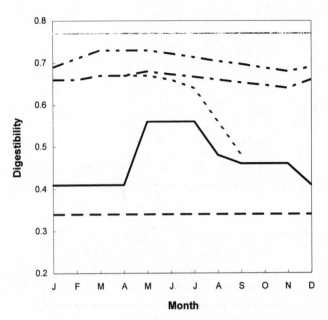

Figure 14.2. Seasonal changes in the digestibility of live and dead grass biomass and of the current season's growth of heather shoots. ———— = Reseeded grassland, —— - - = *Agrostis* spp.,– —— - = *Festuca* spp., - - - -= *Molinia caerulea*, ———— = Heather, —— —— = dead grass.

heather. Since, at this time of year, biomass is high, digestibility is the main determinant of this order of preference. As summer progresses, the amount of *Molinia* in the diet increases until August when it begins to decline as the *Molinia* starts to senesce. In November, the proportion of *Agrostis/Festuca* in the diet declines as the sward is grazed short and intake becomes limited by harvestable biomass. In December, the proportion of *Festuca/Agrostis* also starts to decline as dead biomass starts to increase in the sward and digestibility declines. At the same time, intake from heather increases as it becomes relatively more attractive. These trends continue into January but by February the proportion of heather starts to decline and that of grass to increase again. This occurs because some of the dead material has been removed from the grass by grazing giving the sheep access to new, live material. This continues at an increasing rate through to March. In April, *Festuca/Agrostis* becomes briefly the most preferred vegetation type because, although both it and the *Agrostis/Festuca* have started their spring growth, the *Agrostis/Festuca* is still short after the heavy grazing the previous year.

If the stocking rate is doubled to 1.23 ewes ha^{-1} (Figure 14.3b), changes occur in the diet selected, particularly in the autumn and winter. The *Agrostis/Festuca* is more heavily grazed in summer, so it becomes very short and as a result there is an increase in the proportion of *Festuca/Agrostis* in the diet in September. The live material from both grass vegetation types is then eaten rapidly, leaving a high proportion of dead material thereby reducing the overall digestibility of the diet. As a result, by January, the sheep are eating a greater proportion of heather than *Agrostis/Festuca* in their diet at this stocking rate. The annual utilization rates for

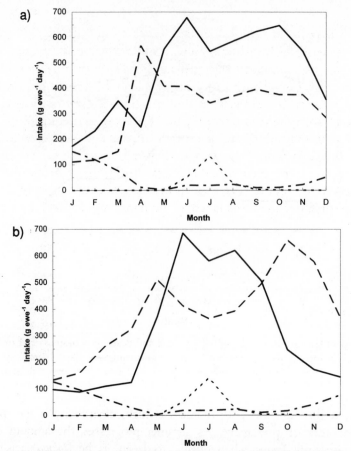

Figure 14.3. Seasonal distribution of intake between *Agrostis/Festuca, Festuca/Agrostis, Molinia* and heather vegetation types on a farm described in the text at two stocking rates, (a) 0.62 ewes ha^{-1} and (b) 1.23 ewes ha^{-1} ——————— = *Agrostis/Festuca,* —— —— = *Festuca/Agrostis,* – —— — = *Molinia caerulea,* – – – – = Pioneer heather.

each of the vegetation types at both stocking rates are shown in Table 14.1. The Table shows that there is not always a direct relationship between stocking rate and utilization rate. In this example, a doubling of stocking rate resulted only in a 1.5 times increase in the utilization rate of *Agrostis/Festuca.*

Table 14.1 Predicted utilization rates (proportion of the annual production removed by sheep) on different vegetation types at two sheep stocking rates at a site described in the text.

| | Stocking rate (sheep ha^{-1}) | |
Vegetation type	0.62	1.23
Agrostis/Festuca	0.54	0.80
Festuca/Agrostis	0.27	0.61
Molinia	0.03	0.07
Pioneer heather	0.19	0.37

14.2.2 The effect of the ratio of grass to heather

The utilization rate on each vegetation type varies not only with the seasonal stocking rate and size of the sheep (via offtake) and with latitude and altitude (via biomass production) but also with the area of each vegetation type. By keeping all but the latter constant, the effect of the proportion of different vegetation types on utilization rates can be illustrated. Figure 14.4 shows a prediction of the effect of stocking rate on utilization rates and on the annual intake of digestible material per ewe for two different sites with contrasting proportions of heather and *Agrostis/Festuca*. It can be seen that the site with the higher proportion of grass (0.90) can support more sheep at a given annual intake of digestible material. If 230 kg of digestible dry matter is taken as the minimum annual requirement for a

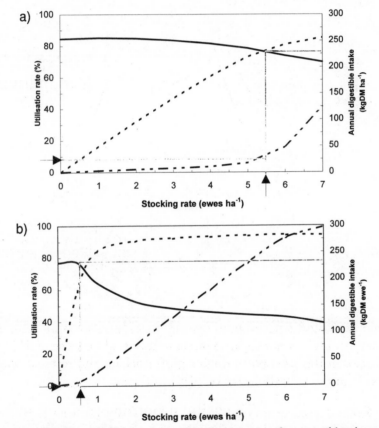

Figure 14.4 The effect of stocking rate on annual utilisation rate of grass and heather and on annual intake of digestible dry matter. The model has been run for two sites in Grampian Region grazed by 50 kg ewes. The sites consisted of (a) 0.90 *Agrostis/Festuca* : 0.10 heather and (b) 0.10 *Agrostis/Festuca* : 0.90 heather. The model was run using typical altitudes of 400 m for heather and 300 m for *Agrostis/Festuca*, − − − − = utilization rate on grass, − −−−− − = utilization rate on heather, −−−−−−−− = annual intake per ewe of digestible material. The arrows indicate the stocking rate and level of heather utilization which result when ewes are stocked to obtain a suggested minimum requirement of 230 kg of digestible dry matter per year.

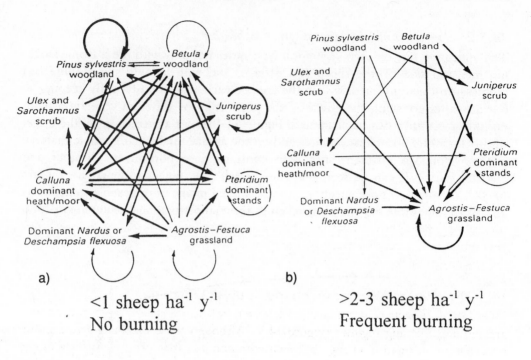

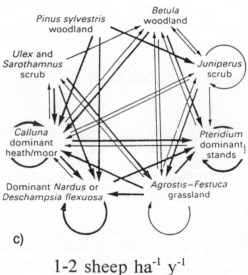

Figure 14.5. Successional transitions in the uplands (particularly northeast Scotland) between eight vegetation types given (a) low grazing pressures (< 1 sheep equivalent ha–1 year–1) and no burning, (b) high grazing pressures (> 2–3 sheep equivalents ha–1 year–1) and frequent burning, and (c) intermediate levels of grazing (1–2 sheep equivalents ha–1 year–1) and occasional burning. Broad arrows represent common transitions, thin arrows apparently less frequent transitions, and curved arrows self-replacement. The vegetation types are arranged so that types tending to podzolize and/or acidify soils are on the left, and types with contrasting effects on the soil are on the right (from Miles, 1988).

ewe with a single lamb, at the maximum stocking rate compatible with maintaining this intake, the heather will be more heavily grazed at the site with the larger proportion of grass. It can also be seen that little heather is eaten until grass utilization rates reach about 70 %. As stocking rates increase above this point, heather utilization rates increase and annual intakes of digestible material decrease more rapidly where the proportion of heather is small than where the proportion of heather is large. Heather is therefore more likely to be at risk from heavy grazing where the ratio of heather to grass is small.

14.2.3   Uses of the model

The model has been found to be of value as an educational tool and in providing site specific predictions. These are useful in supporting field assessments and expert opinion. Predictions made by the model are likely to become more reliable as the model is further tested and developed.

14.3   Predicting Vegetation change due to Grazing

Miles (1988) depicts possible changes between upland vegetation types under three grazing and burning regimes (Figure 14.5). Although these diagrams give a good overview of vegetation change between communities, they can only offer a range of possibilities for change at a particular site. This is for two reasons: first, the use of stocking rates as a measure of grazing pressure and, second, the lack of information on the conditions under which any particular change is likely to occur. As has been demonstrated above, stocking rates do not necessarily give a good indication of grazing pressure on any particular vegetation type.

The principal factors which can cause vegetation change to occur, often in interaction with the effect of grazing are changes in soil type (nutrient level, base status, moisture level, aeration, depth), climate (length of growing season, seasonal rainfall and temperature pattern, snow cover, frost, exposure), pollution (acid rain and nitrogen inputs) and burning. As well as considering the average levels of these factors, the probability distributions around these averages have to be taken into account since unusual occurrences can deflect the direction of change.

The prediction of vegetation change using general rules derived from the relatively few observations of vegetation change is likely to be inadequate because of the large number of possible combinations of levels of environmental and management factors. Another approach to dealing with vegetation change due to grazing is to consider the functional attributes of both plant and animal species. Grime et al., (in press), Noble and Slatyer (1980) and Moore and Noble (1990) have used similar approaches based on the functional attributes of plants to predict vegetation change under a variety of disturbances which have not included grazing. The functional attribute approach to predicting the effects of grazing would involve identifying the attributes of both plants and animals which are likely to be important in predicting the effect of a change in grazing (Tables 14.2 to 14.4). Information on plant functional attributes in the UK can be obtained from existing sources such as Grime, Hodgson and Hunt (1988) and the Ecological Flora Database (Fitter and Peat, 1993). The next step would be to ascribe a relative value for these attributes to the plant and animal species to be considered at a particular site. Often, only the dominant species need to be considered as functionally independent because many of the less dominant species will increase or decrease together as a result of changes in the dominant species. On British heaths and moorlands there are relatively few dominant species and there is sufficient information on most of these to be able to characterise them functionally.

Table 14.2   Examples of functional attributes of plants relevant to predicting the effects of grazing.

Physical	Growth and reproduction	Grazing related
Life form (e.g. dwarf shrub)	Regeneration mechanism	Digestibility to grazing animals
Longevity (e.g. perennial)	Meristem position	Anti-herbivore attributes
Leaf longevity (e.g. evergreen)	Underground stores	
Leaf form (e.g. fine-leaved)	Seed longevity and dispersal	
Maximum height	Tolerance of adverse soil conditions	
Phenotypic plasticity	Tolerance of adverse climatic conditions	
Genetic variability	Shade tolerance	

Table 14.3   Examples of functional attributes of animals relevant to grazing.

Species	Biting method	Selective ability	Minimum sward height possible
Sheep	Biting/shearing	High	Short
Red deer	Biting/shearing	High	Short
Cattle	Wrap tongues around vegetation and pull	Low	Longer
Goats	Biting/shearing	Can be highly selective but prefer a varied diet	Short
Rabbits	Biting/shearing	Very high	Very short

Table 14.4   Observed grazing preferences not related to digestibility.

Species	Preferences
Sheep	Avoid *Nardus stricta* generally but will graze small plants as part of a short sward. Avoid *Juncus* spp.
Red deer	Graze heather more than do sheep
Cattle	Will eat more *Nardus stricta* than sheep or deer
Goats	Will eat *Juncus* spp. in spring. Will eat *Nardus stricta*
Rabbits	Avoid aromatic or prickly species

As an example we shall consider the prediction of the likely changes in the cover of heather and *Nardus stricta* on a dry peaty podzol with 70 % cover of heather and 30 % cover of *Nardus* in a mixture or fine-grained mosaic grazed by sheep in Grampian Region. Table 14.5 gives some of the functional attributes of heather and *Nardus*. From these, and from the functional attributes of sheep given in Tables 14.3 and 14.4, the following six predictions can be made.

Table 14.5   Examples of functional attributes of heather and *Nardus stricta*

Attribute	Heather	Nardus
Maximum height (cm)	80	40
Meristem position	Apical	Basal
Underground stores	Substantial	Substantial
Soil conditions	Acidic dry	Acidic, moist
Climatic conditions	Cold tolerant Cannot tolerate prolonged snow	Cold tolerant
Digestibility	Low all year	Live material higher than heather. Dead material lower
Anti-herbivore devices	Tannins	Silicates. Lower silicate levels in new, spring growth

1. *Nardus* will be avoided unless grazing pressure is extremely high.

2. Heather will be grazed in preference to *Nardus* except in early Spring when silicate levels are lower in the new growth of *Nardus*.

3. High levels of removal of annual shoot production are likely to cause a decline in heather cover because the active meristems are apical.

4. Both heather and *Nardus* will be able to withstand removal of intermediate levels of annual shoot production because of substantial below-ground storage.

5. Conditions are suitable for heather and not ideal for *Nardus* since the site is dry.

6. Heather can grow taller than *Nardus*.

It follows from the first three predictions that, if grazing pressure is high, heather cover will decline and *Nardus* cover increase. If grazing pressure is intermediate, it follows from Predictions 4 and 5 that heather has a high chance of remaining dominant and, if grazing pressure is low, the fifth prediction would suggest that heather will remain dominant and may increase in cover. If grazing is removed, it follows from the sixth prediction that heather is likely to grow tall enough to shade out *Nardus*. The heather may then become degenerate, however, and *Nardus* may re-invade. These predictions are borne out by Fenton (1937) who observed that, if *Nardus*/heather areas were fenced from grazing, heather increased in cover on hill grazings in Scotland, by King (1960) who observed that grazing moved the heather/*Nardus* balance in favour of *Nardus*, and by Grant *et al.*, (1978, 1982) who showed that pioneer heather in Grampian Region can withstand removal of 40 % of annual shoot production without a decline in cover but that removal of 80 % caused a decline in cover.

Using this approach, such qualitative predictions could be made for any site on the basis of information on functional attributes. In many ways this approach formalises the methods used by 'experts' to make predictions. Such a rule-based approach lends itself well to computerization in the form of an 'expert' system, included in which would be a database, not only of functional attributes of plant and animal species but also of the results of case studies with which model predictions can be compared. The system would also allow the user to explore the reasoning used by the model to make a prediction. In this form, the model would provide a structure into which new information could be fed and would allow important gaps in knowledge to be easily identified.

14.4 Effects of Grazing on Diversity of Plant Species

As with the effects of grazing on plant species composition, the effects on vegetation species diversity depend upon many factors. Rather than generalize, it may be better to consider each situation as unique and ask the following questions.

1. Is the dominant plant species grazed in preference to other species?

2. Are site conditions favourable for the dominant species relative to others?

3. Is the dominant species likely to suffer adverse effects from grazing?

4. If the dominant species changes, are there any associated species which are likely to be lost?

5. Will grazing increase the number of regeneration niches available?

6. Are there likely to be sources of propagules for invading species?

7. Are conditions likely to be suitable for establishment of new species?

8. Are any other successional processes occurring simultaneously?

The answers to the first three questions allow the prediction of how the dominant species are likely to respond under different grazing pressure and those to the remaining questions allow the prediction of the likelihood of other species disappearing or colonizing. The final question ensures that vegetation changes, other than those caused by grazing, are also considered.

14.5 Conclusion

In this Chapter we have discussed the use of traditional simulation modelling and the more novel approach of 'expert' system modelling to predict the complex functioning of grazing systems. Although the grazing simulation model described is already in use as an educational and research tool and to provide some assistance for site management (Armstrong and Sibbald, 1992), the functional attribute approach to predicting the effects of grazing on plant species composition has yet to be developed but has the potential to provide a flexible decision support tool for land managers.

References

Armstrong, H. M. and Sibbald, A. R. (1992). A model of pasture utilization in the hill country of the UK, *Agricultural Systems and Information Technology*, **4,** 11–13.

Fenton, E. W. (1937). The influence of sheep in the vegetation of hill grazings in Scotland, *Journal of Ecology*, **25,** 424–30.

Fitter, A. and Peat, H. (1993). The ecological flora database, *NERC NEWS*, January, 24–5.

Grant, S. A., Barthram, G. T., Lamb, W. I. C. and Milne, J. A. (1978). Effect of season and level of grazing on the utilization of heather by sheep. I. Responses of the sward, *Journal of the British Grassland Society*, **33,** 289–300.

Grant, S. A., Milne, J. A., Barthram, G. T. and Souter, W. G.. (1982). Effects of season and level of grazing on the utilization of heather by sheep. III. Longer-term responses and sward recovery, *Grass and Forage Science*, **37,** 311–20.

Grime, J. P., Hodgson, J. G. and Hunt, R. (1988). *Comparative Plant Ecology. A Functional Approach to Common British Species*. Unwin Hyman, London.

Grime, J. P., Hodgson, J. G., Hunt, R., Thompson, K., Hendry, G. A. F., Campbell, B. D., Jalili, A., Hillier, S. H., Diaz, S. and Burke, M. J. W. (in press). Functional types: testing the concept in northern England. In Smith, T. M., Shugart, H. H. and Woodward F. I. (Eds), *GCTE Workshop on Plant Functional Types*, Charlottesville, in press.

King, J. (1960). Observations on the seedling establishment and growth of Nardus stricta in burned Callunetum, *Journal of Ecology*, **48,** 667–77.

Miles, J. (1988). Vegetation and soil changes in the uplands. In Usher, M. B. and Thompson, D. B. A. (Eds), *Ecological Change in the Uplands*, Special Publications Series of the British Ecological Society, 7. Blackwell Scientific Publications, Oxford. 55–70.

Moore, A. D., and Noble, I. R. (1990). An individualistic model of vegetation stand dynamics, *Journal of Environmental Management*, **31,** 61–81.

Noble, I. R. and Slatyer, R. O. (1980). The use of vital attributes to predict successional changes in plant communities subject to recurrent disturbances. *Vegetatio*, **43,** 5–21.

15 THE VEGETATION DYNAMICS OF WET HEATHS IN RELATION TO SHEEP GRAZING INTENSITY

A. J. Nolan, D. J. Henderson and B. G. Merrell

Summary

1. Wet moorland plant communities account for over half of the indigenous vegetation of northern Britain. While research has been carried out on the effects of burning and grazing management on dry heather moorland, little is known about the dynamics of *Calluna* and associated species on wet moorlands.

2. Experimental plots have been established at three sites to investigate the effects of a range of sheep grazing intensities (0, 0.4, 0.8 and 1.2 sheep per ha) on wet moorlands differing in structure and species composition.

3. The preliminary results after three years' grazing on one site show that, although there is a generally positive relationship between stocking rate and utilization of *Calluna* and a negative relationship with cover of *Calluna*, the previous history and stand structure of wet heather moorlands can have an important effect on the response of *Calluna* to stocking rate changes.

15.1 Introduction

Plant communities of wet heather moorland cover much of the landscape of northern Britain and account for about one half of the indigenous vegetation resource. Although extensive research has been carried out on the effects of burning and grazing management on dry heather moorland, particularly in eastern Scotland, little is known about the vegetation dynamics of *Calluna* and associated species on wet moorlands. Unfavourable burning and grazing regimes have lead to a decline in cover of *Calluna* and replacement by grass, sedge and moss species on wet moorlands in many upland areas of Britain (Birse, 1980). Understanding the responses of these communities to different burning and reduced grazing regimes and the interactions of the component plant species is important to the future management of vegetation over large areas of western and northern Scotland and the northern

Pennines. The objectives of this research are to quantify vegetation changes in response to a range of sheep grazing intensities, and define stocking levels necessary for the maintenance and enhancement of cover of *Calluna* on a range of wet heather moorland communities. This is a necessary precursor to the development of ecologically sound management guidelines and the reconciliation of agricultural, sporting, conservation and amenity interests.

15.2 Study Sites

The work is being carried out at three sites, namely Redesdale, Northumberland, Claonaig Estate, Tarbert, Argyll and Dundonnell, Wester Ross, but only the results from the Redesdale site will be discussed here. This site was set up in the summer of 1989, on a degraded area of wet moorland on the Burnhead heft, ADAS Redesdale, Northumberland. The vegetation was dominated by *Calluna* and *Molinia*, with some *Eriophorum vaginatum* and *Vaccinium myrtillus*, having affinities with communities recognized as M15 of the National Vegetation Classification (Rodwell, 1991). Peaty gley soils predominate, with organic surface horizons generally within the range of 20–40 cm depth, overlying drift derived from Carboniferous sediments. The site chosen for study included contiguous stands of mature *Calluna* (20 years old) and *Calluna* at the pioneer phase of growth (5 years old, burned in spring 1987). The latter consisted of two distinct areas; first *Calluna* regenerating predominantly by vegetative means on a stand that had been burned at 15 years old, and second, *Calluna* recolonizing principally by seed on a stand that had been burned at 30 years old. Terminology for the phases of life-history of *Calluna* follow those of Watt (1955) and Gimmingham (1972). Experimental treatments were imposed on all three stand types.

15.3 Methods

The experimental design (common to all three sites) was based on four levels of sheep grazing including a no-grazing control and low, intermediate and high levels of grazing corresponding to 0.4, 0.8 and 1.2 sheep/ha respectively. The grazing treatments were imposed on fenced plots of 0.2 ha by stocking on six occasions per year (January, March, June, July, August and October) with groups of five ewes (including lambs during the summer grazing episodes).

Floristic measurements, using an inclined-point quadrat frame, were recorded for each plot along permanent transects in late-summer (200 pins per plot). Estimates of utilization of *Calluna* and other principal plant species present were recorded after the summer grazing period (September) and at the end of the winter grazing period (April). For *Calluna* the method of assessment of utilization by grazing adopted was that described by Grant *et al.*, (1981) and was based on the number of shoots grazed and the proportion of each shoot removed. At each recording date 100 randomly selected shoots per plot were assessed and 100 measurements of *Calluna* height were recorded concurrently. Data were also recorded from open hill areas of similar vegetation adjacent to the fenced plots. On these areas the stocking rate in place at the start of the experiment (1.8 sheep/ha) has been maintained. The data presented are interim results and all data will be statistically analyzed at the end of the experiment in 1994.

15.4 Results and Discussion

The mean percentage utilization of *Calluna* (April 1992) for the grazing treatments on the different stand types at Redesdale are presented in Figure 15.1. With the exception of the high grazing treatment on the mature heather (MH) stand, utilization levels of *Calluna* increased with increasing stocking rate. The MH plots

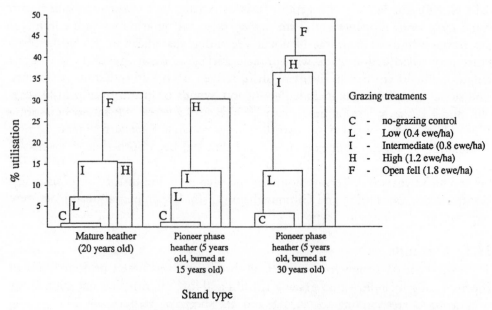

Figure 15.1. Mean % utilization of *Calluna* for grazing treatments on the different stand types, Redesdale site, April 1992.

generally showed lower levels of utilization than those on the pioneer phase heather stands subject to equivalent grazing treatments, presumably because other species were preferred to the mature *Calluna*. On the pioneer heather stand burned at 15 years old (Phb15), utilization of *Calluna* at the high stocking rate was almost 30 %. On the pioneer phase heather stand burned at 30 years old (PHb30), the plots at the intermediate and high stocking rates, and the open fell area had notably high levels of *Calluna* utilization of 36.0, 39.7 and 47.9 % respectively. These high levels of utilization were in part a reflection of initial low percentage cover values on this stand type, associated with the observation that the regeneration had been principally from seed. Utilization of *Calluna* by other herbivores (chiefly grouse, hares, small mammals and invertebrates) within the no-grazing control plots was low on all three stand types (0–3.0 %), indicating the low grazing pressure exerted by these other herbivores on *Calluna* at this site.

The mean *Calluna* heights (October 1989 and April 1992) for the grazing treatments on the different stand types at Redesdale are presented in Figure 15.2. *Calluna* height on the MH stand was little influenced by stocking rate, though on the no-grazing control, *Calluna* increased markedly in height compared with the

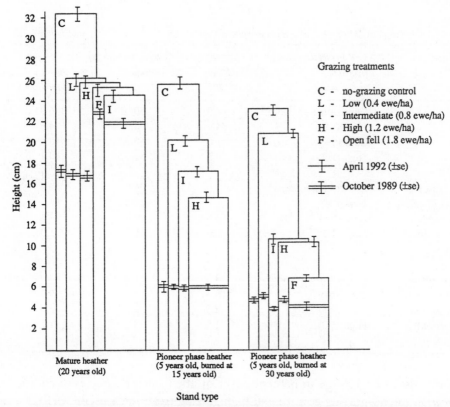

Figure 15.2. Mean *Calluna* heights for grazing treatments on the different stand types, Redesdale site, October 1989 and April 1992.

grazed plots, reflecting the lower level of utilization. On the pioneer phase heather stands (PHb15 and PHb30) there was a clear relationship between increased stocking rate and decreased height increments of *Calluna*. On these stand types the no-grazing control plots showed increases in height between 1989 and 1992 of 18 cm and 19 cm respectively. In contrast, *Calluna* on the high grazing treatments increased in height by only 8 cm and 6 cm respectively during this period.

Changes in percent cover of *Calluna* (calculated from first hits) between 1989 and 1992 are given in Table 15.1. On the MH stand there was no clear directional pattern in relation to stocking rate, reflecting the lower levels of utilization and the relative stability of this stand type. On the pioneer phase heather stands, a similar pattern to that observed for *Calluna* height increments was evident, with relatively greater increases in cover on the no-grazing control and low grazing treatments compared to the intermediate and high stocking levels. Increases in cover of *Calluna* were much greater on the plots on the PHb15 stand relative to those on the PHb30 stand, reflecting the more rapid re-establishment of *Calluna* from vegetative regeneration than seed, and the relatively high levels of utilization and low initial cover values of the intermediate and high grazing treatments on the PHb30 stand.

Table 15.1 Change in cover of *Calluna* on experimental plots at Redesdale site (in %) 1989–92

Stand type	Grazing level (sheep/ha)	Caluna cover (in %)		
		October 1989	*August 1992*	*Increase 1989–1992*
Mature	Control (no-grazing)	44.0	50.0	6.0
heather	Low (0.4)	34.0	38.5	4.5
(MH)	Inter (0.8)	41.0	60.0	19.0
	High (1.2)	40.5	51.0	10.5
Pioneer phase	Control (no-grazing)	9.0	36.0	27.0
heather (5 years	Low (0.4)	8.0	24.5	16.5
old burned at	Inter (0.8)	6.5	20.0	13.5
15 years old) (PHb15)	High (1.2)	8.0	19.0	11.0
Pioneer phase	Control (no-grazing)	4.0	11.0	7.0
heather (5 years	Low (0.4)	9.5	18.5	9.0
old burned at	Inter (0.8)	2.5	5.5	3.0
30 years old) (PHb30)	High (1.2)	1.5	3.0	1.5

Comparisons of change in percent cover of the principal species in addition to *Calluna* on the no-grazing control and high grazing treatments of the PHb15 stand between 1989 and 1992 are shown in Figure 15.3. In contrast to *Calluna*, both *Molinia caerulea* and *Carex nigra* showed a relatively greater increase in cover between 1989 and 1992 at the high grazing treatment compared with the no-grazing control, as unlike *Calluna*, they were not being grazed preferentially. A number of species also decreased in cover as this stand developed post-burning. For *Eriophorum vaginatum* and *Deschampsia flexuosa* the decrease was more marked on the no-grazing control compared to the high grazing treatment, as taller-growing species began to dominate the vegetation in the absence of sheep grazing. Decreases in cover were also recorded for *Vaccinium myrtillus*, litter and mosses between 1989 and 1992 on both the no-grazing control and high grazing plots. The floristic measurements and date from biomass samples are currently being analyzed more fully to gain a greater understanding of the changes in species composition in relation to grazing intensity.

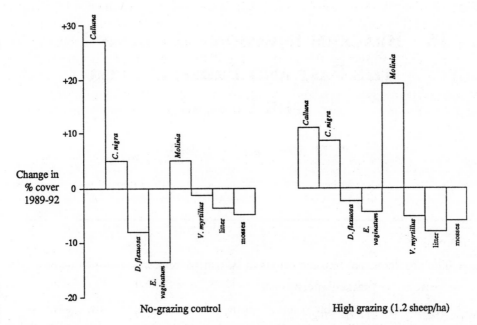

Figure 15.3. Comparison of change in % cover of principal species on no-grazing control and high grazing treatments, pioneer phase heather stand (5 years old, burned at 15 years old), Redesdale site, 1989–1992.

These preliminary results show that, although there is a generally positive relationship between stocking rate and utilization of *Calluna* and negative relationship with cover of *Calluna*, the previous history and stand structure of wet heather moorlands can have an important effect on their response to stocking rate changes. The outcome of this research will enable positive measures to be taken for the maintenance and enhancement of cover of *Calluna* on wet moorlands and the production of a species balance and vegetation structure appropriate to meet a range of land use objectives.

References

Birse, E. L. (1980). *Plant Communities of Scotland: a Preliminary Phytocoenonia*. Soil Survey of Scotland Bulletin No. 4, Macaulay Institute for Soil Research, Aberdeen. 158–172.

Gimmingham, C. H. (1972). *Ecology of Heathlands*. Chapman and Hall, London.

Grant, S. A., Hamilton, W. J. and Souter, C. (1981). The responses of heather-dominated vegetation in north-east Scotland to grazing by red deer. *Journal of Ecology* **69,** 189–204.

Rodwell, J. S. (Ed.) (1991). *British Plant Communities Volume 2: Mires and Heaths*. Cambridge University Press, Cambridge.

Watt, A. S. (1955). Bracken versus heather, a study in plant sociology. *Journal of Ecology* **43,** 490–506.

16 BRACKEN INVASION – LESSONS FROM THE PAST AND PROSPECTS FOR THE FUTURE

R. H. Marrs and R. J. Pakeman

Summary

1. The problems that bracken causes in Britain are reviewed along with some of the reasons for bracken's persistence.

2. Bracken is a remarkably resilient species which has defied many attempts at control. Some of the reasons why bracken is such a successful invasive species are discussed in relation to its growth cycle.

3. Information on the annual growth cycle of bracken has been drawn together in a computer model, which allows us to make preliminary predictions about bracken growth and spread in response to climate change and the effectiveness of bracken control treatments.

4. These predictions suggest that bracken could expand if global warming occurs and bracken control could also be more difficult.

16.1 Introduction

Bracken (*Pteridium aquilinum* (L.) Kuhn) is a fern whose sporophyte is extremely successful. It has an exceptionally large range occurring on every continent except Antarctica (Page, 1979). In the UK it is widespread particularly in Wales, western and northern England and western Scotland. Estimates of the area covered by bracken vary enormously from 2880 to 6361 km^2 or 1.3 to 2.8 % of the land area (Bunce *et al.*, 1981; Taylor, 1986). The huge discrepancy between these figures results from:

(a) problems associated in the extrapolation from local studies to the countrywide scale;

(b) difficulties of mapping bracken from aerial photographs, especially when bracken cover is low (<25 %); and

(c) deciding what is meant by bracken-covered land, since it can be present at any-thing from a few fronds per 100 m² to dense patches with no other species present.

There has also been considerable debate on how fast bracken is spreading. It is certainly perceived to be spreading into new land in many areas. Estimates for expansion rates vary between 1 and 3% per year (Miller *et al.*, 1990; Taylor, 1986; Hopkins *et al.*, 1988; Pakeman and Marrs, 1992a). Indeed one study has actually shown a decrease in the amounts of bracken in National Parks in England and Wales between the 1970s and 1980s (Countryside Commission, 1991). However, these results must be viewed with caution as there are many problems inherent in using aerial photographs for this purpose. One major difficulty is that the techniques may only detect large-scale change. Irrespective of exactly how much bracken is present it causes many problems for land managers. Financial loss to agriculture (mainly hill farms) was estimated by Lawton and Varvarigos (1989) to be £8.8 million in the Less Favoured Areas in England and Wales. Most of this loss is because of reduced grazing on bracken-infested land, but a significant amount is due to costs associated with animal welfare due to poisoning and tick-borne diseases. In forestry vigorous bracken competes with and damages young trees, although a light cover can provide shelter from wind and frost. Good forestry practice involves some degree of bracken control until the bracken is overtopped by the trees.

The effects of bracken on animal health are well documented (Evans, 1986; Taylor, 1989) with many animals suffering poisoning and even death. Sheep ticks are often found in bracken litter and these carry diseases of sheep and grouse (Hudson, 1986) and Lyme disease which affects humans (Muhlemann and Wright, 1987). There are also reports that bracken may be correlated with some human diseases: for example, risks from oesophageal cancers are increased if it is eaten (Hirayama, 1979). Carcinogenic principles from bracken can be leached into water and can be found in milk. In some areas correlations have been found between bracken incidence and higher levels of certain cancers. (Galpin *et al.*, 1990; Villalo-bos-Salazar *et al.*, 1989). However, risks to humans are considered small except where there is no bulk dairy processing in regions of high bracken infestation (Fenwick, 1989). A single experiment has also shown that bracken spores can cause cancers in mice (Evans, 1987, 1989), but this result has so far remained unsubstantiated.

From a conservation point of view bracken occurs as a member of 36 communities of the NVC (Rodwell, 1991a,b; 1992; in press), but most bracken communities are classified into one of two communities W25 *Pteridium aquilinum – Rubus fruticosus* and U20 *Pteridium aquilinum – Galium saxatile*. Some rare plants are found associated with bracken, often when the bracken acts as a surrogate tree canopy after woodland clearance. Species such as *Corydalis claviculata, Colchicum autumnale, Polygonatum multiflorum, Trientalis europaeus* and *Gladiolus illyricus* have been recorded (Pakeman and Marrs, 1992a). Bracken communities have also been reported as important for two butterfly species (High brown Fritillary – *Argynnis adippe* and Heath Fritillary – *Mellicta athalia* (Warren, 1991), species characteristic of coppice woodland. Both butterfly species use food plants (*Viola* spp. and *Melampyrum pratense* respectively) which persist under a light bracken cover. As the amount of coppice woodland has declined in recent years, there has been a corresponding decrease in the abundance of suitable food plants, and the ones that survive under bracken are extremely important for the survival of these butterflies. The Whinchat is one species of bird that appears to be positively associated with bracken (Pakeman and Marrs, 1992a). Although these conservation benefits are important locally, most bracken areas are less important from a conservation point of view than the communities which bracken replaces.

Where bracken encroaches on moorland the sporting value of an estate is reduced (Hudson and Newborn, 1989). This is partly because of reduced *Calluna* area, but tickborne infections are also a problem. From a landscape view point, however, bracken is often thought important as an autumn colour, although its dense canopy can often prevent access to walkers. Bracken can also have a large effect on hydrology, intercepting 50 % of incident rainfall, the same amount as a stand of Sitka spruce (*Picea sitchensis*) (Williams, *et al.*, 1987; Ford and Deans, 1978).

Thus, in the UK bracken is considered an important problem particularly in the uplands. This chapter reviews some aspects of the biology of bracken, concentrating on those that allow it to become a dominant plant, and identifying some of the reasons why it may continue to pose problems well into the 21st century.

16.2 Why is bracken a 'difficult weed'?

16.2.1 Bracken's origins

Bracken is thought to be a native of woodland, where it is common in glades and woodland margins. It is usually not an aggressive understorey species in this situation. Most woodland plants are adapted to survive shade, and often show saturated photosynthesis at low light intensities. Bracken, however, does not show saturated photosynthesis rates at low light intensities, and it can limit transpiration at lower levels than other ferns (Hollinger, 1987). Thus, it is ideally adapted to life outside woodland.

16.2.2 Adaptation to invasion and persistence

A successful invader species needs to be able to become established in another plant's space, perhaps replacing it completely, and then to persist by inhibiting the invasion of others.

16.2.2.1 Invasion

Bracken has two means of spread, rhizomes and spores. It is generally accepted that most bracken encroachment occurs through the invasion of rhizomes, with the rhizomes creeping out from established patches. Rates of invasion range from 1–3 m per year. If invasion only comes from vegetative means through rhizomes then the consequences are that (a) no new patches will be created, and (b) genetic change will involve only somatic mutations within established clones.

However, bracken does produce many spores, and there is limited evidence that a few spores survive in spore banks (Dyer, 1990). What is not understood is the importance of the spore-prothallus pathway in regeneration of new individuals. It is possible, though unlikely, that some new sporophytes are created within existing patches occasionally which will help to increase genetic diversity. New patches can normally only be created from spores and such occurrences are often associated with disturbances such as burning. (Oinonen, 1967). It is possible that 'guerilla' rhizomes occur, which spread out rapidly and at great distance from an existing patch, from where it can establish a distant daughter colony. However, this mechanism has not been demonstrated. It is also conceivable that physical dispersal of rhizome material could occur, although this too has not been documented.

16.2.2.2 Growth and suppression of other species

As bracken grows it can develop a dense frond canopy in the summer; frond densities of between 20–60 fronds m^{-2} with mean heights of between 1–2.5 m are not unusual. As the fronds die in the autumn a large amount of litter is added to previous accumulations (up to 8 t ha^{-1}). In very dense stands the loose litter layer can be up to 0.75 m thick on top of 10–20 cm of decaying bracken humus. The deep shade excludes many species and the deep litter layer can hinder germination and establishment.

The main part of the bracken plant occurs underground as a rhizome; rhizome mass varies but 10–20 t ha^{-1} is common (Marrs, Pakeman and Lowday, 1992). Two main types of rhizome are found – long shoots or storage rhizomes and short shoots or frond-bearing rhizomes (Thomson, 1990). The rhizomes contain large reserves of carbohydrate, nutrients and frond buds, some of which are used each spring to produce the developing fronds, As the newly emergent fronds start growing they are a drain on the rhizome carbohydrate reserves. As the fronds grow, they become self-sustaining as photosynthesis develops, and they transport carbohydrates and nutrients back to the rhizomes in the latter part of the growing season.

Bracken is very resilient to damage. There are many dormant buds on the rhizomes and some active ones that are not used in any year. Thus new fronds can always be grown to replace ones that are damaged. Moreover, all parts of the plant have many anti-herbivore defences: cyanide (Hadfield and Dyer, 1986), thiaminase (Evans, 1986), low protein content, phenolics and tannins, ecdysones (which disrupt insect development), various carcinogenic compounds and ants attracted to extra-floral nectaries (Lawton, 1976).

16.2.2.3 Persistence

Very few species can invade once dense bracken has become established because of the dense shade and deep litter, and there is some evidence that bracken produces allelopathic chemicals (Gliessman, 1976).

There are some possible exceptions where succession from dense bracken to woodland has been noted.

1. Where the bracken itself exhibits a cycle in its growth habit (Watt, 1955, 1976), and in its pioneer stage may be so reduced that other species can colonize. Such a situation is relatively rare although a good example has been described for Lakenheath Warren in Suffolk (Marrs and Hicks, 1986).

2. Where the bracken litter is disturbed by external factors. In a 88 m pathway (2 m wide) cut in dense bracken at Holme Fen near Peterborough in 1980, 76 *Betula* and 6 *Salix* established in two years, but tree regeneration was absent in uncut bracken (R. H. Marrs unpublished).

3. Invasion of *Pinus sylvestris* seedlings have been noted under relatively dense bracken at Lakenheath Warren with a mean of 2.5 seedlings m^{-2} (Marrs and Hicks, 1986). Visual inspection of the site suggested that at least some of these seedlings were becoming established adults (Marrs and Hicks, 1986).

16.2.3   *What are the constraints on bracken?*

16.2.3.1   Abiotic

The major factor affecting the altitudinal distribution of bracken is frost (Watt, 1976). Bracken is exceptionally sensitive to frost with the fronds being killed by the first autumn frosts. Where late spring frosts occur bracken fronds are often killed and sometimes even rhizomes are affected (Watt, 1976).

Soil moisture is also an important controlling factor as the rhizomes appear very sensitive to waterlogging or at least reduced soil aeration (Poel, 1951, 1961; Watt, 1976, 1979). Drainage of moorland may have contributed to the spread of bracken.

16.2.2.2   Biotic

There are three biotic factors that can potentially limit bracken growth – the presence of other vegetation, stocking type and rate, and insect herbivory.

Presence of other vegetation. The most famous example of this was provided by Watt (1955), where bracken invaded into *Calluna* only when the *Calluna* was in its pioneer and degenerate phases (competition weak) and retreated when *Calluna* was in the building and mature phases (competition strong). Resurvey of Watt's study area after almost 30 years has shown that the bracken had invaded the entire area (Marrs and Hicks, 1986). Whether this was the result of bracken invasion or *Calluna* dieback or a combination of both remains unknown.

Direct evidence for suppression of bracken by other vegetation remains mostly anecdotal. However, Marrs (1987) showed that where birch regrowth from cut stumps was suppressed by stump treatment bracken infestation was greater than untreated plots (frond biomass treated = 266 g m^{-2}; untreated 172 g m^{-2}. More recently Lowday and Marrs (1992) showed in a replicated experiment that where a grassland mix was sown (mainly *Festuca ovina* survived but the unsown *Deschampsia flexuosa* was also present) and a grass biomass of between 250–500 g m^{-2} achieved, bracken biomass was significantly lower than where grass biomass was negligible.

Stocking type and rate. It has often been suggested that the change from either cattle to sheep or from wether sheep to ewes and lambs in upland Britain has been a factor enhancing bracken expansion. This change effectively has been a reduction in the trampling pressure, which damages the fronds.

Insect herbivory. Forty insect species can feed on bracken (Lawton, 1976), yet bracken is rarely affected in the field. This is partly because of bracken's herbivore defence compounds, but also because many insects are controlled by predators and pathogens (Lawton *et al.*, 1986). When released from predation/pathogen attack the insects can have marked effects on bracken vigour. This has led to suggestions that insects which feed on bracken elsewhere could be imported into Britain as a biological control agent (Lawton, 1988; 1990).

16.3 Strategies for Bracken Control

There are three potential strategies that can be used to control bracken; each tackles a different aspect of the growth cycle of the plant or the way that biotic factors influence bracken.

16.3.1 Mechanical control – attacking rhizome carbohydrate reserves

The most effective way to tackle the rhizome system is to attack it directly through ploughing; the rhizomes are broken up and some are exposed to the action of frost (Gimingham, 1992). Usually this approach is not feasible, and an indirect approach is needed. Here the aim is to ensure a maximum withdrawal of carbohydrates and nutrients from the rhizome reserves, with the ultimate aim of complete exhaustion of rhizome reserves (Hunter, 1953; Williams and Foley, 1976). The fronds should be cut before new assimilates are translocated to the rhizomes in large amounts (late-July/early August in Britain – Williams and Foley, 1976). Cutting can be done one, two or three times annually (Braid, 1959; Williams, 1980). Biological control using either insect herbivores, micro-organisms or trampling from cattle are variants of this strategy; the intention is to inflict damage to the fronds thus depleting rhizome reserves.

16.3.2 Herbicidal control – attacking the rhizome bud reserves

Here a different approach is used. Herbicides are unlikely to have a significant direct effect on the rhizome carbohydrate reserves in the short term, so herbicides which attack these resources indirectly through killing frond buds on the rhizome are most successful. As frond production, and hence photosynthesis, is reduced rhizome reserves are lost slowly through respiration and decomposition.

Asulam (methyl(4-aminobenzenesulphonyl) carbamate) is the most widely used herbicide for bracken control; it is translocated into the rhizomes and accumulated in both active and dormant buds, where it effects a lethal action. (Veerasekaran *et al.*, 1976; 1977a,b; 1978). Asulam often gives a very good reduction in fronds in the year after spraying, but some escape and there is thereafter a rapid frond recovery unless other treatments are applied in subsequent years (Robinson, 1986).

16.3.3 Inhibition by other vegetation

As discussed previously bracken can be reduced in vigour if other vegetation is established. As the management objective in bracken control programmes is to replace the bracken with another vegetation type there is scope for using this process to reduce the rates of bracken recovery. There have been few attempts to develop this approach with post-control vegetation development being looked on as a bonus. Often vegetation development on asulam-treated areas has been poor (Pakeman and Marrs, 1992c), and even where cutting has been used it can take many years to establish dense vegetation (Lowday and Marrs, 1992). Ninnes (this volume) has observational evidence to suggest that bracken invasion may be checked if *Calluna* is burnt regularly to keep it in the building phase. Older, weaker *Calluna* allowed rapid bracken invasion.

16.4   Bracken – Prospects for the Future

It is quite apparent that a great deal is known about bracken biology and methods of control, at least in the short term (3–5 years). However, information is lacking on the ability to predict the likely outcome of bracken performance and effects of control treatments in the longer term (5–50 years). Despite our advances in knowledge about bracken control over the last 30 years, there is some evidence that bracken is still increasing (Taylor, 1986). This must also be viewed against a background of climate change; recent estimates suggest that by the year 2030 AD summer temperatures might have increased by about 1.4 °C and winter temperatures by 1.5–2.1 °C (United Kingdom Climate Change Impacts Review Group, 1991).

We have developed a computer model to predict the likely outcome of management practices on bracken under current climatic conditions, and the response of bracken to climate change. The model describes the yearly cycle of bracken in terms of daily changes in three physiological compartments (frond biomass, rhizome biomass and rhizome carbohydrate concentration) (Pakeman *et al.*, in press). The model can either be run on an individual stand basis to predict bracken performance and spread, or provide a national picture on a 40 km grid (Pakeman *et al.*, 1993). For comparisons of different climates the model is usually run to an equilibrium point to provide steady state measures of bracken biomass. Initially all of the model predictions are based at sea level. Effects of altitude can be included by introducing a lapse rate to adjust for temperature, actual:potential evaporation ratios and the length of the growing season. Tests of model predictions against field data (Pakeman *et al.*, in press; Pakeman and Marrs, in press) gave reasonable results for sites across the UK where there were published measures of bracken biomass, and for bracken control experiments in Breckland and the North York Moors.

16.4.1   Bracken performance under present climatic conditions

The model predicts greatest equilibrium biomass in the south-west and west, with the greatest values (3150 g m^{-2}) found in North Cornwall at sea level (Figure 16.1). In the south-east of England biomass was restricted by low actual:potential evaporation ratios, whereas in Wales, north England and most of Scotland biomass is

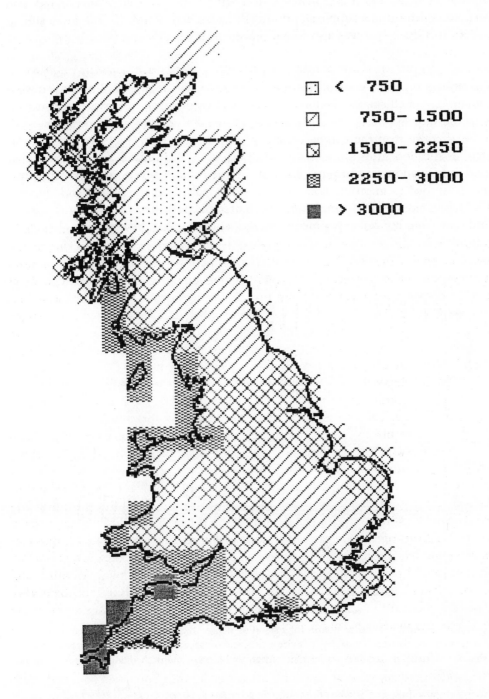

Figure 16.1. Model predictions of equilibrium biomass (g m^{-2}) throughout the UK on 1 January at sea level under present climatic conditions; predictions are based on climate for a 40 km x 40 km grid.

limited by the short growing season, largely through its interruption by frost. The smallest biomass was found in the Cairngorms with 169 g m^{-2}. Spread has also been modelled using a simple algorithm (Pakeman and Marrs, 1992b) and a similar pattern to Figure 16.1 was also found (Pakeman *et al.*, 1993).

16.4.2   *Effects of bracken control treatments under present climatic conditions*
The effects of three control treatments are shown in Figure 16.2 and contrasted with an untreated stand. The model shows that cutting once and twice per year reduce the biomass of the rhizome through time, with cutting twice per year much more effective than the cutting once per year. Cutting twice per year shows complete eradication after about six years. This is overoptimistic and suggests that more information on the physiology of bracken under severe management pressure is needed to improve model predictions. Asulam on the other hand shows a very rapid reduction in frond numbers, but rapid recovery. When tested against field data from control experiments the model reasonably predicted the results.

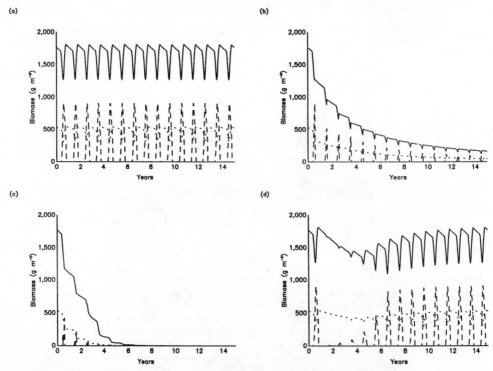

Figure 16.2. Predicted model responses for a stand of dense bracken given four different treatments; (a) untreated, (b) cut once a year, (c) cut twice a year, and (d) sprayed once with asulam. Solid lines — rhizome biomass, dotted lines — rhizome carbohydrate levels, and dashed lines — frond biomass.

16.4.3   *Bracken performance under the predicted climate of 2030 AD*
Equilibrium biomass and rates of spread in a selected number of areas for both present conditions and the predicted climates of 2030 AD are shown in

Table 16.1. There is an increase both in the amount of bracken predicted in each region and an increase in spread. The model has also been used to assess the interaction of climate change with altitude. Under present conditions the bracken equilibrium biomass in the southern Grampians appears relatively constant up to approximately 200 m, after which it declines slowly to an altitudinal limit of 340 m (Figure 16.3). In the climate of 2030 AD not only would there be an increase in the equilibrium biomass at the lower altitudes but the altitudinal limit would be increased to 550 m (Pakeman and Marrs, 1993). The greatest equilibrium biomass is predicted to be at mid-altitudes, because at lower altitudes the longer growing season afforded by increased temperatures is offset by effects of late-spring frosts. These results suggest that bracken could become a much more serious problem in the future.

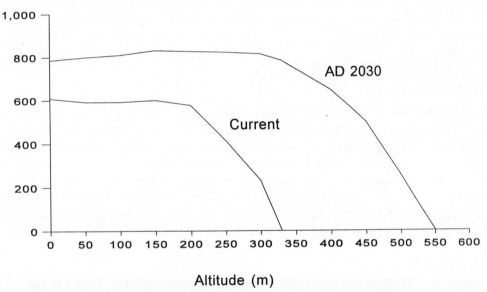

Figure 16.3. Model predictions of equilibrium biomass (g m^{-2}) with altitude under present climatic conditions and those forecast for AD 2030.

Table 16.1 Model predictions of equilibrium biomass and rates of spread derived for a range of geographical locations under current climatic conditions and under the potential climate of 2030.

Site	Equilibrium biomass (g m^{-2})		Rate of spread (m yr^{-1})	
	Current	2030	Current	2030
South Devon	2271	2830	0.59	0.83
Snowdonia	1504	1559	0.26	0.33
Southern Grampians	586	794	0.07	0.14
Scottish Borders	868	1033	0.10	0.17
Breckland	1695	1622	0.52	0.62

16.4.4 Effects of bracken control treatments in a changing climate

Running the model to simulate two bracken control treatments (applying asulam and cutting once per year) under both the present climate and that of 2030 AD for a stand in the Scottish Borders (Table 16.2) showed a slightly faster recovery to 90 % of pre-treatment conditions under the predicted climates of 2030 than under the present conditions. Whether this more rapid recovery is economically important remains to be seen.

Table 16.2 The predicted time to recovery of a bracken stand in the Scottish borders after two types of control treatment under current climatic conditions and the potential climate of 2030.

Treatment	Time to 90% recovery after treatment (yr)	
	Current conditions	*2030*
Asulam spraying (98% kill of fronds in the years after spraying)	16	15
Cutting (one cut yr^{-1}) for 3 years	33	28

16.5 Conclusions

Bracken is a successful invasive species that causes problems for many aspects of man's activities. It has the potential to spread because of changing land use practices and climate change. Even although a great deal is known about the biology and control of bracken there is still the perception that it is increasing. The aim of our work has been to try and bring together what is known about bracken into a mathematical model, which will allow us to predict the likely outcome of various climate change and management scenarios. This process has highlighted other areas where our existing knowledge needs to be improved.

References

Braid, K. W. (1959). *Bracken: A Review of the Literature*. Commonwealth Agricultural Bureaux, Hurley,

Bunce, R. G. H., Barr, C. J. and Whittaker, H. A. (1981). An integrated system of land classification. *Institute of Terrestrial Ecology Annual Report 1980*, NERC, Swindon, 28–33.

Countryside Commission (1991). *Landscape Change in the National Parks*, Countryside Commission Publications, Levenshulme,

Dyer, A. (1990). Does bracken spread by spores? In Smith, R. T. and Taylor, J. A. (Eds), *Bracken Biology and its Control*, Australian Institute of Agricultural Science Occasional Publication No. 40, Sydney, 35–42.

Evans, I. A. (1987). Bracken carcinogenicity. *International Quarterly Science Review*, **VII**, 161–199.

Evans, I. A. (1989). Bracken in the environment. In Taylor, J. A. (Ed.), *Bracken, toxicity and carcinogenicity as related to animal and human health*. Institute of Earth Studies Publication No. 44, Aberystwyth, 4–9.

Evans, W. C. (1986). The acute diseases of animals. In Smith, R. T. and Taylor, J. A. (Eds), *Bracken: Ecology, Land Use and Control Technology*, Parthenon Press, Carnforth, 121–132.

Fenwick, G. R. (1989). Bracken (*Pteridium aquilinum*) – Toxic effects and toxic constituents. Journal of the Science of Food and Agriculture, **46**, 147–73.

Ford, E. D. and Deans, J. D. (1978). The effects of canopy structure on stemflow, throughfall and interception loss in a young sitka spruce plantation. *Journal of Applied Ecology*, **15**, 905–17.

Galpin, O. P., Whitaker, C. J., Whitaker, R. and Kassab, J. Y. (1990). Gastric cancer in Gwynedd. Possible links with bracken. *British Journal of Cancer*, **61**, 737–40.

Gimingham, C. H. (1992). *The Lowland Heath Management Handbook*. English Nature, Peterborough,

Gliessman, S. R. (1976). Allelopathy in a broad spectrum of environments as illustrated by bracken. *Botanical Journal of the Linnean Society*, **73**, 95–104.

Hadfield, P. R. and Dyer, A. F. (1986). Polymorphism of cyanogenesis in British populations of bracken (*Pteridium aquilinum* (L.) Kuhn). In Smith, R. T. and Taylor, J. A. (Eds), *Bracken: Ecology, Land Use and Control Technology*, Parthenon Press, Carnforth, 293–300.

Hirayama, T. (1979). Diet and cancer. *Nutrition and Cancer*, **1**, 67–81.

Hollinger, D. Y. (1987). Photosynthesis and stomatal conductance patterns of two fern species from different forest understoreys. *Journal of Ecology*, **75**,925–35.

Hopkins, A., Wainwright, J., Murray, P. J., Bowling, P. J. and Webb, M. (1988). 1986 survey of upland grassland in England and Wales: changes in age structure and botanical composition since 1970–72 in relation to grassland management and physical features. *Grass and Forage Science*, **43**, 185–98.

Hudson, P. J. (1986). Bracken and ticks on grouse moors in the north of England. In Smith, R. T. and Taylor, J. A. (Eds), *Bracken: Ecology, Land Use and Control Technology*, Parthenon Press, Carnforth, 161–170.

Hudson, P. J. and Newborn, D. (1989). The environmental impact of bracken. *The Game Conservancy Review of 1988*. No. 20, The Game Conservancy, Fordingbridge, 117–19.

Hunter, J. G. (1953). The composition of bracken: some major- and trace-element constituents. *Journal of the Science of Food and Agriculture*, **4**, 10–20.

Lawton, J. H. (1976). The structure of the arthropod community on bracken. *Botanical Journal of the Linnean Society*, **73**, 187–216.

Lawton, J. H. (1988). Biological control of bracken in Britain: constraints and opportunities. *Philosophical Transactions of the Royal Society of London B.*, **318**, 335–55.

Lawton, J. H. (1990). Developments in the UK biological control programme for bracken. In Smith, R. T. and Taylor, J. A. (Eds), *Bracken Biology and its Control*, Australian Institute of Agricultural Science Occasional Publication No. 40, Sydney, 309–14.

Lawton, J. H., MacGarvin, M. and Heads, P. A. (1986). The ecology of bracken-feeding insects: background for a biological control programme. In Smith, R. T. and Taylor, J. A. (Eds), *Bracken: Ecology, Land Use and Control Technology*, Parthenon Press, Carnforth, 285–92.

Lawton, J. H. and Varvarigos, P. (1989). *Socio-Economic Aspects of Bracken Control*. Report submitted to the Ministry of Agriculture, Fisheries and Food. Department of Biology, University of York, York,

Lowday, J. E. and Marrs, R. H. (1992). Control of bracken and the restoration of heathland. I. Control of bracken. *Journal of Applied Ecology*, **29**, 195–203.

Marrs, R. H. (1987). Studies on the conservation of lowland *Calluna* heaths. I. Control of birch and bracken and its effect on heath vegetation. *Journal of Applied Ecology*, **24**, 163–75.

Marrs, R. H. and Hicks, M. J. (1986). Study of vegetation change at Lakenheath Warren: A re-evaluation of A. S. Watt's theories of bracken dynamics in relation to succession and vegetation management. *Journal of Applied Ecology*, **23**, 1029–46.

Marrs, R. H., Pakeman, R. J. and Lowday, J. E. (1992). Control of bracken and the restoration of heathland. V. Effects of bracken control treatments on the rhizome and its relationship with frond performance. *Journal of Applied Ecology*, **30**, 107–18.

Miller, D. R., Morrice, J. G. and Whitworth, P. L. (1990). Bracken distribution and spread in upland Scotland: an assessment using digital mapping techniques. In Smith, R. T. and Taylor, J. A. (Eds), *Bracken: Ecology, Land Use and Control Technology*, Parthenon Press, Carnforth, 121–32.

Muhlemann, M. F. and Wright, D. J. M. (1987). Emerging pattern of Lyme disease in the United Kingdom and Irish Republic. *The Lancet*, **1987 (i)**, 260–62.

Ninnes, R. B. (this volume) Bracken, Heath and Burning on the Quantock Hills, England.

Oinonen, E. (1967). Sporal regeneration of bracken (*Pteridium aquilinum* (L.) Kuhn) in Finland in the light of the dimensions and age of its clones. *Acta Forestalia Fennica*, **83**, 1–96.

Page, C. N. (1979). Experimental aspects of fern ecology. In Dyer, A. F. (Ed). *The Experimental Biology of Ferns*, Academic Press, London, 551–89.

Pakeman, R. J. and Marrs, R. H. (1992a). The conservation value of bracken *Pteridium aquilinum* (L.) Kuhn – dominated communities in the UK, and an assessment of the ecological impact of bracken expansion or its removal. *Biological Conservation*, **62**, 101–14.

Pakeman, R. J. and Marrs, R. H. (1992b). The effects of climate change on bracken and its control. *Aspects of Applied Biology*, **29**, 309–16.

Pakeman, R. J. and Marrs, R. H. (1992c). Vegetation development on moorland after control of *Pteridium aquilinum* with asulam. *Journal of Vegetation Science*, **3**, 707–10.

Pakeman, R. J. and Marrs, R. H. (1993). Potential effects of climate change on bracken and its control. In *Proceedings of Crop Protection in Northern Britain, 1993*, Association of Applied Biologists, Wellesbourne, 259–264.

Pakeman, R. J. and Marrs, R. H. (1993). Long-term recovery of bracken (*Pteridium aquilinum* (L.) Kuhn) after asulam spraying. *Annals of Applied Biology*, **122**, 519-30.

Pakeman, R. J., Marrs, R. H. and Hill, M. O. (1993). *Bracken Distribution and Management, 3 vols.* NERC report to DOE, NERC, Swindon.

Pakeman, R. J., Marrs, R. H. and Jacob, P. J. (1994). A model of bracken (*Pteridium aquilinum*) growth and the effects of control strategies and changing climate. *Journal of Applied Ecology*, **31**, 145-54.

Poel, L. W. (1951). Soil aeration in relation to *Pteridium aquilinum* (L.) Kuhn. *Journal of Ecology*, **39**, 182–91.

Poel, L. W. (1961). Soil aeration as a limiting factor in the growth of *Pteridium aquilinum* (L.) Kuhn. *Journal of Ecology*, **49**, 107–11.

Robinson, R. C. (1986). Practical herbicide use for bracken control. In Smith, R. T. and Taylor, J. A., (Eds), *Bracken: Ecology, Land Use and Control Technology*, Parthenon Press, Carnforth, 331–240.

Rodwell, J. S. (Ed.) (1991a). *British Plant Communities. Vol. 1. Woodlands and Scrub.* Cambridge University Press, Cambridge,

Rodwell, J. S. (Ed.) (1991b). *British Plant Communities. Vol. 2. Mires and Heaths.* Cambridge University Press, Cambridge,

Rodwell, J. S. (Ed.) (1992). *British Plant Communities. Vol. 3. Grasslands and Montane Communities.* Cambridge University Press, Cambridge,

Rodwell, J. S. (Ed.) in press. *British Plant Communities. Vols. 4–5).* Cambridge University Press, Cambridge.

Taylor, J. A. (1986). The bracken problem: a local hazard and global issue. In Smith, R. T. and Taylor, J. A. (Eds), *Bracken: Ecology, Land Use and Control Technology*, Parthenon Press, Carnforth, 21–42.

Taylor, J. A. (Ed.) (1989). *Bracken, Toxicity and Carcinogenicity as related to Animal and Human Health.* Institute of Earth Studies Publication No. 44, Aberystwyth,

Thomson, J. A. (1990). Bracken morphology and life cycle: preferred terminology. In Smith, R. T. and Taylor, J. A. (Eds), *Bracken Biology and its Control*, Australian Institute of Agricultural Science Occasional Publication No. 40, Sydney, 333–9.

United Kingdom Climate Change Impacts Review Group (1991). *The Potential Effects of Climate Change in the United Kingdom, First Report.* HMSO, London,

Veerasekaran, P., Kirkwood, R. C. and Fletcher, W. W. (1976). The mode of action of asulam (methyl(4-aminobenzenesulphonyl) carbamate) in bracken. *Botanical Journal of the Linnean Society*, **73**, 247–68.

Veerasekaran, P., Kirkwood, R. C. and Fletcher, W. W. (1977a). Studies on the mode of action of asulam in bracken (*Pteridium aquilinum* (L.) Kuhn). I. Absorption and translocation of ^{14}C asulam. *Weed Research*. **17**, 33–9.

Veerasekaran, P., Kirkwood, R. C. and Fletcher, W. W. (1977b). Studies on the mode of action of asulam in bracken (*Pteridium aquilinum* (L.) Kuhn). II. Biochemical activity in the rhizome buds. *Weed Research*, **17**, 85–92.

Veerasekaran, P., Kirkwood, R. C. and Fletcher, W. W. (1978). Studies on the mode of action of asulam in bracken (*Pteridium aquilinum* (L.) Kuhn). III. Long-term control of field bracken. *Weed Research*, **18**, 315–19.

Villalobos-Salazar, J., Meneses, A., Rojas, J. L., Mora, J., Porras, R. E., and Herrero, M. V. (1989). Bracken derived carcinogens as affecting animal health and human health in Costa Rica In Taylor, J. A. (Ed.), *Bracken, Toxicity and Carcinogenicity as related to Animal and Human Health.* Institute of Earth Studies Publication No. 44, Aberystwyth, 40–51.

Warren, M. S. (1991). The successful conservation of an endangered species, the heath fritillary butterfly *Mellicta athalia*, in Britain. *Biological Conservation*, **55**, 37–56.

Watt, A. S. (1955). Bracken versus heather, a study in plant sociology. *Journal of Ecology*, **43**, 490–506.

Watt, A. S. (1976). The ecological status of bracken. *Botanical Journal of the Linnean Society*, **73**, 217–39.

Watt, A. S. (1979). A note on aeration and aerenchyma in the rhizome of bracken (*Pteridium aquilinum* (L.) Kuhn var. aquilinum). *New Phytologist*, **82**, 769–76.

Williams, A. G., Kent, M., and Ternan, J. L. (1987). Quantity and quality of bracken throughfall, stemflow and litterflow in a Dartmoor catchment. *Journal of Applied Ecology*, **24**, 217–230.

Williams, G. H. (1980). *Bracken control: a review of progress, 1974–79.* (Research and Development Publication no. 12). West of Scotland Agricultural College, Auchincruive,

Williams, G. H. and Foley, A. (1976). Seasonal variations in the carbohydrate content of bracken. *Botanical Journal of the Linnean Society*, **73**, 87–94.

17 BRACKEN, HEATH AND BURNING ON THE QUANTOCK HILLS, ENGLAND

R. B. Ninnes

Summary

1. The relationship between burning and loss of dwarf-shrub heath to *Pteridium aquilinum* between 1947 and 1987 was studied on the Quantock Hills, in Somerset, Southwest England.

2. Dwarf-shrub heath was much more likely to have been lost to *Pteridium* if it was not burned between 1938 and 1987 than if it was burned at least once during that period.

3. Competitive vigour of dwarf-shrub heath under a regular burning regime appears to have outweighed the risk of *Pteridium* invasion immediately following fire.

4. The nationally rare *Ulex gallii-Agrostis curtisii* and *Calluna vulgaris-Ulex gallii* heath communities were particularly vulnerable to *Pteridium*, while other *Calluna* dominated heaths were much less so.

17.1 Introduction

Dwarf-shrub heath on the Quantock Hills appeared to be under threat from invasion by *Pteridium*. This was of concern because of the scarcity of lowland heath in Western Europe (Gimingham, 1992) and its high nature conservation priority in Britain (Nature Conservancy Council, 1989; Gimingham, 1992). This study identified the loss of dwarf-shrub heath to *Pteridium* and relates this to burning and dwarf-shrub heath type. The possible role of past grazing levels has also been assessed.

17.1.1 Burning

Fire can allow *Pteridium* to spread into dwarf-shrub vegetation, because survival of its rhizomes can enable *Pteridium* to regenerate more quickly than dwarf-shrubs (e.g. Fenton, 1949; Gimingham, 1971; Brown, 1991). However, spread of *Pteridium* has also been associated with degeneration of dwarf-shrub heath in the absence of burning (e.g. Gimingham *et al.*, 1979; Marrs *et al.*, 1986).

17.1.2   *Vegetation*

Most dwarf-shrub heath on the Quantocks was lowland in character (130 to 358 m above sea level) and can be defined by four NVC communities (Rodwell, 1991). A *Calluna* dominated, floristically impoverished *Scirpus cespitosus-Erica tetralix* wet heath occupied the poorly drained iron-pan podzols of the hilltops. *Calluna vulgaris-Vaccinium myrtillus* heath occurred on better drained mid-slopes and was most diverse on north-facing slopes. *Ulex gallii-Agrostis curtisii* heath and *Calluna vulgaris-Ulex gallii* heath were found on the most free-draining soils, either on steeper slopes, or associated with Medieval ridge and furrow cultivation.

17.1.3   *Grazing*

The study area was part of an 1800 ha grazing unit, which included some woodland and pasture. Stock numbers varied between 1947 and 1987 and have been estimated as follows: 600 to 1500 ewes (plus lambs); 9 to 50 ponies (plus foals) (Somerset County Council 1989) and 200 of the 800 to 900 strong Quantock red deer population (Winder and Chanin, 1993). The overall stocking rate was just under 1 ewe-equivalent ha^{-1}, on average, and was always less than 1.5 ha^{-1}. Most grazing was all year round. Thus, grazing has mainly been well below levels at which widespread damage to *Calluna* might be expected (e.g. 1.5–2 ewes ha^{-1} yr^{-1}, Felton and Marsden, 1989; and 2 ewes ha^{-1} yr^{-1}, Gimingham, 1992). However, grazing has not been uniformly distributed and severe over-grazing of dwarf-shrubs could be observed locally, indicating that grazing may have had a role in weakening dwarf-shrubs that were replaced by *Pteridium*.

17.2   Methods

A map of vegetation and features present in 1987 was made of the 1400 ha study area. Vegetation boundaries were traced from 1987 vertical air photos (6/5/1987, 1:10 000, false colour infra-red) on to acetate and transferred, by enlargement and local adjustment of scale, on to 1:4460 scale enlargements of Ordnance Survey maps. The vegetation boundaries and types were then verified by field survey of the whole study area.

The vegetation was categorized into the main types. Where intermediates occurred, both the dominant and sub-dominant elements of the vegetation were shown. For example, *Ulex gallii-Agrostis curtisii* heath (code 'UA') with sub-dominant *Pteridium* (code 'P') was mapped as 'UAP'. If *Pteridium* had dominated, the map code would have been 'PUA'.

Fires between 1938 and 1987 were added to the map. The boundaries and dates of these were determined from a combination of vertical air photos (23/1/1947, variable scale 1:6000 to 1:10 000, black and white; 7/9/1971, 1:12 000, black and white; 17/8/1981, 1:12 000, black and white; and 6/5/1987, as above); colour slide photos from 1960 to 1982; Forestry Commission and Fire Brigade records from 1964 to 1979; and examination of heath structure. Most of the fire dates were determined to within two years using this variety of evidence. There was good evidence of fires as far back as 1938; these were determined from the 1947 photos, using the experience of 1971, 1981 and 1987 air photo fire patterns where dates could be determined precisely from other sources. These earlier fires were included in the study, because they would have influenced heath development after 1947.

Loss of dwarf-shrubs to *Pteridium* between 1947 and 1987 was determined by comparing the 1987 vegetation map and air photos with the 1947 air photos. Areas of change were shaded on to the vegetation map. *Pteridium* was only evident as dead litter at the time of the 1947 (January) and 1987 (May) photos and, therefore, did not obscure dwarf-shrubs. This enabled very accurate mapping of dwarf-shrubs. On both sets of photos, *Pteridium* produced pale textured patterns, which showed well even in small gaps within dwarf-shrub heath; although *Pteridium* could only rarely be identified where it was scattered within dense dwarf-shrub heath. Therefore, the changes that could be observed were relatively long-term in nature, involving the complete loss, or fragmentation, of dwarf-shrub heath and its re-placement by *Pteridium*. Decline of *Pteridium* associated with increased cover of dwarf-shrubs was only recorded over 4 ha and does not feature in the analyses.

The 1947 air photos were good enough, in most cases, to confirm that dwarf-shrub heath types present in 1947 were the same as in 1987 and also to determine heath type on areas from which dwarf-shrub heath had disappeared by 1987. Colour photos from the early 1960s also showed that dwarf-shrub heath types have not changed since then.

Thus, the result of data gathering was a 1:4460 scale map of 1987 vegetation, which also showed burning between 1938 and 1987 and areas within which dwarf-shrubs had been lost to *Pteridium*. This map was sampled with randomly located points (overall density of about 3 ha^{-1}), of which 2415 were within the 771 hectares that were dominated by dwarf-shrubs in 1947. The following information was recorded for each point.

1. 1947 and 1987 vegetation types.

2. If *Pteridium* had replaced dwarf-shrub heath between 1947 and 1987. This was recorded if:

   (a) *Pteridium* was absent or sub-dominant in 1947, but had completely replaced dwarf-shrub heath by 1987, or

   (b) *Pteridium* was absent in 1947 and had partially replaced dwarf-shrub heath by 1987.

3. The distance between the sampling point and the nearest *Pteridium* in 1947.

4. The number of times the sample point was burned between 1938 and 1987 (0, 1, 2, 3, or 4 times) and the years when burning occurred.

Four sample groups were defined according to heath type, as follows: all of the dwarf-shrub dominated heath; *Ulex gallii-Agrostis curtisii* heath; *Calluna vulgaris-Ulex gallii* heath; and other *Calluna* dominated heaths. Tables were prepared for each sample group to show the proportion of samples in which dwarf-shrubs were replaced by *Pteridium*, dependent upon the amount of burning (unburned; 1 burn; and more than 1 burn) and the distance from *Pteridium* in 1947 (*Pteridium* already present; up to 4.5 m away; between 4.5–40 m away; and 40–100 m away).

17.3 Results

The proportion of samples in which dwarf-shrub heath was replaced by *Pteridium* was much greater among the unburned samples (63 % of samples) than it was among the samples which had been burned at least once (21 % of samples) (Table 17.1). Furthermore, the proportion of samples in which *Pteridium* increased was lowest among those at which heath had been burned more than once. These trends persisted regardless of the original distance from *Pteridium*.

Table 17.1 Percentages of samples (total 2145 within 771 ha) which lost dwarf-shrub heath and gained *Pteridium* (*Pt.*) between 1947 and 1987. The amount of burning refers to the period 1938 to 1987 and the metres from *Pteridium* refers to the distance between samples and the nearest *Pteridium* in 1947.

Metres from Pt.	No burning	Burned	1 burn only	Over 1 burn	Total
0	59.1	45.7	51.9	41.9	51.4
4.5	77.6	30.0	45.1	18.5	39.7
4.5–40	73.3	13.8	23.1	9.9	19.7
40–100	66.7	2.7	1.4	3.0	3.3
all	63.4	21.4	32.4	16.4	30.4

Only 11 % of *Calluna* dominated heath samples lost dwarf-shrubs to *Pteridium* (Table 17.2), compared with 29 % of *Ulex gallii-Agrostis curtisii* heath samples (Table 17.3) and 68 % of *Calluna vulgaris-Ulex gallii* heath samples (Table 17.4). The losses were consistently high among unburned samples of the latter two heath types. The proportions of samples which lost dwarf-shrubs to *Pteridium* were lowest in the burned sample groups in all situations except for *Calluna vulgaris-Ulex gallii* heath samples which already had *Pteridium* in 1947.

Table 17.2 Percentages of *Calluna vulgaris* dominated heath (H12 and M15) samples (total 1006 within 321 ha) which lost dwarf-shrubs to *Pteridium* (*Pt.*) between 1947 and 1987. Key '–' = no samples.

Metres from Pt.	No burning	Burned	1 burn only	Over 1 burn	Total
0	36.7	24.6	25.3	24.2	25.2
4.5	75.0	18.3	33.3	5.9	20.6
4.5–40	16.7	6.3	13.6	3.6	6.7
40–100	–	0.9	0.0	1.2	0.9
all	30.4	10.3	17.3	7.6	11.2

Table 17.3   Percentages of *Ulex gallii-Agrostis curtisii* heath (H4) samples (total 742 within 237 ha) which lost dwarf-shrubs to *Pteridium* (*Pt.*) between 1947 and 1987.

Metres from Pt.	No burning	Burned	1 burn only	Over 1 burn	Total
0	92.9	36.8	40.0	35.1	47.9
4.5	81.8	42.1	59.3	32.7	51.0
4.5–40	80.0	18.6	28.0	15.4	23.3
40–100	–	5.9	5.9	6.0	5.9
all	85.0	22.4	33.3	18.4	29.1

Table 17.4   Percentages of Calluna vulgaris-Ulex gallii heath (H8) samples (total 577 within 184 ha) which lost dwarf-shrubs to Pteridium (Pt.) between 1947 and 1987.

Metres from Pt.	No burning	Burned	1 burn only	Over 1 burn	Total
0	69.8	84.2	89.2	79.8	75.3
4.5	88.2	43.8	75.0	12.5	66.7
4.5–40	82.9	34.4	45.7	19.2	53.9
40–100	66.7	5.0	0.0	9.0	13.0
all	69.3	61.7	68.0	55.6	67.6

17.4   Discussion

The results suggest that heath burning may have reduced the spread of *Pteridium*, although a full exploration of this relationship through experiments would be required to verify this assertion.

The most likely explanation for the relative vulnerability of unburned heath lies in the loss of competitive vigour which occurs as dwarf-shrubs degenerate (Watt, 1955; Gimingham, 1972). In contrast, any short-term increase of *Pteridium* in response to burning appeared to be outweighed by the good recovery and longer term vigour of the dwarf-shrubs when maintained in their pioneer, building or mature phases through regular burning.

Although the risk of *Pteridium* spreading into dwarf-shrub heath was apparently reduced by burning, it was not eliminated: dwarf-shrub heath was lost from 21 % of all burned samples. This observation suggests that there is a delicate balance between short-term increase of *Pteridium* after burning and this increase being outweighed by the recovery and longer term vigour of regularly burned dwarf shrub heath.

These conclusions suggest that dwarf-shrub heath should be managed by regular burning, as commonly recommended (e.g. Department of Agriculture and Fisheries for Scotland and Nature Conservancy Council, 1977 and Scottish Natural Heritage, 1993), even if it is vulnerable to *Pteridium* spread. Marrs *et al.*, (1986) came to similar conclusions for *Calluna* heathland on the Breckland; these are to maintain it in a young and vigorous condition (building and mature phases) by a combination of burning and cutting. Specific control measures against *Pteridium*, such as herbicide treatment, may also be required where spread is taking place despite burning, or because burning is inadvisable for other reasons.

Acknowledgements

I would like to thank Alison Hester and an anonymous referee for very helpful comments on earlier drafts of this manuscript.

References

Brown, R. W. (1991). Bracken *(Pteridium aquilinum)*. Is it a Friend or Foe on the Hillside? *Annual Report of the Joseph Nickerson Reconciliation Project*, 25–29.

Department of Agriculture and Fisheries for Scotland and Nature Conservancy Council (1977). *A Guide to Good Muirburn Practice*, HMSO.

Felton, M. and Marsden, J. (1989). *Heather Regeneration in England and Wales – a Feasibility Study for the Department of the Environment*. Nature Conservancy Council, Peterborough.

Fenton, E. W. (1949). Vegetation changes in hill grazings with particular reference to heather *(Calluna vulgaris)*. *Journal of the British Grassland Society*, **4**, 95–103.

Gimingham, C. H. (1971). *Calluna* heathlands: use and conservation in the light of some ecological effects of management. In Duffey, E. A. G. and Watt, A. S. (Eds), *Scientific Management of Plant and Animal Communities for Conservation*. British Ecological Society Symposium No. 11. Blackwell, Oxford and Edinburgh, 91–103.

Gimingham, C. H. (1972). *Ecology of Heathlands*. Chapman and Hall, London.

Gimingham, C. H. (1992). *The Lowland Heathland Management Handbook*. English Nature, Peterborough.

Gimingham, C. H., Chapman, S. B. and Webb, N. R. (1979). European Heathlands. In Specht, R. I. (Ed.), *Heathlands and Related Shrublands – A. Descriptive Studies*. Elsevier, Amsterdam, 365–413.

Marrs, R. H., Hicks, M. J. and Fuller, R. M. (1986). Losses of lowland heath through succession at four sites in Breckland, East Anglia, UK. *Biological Conservation*, **36**, 19–38.

Nature Conservancy Council (1989). *Guidelines for the Selection of Sites of Special Scientific Interest*. Nature Conservancy Council, Peterborough.

Rodwell, J. S. (1991). *Plant Communities in Great Britain – Mires and Heaths*. Cambridge University Press, Cambridge.

Scottish Natural Heritage (1993). *A Muirburn Code*. Scottish Natural Heritage, Battleby.

Somerset County Council. (1989). *Quantock Hills Management Plan*. Somerset County Council, Taunton.

Watt, A. S. (1955). Bracken versus heather: a study in plant sociology. *Journal of Ecology*, **43**, 490–506.

Winder, F. and Chanin, P. (1993). Red Deer on the Quantocks – the survey's findings. *Nature in Somerset 1993*. Somerset Trust for Nature Conservation, Bridgwater, 30–34.

18 HABITAT SELECTION BY WHINCHATS: A CASE FOR BRACKEN IN THE UPLANDS?

D. S. Allen

Summary

1. Whinchats have declined in many previously occupied lowland habitats leaving the uplands as their breeding stronghold in Britain.

2. Whinchats in the uplands are associated with areas of low altitude and high bracken cover.

3. This positive association with bracken cannot be explained solely in relation to the species' selection of low altitudes.

4. The strength of this pattern and its repeatability over areas as dissimilar as the North York Moors and the eastern Highlands of Scotland should provide some balance to the almost wholly negative perception of bracken in the uplands.

5. The possible impact of widespread bracken control on important breeding populations of whinchats is considered.

18.1 Introduction

The whinchat *Saxicola rubetra* is associated historically with a wide range of habitats in both the uplands and lowlands of Britain. Declines in the lowland populations, largely a consequence of agricultural improvement (Marchant *et al.*, 1990), have left the uplands as the species' breeding stronghold in Britain. The distribution and abundance of the species in these areas is associated with several inter-related variables, corresponding most notably to low altitude and a high cover of bracken *Pteridium aquilinum* (e.g. Brown and Stillman, 1993; Tyler, 1988). Given the generally negative perception of bracken in the uplands, further examination of the relationship between whinchats and bracken is pertinent. This chapter addresses the question of whether the relationship with bracken is simply a consequence of the species' selection of low altitudes, or whether whinchats respond positively to bracken over and above their response to altitude.

18.2 Methods

Surveys of the North York Moors and eastern Highlands of Scotland (Figure 18.1), carried out by RSPB in 1983 and NCC in 1989 respectively, provide information on the distribution of whinchats and bracken in the two areas. For each area, 1 km^2 sites are classified according to the presence or absence of whinchats and bracken, and their median altitude (Table 18.1). The proportion of 1 km^2 sites containing bracken, within fixed altitudinal classes, is compared between sites where whinchats are present and absent using generalized linear modelling procedures. For each area, independently, various models reflecting different hypotheses concerning the relationship between whinchat distribution, altitude and the frequency of bracken occurrence are examined. The adequacy of the different models is assessed by a simultaneous test procedure (Aitkin *et al.*, 1989) and a model rejected

Figure 18.1. Location of survey areas.

as inadequate if its deviance (or likelihood ratio) is greater than the critical value $\chi^2_{0.15,3}=5.32$. Where more than one adequate model exists, choice between them is based upon comparisons of their respective deviances and their approximation to the raw data.

Table 18.1   The number (and proportion) of 1 km² sites, classified according to altitude and the presence/absence of whinchats (WC), that contain bracken in the North York Moors and the eastern Highlands of Scotland.

Location	Median altitude (m)	WC absent	WC present	Total
North York	110–200	2/2 (1.00)	5/5 (1.00)	7/7 (1.00)
Moors	210–300	21/40 (0.53)	15/18 (0.83)	36/58 (0.62)
	310–400	7/22 (0.32)	4/4 (1.00)	11/26 (0.42)
Eastern	190–320	2/5 (0.40)	5/7 (0.71)	7/12 (0.58)
Highlands	330–460	3/20 (0.15)	3/7 (0.43)	6/27 (0.22)
	470–600	1/12 (0.08)	1/4 (0.25)	2/16 (0.13)

18.3   Results

Several models can be defined as adequate to describe the patterns in the two regions. In the North York Moors, three models adequately represent the data (Table 18.2). The full model (model 1) can be rejected on the grounds that, even with an additional explanatory variable, it provides no better a fit than either of the two smaller models (models 2 and 3). Choice between these two is fairly subjective and based on the magnitude of their respective deviances and their approximation to the raw proportions data in Table 18.1. Thus, Model 3 is judged to best represent the North York Moors data. In the eastern Highlands, all five models are adequate and choice between them follows a similar process to that above. The altitude-only and whinchat-only models are rejected on the grounds that they provide poorer fits than Models 2 and 3 (Deviance values differ by greater than the critical value of χ^2 with 1 df, corresponding to the difference in the number of explanatory terms in the models), and the full model is similarly rejected as offering no improvement upon smaller models. Consequently, model choice is again between Models 2 and 3, but in contrast to the North York Moors data, it is Model 2 that has the smallest deviance and provides the best subjective match to the raw data.

Table 18.2   Deviances of models describing different relationships between whinchat distribution, altitude and frequency of bracken occurrence. Those models judged to provide the best fit to the two data sets are shown in bold type.

	Deviance		
Model	North York moors	Eastern Highlands	d
(1) ALT + WC + ALT.WC	3.75	0.16	2
(2) ALT + WC	4.35	**0.16**	3
(3) ALT + ALT.WC	**3.75**	0.54	3
(4) ALT	16.02	4.45	4
(5) WC	8.22	4.80	4

ALT Median altitude
WC Whinchat presence/absence
ALT.WC Interaction term

Graphical representation of the two models (Figure 18.2) aids their interpretation. In the eastern Highlands, a greater proportion of whinchat-occupied sites

(a).

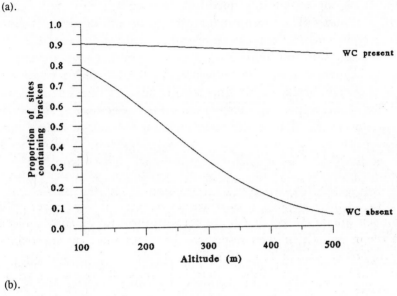

(b).

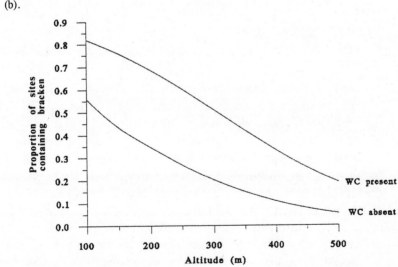

Figure 18.2. Graphical representation of models of the proportion of 1 km² sites classified according to altitude and the presence/absence of whinchats (WC), that contain bracken in (a) the North York Moors and (b) the eastern Highlands.

contain bracken than unoccupied sites across all altitudes. In contrast, only as altitude increases on the North York Moors is a difference apparent between sites with and without whinchats.

18.4   Discussion

In areas as different as the North York Moors and the eastern Highlands, a greater proportion of whinchat-occupied sites tend to contain bracken than unoccupied sites of similar altitude. Thus whinchats appear to respond positively to bracken to a degree that cannot be fully explained by reference solely to the species' preference for low altitudes. The precise nature of the pattern differs between the two areas, however, in a manner that can be related to regional differences in the overall extent of bracken. First, the altitude at which selection becomes apparent (as indicated by the degree to which lines diverge). In the North York Moors, all low altitude sites contain bracken and, consequently, areas with and without whinchats cannot differ in this respect. (Differences at a finer scale may contribute to selection at this level.) As altitude increases and bracken becomes less ubiquitous, positive selection of sites with bracken becomes increasingly clear. Second, the trend in the proportion of whinchat-occupied sites that contain bracken. In the North York Moors, bracken remains sufficiently common in the higher altitude classes to enable most whinchats to settle on sites containing bracken while in the eastern Highlands, the proportion of whinchat-occupied sites containing bracken declines in parallel with unoccupied sites due to the relative infrequency of bracken in the higher altitude classes.

The apparent generality of this association provides a contrast to the almost universally negative perception of bracken in the uplands. A recent attempt to take a balanced view of 'the bracken problem' (Pakeman and Marrs, 1992) notes the association but also reports various supposedly negative effects of bracken on upland birds. These arguments, based largely on comparisons of the number and densities of species breeding in different vegetation types are unrealistic, however, taking no account of fundamental topographic patterns of distribution. Golden plover *Charadrius apricaria*, for example, may occur at higher densities in the North York Moors on heather *Calluna vulgaris*-dominated moorland, but it does not follow that they are at risk from bracken encroachment since, unlike bracken, they are strongly associated with areas of relatively high altitude (Brown and Stillman, 1993; Haworth and Thompson, 1990). The assertion that 'many birds are lost when bracken replaces other communities' and, in particular, the implication that it is the rarer species that are most at risk from bracken expansion is unsupported.

If bracken is to be controlled on a large scale in the uplands, some estimate of the likely effects on whinchat populations should be attempted. Monitoring of areas where bracken control is currently under way is needed to assess the impact of control measures on the upland populations of a species that has declined already, not only in Britain but throughout much of Europe.

Acknowledgements

I am grateful to RSPB and JNCC for allowing me access to their survey data and to John Byrne for his advice on the analysis. Andy Brown, Rupert Ormond and Des Thompson commented helpfully on an earlier draft of the manuscript. This work was carried out whilst in receipt of a NERC-SNH CASE studentship.

References

Aitkin, M., Anderson, D., Francis, B. and Hinde, J. (1989). *Statistical Modelling in GLIM*. Clarendon Press, Oxford.

Brown, A. F. and Stillman, R. A. (1993). Bird-habitat associations in the eastern highlands of Scotland. *J. Appl. Ecol.*, **30**, 31–42.

Haworth, P. F. andd Thompson, D. B. A. (1990). Factors associated with the distribution of upland birds in the south Pennines, England. *J. Appl. Ecol.*, **27**, 562–77.

Marchant, J. H., Hudson, R., Carter, S. P. and Whittington, P. A. (1990). *Population Trends in British Breeding Birds*. British Trust for Ornithology, Tring.

Pakeman, R. J. and Marrs, R. H. (1992). The conservation value of bracken *Pteridium aquilinum* (L.) Kuhn-dominated communities in the UK, and an assessment of the ecological impact of bracken expansion or its removal. *Biological Conservation*, **62**, 101–14.

Tyler, S. J. (1988). Birds and bracken in Wales. In A Report Prepared by the Senior Technical Officers' Group, Wales. *Bracken in Wales*. Nature Conservancy Council, Bangor.

19 THE IMMINENT DESTRUCTION OF NORTHWEST EUROPEAN HEATHS DUE TO ATMOSPHERIC NITROGEN DEPOSITION

J. T. de Smidt

Summary

1. Heathland ecosystems in the lowlands of Europe are endangered by loss of their species.

2. In the major part of the geographical area of these heaths the annual atmospheric deposition is more than 15 kg nitrogen per hectare, which is beyond the ecological tolerance of most heathland species.

3. Accordingly, heath species can survive in Europe only in Galicia, in parts of the middle European mountain ranges (e.g. the Vosges, Schwarzwald, Auvergne, Appenines, west Norway), and in parts of the British Isles, particularly in Scotland.

4. This limited tolerance to nitrogen-input has become clear from empirical field observations and from fertilizer experiments in The Netherlands.

19.1 Introduction

This chapter considers aspects of the demise of north west European heaths, most notably in relation to pollution in the Netherlands.

Empirical observations of the demise of north west European heaths go back to the late 1970s, when an increase in the abundance of grass was observed in heathland. Two grass species were responsible: *Deschampsia flexuosa* in the dry heaths and *Molinia caerulea* in the wet heaths. There has been some hesitation among heathland ecologists to recognise the increased dominance by grasses as a trend rather than as a fluctuation.

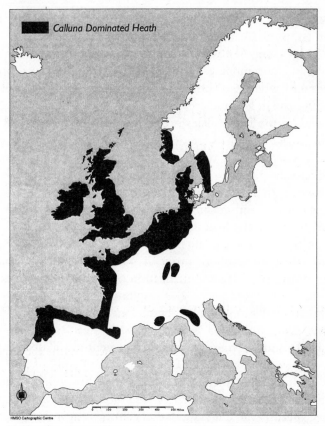

Figure 19.1. Geographical area of present-day occurrence of *Calluna*-dominated heathland.

19.2 Species changes in Netherlands heathlands: the spread of *Deschampsia*

Grasses were traditionally known in the Netherlands as temporary dominants of heathland after disturbance, such as fire, mowing or an attack by the heather beetle (*Lochmaea suturalis*) (de Smidt, 1977a). However, this dominance lasted no more than two or three years, until *Calluna vulgaris* or *Erica tetralix* regained their dominant position, and the temporary grassy aspect occurring during the pioneer phase of *Calluna* had no negative consequences for the heathland ecosystem.

Many characteristic heathland species flowered and produced seeds, thus renewing the seedbank and spreading to new locations. Amongst these are a number of relatively rare species in the lowland heath such as *Arnica montana, Antennaria dioica, Scorzonera humilis* and *Lycopodium complanatum*. These species co-existed with grasses very well, since the grasses covered no more than 20 % of the ground. The frequent heathland grasses were *Festuca tenuifolia, Sieglingia decumbens, Nardus stricta* and *Agrostis vinealis* (but not *Deschampsia* spp) (de Smidt, 1977b). These grasses rarely dominated the heaths, for they would have needed a relatively rich loamy soil and permanent suppression of the dwarf shrubs, as happens along tracks or around sheep folds. *Deschampsia* was a woodland species, growing on the raw humus and in the shaded and damp microclimate of pinewood.

In the pre-nitrogen era *Deschampsia* was a consistent member only in the *Vaccinium*-rich heathland communities. This *Vaccinio-Callunetum* is a boreal-montane heathland community where the cool and damp macroclimate resembles that of the woodland microclimate in lowland areas (e.g. Gimingham, this volume). This behaviour of *Deschampsia* in the British Isles is clearly described by Rodwell (1991). From the Midlands of England to northern Scotland it is a frequent heathland species. In the context of *Deschampsia* as an indicator of air pollution, it is interesting that Shimwell (1973) had already explained the floristic composition of the *Calluna vulgaris – Deschampsia flexuosa* heath as occurring under the combined effects of a cool and wet climate, frequent burning and grazing, and heavy atmospheric pollution around the industrial conurbations of the Midlands and northern England.

This brings us close to the explanation of the success of *Deschampsia* in Dutch heathlands. The annual atmospheric input of 40 kg nitrogen per hectare has both an acidifying and fertilizing effect. Nitrification of nitrogen-oxides and of ammonia creates pH values of 3 and lower. The resulting nitrate is an important nutrient. Such low pH values explain the loss of herbs like *Arnica montana, Antennaria dioica, Scorzonera humilis, Campanula rotundifolia, Hypochaeris radicata* and of the lycopods (van Dobben, 1991). Indeed, these species of sub-neutral soil decreased rapidly between 1970 and 1980. The weakly buffered heathland soils of the moderpodzol type easily lose their cations, calcium and potassium, through acid deposition. Below pH 3 even aluminium is released from the soil complex, thus poisoning the habitat for many species (van der Aart *et al.*, 1988). *Deschampsia*, however, can withstand such low pH values.

These findings do not explain, however, why *Deschampsia* should have reached dominance, since *Calluna* also thrives in acid conditions. Both benefit from nitrate when it is available in great quantity, so *Calluna* ought to keep its dominant position. But *Calluna* undergoes important physiological changes. The high nitrogen uptake raises considerably the nutritive value of the *Calluna* leaves for herbivores. This enables the heather beetle (*Lochmaea suturalis*) to build up a dense population much more rapidly than it did before the atmospheric deposition of nitrogen became so high (Brunsting and Heil, 1985). Indeed, the frequency of heather beetle outbreaks rose from once in ten years in the first half of the 20th century to every 3–5 years after 1970 (de Smidt, 1977a; Berdowski, 1987; Aerts and Heil, 1993). Other effects of the physiological changes resulting from nitrogen uptake are higher sensitivity to frost and to drought (Heil, 1984).

19.3 The loss of biodiversity: pre- and post-1980

Until about 1980 the damage, as described above, to the *Calluna* canopy was temporary (*Calluna* regenerated from the seed bank within a few years). In the meantime, the sub-dominant herbs, the dwarf shrubs *Genista anglica* and *Genista pilosa*, and lycopods had an opportunity to enlarge their populations. Such damaged

Calluna stands were also the best location for lichen formation: a great variety of *Cladonia* species developed rapidly in such open places.

After 1980, however, the death of *Calluna* meant virtually the end of the heathland ecosystem. Before this, *Deschampsia* had been confined to the canopy layer, unable to compete with *Calluna*. After the death of *Calluna*, *Deschampsia* was able to grow fast, produce seedlings in the surrounding areas and then close canopy before *Calluna* could regenerate. *Calluna* was then 'trapped' by its inherent, inflexible slow growth rate, whereas *Deschampsia* had flexibility – growing slowly and staying small, or growing fast and becoming tall. In the dense sward of *Deschampsia*, insufficient space was left for seedlings of dwarf shrubs, for herbs or for cryptogams.

It was not the loss of beauty that was distressing, however, for a *Deschampsia* prairie has its own beauty! In any case there is no great antipathy against *Deschampsia*, for it is an indigenous species. Rather, it was the drastic loss of the characteristic heathland ecosystem that concerned ecologists in the Netherlands. An ecosystem and a habitat for one of the most characteristic suite of species that contributes to the biodiversity of Atlantic and sub-Atlantic Europe was being lost.

Empirical evidence for the loss of many sub-dominants, in the first instance, and eventually of the total ecosystem, including insects, reptiles and birds, came from permanent plots, remote sensing and repeated vegetation surveys.

Permanent plots, that were started between 1950 and 1960, showed a decrease of cryptogams during the 1960s and 1970s and, from the mid 1970s onwards, a

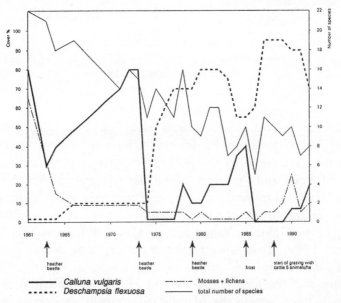

Figure 19.2. The change from *Calluna*-dominance to *Deschampsia* and the decrease of number of species in a permanent plot on the Veluwe (Netherlands). The loss of cryptogams occurred 10 years earlier than the shift to grass, both as effects of atmospheric nitrogen deposition.

dramatic increase of *Deschampsia* after damage to *Calluna* by the heather beetle or frost (Figure 19.2) (de Smidt, unpublished).

Remote sensing made it possible to make accurate estimates of the cover of heather versus grass over large areas. This showed the dramatic increase of grass cover in most heathland areas after the death of *Calluna* (Moen *et al.*, 1991).

Another opportunity to study this process was offered by a study in the 1970s of plant communities on heathlands of the Veluwe, Netherlands. Re-sampling of the same areas in 1988 showed an increase of grasses and a decrease of sub-dominants (van Ree and Meertens, 1989; de Smidt and van Ree, 1991) (Figure

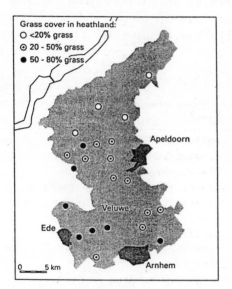
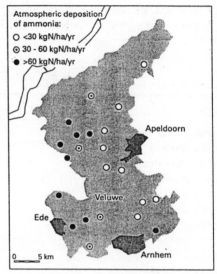

Figure 19.3. Relationship between increase in grass cover and deposition of nitrogen in the Veluwe (Van Ree and Meertens, 1989).

19.3). The decrease of the subdominants could only be recorded from the permanent plots, as they could not be detected using remote sensing. This study on the Veluwe also gave the opportunity to demonstrate the correlation between the increase of grass and the input of nitrogen (Figure 19.3). In the southern Veluwe grass increased more than in the northern part, coinciding with a higher nitrogen input in the southern part, because of intensive bio-industry (chicken, veal and pig) in the Gelderse Vallei, compared with the north and east (van Ree and Meertens, 1989). This comparative inventory also revealed that the first response of the heathland ecosystem to nitrogen input is the loss of sub-dominants, and the next is the shift to grassland. This is demonstrated in the northern Veluwe, where the increase of grass is moderate, but the cryptogams have been strongly reduced.

In twenty years between the two records, 25 cryptogams show a drastic decrease or a total loss (Table 19.1). The most common heathland mosses *Hypnum jutlandicum* and *Dicranum scoparium* are still frequently present but have suffered a strong quantitative reduction. The total cover of the moss layer was reduced from around 50–60 % to 2–10 %. Six *Cladonia* species (*C. bacillaris, C. macilenta, C. floerkeana, C. chorophaea, C. portentosa, C. coccifera*) manage to survive at low abundance. One cryptogam shows the opposite response: *Campylopus introflexus*. Since the first establishment of this Southern Hemisphere moss some twenty years ago, it spread rapidly in Dutch heathlands. Its abundance increased explosively after the rapid loss of indigenous species. It has become the most frequent species and usually covers more ground than all the other cryptogams together (see also Equihua and Usher, 1993). The effect on the vegetation of the loss of so many characteristic species is the extinction of six sub-associations out of the total of ten that had been described in 1977 (de Smidt, 1977b) (Table 19.2).

Table 19.1   Cryptogams that strongly decreased or disappeared after 1980 from heathland on the Veluwe (Van Ree and Meertens, 1989

Lichens	*Hepatics*
Cladonia uncialis	*Ptilidium ciliara*
Cladonia squamosa	*Calypogeia fissa*
Cladonia arbuscula	*Gymnocolea inflata*
Cladonia gracilis	*Lophozia ventricosa*
Cladonia glauca	*Kurzia pauciflora*
Cladonia destricta	*Odontoschisma sphagni*
Cladonia foliacea	*Cephalozia bicuspidata*
Cladonia strepsilis	*Lophocolea bidentata*
Cladonia subulata	*Barbilophozia attenuata*
Cladonia verticillata	*Barbilophozia barbata*
Cornicularia aculeata	*Scapania nemorosa*
Hypogymnia physodes	*Cephaloziella divaricata*

Table 19.2   Associations and sub-associations of dry inland heath in 1975. Six of these (*) disappeared between 1980 and 1988.

Asociation Genisto-Callunetum (G-C)	
Sub-associations	G.-C. sieglingietosum
	G.-C. typicum
	*G.-C. cladonietosum uncialis
	*G.-C. cladonietosum bacillaris
	*G.-C. lophozietosum
	*G.-C. bazzanietosum
Association Vaccinio-Callunetum (V-C)	
Sub-associations	V.-C. potentilletosum
	V.-C. typicum
	*V.-C. cladonietosum
	*V.-C. bazzanietosum

Table 19.3 Critical nitrogen loads (kg N ha^{-1}yr^{-1}) to semi-natural terrestrial vegetation (adapted from Heil and Bobbink, 1993)

	Critical load	*Indication*
Acidic (managed) coniferious forest	15–20	Changes in ground flora and fungal fruit bodies
Acidic (managed) deciduous forest	<15–20	Changes in ground flora
Calcareous forests	Unknown	Unknown
Lowland dry heathland	15–20	Transition from heather to grass
Lowland wet heathland	17–22	Transition from heather to grass
Species-rich lowland heaths/acid grassland	<20	Decline in sensitive species
Arctic and alpine heaths	<15–20	Increase in grasses
Calcareous species-rich grassland	14–25	Increase in tall grass
Neutral-acid species-rich grassland	20–30	Increase in tall grass
Montane-subalpine grassland	10–15	Increase in tall graminoids, decline in diversity
Shallow soft-water bodies	<20	Decline in isoetid species
Fens	20–35	Increase in tall graminoids, decline in diversity
Ombrotrophic bogs	10–15	Decrease in typical mosses, increase in tall graminoids

19.4   Conditions under high N levels

Some experimental evidence for high nitrogen input being the causal factor has been collected from 1981 onwards. Fertilizer experiments were carried out in the Hoorneboeg heathland reserve with a mix containing 14 % N, 16 % P and 18 % K. Lichens disappeared first, followed by the bryophytes. The more fertilizer that was applied annually, the more rapid this process became (Figure 19.4a). An unexpected observation in this experiment was the disappearance of lichens in the untreated plots between 1983 and 1988 (Figure 19.4b). This effect was ascribed to nitrogen deposition from the atmosphere. From the third to the fifth year *Deschampsia* increased explosively in the fertilized plots (Figure 19.4c). A small number of bryophytes survived, but in very low abundance, with a cover of not more than 1 %. Furthermore, some new mosses appeared in the fertilized plots (*Brachythecium rutabulum, Ceratodon purpureus, Funaria hygrometrica* and *Eurhynchium praelongum*), together with some 'weedy' angiosperms of nitrogen-rich disturbed habitats (*Agrostis stolonifera, Poa pratensis* and *Rubus fruticosus*) (Figure 19.4a,d). These data indicate that the loss of cryptogams was a direct effect of added fertilizers, and not an indirect effect because of the dense grass sward. The direct effect hypothesis is supported by the observation that lichens vanished from the fertilized plots two to three years before the grass became dominant.

19.5   Survival strategies and safe refugia

Field and laboratory experiments by Heil and Diemont (1983), Heil (1984), Heil and Bruggink (1987) and Aerts (1989) confirmed the importance of nutrients, especially

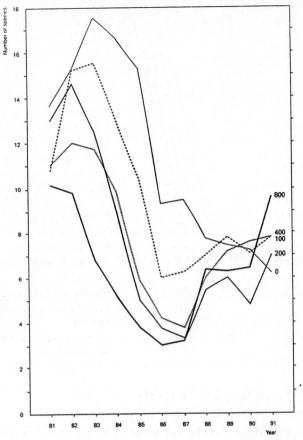

Figure 19.4a. Decrease of total number of species (mainly cryptogams) in *Calluna* heath turning into grass. Fertilized from 1981–1987 with 0, 100, 200, 400, 800 kg NPK ha^{-1}yr^{-1}).

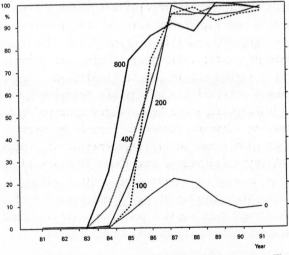

Figure 19.4b. Decrease of lichens in *Calluna* heath turning into grass (as Fig. 19.4 a) above). The reference plots (0 kg) also lost their lichens as an effect of atmospheric deposition of nitrogen, becoming manifest in those years.

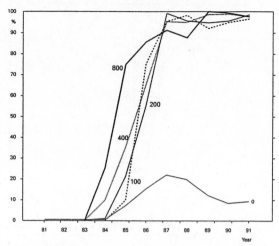

Figure 19.4c. Establishment and increase of *Deschampsia* in *Calluna* heath (as Fig. 19.4a above).

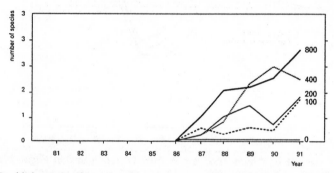

Figure 19.4d. Establishment and increase of eutraphent species in heathland after the change into Deschampsia vegetation (as Figure 19.4a above).

of nitrogen, in the shift from heathlands to grassland. Heil and Bobbink (1993) used the data of these experiments to construct a model predicting the interaction between *Calluna, Molinia, Deschampsia* and the heather beetle at different input levels of nitrogen (Figure 19.5a,b). At an input of more than 15 kg N ha^{-1} yr^{-1} *Calluna* lost its dominance. The sub-dominants disappeared as well, as demonstrated by the permanent plots.

This result contributes to a strong plea for a drastic reduction of nitrogen emissions. The loss of the heathland ecosystem is in itself already an important factor in arguments for such a reduction. But the fate of the heathland species is mirrored by a great number of other indigenous species (Heil and Bobbink, 1993). A drastic reduction of nitrogen emissions from agriculture, traffic and industry will take at least several decades. 'Survival' programmes for endangered species therefore need to be developed as a matter of urgency.

Some relief comes through land management. One can have intensified removal of accumulated nutrients by cutting and removing sods. The low nutrient levels in the underlying bare ground offer both *Calluna* and *Erica* an opportunity to regen-

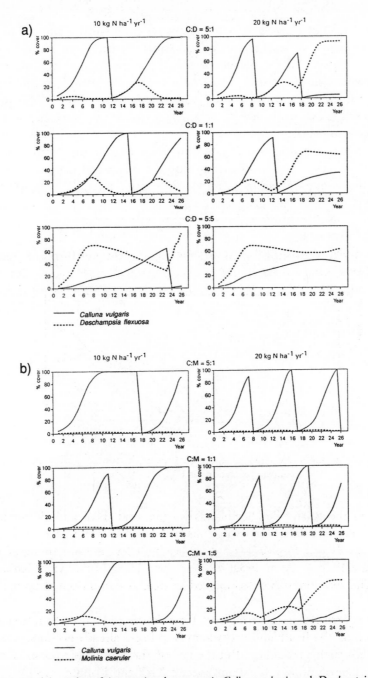

Figure 19.5. Model results of interaction between a) *Calluna vulgaris* and *Deschampsia flexuosa* at two levels of atmospheric nitrogen deposition and different initial ratios between *Calluna* (C) and *Deschampsia* (D). C:D = ratio between *Calluna* and *Deschampsia* at the beginning of the simulation. The sudden reduction of *Calluna* cover is due to stochastic heather beetle attacks. At the level of 20 kg N ha⁻¹yr¹ *Deschampsia* will always become dominant after one or two disturbance events. b) *Calluna vulgaris* and *Molina caerulea* at two levels of atmospheric nitrogen deposition and different initial ratios between *Calluna* and *Molinia* (details as in a).

erate from the seed bank, to dominate the grasses for a short while and to produce more seed. However, time seems to be too short for the cryptogams to establish and the pH is too low for the sub-dominants to return. A helpful additional means of management is cattle grazing. These large grazing animals keep the vegetation sufficiently low and open for a number of cryptogams to return. Experiments are still at too early a stage, however, to conclude for which species cattle grazing offers major opportunities for survival.

An important conclusion is that safe refugia are only found in areas with sufficiently clean air. These are on the fringes of the heathland geographical area, of which Scotland is one of the more important parts (Hetteling *et al.*, 1991, Figure 19.6).

Acknowledgements

I am grateful to the following for comments on an earlier draft of the manuscript: Dr Hilary Birks, Lynne Farrell, Dr Alison Hester, Mrs Marianne Robson and Dr Des Thompson.

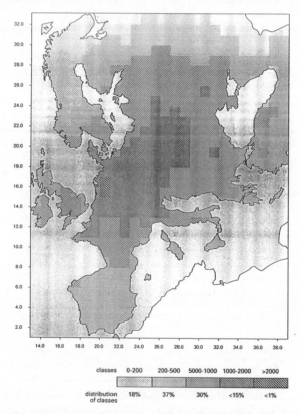

Figure 19.6. Present load computation of nitrogen (NO_x+NH_x) expressed in mol_c $ha^{-1}yr^{-1}$ mapped in five load classes. Only the load classes 0–200 and 200–500 offer safe refugia for heathland; these are found in west Norway, Scotland, west Ireland, north Spain and north Portugal (Hetteling *et al.*, 1991).

References

Aart, P. J. M. van der, Aerts, R., Bobbink, R., Dijk, H. F. G. van and Koerselman, W. (1988). Eutrophication of terrestrial ecosystems (in Dutch), *Landschap*, **5(4),** 253–69.

Aerts, R. (1989). Plant strategies and nutrient cycling in heathland ecosystems. Thesis, University of Utrecht.

Aerts, R. and Heil, G. W. (1993). *Heathlands: Patterns and processes in a changing environment.* Geobotany 20. Kluwer Academic Publishers, London.

Berdowski, J. J. M. (1987). The catastrophic death of *Calluna vulgaris* in Dutch heathlands. Thesis, University of Utrecht.

Brunsting, A. M. W. and Heil, G. W. (1985). The role of nutrients in the interaction between a herbivorous beetle and some competing plant species in heathlands. *Oikos*, **44,** 23–26.

Dobben, H. F. van (1991). Effects on heathland. In Hey, G. J. and Schneider, T. (Eds), *Acidification Research in The Netherlands, Final report of the Dutch Priority Programme on Acidification.* Elsevier, Amsterdam, 139–45.

Equihua, M. and Usher, M. B. (1993). Impact of carpets of the invasive moss *Campylopus introflexus* on *Calluna vulgaris* regeneration. *J. Ecol*, **81,** 359–65.

Gimingham, C. H. (this volume) Heaths and Moorland: an overview of ecological change.

Heil, G. W. (1984). Nutrients and the species composition of heathland. Thesis, University of Utrecht.

Heil, G. W. and Bobbink, R. (1993). Impact of atmospheric nitrogen deposition on dry heathlands. In Aerts, R. and Heil, G. W. (Eds), *Heathlands: Patterns and processes in a changing environment.* Kluwer Academic Publishers, London, 181–200.

Heil, G. W. and Bruggink, M. (1987). Competition for nutrients between *Calluna vulgaris* (L.) Hull and *Molinia carulea* (L.) Moench. *Oecologia*, **73,** 105–8.

Heil, G. W. and Diemont, H. (1983). Raised nutrient levels change heathland into grassland. *Vegetatio*, **53,** 113–20.

Hetteling, J. P., Downing, R. J. and de Smet, A. M. (1991). Mapping critical loads for Europe. CCE technical reports No. 1. RIVM Report No. 259101001.

Moen, J. P., Wel, F. J. M. van der, Smidt, J. T. de, Vels, L. L. and Harms, D. J. (1991). Monitoring van heidevergrassing met behulp van remote sensing en een geografisch informatiesysteem (HEIMON). *Delft. BCRS Rapport*, 91–12.

Ree, P. J. van and Meertens, M. H. (1989). Verarming van de Veluwse heide in relatie met ammoniak-depositie. *Provincie Gelderland.* Report No. 4688.

Rodwell, J. S. (1991) (Ed.). *British Plant Communities, Vol. 2. Mires and Heaths.* Cambridge University Press, Cambridge.

Shimwell, D. W. (1973). Man induced changes in the heathland vegetation of Central England. *Colloques Phytiosociologiques*, **2,** 58–74.

Smidt, J. T. de (1977a). Interaction of *Calluna vulgaris* and the heather beetle (*Lochmaea suturalis*). In Tüxen, R. (Ed.), *Vegetation und Fauna.* J. Cramer, Vaduz, 179–86.

Smidt, J. T. de (1977b). Heathland vegetation in the Netherlands. *Phytocoenologia*, **4(3),** 258–316.

Smidt, J. T. de and Ree, P. van (1991). The decrease of bryophytes and lichens in Dutch heathland since 1975. *Acta Bot. Neerl.* **40,** 379.

20 THE DISTRIBUTION OF HEATHER MOORLAND AND THE SENSITIVITY OF ASSOCIATED SOILS TO ACIDIFICATION

S. J. Langan, A. Lilly and B. F. L. Smith

Summary

1. The distribution of heaths and moorland in Scotland, as predicted by the Land Cover of Scotland database, is described. A regional assessment of the soils associated with these areas shows that many have a low pH and base saturation.

2. To examine the sensitivity of some of these soils to further acidification, soils sampled in the late 1950s and early 1960s were resampled in 1988. The data generally show a decrease in exchangeable calcium and base saturation and an increase in exchangeable aluminium between the two sampling periods.

20.1 Introduction

Heaths and moorland dominated by heather and other dwarf shrubs are a major component of Scotland's landscape and occupy about 40 % of the land cover, either as dominant communities or as mosaics with other vegetation types. The soils are often naturally acidic due to their nutrient poor parent material and also the moderate to high rainfall. This natural acidity is further exacerbated by anthropogenically derived acid deposition. Data from the United Kingdom Review Group on Acid Rain (1990) show that the atmospheric deposition of total non-marine sulphur is in the range from 0.5 to 1.0 keq H^+ ha^{-1} yr^{-1} for large parts of the uplands in eastern Scotland. To assess the change in soil acidity that these anthropogenic inputs may have caused, soil chemistry data of the uppermost soil horizons in areas dominated by heather moorland in northeast Scotland are presented. The soils were sampled in the 1950s and resampled in 1988.

20.2 Spatial Distribution of Soils and Heaths

In early 1989 a programme of work to develop a spatially referenced database of land cover for Scotland was begun. The land cover types were interpreted from

1:24 000 scale air photographs taken in 1988. Some of the main features that were identified were heather and dwarf shrub heath land, blanket bog and other peat land vegetation and montane vegetation (Macaulay Land Use Research Institute, 1993). The subsequent digitization of the interpreted land cover data allowed an estimate to be made of the areal extent of Heather Moorland (vegetation where *Calluna vulgaris* is a major component either in association with other dwarf shrubs or other moorland plant species) in 1988 (see Frontispiece). There is a total area of 14 480 km^2 where the vegetation is predominantly *C. vulgaris*, and a further 17 000 km^2 where heather is found in association with other moorland communities such as semi-natural grasslands.

Given the spatial distribution of land with heather moorland, it is not surprising that there is a variety of soil types associated with this vegetation, the most significant of which are the humus-iron and peaty podzols, peaty gleyed podzols, peaty gleys, basin, valley and blanket peats. Some important but less extensive soils include brown podzolic soils, subalpine podzols and alpine podzols. The majority of these soils are naturally acidic irrespective of parent material, and all, apart from the peaty gleys and peats, are leached to some degree. Data presented by Langan and Wilson (1992) suggest large areas of moorland to have soils which are dominated by acid soil horizons with a base saturation of <20 %. The distribution of these soils with a low base saturation is coincident with those soils of a low critical load for acidity reported by Langan and Wilson (1993). This is due to soils having developed on nutrient poor parent material in areas of high rainfall in which leaching is a dominant soil process. Soils with higher base saturation are concentrated in the foothills and lower slopes on the margins of agricultural land.

20.3 Soil resampling

The sites revisited were selected to encompass a range of parent material and soil types. Any site where the land-use had changed was excluded. Where the sites and soil conditions could be matched to the original soil sampling, then new soil profiles were described and sampled. The sites used in the study were originally sampled between 1957 and 1964. For these sites resampling was undertaken in the summer of 1988.

Table 20.1 summarizes the site characteristics of the nine sites used in this study. The soils have formed on a range of parent materials common in Scotland and include acid granites (Countesswells Association) through metamorphic schists of varying acidity (Foudland Association) to the more base-rich parent material of the Insch Association. The average period between sampling was 27 years although individual sites were sampled at a 33-year interval at Benaquhallie (site 3) and a 22-year interval at Peatfold (site 9). Samples collected in 1988 were air dried, and, together with the earlier 1950s and 1960s stored air-dried samples were analysed for exchangeable cations, aluminium and soil water pH. This ensured that the same techniques for the determination of the soil chemistry were used on all soils.

Table 20.1   Details of the sites resampled.

Site name	No.	Association	Parent material	Series	Major soil group	Vegetation	Sampled	Interval	Horizon
Ledmacay 2	1	Insch	Epidiorite	Invernettie	Brown forest soil	Boreal heather moor	9:64/10:88	24 years	A
Suie 2	2	Foudland	Andalusite schist	Foudland	Humus iron podzol	Boreal heather moor	3:60/9:88	28	H
Benaquhallie	3	Foudland	Schist	Foudland	Brown podzol	Boreal heather moor	10:55/10:88	33	A
Glack 1	4	Insch	Basic igneous	Insch	Brown forest soil	Boreal heather moor	12:59/9:88	29	A
Orditeach	5	Insch	Basic igneous	Bruntland	Humus iron podzol	Boreal heather moor	8:57/9:88	31	AEh
Kircram 2	6	Countesswells	Granite	Charr	Peaty podzol	Atlantic heather moor	1:64/9:88	24	Eh
Glack 2	7	Insch	Basic igneous	Bruntland	Humus iron podzol	Boreal heather moor	12:59/9:88	29	H2
Ledmacay 1	8	Insch	Basic igneous	Insch	Brown forest soil	Boreal heather moor	9:64/10:88	24	Ah
Peatfold	9	Insch	Epidiorite	Mosstown	Peaty Gley	Molinia bog	5:66/10:88	22	O

Table 20.2   Soil chemistry data between 1957 to 1964 and 1988.

Site	No.	Base Saturation (%) First	Resample	Acidity (me/100g) First	Resample	Calcium (me/100g) First	Resample	Aluminium (me/100g) First	Resample	Soil Water pH First	Resample
Ledmacay 2	1	44	14	10.56	19.89	6.37	2.13	0.21	0.6	5.04	5.1
Suie 2	2	30	3	17.19	43.04	2.92	0.38	1.01	0.34	3.63	4.11
Benaquhallie	3	8	4	12.52	20.81	0.36	0.2	0.46	0.61	4.71	4.36
Glack 1	4	59	10	14.06	18.69	16.14	1.13	0.14	0.57	5.41	4.91
Orditeach	5	17	7	11.59	34.18	1.3	1.32	0.34	0.79	4.82	4.51
Kircram 2	6	4	1	0.1	12.23	0.02	0.05	0.2	0.14	4.69	4.12
Glack 2	7	9	8	34.93	52.91	1.55	1.15	0.85	0.72	4.33	4.82
Ledmacay 1	8	17	17	16.53	22.93	1.83	3.2	0.68	0.43	4.89	5.03
Peatfold	9	56	76	3.38	2.4	3.08	5.33	0.1	0.01	4.97	5.44

Results of the changes in soil chemistry at each site are provided in Table 20.2. The soil water pH of the sites shows a variable response between sampling dates. Sites 3 to 6 exhibiting a decrease in pH, sites 2, 7 and 9 an increase and sites 1 and 8 approximately the same. It is difficult from these data to depict any trend in acidification related to either parent material, soil type or sampling period. Similarly, exchangeable aluminium lacks a consistent trend. The lowest exchangeable aluminium levels are in the gleyed soil of site 9. The largest increases in exchangeable aluminium occurred at those sites in which exchangeable acidity increased and pH was constant or fell. At sites 2, 7 and 8 where there was a rise in pH, aluminium levels decreased.

At eight of the nine sites there has been an increase in the surface horizon exchangeable acidity between the sampling dates. At site 9 there was a slight decrease in acidity. It is probably significant that this site was the only gley soil in the study. This soil was in a receiving site and probably subjected to frequent influxes of water from the more base-rich deeper mineral soil horizons which would rejuvenate the exchange complexes of the soil. Conversely, the highest acidity levels occur at sites 2, 5 and 7. Here the soils are humus iron podzols in which acidity in the upper horizons is the result of leaching of acidity from the acidic mor humus surface layer into the upper mineral horizons. To illustrate the magnitude of change in acidity between the dates, Figure 20.1 shows the acidity measured in 1988 against that of the first sample.d The data indicate the more acid soil horizons have shown a greater change (i.e. further away from the 1:1 line) than the less acid soils. Compared with the exchangeable acidity and with the exception of site 4, Calcium plays a relatively minor role in the exchange complexes of these soils. Comparison

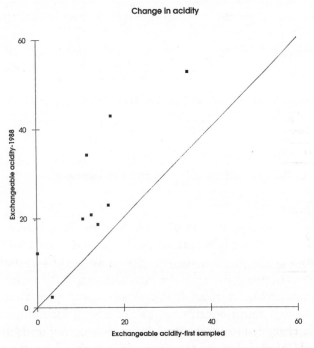

Figure 20.1. The change in surface exchangeable acidity for all sites between two sampling dates.

of the base saturation data for the two sampling dates for each site is shown in Figure 20.2. The data show that with the exception of site 9 there has been a substantial decrease in base saturation. In terms of the base saturation classes used by Langan and Wilson (1992) to identify soil sensitivity to acidification, only site 9 falls into the not sensitive class and on the basis of the resampled data all of the other sites would be classed as sensitive (i.e. <20 % base saturation). The soil

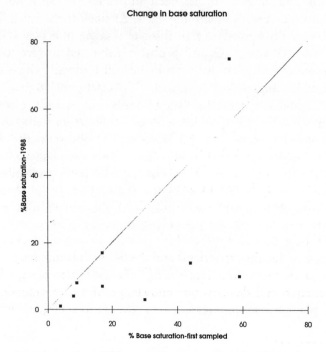

Figure 20.2. The change in surface soil horizon base saturation for all sites between two sampling dates.

developed from a granitic parent material (site 6) had the lowest measured base saturation both in the original sample and the 1988 sample.

20.4 Discussion

The soil chemical data suggests that the soils revisited have acidified over the last 20 to 30 years and that this has occurred in soils derived from a wide range of parent materials from acidic granites to base-rich epidiorites. This indicates that the removal of bases is occurring at a greater rate than supply through weathering. The only soil to show no evidence of acidification was a peaty gley where the net influx of relatively base-rich water contributes to the overall buffering capacity of the soil. This emphasizes that soil type and in particular, soil hydrology may be of equal importance in buffering acid inputs to the soils of heaths and moorlands than parent materials, particularly in the uplands where weathering rates are low. The general increase in exchangeable acidity and loss of base saturation exhibited by the other moorland soils suggests these sites will be even more sensitive to further acidification.

It is important to recognize that the changes in the soils described are highly site specific and are largely illustrative of the response of soils to acidification. The number of data presented are insufficient to permit conclusive interpretation. However, Billett *et al.*, (1990) working on a series of forest soils in the same area of northeast Scotland suggested that changes in soil chemistry, over a similar period to that reported here, were similarly characterized by decreases in pH, base cations and base saturation. Such changes were attributed to a combination of nutrient depletion caused by tree growth, natural pedogenic processes and atmospheric pollution effects. It would seem from the results of the present study that these last two processes have, in differing proportions and to differing degrees, led to the changes described for the heather moorland sites.

If further acidification occurs at the sites reported which results in the reduction of pH and associated increase of aluminium in soil solution, it is likely that the productivity of heather and other dwarf shrubs will be adversely affected. Work at Aberdeen University (Sanyi, 1989) has shown that with increasing acidification *C. vulgaris* roots show a decline in growth and productivity. Similarly the national critical load work suggests many of Scotland's soils are the recipients of acid deposition in excess of that which will induce damage to their plant communities (Langan and Wilson, 1993). It therefore seems the potential for change in the species composition of heather moorland and the Scottish landscape in future years is large. In order to monitor and manage such a change, if necessary, it is vital that we continue to research and develop our knowledge of the interaction between soil chemistry and plant community response in relation to acidification.

Acknowledgement

This work has been carried out as part of the Critical load work at MLURI under sponsorship from the Scottish Office Environment Department.

References

Billett, M. F., Parker-Jervis, F., Fitzpatrick, E. A. and Cresser, M. S. (1990). Forest soil chemical changes 1949/50 and 1987. *Journal of Soil Science*, **41**, 133–45.

Langan, S. J. and Wilson, M. J. (1992). Predicting the regional occurrence of acid surface waters in Scotland using an approach based on geology, soils and land use. *Journal of Hydrology*, **138**, 515–28.

Langan, S. J. and Wilson, M. J. (1993). The application of Skokloster critical load classes to the soils of Scotland. In Hornung, M. and Skeffington, R. A. (Eds), *Critical Loads: Concept and Applications. ITE symposium No. 28*. HMSO, London, 40–7.

Macaulay Land Use Research Institute (1993). The Land Cover of Scotland 1988: Final Report. Macaulay Land Use Research Institute, Aberdeen.

Sanyi, H. A. R. (1989). *Effects of Liming of Upland Soils on Nutrient Mobilities in Relation to Water Quality* (PhD Thesis, University of Aberdeen).

United Kingdom Review Group on Acid Rain. (1990). Acid precipitation in the United Kingdom 1986–1988. Third report of the United Kingdom Review Group on Acid Rain, Warren Spring Laboratory, Stevenage.

21 HEATHS AND MOORLAND: LONG-TERM ECOLOGICAL CHANGES, AND INTERACTIONS WITH CLIMATE AND PEOPLE

A. C. Stevenson and H. J. B. Birks

Summary

1. *Calluna vulgaris*-dominated heathlands are a ubiquitous landscape component of northwest Europe. Although heathlands dominated by *Calluna* are recorded from Tertiary times, it is only during the Holocene (last 10 000 years) that *Calluna vulgaris*-dominated heathlands have come to prominence. Prior to this, heathlands dominated by other ericaceous taxa occurred, often including taxa from, what are today, very different biogeographical provinces, e.g. *Bruckenthalia spiculifolia*, *Chamaedaphne calyculata*, *Erica mackaiana* and *Rhododendron ponticum*.

2. Studies on the origins of Holocene *Calluna vulgaris* heathlands are reviewed. There is an intimate linkage between human land-use and land management. Some evidence is presented to indicate that while fire is a common feature of heathlands once created, heathland formation has sometimes been without the aid of fire. It is suggested that the importance of grazing in heathland creation may have been underestimated.

3. Palaeoecological analyses of recent lake sediments provide some insights into the nature and causes of the widespread decline in heather moorland, a phenomenon thought to be recent. This loss has been occurring in some locations since 1500 AD. At most sites it was initiated before the advent of industrialization suggesting that changing grazing and burning strategies in the uplands may have been the prime cause for the observed reductions.

21.1 Introduction

Dwarf-shrub heaths are a characteristic feature of many parts of the world, yet it is the *Calluna vulgaris*-dominated heathlands of northwest Europe that normally evoke instant recognition. These heathlands, currently under intense pressure, with major losses through overgrazing, overburning, acid deposition and afforestation (Stevenson and Thompson, 1993), form an extensive and unique ecosystem of international importance (Thompson *et al.*, 1995). Yet, far from being natural, they are cultural landscapes: the product of thousands of years of human management by grazing, mowing and fire, providing a sustainable land-use resource for sheep (*Ovis aries*), red grouse (*Lagopus lagopus*) and red deer (*Cervus elaphus*) production (Usher and Thompson, 1993; Thompson *et al.*, 1995; Sydes and Miller, 1988).

Although heathlands dominated by *Calluna vulgaris* are a characteristic feature of northwestern Europe in the Holocene (post-glacial) this has not always been true and landscapes dominated by other ericaceous shrubs have played prominent roles in the past. This chapter reviews the history of the 'heathland formation' in northwest Europe, in particular the ecological role it has played, together with an evaluation of the possible causes of change at the time scales of the late Tertiary and Quaternary and of the recent past.

Terminology of late Tertiary and Quaternary stages follows Jones and Keen (1993) except that the international term Holocene is used in preference to the British term 'Flandrian' to refer to the last 10 000 years of Earth's History.

21.2 Late Tertiary and Quaternary History

21.2.1 *Pliocene*

Fragmentary but tantalizing evidence of heathlands during the late Tertiary can be seen from a number of sites across Europe but unfortunately our knowledge is often hampered by poor taxonomic and stratigraphic resolution. Analyses of Reuverian lignite deposits in Holland (Zagwijn, 1960) and estuarine clays and silts in Normandy (Elhaï, 1963; Roger and Freneix, 1946) suggest that Ericales-dominated heathlands were locally present.

In the British Isles a late Miocene/early Pliocene deposit at Hollymount, Eire (Boulter, 1980; Hayes, 1978) contains ericaceous pollen, together with pollen derived from a mixed deciduous woodland of oak and pine and significant quantities of exotic taxa like *Taxodium, Tsuga, Symplocos, Sciadopitys, Liquidambar* and Palmae. Andrew and West's (1977) analysis of the late Pliocene Coralline Crag deposits at Orford, East Anglia contains *Empetrum* and *Bruckenthalia spiculifolia* pollen. The pollen assemblages may derive from a range of lowland eutrophic and oligotrophic mires dominated by *Pinus, Sequoia* and *Taxodium* whereas the surrounding slopes may have supported taxa of better drained sites such as *Picea, Tsuga, Betula, Ulmus, Quercus, Liquidambar, Pterocarya, Platycarya* and *Ilex*.

Oldfield's work (Oldfield, 1968; Huckerby and Oldfield, 1976) on the cliff deposits around Biarritz, southwest France give us the first detailed record of the nature of heathlands at the Pliocene/Lower Pleistocene boundary. At Bidart Plage, pollen and macrofossil evidence from a relict heathland soil (Oldfield, 1968; Huckerby and Oldfield, 1976) show the first records of substantial amounts of *Calluna* pollen in association with a predominantly euoceanic flora of *Erica tetralix,*

E. scoparia, E. mackaiana, E. ciliaris and *E. vagans* in a landscape otherwise dominated by *Pinus, Alnus, Pterocarya, Tsuga, Sequoia* and *Sciadopitys.*

21.2.2   Pleistocene

Early Pleistocene environments (e.g. the Ludhamian and Antian temperate stages) were characterized by a warm-temperate woodland of *Pinus, Tsuga, Picea, Ulmus* and *Quercus* together with a significant contribution from *Empetrum* and other ericaceous dwarf shrubs (Figure 21.1a, West, 1980a). Unlike later cold phases in the Quaternary where the advent of widespread glaciation prevented vegetation development across most of northwestern Europe (West, 1961; West, 1980a, 1980b; Figure 21b–d), the contribution of *Empetrum*- and Ericaceae-dominated heath increases dramatically during the succeeding cold stages (Thurnian and Baventian — Figure 21.1a). Since pollen analysts have not always distinguished the different pollen types within the Ericaceae and Empetraceae a composite curve reflecting inputs from taxa from both these sources is depicted on Figure 21.1a–d. Later pollen and macrofossil work demonstrates that *Empetrum* was a major component of these early Pleistocene heathland communities.

With the onset of major glaciations in northern Europe, heathlands (chiefly *Empetrum*-dominated) were most frequent in the initial warming (the so-called protocratic phase) and final cooling stages (the so-called cryocratic phase) of interglacials (Birks, 1986). During these temperate stages they became localized spatially and temporally, only occurring where topographic conditions allowed mire development or where inevitable pedogenic processes led to leached and podsolized soils (oligocratic stage — Birks, 1986) (Figure 21.1). Glimpses of their ecological nature can be seen from peat deposits at Beeston (West, 1980b) where pollen analyses of the oligocratic phase of the late-Pastonian stage reveal a rich ericaceous flora, including the euoceanic taxa *Calluna, Erica umbellata* and *Erica lusitanica, Bruckenthalia spiculifolia* (restricted to the Balkans at present) and the boreal/circumpolar species *Chamaedaphne calyculata* in association with *Vaccinium, Eriophorum* and *Sphagnum.*

The occurrence of heathland vegetation in the early protocratic phase of interglacials persisted through the middle Pleistocene temperate stages, e.g. the *Empetrum* phases from the early protocratic phases of the Cromerian at Sidestrand (West, 1980b) and Bacton (Duigan, 1963; Figure 21.1c). The development of species-rich heathland communities during the late oligocratic phase also continued, as exemplified by sites in Ireland e.g. Gort, Kilbeg, Baggotstown, Kildromin — Jessen *et al.,* 1959; Watts, 1959, 1964, 1967) where the late Gortian (=Hoxnian stage) heathlands were dominated by *Rhododendron ponticum* communities together with *Bruckenthalia spiculifolia* and many other euoceanic/Lusitanian taxa such as *Daboecia cantabrica, Erica scoparia, E. mackaiana* and *E. ciliaris. Calluna vulgaris* was present but not abundant. This development of late Hoxnian, species-rich, ericaceous floras is a common characteristic across much of western Europe (Oldfield, 1968; Huckerby and Oldfield, 1976 — Marbella; Murr, 1926 — Höttingen; Depape and Bourdier, 1952 — southern France) but strikingly it does not feature in many of

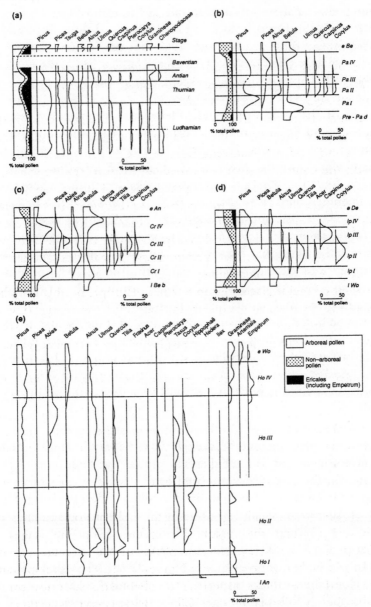

Figure 21.1. Generalized pollen diagrams for the UK from various Pleistocene cold and warm stages (a) Ludhamian, Thurnian, Antian, Baventian (b) Pastonian, (c) Cromerian, (d) Hoxnian, (e) Ipswichian. (Adapted from West, 1980a).

the extensive Hoxnian and Ipswichian stage deposits in East Anglia where only an *Empetrum* heath developed (Turner, 1970).

Similar developments of heathlands are seen during the Ipswichian interglacial stage, where for only the second time in the Quaternary appreciable quantities of

Calluna pollen are found. These developed during the *Carpinus*-dominated phase, as shown from pollen analyses of a peat raft at Hutton Henry, County Durham (Beaumont *et al.*, 1969). Deposits at Fulga Ness, Shetland thought by some to date to the Hoxnian stage (Birks and Ransom, 1969) but now thought by others to date to the Ipswichian stage (Hall *et al.*, 1993), reveal a similar heathland composition to many of the Irish Hoxnian deposits, except that *Bruckenthalia* appears to play a more prominent role.

The richness of these early and middle Pleistocene heathlands is interesting not only because it might point to markedly different climate conditions, but also because of the unusual juxtaposition of many heathland taxa derived from what are now different biogeographical provinces. Ecologically *Bruckenthalia* is a plant of the sub-alpine zone (1250–2500 m) of southeastern Europe today where it forms extensive communities with *Vaccinium vitis-idaea*, *V. myrtillus*, *Arctostaphylos uva-ursi*, *Juniperus communis* ssp. *nana* and *Deschampsia flexuosa* (Birks and Peglar, 1979). Birks and Peglar (1979) showed that *Bruckenthalia* is heavily underrepresented in modern pollen spectra and suggest that *Bruckenthalia* percentages of 1–5 % are likely to indicate the presence of extensive local populations. Turrill (1929) proposes that in the Balkans *Bruckenthalia* is an ecological counterpart of *Calluna* occurring in similar habitats; a range of acid humus-rich soils on both well-drained and waterlogged sites. It should be noted that in many early studies of interglacial deposits the pollen and seeds of *Bruckenthalia spiculifolia* were misidentified as *Frangula/Rhamnus* and *Erica scoparia* var. *macrosperma*, respectively (Birks and Peglar, 1979). It is likely that *Bruckenthalia spiculifolia* may have been one of the dominant ericaceous dwarf-shrubs in northwest Europe prior to the mid-Devensian (last glacial) stage.

21.2.3 Holocene

Compared with the preceding interglacial/glacial cycles the nature of the heathland formation takes on a new and ubiquitous role in the Holocene of northwest Europe. However, the *Empetrum*-dominated heathlands of the cryocratic and protocratic phases of temperate stages continue to play a widespread and major role in the late-glacial Alleröd interstadial 12 000 and 11 000 years ago in the UK, northwest Ireland and southern and western Scandinavia. The succeeding Younger Dryas stadial period (11 000–10 000 years ago) resulted in some contraction of abundance and range but on the resumption of climate warming at the beginning of the early Holocene further expansion in the abundance of *Empetrum* occurred. This was subsequently followed by a generally northward displacement of its range during the early and mid Holocene (Huntley and Birks, 1983).

The major difference between previous temperate stages and the Holocene is, however, the widespread and dominant role played by *Calluna vulgaris* in the heathland formations of northwestern Europe. The origin of these heathlands has been the subject of controversy (Faegri, 1940; Jonassen, 1959; Dimbleby, 1962; Odgaard, 1988) and for a long time they were regarded as a natural climax vegetation (Odgaard, 1988). European isopoll maps of *Calluna* (Huntley and Birks, 1983) show that its expansion was a delayed phenomenon. Early occurrences, about

10 000 years ago, are recorded in most oceanic, western areas of Europe where local topographic conditions may have favoured the development of heathland and mire communities into which *Calluna* expanded e.g. Outer Hebrides (Little Loch Roag – Birks and Madsen, 1979; Loch Airigh na h-Aon Oidche, South Uist – Edwards *et al.*, this volume), Loch of Winless, northeastern Scotland (Peglar, 1979), and southwestern France (La Moura – Oldfield, 1964). *Calluna* did not really rise to prominence until about 6000 BP with its expansion of range into much of northwestern Europe (Netherlands, Belgium, northern France, northern Germany, and southwestern Scandinavia) and the Central Scottish Highlands, Cheviots, and North and South Pennines in the UK to dominate most of the geologically infertile uplands and creating extensive heathland by about 4000 BP. Further range expansion and consolidation took place subsequently, especially on the poor sandy soils of the lowlands of the UK, Netherlands and western Germany.

The pioneering work of Faegri (1940), Iversen (1941, 1949) and Jonassen (1950) showed conclusively that many *Calluna*-dominated heathlands were derived from areas that once supported woodland. The initial expansion of *Calluna* around 6000 BP is thought by some (e.g. Huntley and Birks, 1983) to be either the result of progressive soil deterioration or changes in oceanicity across Europe. Human influence is discounted because of the lack of any widespread and unambiguous evidence for forest clearance at this time although Behre (1988) presents evidence for the creation of heaths by Neolithic cultures. Similar pedogenic/climate explanations were originally advanced for the later conversion of forest to heathland in West Jutland (Jonassen, 1950) and upland areas around Sheffield (Conway, 1947) at the Sub-Boreal/Sub-Atlantic boundary (2500 BP). This is a period thought by many at that time to be a period of major climate change (Blytt, 1876; Sernander, 1910) and Jonassen invoked this climatic shift as the mechanism that led to farm abandonment, thereby favouring the subsequent spread of *Calluna vulgaris*. The key to understanding the mechanisms which aided the spread of *Calluna* lies in a detailed examination of the causes and timing of the conversion of forest to heath. Although a climatic explanation for the *Calluna* spread was initially favoured, this changed to the recognition of a direct link between human land-use and heathland creation as more and more data from across western Europe demonstrated that the expansion of *Calluna* was a diachronous phenomenon (e.g. Kaland, 1986; Odgaard, 1988; Dimbleby, 1962). Moreover, not only did the expansion not appear to correlate with periods of known climate change (Kaland, 1986) but palaeoecological evidence showed that its spread was intimately linked with many pastoral pollen indicators and with charcoal, indicating the occurrence of prehistoric fires (e.g. Kaland, 1986; Odgaard, 1988; Dimbleby, 1962; Caseldine and Hatton, 1993).

21.2.4 The role of fire

The use of fire is often a major element in the management and maintenance of heathlands (Hobbs and Gimingham, 1987), although some heather stands are known to have survived for at least 60–70 years without having been subject to fire and are still vigorous as a result of *Calluna*'s ability to root adventitiously into the mor humus (MacDonald *et al.*, 1994). However, the use of fire in the original creation of heathland landscapes is more problematical. It is generally assumed that fire played an essential role in the initial creation of heathlands with small-scale clearances (Landnam episodes — Iversen, 1941, 1964, 1969) creating small open areas into which heather expanded after abandonment of management. However, the palaeoecological evidence is somewhat equivocal. Some studies, mostly derived from lakes, demonstrate that *Calluna* pollen began to expand at roughly the same time as microscopic charcoal becomes frequent in the lake sediment record (Odgaard, 1988, 1992; Kaland, 1986; Edwards and Rowntree, 1980; Caseldine and Hatton, 1993). The elegant work of Odgaard (1992) in his detailed studies of the origins of the West Jutland heathlands demonstrates (Figure 21.2), using multivariate analyses of the pollen and charcoal data, the close agreement between the creation and subsequent maintenance of local heathland and increased fire frequency.

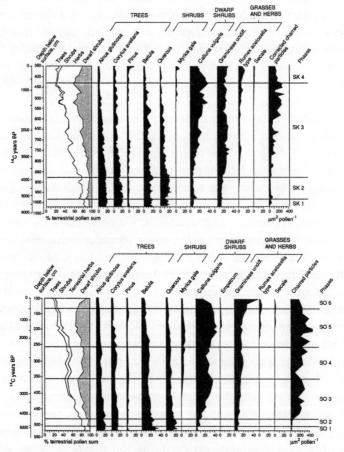

Figure 21.2. Pollen diagrams from two lakes in West Jutland, Denmark, — Lake Skansø and Lake Solsø (Adapted from Odgaard, 1992).

Studies of heathland creation from *in situ* analyses of mor humus profiles (Dimbleby, 1962) are, however, at variance with the presumed role of fire in the initial creation of heathland. It is interesting to note that little evidence of charcoal, as a proxy indicator for fire, is presented by Dimbleby in his original contribution to this subject (Dimbleby, 1962). The classic studies by Iversen (1964, 1969) on mor humus profiles from Draved Forest in Jutland clearly show the transition from forest to heath at 700 AD is marked by charcoal. However, only one profile (Iversen, 1969) is sampled at a high enough temporal resolution to show that fires were occurring contemporaneously with the loss of forest and the rise of heather. Some mor humus profiles show, however, that forest was converted to heathland without the aid of fire. Figure 21.3 is a pollen and charcoal diagram from a mor humus profile sampled from underneath a *Calluna* stand on Trochry Moor, Perthshire that has not been burnt for at least the last 60–90 years. The upper part of the diagram clearly demonstrates that until burning ceased at this particular site in the 1920s, fire was being regularly used as a management tool but *only* after the site was dominated by heather. The creation of the heathland appears to have gone through three phases: (1) The original *Betula/Corylus* woodland with a fern-dominated understorey began to lose the fern component as grasses and a small amount of *Calluna* and Salix took over. (2) Grasses came to dominate the site but *Calluna* pollen values remained low. (3) The site finally began to see a loss of *Betula* and *Corylus* as *Calluna* pollen values increased dramatically along with *Potentilla*-type. It is striking that the initial creation of the heather moorland from its original progenitor *Betula/Corylus* woodland does not indicate any use of fire. This suggests that grazing intensity may have had a more important role to play than has hitherto been assumed, according well with the earlier views of Ellenberg (1954) and Pearsall (1934) on the importance of grazing in woodland destruction and heathland creation. This ambivalent evidence for the role of fire in heathland creation could result not only from the diverse nature of heathlands creation but also the different dispersal, sedimentation, preservation and other taphonomic processes by which pollen and charcoal in lake basins and mor-humus profiles record the environment at differing temporal and spatial scales.

Interestingly, there are elements in some northwestern European heathlands that bear some resemblance to the species-rich, oceanic heathlands of the Hoxnian and Ipswichian stages and are mainly restricted to the Atlantic areas of southwestern Ireland, southwest France, northwest Spain and western Portugal. These heathlands contain many ericaceous species, known as 'the Lusitanian flora', that were found in Hoxnian and Ipswichian deposits in western Europe (Mitchell and Watts, 1970). However, some elements of this flora do not appear to fit in with the accepted history of these taxa. For instance, Webb (1983) considered that unlike the disjunct distribution of many of the Lusitanian elements of the Irish flora, that of *Erica erigena* has long remained an anomaly because of its high susceptibility to frost, the lack of adequate refugial explanations and the absence of any fossils of the taxon in palaeoecological analyses within its present areas of distribution in Ireland. The modern-day distribution of *E. erigena* is western Ireland, Bordeaux and

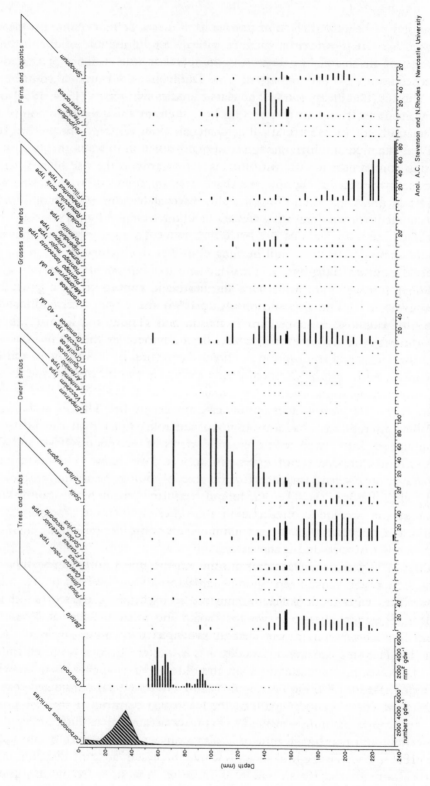

Figure 21.3. A mor-humus pollen, charcoal and carbonaceous particle profile from Trochry Hill, Perthshire.

Anal. A.C. Stevenson and N.Rhodes - Newcastle University

Iberia (Foss *et al.*, 1987). Foss and Doyle (1990) conducted detailed studies on the blanket mires of Connemara where *E. erigena* is locally abundant. Using a combination og pollen analysis together with the novel application of scanning electron microscopy to fossil pollen material (Foss and Doyle, 1988) and radiocarbon dating they showed that *E. erigena* only appears in the pollen record at about AD 1431–1480, in association with many pollen indicators of disturbance. Possible explanations for the observed patterns include poor flowering accounting for the absence of any long-term pollen record or recent seed dispersal on birds' feet as a possible mechanism for the arrival of *E. erigena* in Ireland. Foss and Doyle (1990) propose, however, that the appearance of *Erica erigena* in Connemara was linked to the establishment of trade routes with Galicia in northwest Spain and the subsequent transport of pilgrims, wine and goods, where heather, including *E. erigena* was often used as a bedding and packaging material.

21.3 Recent Changes

Although it is well known that heather moorland has been slowly declining across northwestern Europe (Thompson *et al.*, 1995) the timing, trends and possible causes of this loss are uncertain. Stevenson and Thompson (1993) attempted to test a number of hypotheses that have been advanced to explain this decline: (1) afforestation (e.g. Thompson *et al.*, 1988) (2) grazing in sub-montane areas combined with burning (e.g. Thompson *et al.*, 1995); (3) atmospheric pollution e.g. soot deposition (Chambers *et al.*, 1979); (4) acid deposition (Thompson and Baddeley, 1991; Lee *et al.*, 1989; Roelofs, 1986) and (5) climate change, e.g. 'Little Ice Age'. Previous attempts to evaluate these hypotheses have involved either short-term manipulative and observational studies on moorland (Hobbs and Gimingham, 1987; Grant and Maxwell, 1986; Grant *et al.*, 1985; Welch, 1984) or mid-term analyses of remotely sensed imagery (including aerial photographs) (Bunce, 1989; Sydes and Miller, 1988; NCC/CCS, 1988; Anderson and Yalden, 1981). However, none of these can provide a long-term (i.e. >100 years) perspective in the timing and spatio-temporal dynamics of vegetation change (Birks, 1988; Miles, 1988).

A number of well-dated, high-resolution pollen profiles, covering at a maximum the last 1000 years, are available from the western uplands of the UK and Ireland (Figure 21.4 – Stevenson and Thompson, 1993). All the sites, except one, are headwater lakes with small pollen catchments and whose pollen record is likely to reflect vegetation change within the catchment (Jacobson and Bradshaw, 1981). Only the *Calluna*/Gramineae pollen ratio is depicted in Figure 21.4 since these two taxa dominate the pollen sum at each site (about 50–90 %) throughout the period of study. Tree pollen was at a minimum (about 5–10 % in all cores). A full discussion of these data is given by Stevenson and Thompson (1993) and is not repeated here. However, a number of interesting features of the data are briefly explored.

The *Calluna*:Gramineae ratio varies considerably over the timespan covered by the cores. At a number of sites *Calluna* expands, relative to Gramineae, until the mid-1800s (Llyn Clyd, Llyn Dulyn, Loch Tanna, Loch Skerrow, Lough Muck). It is unclear what mechanisms could have promoted *Calluna* at this time but changing

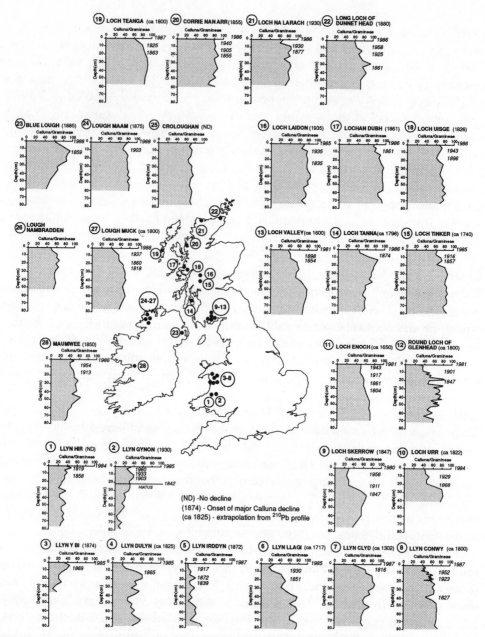

Figure 21.4. Location map of the study sites together with the *Calluna*: Gramineae pollen ratio for each site. Studies that have examined the relationship between *Calluna* abundance and *Calluna* pollen deposition have found it to be linear (Moore, Evans and Chater 1986). The Gramineae record represents the main acid, upland grass species *viz. Molinia caerulea, Agrostis stolonifera, A. canina, Festuca* spp. and *Nardus stricta*. The date, in parentheses, by the lake name gives an approximation of when the *Calluna* decline commenced. In some lakes, dates prior to the commencement of the ^{210}Pb record have had to be estimated by extrapolation of the ^{210}Pb record. In two lakes (Lough Nambradden and Croloughan) there are no dates available. (From Stevenson and Thompson, 1993 by permission of Edward Arnold.)

practices in upland grazing, especially the widespread use of cattle rather than sheep in the 17th and early 18th centuries, and consequent changes in the proportion of flowering shoots grazed, may have been important (Smout, 1994 personal communication). In addition, changing muirburn frequencies and intensities may have had a significant effect.

A feature of the more recent data is a widespread decline in the relative abundance of *Calluna* pollen over the last 150–200 years in about 90 % of the catchments studied. The majority of sites (68 %), mostly located in Wales and Galloway, show a >10 % reduction in *Calluna* pollen abundance compared with Gramineae pollen. A further 25 %, mostly located in northwest Scotland and Ireland, show a smaller (<10 %) decline in *Calluna* pollen abundance. In a small number of lakes there is no evidence of any reductions in *Calluna* pollen abundance. When the temporal pattern of the *Calluna* decline is examined a clear spatial pattern in the timing of change is evident. The earliest declines, prior to 1750 AD, occur in north Wales and Galloway, increasing by 1800 to two further sites in north Wales (Llyn Llagi) and Galloway (Round Loch of Glenhead) together with additional sites on Arran (Loch Tanna), South Uist (Loch Teanga) and Ireland (Lough Muck). From 1800–1850 additional Galloway and north Welsh sites show declines, together with Loch Uisge, Strontian. From 1850–1900 most of the other lakes, except for a site in south Wales and two sites in central and north-west Scotland, show *Calluna* pollen declines.

This complex spatio-temporal response of individual catchments, especially with most change post-dating the 'Little Ice Age' (about 1500–1800; Grove, 1988), casts doubt upon the hypothesis that recent climate change could have been responsible for the patterns seen. Moreover, although afforestation and acidic deposition may be currently having an important effect (Sydes and Miller, 1988; Roelofs, 1986), *Calluna* declines were already occurring well before the advent of afforestation and acidic deposition. Stevenson and Thompson (1993) observed that the spatio-temporal patterns of *Calluna* pollen declines across the UK and Ireland well match changes in grazing histories. The earliest declines were recorded in areas that had been subject to intensive grazing from medieval times (e.g. Wales and southwest Scotland), in contrast to areas in northwest Scotland and Ireland where sheep and deer grazing pressures have been lower until more recently. Some doubt must exist as to whether the decline in *Calluna* pollen reflects a significant population reduction or whether it reflects intense grazing reducing the flowering and hence pollen production of *Calluna*. However, since the declines in *Calluna* pollen over the last 50–60 years mirror observed changes in the abundance of *Calluna* across the UK (Thompson *et al.*, 1995), it is likely that the declines in the *Calluna*:Gramineae pollen ratio are a real reflection of actual changes in the abundance of *Calluna* within the catchments of the lakes studied.

An immediate challenge is to explain why the rates of apparent loss of *Calluna* vary so much between regions as well as between decades. Comparative catchment studies could provide some of the answers, not least in providing us with snapshots of how landscapes and habitats must have appeared over the past 600 years.

Moreover, a number of important questions still need to be resolved, especially about the role of burning in upland management. Given that the advent of widespread muirburn in Scotland was not associated with the coming of sheep, as is commonly thought, but was a consistent feature of landscapes way back into 'pre-improver' times (C. Smout, personal communication; Mather, 1993), it is essential to identify the effects of changing muirburn frequencies on vegetation. To this end a programme of work is now addressing this problem by examining in detail the charcoal and vegetation records of these study sites to identify trends.

21.4 Conclusions

It appears that the heathland formation has been a temporally intermittent but characteristic feature of northwest European landscapes for at least the last 20 million years. Although the heathland formations of northwestern Europe are currently dominated by *Calluna vulgaris*, it is clear that *Calluna* pollen is rare in all interglacial stages except for the Holocene. It is likely that in many of the temperate stages of the Pleistocene, the dwarf-shrub heaths of northwestern Europe were dominated by species such as *Bruckenthalia spiculifolia*, *Daboecia cantabrica* and *Erica mackaiana*. Why *Calluna vulgaris* was apparently so rare during the bulk of the 1–2 million years of the Quaternary until the last 9000 years is a complete mystery in our understanding of the palaeoecology of northwest Europe. Despite our inability to resolve this problem, it is clear from the palaeoecological record of the recent past that *Calluna vulgaris* appears to be declining in many upland areas. The geographical extent and magnitude of this decline are matters of grave concern for all concerned with the conservation and management of the uplands. Palaeoecology can provide a long-term perspective on the timing and rates of this decline.

References

Anderson, P. and Yalden, D. W. (1981). Increased sheep numbers and the loss of heather moorland in the Peak District, England. *Biological Conservation*, **20**, 195–213.

Andrew, R. and West, R. G. (1977). Pollen spectra from Pliocene Crag at Orford, Suffolk. *New Phytologist*, **78**, 709–14.

Beaumont, P., Turner, J. and Ward, P. F. (1969). An Ipswichian peat raft in glacial till at Hutton Henry, Co. Durham. *New Phytologist*, **68**, 797–805.

Behre, K. E. (1988). The role of man in European vegetation history. In Huntley, B. and Webb III, T. (Eds), *Vegetation History*. Kluwer, Dordrecht, 633–72.

Birks, H. J. B. (1986). Late-Quaternary biotic changes in terrestrial and lacustrine environments, with particular reference to north-west Europe. In Berglund, B. E. (Ed.) *Handbook of Holocene Palaeoecology and Palaeohydrology*. John Wiley, Chichester, 3–65.

Birks, H. J. B. (1988). Long-term ecological change in the British uplands. In Usher, M. B. and Thompson, D. B. A. (Eds) *Ecological Change in the Uplands*. Blackwell, Oxford, 37–56.

Birks, H. J. B. and Madsen, B. J. (1979). Flandrian vegetational history of Little Loch Roag, Isle of Lewis, Scotland. *Journal of Ecology*, **67**, 825–42.

Birks, H. J. B. and Peglar, S. M. (1979). Interglacial pollen spectra from Sel Ayre, Shetland. *New Phytologist*, **83**, 559–75.

Birks, H. J. B. and Ransom, M. E. (1969). An interglacial peat at Fulga Ness, Shetland. *New Phytologist*, **68**, 777–96.

Blytt, A. (1876). *Essay on the Immigration of the Norwegian Flora during Alternating Rainy and Dry Periods.* Christiania, Alb. Cammermeyer. 89pp.

Boulter, M. C. (1980) Irish Tertiary plant fossils in a European context, *Journal of Earth Sciences – Royal Dublin Society,* **3,** 1–11.

Bunce, R. H. G. (Ed.) (1989). *Heather in England and Wales.* HMSO, London, 40

Caseldine, C. and Hatton, J. 1993. The development of high moorland on Dartmoor: fire and the influence of mesolithic activity on vegetation change. In Chambers, F. M. (Ed.), *Climate Change and Human Impact on the Landscape.* Chapman and Hall, London, 119–32.

Chambers, F. M., Dresser, P. Q. and Smith, A. G. (1979). Radiocarbon dating evidence on the impact of atmospheric pollution on upland peats. *Nature,* **282,** 829–32.

Conway, V. M. (1947). Ringinglow Bog near Sheffield. Part 1. Historical. *Journal of Ecology,* **34,** 149–81.

Depape, G. and Bourdier, F. R. (1952). La Flore interglaciare à *Rhododendron ponticum* L. de Barraux dans la vallée de l'Isère entre Grenoble et Chambery. *Compte Rendue de l'Acadamie des Sciences, Paris,* **235,** 1531–00.

Dimbleby, G. W. (1962). *The Development of British Heathlands and their Soils.* Clarendon Press, Oxford.

Duigan, S. (1962). Pollen analyses of the Cromer Forest Bed Series in East Anglia. *Philosophical Transactions of the Royal Society of London,* B **246,** 149–202.

Edwards, K. J. and Rowntree, K. M. (1980). Radiocarbon and palaeoenvironmental evidence for changing rates of erosion at a Flandrian stage site in Scotland. In Cullingford, R. A., Davidson, D. A. and Lewin, J. (Eds), *Timescales in Geomorphology.* John Wiley, Chichester. 207–23.

Edwards, K. J., Whittington, G. and Hirons, K. (this volume). The relationship between fire and long-term heathland development in South Uist, Outer Hebrides.

Elhaï, H. 1963. *La Normandie Occidentale.* Bière: Bordeaux.

Ellenberg, H. 1954. Steppenheide und Waldweide. *Erdkunde,* **8,** 188–94.

Faegri, K. 1940. Quartärgeologische Untersuchungen im Westlichen Norwegen. II Zur Spätquartären Geschichte Jaerens. *Bergens Mus. jab. Natur,* **7,** 1–201.

Foss, P. J., Doyle, G. J. and Nelson, E. C. (1987). The distribution of *Erica erigena* R. Ross in Ireland. *Watsonia,* **16,** 311–26.

Foss, P. J. and Doyle, G. J. (1988). A palynological study of the Irish Ericaceae and *Empetrum, Pollen et Spores,* **30,** 151–78.

Foss, P. J. and Doyle, G. J. (1990). The history of *Erica erigena* R. Ross. an Irish plant with a disjunct European distribution. *Journal of Quaternary Science,* **5,** 1–16.

Grant, S. A., Bolton, G. R. and Torvell, L. (1985). The responses of blanket bog vegetation to controlled grazing by hill sheep. *Journal of Applied Ecology,* **22,** 739–51.

Grant, S. A. and Maxwell, T. J. (1988). Hill vegetation and grazing by domesticated herbivores: the biology and definition of management options. In Usher, M. B. and Thompson, D. B. A. (Eds), *Ecological Change in the Uplands.* Blackwell, Oxford, 201–214.

Grove, J. M. (1988). *The Little Ice Age.* Methuen, London, 498.

Hall, A. M., Whittington, G. and Gordon, J. E. (1993). Interglacial peat at Fulga Ness, Shetland. In Birnie, J., Gordon, J., Bennett, K. and Hall, A. *The Quaternary of Shetland: A Field Guide.* Quaternary Research Association, London, 62–76.

Hayes, F. L. (1978). *Palynological Studies in the South East United States, Bermuda and Southeast Ireland.* (Unpublished MSc thesis, Trinity College, Dublin.)

Hobbs, R. J. and Gimingham, C. H. (1987). Vegetation, fire and herbivore interactions in heathland. *Advances in Ecological Research,* **16,** 87–173.

Huckerby, E. and Oldfield, F. (1976). The Quaternary vegetational history of the French Pays Basque. *New Phytologist,* **77,** 499–526.

Huntley, B. and Birks, H. J. B. (1983). *An Atlas of Past and Present Pollen Maps for Europe: 0–13,000 years ago.* Cambridge University Press, Cambridge, 667.

Iversen, J. (1941). Landnam i Danmarks Stenalder. *Danmarks Geologiske Undersögelse,* II **66,** 1–67.

Iversen, J. (1949). The influence of prehistoric man on vegetation. Danmarks Geologiske Undersögelse, IV 6, 1–25.

Iversen, J. (1964). Retrogressive vegetation succession in the post-glacial. *Journal of Ecology* (supplement), **52,** 59–70.

Iversen, J. (1969). Retrogressive development of a forest ecosystem demonstrated by pollen diagrams from fossil mor. *Oikos,* **12,** (suppl.), 35–49.

Jacobson, G. J. and Bradshaw, R. H. W. (1981). The selection of sites for palaeovegetational studies. *Quaternary Research* **16,** 80–96.

Jones, R. L. and Keen, D. H. (1993). *Pleistocene Environments in the British Isles.* Chapman and Hall, London.

Jessen, K., Andersen, S. T. and Farrington, A. (1959). The Interglacial deposit near Gort, Co. Galway, Ireland. *Proceedings of the Royal Irish Academy,* **60,** B, 3–77.

Jonassen, H. (1950). Recent pollen sedimentation and Jutland heath diagrams. *Dansk. Botanisk. Arkiv,* **13,** 1–168.

Kaland, P. E. (1986). The origin and management of Norwegian coastal heaths as reflected by pollen analysis. In Behre, K. E. (Ed.), *Anthropogenic Indicators in Pollen Diagrams.* Balkema, Rotterdam, 19–36.

Lee, J. A., Tallis, J. H. and Woodin, S. J. (1988). Acid deposition and upland vegetation. In Usher, M. B. and Thompson, D. B. A. (Eds), *Ecological Change in the Uplands.* Blackwell, Oxford, 151–64.

MacDonald, A. J., Kirkpatrick, A. H., Hester, A. J. and Sydes, C. (1994). Regeneration by layering of heather (*Calluna vulgaris*): frequency and characteristics in upland Britain. *Journal of Applied Ecology,* 000–000.

Mather, A. M. (1993). The environmental impact of sheep farming in the Scottish Highlands. In Smouth, T. C. (Ed.), *Scotland Since Prehistory: Natural Change and Human Impact.* Scottish Cultural Press, Aberdeen.

Miles, J. (1988). Vegetation and soil change in the uplands. In Usher, M. B. and Thompson, D. B. A. (Eds), *Ecological Change in the Uplands.* Blackwell, Oxford, 57–70.

Mitchell, G. F. and Watts, W. A. (1970). The History of the Ericaceae in Ireland during the Quaternary Epoch. In Walker, D. and West, R. G. (Eds), *Studies in the Vegetation History of the British Isles.* Cambridge University Press, Cambridge, 13–21.

Moore, P. D., Evans, A. T. and Chater, M. (1986). Palynology and stratigraphic evidence for hydrological changes in mires associated with human activity. In Behre, K. E. (Ed.), *Anthropogenic Indicators in Pollen Diagrams.* Balkema, Rotterdam, 209–20.

Murr, J. (1926). Neue Übersicht über die fossile Flore der Höttinger Breccie. *Jahrb. de. Geolog. Bundesanstalt,* **76,** 153.

NCC/CCS (1988). *National Countryside Monitoring Scheme, Scotland, Grampian.* Battleby, Perth, Countryside Commission for Scotland and Nature Conservancy Council.

Odgaard, B. (1988). Heathland history in western Jutland, Denmark. In Birks, H. H., Birks, H. J. B., Kaland, P. E. and Moe, D. (Eds), *The Cultural Landscape: Past, Present and Future.* Cambridge University Press, Cambridge, 311–19.

Odgaard, B. (1992). The fire history of Danish heathland areas as reflected by pollen and charred particles in lake sediments. *The Holocene,* **2,** 218–26.

Oldfield, F. (1964). Late-Quaternary deposits at Le Moura, Biarritz, southwest France. *New Phytologist,* **63,** 374–409.

Oldfield, F. (1968). The Quaternary vegetational history of the French Pays Basque. I. Stratigraphy and pollen analysis. *New Phytologist,* **67,** 677–731.

Pearsall, W. H. (1934). Woodland destruction in Northern Britain. *Naturalist,* 25–28.

Peglar, S. M. (1979). A radiocarbon-dated pollen diagram from Loch of Winless, Caithness, North-east Scotland. *New Phytologist,* **82,** 245–63.

Roelofs, J. G. M. (1986). The effect of airborne sulphur and nitrogen deposition on aquatic and terrestrial heathland vegetation. *Experientia,* **42,** 372–77.

Roger, J. and Freneix, S. (1946). Remarques sur les Faunes de Foraminiféres du Redonien. *Bulletin Societé Géologique France,* Series 5, **16,** 103–33.

Sernander, R. (1910). *Die Schwedischen Torfmoore als Zeugen postglazialer Klimaschwankungen. Veränderungen des Klimas seit dem Maximum der letzten Eiszeit.* II Internationaler Geologenkongress, Stockholm.

Stevenson, A. C. and Thompson, D. B. A. (1993). Long-term changes in the extent of heather moorland in upland Britain and Ireland: palaeoecological evidence for the importance of grazing. The Holocene, **3,** 70–6.

Sydes, C. and Miller, G. R. (1988). Range management and nature conservation in the British uplands. In Usher, M. B. and Thompson, D. B. A. (Eds), *Ecological Change in the Uplands*. Blackwell, Oxford, 323–37.

Thompson, D. B. A. and Baddeley, J. (1991). Some effects of acidic deposition on montane *Racomitrium lanuginosum* heaths. In Woodin, S. and Farmer, A. (Eds), *The Effects of Acid Deposition on Nature Conservation in Great Britain*. Nature Conservancy Council, Peterborough, 17–28.

Thompson, D. B. A., Macdonald, A. J., Marsden, J. H. and Galbraith, C. (1995). Upland heather moorland: a review of international importance, vegetation change and some objectives for nature conservation. *Biological Conservation*, **71**, in press.

Thompson, D. B. A., Stroud, D. A. and Pienkowski, M. W. (1988). Afforestation and upland birds: consequences for population ecology. In Usher, M. B. and Thompson, D. B. A. (Eds), *Ecological Change in the Uplands*. Blackwell, Oxford, 237–60.

Turner, C. (1970). The middle Pleistocene deposits at Marks Tey, Essex. *Philosophical Transactions of the Royal Society of London*, **257**, B, 373–440.

Turrill, W. (1929). *The Plant Life of the Balkan Peninsula*. Oxford University Press, Oxford.

Usher, M. B. and Thompson, D. B. A. (1993). Variation in the upland heathlands of Great Britain: Conservation importance. *Biological Conservation*, **66**, 69–81.

Watts, W. A. (1959). Interglacial deposits at Kilbeg and Newtown, Co. Waterford. *Proceedings of the Royal Irish Academy*, **60**, B, 79–134.

Watts, W. A. (1964). Interglacial deposits at Baggotstown, near Bruff, Co. Limerick. *Proceedings of the Royal Irish Academy*, **63**, B, 167–89.

Watts, W. A. (1967). Interglacial deposits at Kildromin Townland, near Herbertstown, Co. Limerick. *Proceedings of the Royal Irish Academy*, **65**, B, 339–48.

Webb, D. A. (1983). The flora of Ireland in its European context. The Boyle Medal Discourse. *Journal of Life Sciences, Royal Dublin Society*, **4**, 143–60.

Welch, D. (198)4. Studies in the grazing of heather moorland in north-east Scotland. II. Response of heather. *Journal of Applied Ecology*, **21**, 197–207.

West, R. G. (1961). Vegetational history of the early Pleistocene of the Royal Society borehole at Ludham, Norfolk. *Proceedings of the Royal Society of London B*, **155**, 437–53.

West, R. G. (1980a). *The Pre-Glacial Pleistocene of the Norfolk and Suffolk Coasts*. Cambridge University Press, Cambridge, 203.

West, R. G. (1980b). Pleistocene Forest History in East Anglia. *New Phytologist*, **85**, 571–622.

Zagwijn, W. H. (1960). Aspects of the Pliocene and early Pleistocene vegetation in the Netherlands. *Med. Geol. Stichting*, **C, III**, No. 5.

22 THE RELATIONSHIP BETWEEN FIRE AND LONG-TERM WET HEATH DEVELOPMENT IN SOUTH UIST, OUTER HEBRIDES, SCOTLAND

K. J. Edwards, G. Whittington and K. R. Hirons

Summary

1. The long-term development of heathlands and fire incidence in the Outer Hebridean island of South Uist is examined using the techniques of pollen and microscopic charcoal analysis.

2. *Calluna* is a prominent element in the vegetation from a date of 9740 BP at one site, but, as elsewhere, this was possibly preceded by *Empetrum* heath.

3. Fire was a possible agent in heathland spread and the charcoal record may reflect the intentional management of some coastal and upland heaths during Mesolithic and later times.

22.1 Introduction

There is extensive literature on the relationship between *Calluna*-dominated plant communities and the place of fire in their evolution (e.g. Gimingham, 1972; Legg *et al.*, 1992; Stevenson and Thompson, 1993). Palaeoecological studies of long-term vegetation change make frequent mention of the possible impact of fire, deliberate or otherwise, upon the formation of heaths and moorland, and especially in connection with the spread of blanket peats (e.g. Kaland, 1986; Simmons and Innes, 1987). The investigation pursued here focuses on two main points: the antiquity of heathland in a part of the Outer Hebrides and the rôle of fire in its development.

The term heathland is applied here to *Calluna*-rich or *Calluna*-dominated plant assemblages which may be found upon a variety of substrates, including sand, organic soils of low base status and peat. Pollen and microscopic charcoal are used to provide surrogate evidence for changes in vegetation and fire incidence; the strengths and weaknesses of both indicators have been extensively aired elsewhere (Faegri and Iversen, 1989; Patterson *et al.*, 1987).

22.2 Study Area and Methods

The evidence from a west–east transect of sites has produced a record of changing vegetational landscapes for the various landform units in South Uist, coast, blackland/machair and upland (Figure 22.1):

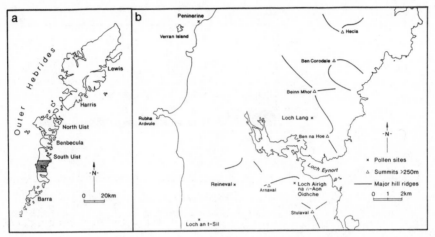

Figure 22.1. (a) The Outer Hebrides with the study area in South Uist shaded. (b) The South Uist study sites.

Peninerine.	An inter-tidal site (O.S. grid reference NF 737 353) located upon a rock-cut platform close to Verran Island.
Loch an t-Sil.	An infilled kettle-hole site (NF 736 235) lying about 0.5 km east of the 'machair' (calcareous shell sand plain) edge, on the 'blackland' (peaty, often cultivated land) and at an altitude of <10 m OD.
Reineval.	A lochan (NF 759 257) located 3.1 km east of the coast in the centre of a largely peat-filled basin and close to the upland edge at an altitude of about 30 m OD.
Loch Airigh na h-Aon Oidhche.	A rock basin loch (NF 796 257) lying at an altitude of 105 m OD in the eastern upland of South Uist.

A peat monolith was recovered from Peninerine and a Russian corer (Jowsey, 1966) was used to sample the other sites. Standard laboratory pretreatments were employed (Faegri and Iversen, 1989).

22.3 Results

Selected bio- and litho-stratigraphic data are presented in Figures 22.2–22.5. Pollen and spore taxa are presented as a percentage of total land pollen and microscopic charcoal is expressed in terms of area accumulation per ^{14}C year. The vertical axis

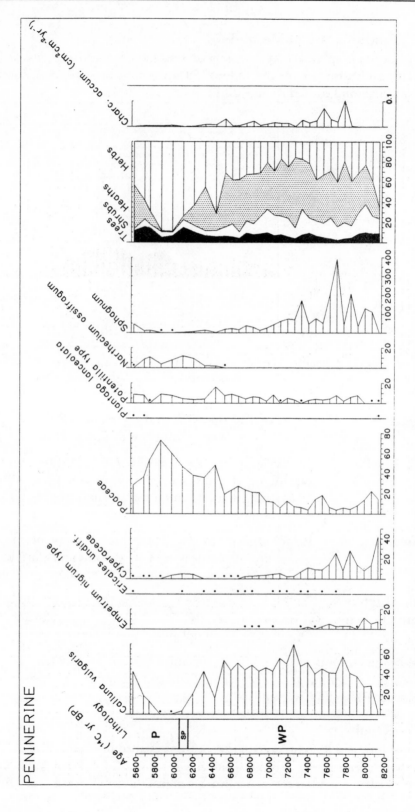

Figure 22.2. Selected pollen, spore and charcoal data from Peninerine. Lithology: P, peat; SP, sandy peat; WP, wood peat.

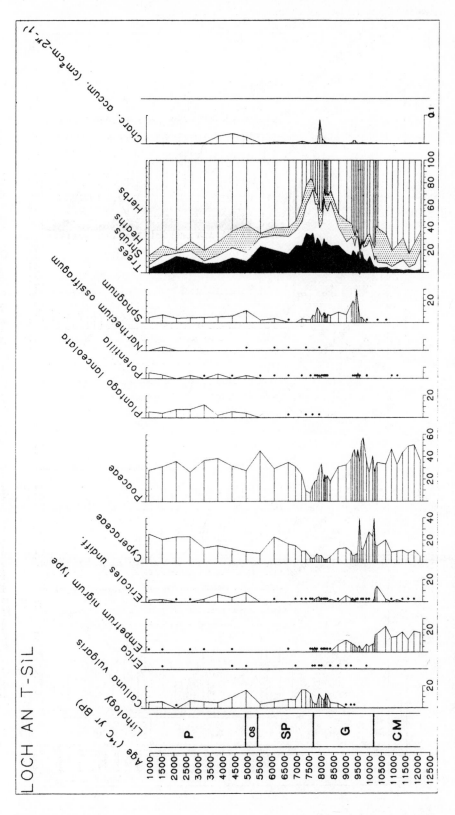

Figure 22.3. Selected pollen, spore and charcoal data from Loch an t-Sil. Lithology: CM, clay/mud bands; G, gyttja, OS, organic sand; P, peat; SP, sandy peat.

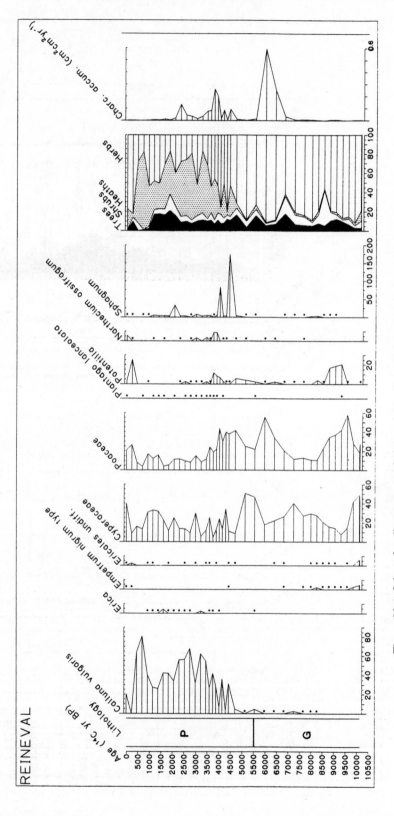

Figure 22.4. Selected pollen, spore and charcoal data from Reineval. Lithology: G, gyttja; P, peat.

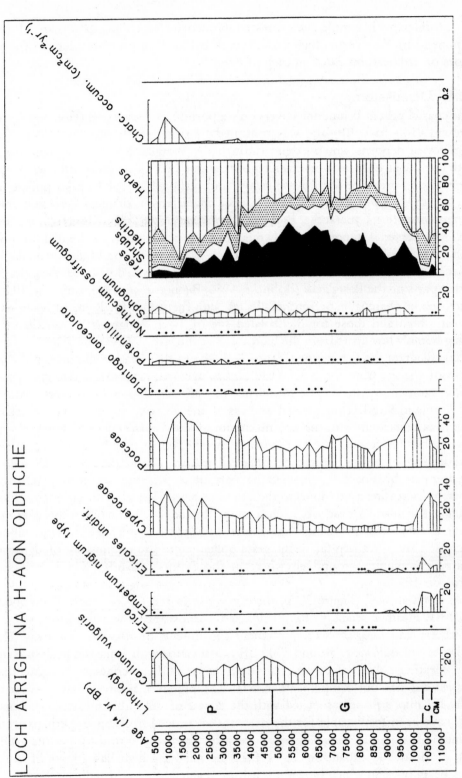

Figure 22.5. Selected pollen, spore and charcoal data from Loch Airigh na h-Aon Oidhche. Lithology: C, clay; CM, clay/mud bands; G, gyttja, P, peat.

of the diagrams is sample age expressed in uncorrected radiocarbon years BP (before present). The chronological framework is based on estimates derived from a series of radiocarbon dates on each profile.

22.4 Discussion

The coastal peat at Peninerine covers only a portion of Postglacial (Holocene) time (around 8130–5570 BP) and was truncated by rising sea levels. The other three sites reveal deposits which extend through the Postglacial into Lateglacial times, with the site at Loch an t-Sìl reaching back about 12 100 ^{14}C years. All sites have a fairly strong presence for *Calluna vulgaris* and, variously, other Ericales pollen, including *Empetrum nigrum* type. Other taxa characteristic of heathland and mire communities (e.g. Cyperaceae, *Potentilla, Narthecium ossifragum* and *Sphagnum*) are also well represented. Of note, but only mentioned in passing here, is the high proportion of tree pollen at Loch an t-Sìl and Loch Airigh na h-Aon Oidhche; unlike its present treeless state, South Uist clearly contained some well-wooded areas during earlier parts of the Postglacial (Bohncke, 1986; Bennett *et al.*, 1990; Edwards, 1990). Microscopic charcoal is present in all sites, with the values for Reineval being particularly high and those for the isolated site of Loch Airigh na h-Aon Oidhche being notably low apart from the increase over the last 1500 years.

The diagram for Peninerine (Figure 22.2) shows that heather dominated the vicinity of the site from about 8100 BP. *Calluna* may well have spread into *Empetrum*- and sedge-rich grassland. The abundance of *Sphagnum* spores in the early part of the profile may reflect the general wetness of the site. Of interest is the first charcoal peak coincident with the first maximum of the *Calluna* curve. Fire was clearly not responsible for the rise in *Calluna* at the site, but it may have assisted in the maintenance of heather dominance. The fall in *Calluna* from about 6500 BP and its replacement by Poaceae seems to be part of a process of substrate change, whereby increasing sand inputs to the site, possibly associated with the encroaching sea and the inland spread of machair sand (Ritchie, 1979), favoured the development of a coastal grassland. The return to *Calluna* dominance as sand inputs decreased and the sharp fall in the grass pollen curve, are reminiscent of dynamic coastal communities found elsewhere in the Scottish islands (Whittington and Edwards, 1993).

At Loch an t-Sìl (Figure 22.3), there is a rise in the *Calluna* curve from about 8800 BP. Heather seems to have colonized a landscape in which grasses, sedges, crowberry and *Sphagnum* were prominent constituents of non-wooded areas. The early peak in *Calluna*, at around 8300 BP, is associated with a marked peak in charcoal. Heather pollen values never approach those of Peninerine and it seems that *Calluna* did not out-compete other taxa. The renewed expansion of *Calluna* at 5000 BP may well be associated with the arrival of Neolithic farmers, who may also have been responsible for the rises in the curves for charcoal (perhaps from domestic fires) and *Plantago lanceolata* (possibly from the spread of pasture). The lack of heathland expansion may reflect the relatively high base status of soils, even peaty ones, in which blown machair sand acted as an acid-reducing agent.

The diagram from Reineval (Figure 22.4) is dominated by the sharp increase in values for *Calluna* pollen from 4500 BP through almost to the present. This post-dates the litho-stratigraphic change from gyttja to sedge peat at the sampling site and would seem to denote the spread of blanket peat within the pollen catchment area. The period 4500–2000 BP is also characterized by high charcoal values. Fire may have been part of a heathland management regime, and/or the charcoal may derive from domestic burning by Neolithic peoples. An earlier maximum in the charcoal curve (around 6500 BP) is not reflected in changes to the fortunes of heathland taxa.

At Loch Airigh na h-Aon Oidhche (Figure 22.5), *Calluna* pollen increases from about 9740 BP and is prominent throughout virtually the whole of the Postglacial. Heather would seem to have been co-dominant with sedges and grasses in open areas, even prior to the sedimentary change from gyttja to peat. There are no sharp increases in charcoal values until around 1500 BP, when *Calluna* expands. This isolated site has no clear indications of human impact before the reduction in arboreal pollen, accompanied by a slight increase in charcoal, at 3680 BP. The spread of heathland for most of the Postglacial, indicated by changes in heathland pollen taxa, is probably a reflection of progressive soil deterioration and blanket peat spread (whether responding in part to climatic change is, as yet, unknown).

The antiquity of *Calluna* heathland across South Uist is proven, along with major expansions from as early as 9740 BP at the easterly upland site of Loch Airigh na h-Aon Oidhche. This compares with the 9500 BP date for a major heather component in the vegetation at Loch Lang (Bennett *et al.*, 1990). The presence of some heathland prior to this, however, is shown by the good representation of *Empetrum* at all sites other than Reineval. Apart from Loch an t-Sil (and Loch Lang), no sites have high values for *Erica*, or undifferentiated Ericales pollen — but such genera as *Erica, Vaccinium* and *Arctostaphylos* are always, where identified, of low abundance in the pollen record. The representation of other heathland indicators is variable, as would be expected for taxa which can also be constituents of wet grassland (Cyperaceae, *Potentilla, Narthecium ossifragum, Sphagnum*). It is impossible to be sure about the precise composition of the heathlands; it is likely that both pure heathlands as well as those with a scrubby woodland element were in existence.

The association of peaks or increases in the curves for charcoal and for *Calluna* at Peninerine (from about 7800 BP), Loch an t-Sil (8300 and 5000 BP), Reineval (4500 BP) and Loch Airigh na h-Aon Oidhche (1500 BP) are of considerable interest and may denote a causal or part-causal connection. It is impossible to say that all or any charcoal is connected with the intentional burning of heathland, although the sustained relationship at Peninerine is of note. There is a lack of synchroneity in charcoal peaks between the sites, and this may indicate that climatic dryness was not a major factor in fire incidence. In addition, it must be pointed out that there is no unambiguous archaeological evidence for the presence of Mesolithic hunter-gatherers in the Outer Hebrides (any such evidence is likely to be hidden beneath sea, sand or peat), although there was certainly early occupation of the Inner Hebrides (Mellars, 1987; Hirons and Edwards, 1990; Edwards and Mithen, in press). It has been argued on palynological grounds, however, that phenomena such as woodland pollen reductions combined with levels of charcoal beyond background levels (e.g. around 8000 BP at Loch an t-Sìl and 6000 BP at Reineval) may signify the impact of Mesolithic communities (Bennett *et al.*, 1990; Edwards, 1990). Peninerine and Reineval might conceivably demonstrate the management of heathland as a grazing resource which bears comparison with that at the site of Callanish in Lewis (Bohncke, 1986) or those further afield (Caseldine and Hatton, 1993).

Acknowledgement

The Leverhulme Trust is thanked for financial support.

References

Bennett, K. D., Fossitt, J. A., Sharp, M. J. and Switsur, V. R. (1990). Holocene vegetational, and environmental history at Loch Lang, South Uist, Scotland. *New Phytologist*, **114**, 281–98.

Bohncke, S. J. P. (1988). Vegetation and habitation history of the Callinish area. In Birks, H. H., Birks, H. J. B., Kaland, P. E. and Moe, D. (Eds), *The Cultural Landscape — Past, Present and Future*. Cambridge University Press, Cambridge, 445–61.

Caseldine, C. and Hutton, J. (1993). The development of high moorland on Dartmoor: fire and the influence of Mesolithic activity on vegetation change. In Chambers, F. M. (Ed.), *Climate Change and Human Impact on the Landscape*. Chapman & Hall, London, 119–31.

Edwards, K. J. (1990). Fire and the Scottish Mesolithic: evidence from microscopic charcoal. In Vermeersch, P. M. and Van Peer, P. (Eds), *Contributions to the Mesolithic in Europe*. Leuven University Press, Leuven, 71–9.

Edwards, K. J. and Mithen, S. (in press). The colonisation of the Hebridean islands of western Scotland: evidence from the palynological and archaeological records. *World Archaeology*.

Faegri, K. and Iversen, J. (1989). *Textbook of Pollen Analysis*, (4th ed). John Wiley & Sons, Chichester, 1–328.

Gimingham, C. H. (1972). *Ecology of Heathlands*. Chapman & Hall, London, 1–266.

Hirons, K. R. and Edwards, K. J. (1990). Pollen and related studies at Kinloch, Isle of Rhum, Scotland, with particular reference to possible early human impacts on vegetation. *New Phytologist*, **116**, 715–27.

Jowsey, P. C. (1966). An improved peat sampler. *New Phytologist*, **65**, 245–8.

Kaland, P. E. (1986). The origin and management of Norwegian coastal heaths as reflected by pollen analysis. In Behre, K. -E. (Ed.), *Anthropogenic Indicators in Pollen Diagrams*. A. A. Balkema, Rotterdam, 19–36.

Legg, C. J., Maltby, E. and Proctor, M. C. F. (1992). The ecology of severe moorland fire on the North York Moors: seed distribution and seedling establishment of *Calluna vulgaris*. *Journal of Ecology*, **80**, 737–52.

Mellars, P. A. (1987). *Excavations on Oronsay: Prehistoric Human Ecology on a Small Island*. Edinburgh University Press, Edinburgh.

Patterson, W. A. III, Edwards, K. J. and Maguire, D. J. (1987). Microscopic charcoal as a fossil indicator of fire. *Quaternary Science Reviews*, **6**, 3–23.

Ritchie, W. (1979). Machair development and chronology in the Uists and adjacent islands. *Proceedings of the Royal Society of Edinburgh*, **83B**, 403–13.

Simmons, I. G. and Innes, J. B. (1987). Mid-holocene adaptations and later mesolithic forest disturbance in Northern England. *Journal of Archaeological Science*, **14**, 385–403.

Stevenson, A. C. and Thompson, D. B. A. (1993). Long-term changes in heather moorland in upland Britain and Ireland: palaeoecological evidence for the importance of grazing. *The Holocene*, **3**, 70–6.

Whittington, G. and Edwards, K. J. (1993). Vegetation change on Papa Stour, Shetland, Scotland: a response to coastal evolution and human interference? *The Holocene*, **3**, 54–62.

23 CHARCOAL ANALYSIS OF MOR-HUMUS SOILS: A PALAEOECOLOGICAL ASSESSMENT OF THE UTILITY OF MOORLAND SOILS FOR THE RECONSTRUCTION OF EXTENDED FIRE HISTORIES

A. N. Rhodes

Summary

1. Aerial photograph analyses of muirburn frequency and extent from Tulach Hill, Perthshire, indicate that approximately 56 % of the heather has not been burned in the post-1950 period.

2. Microscopic charcoal analyses of mor-humus soils cores are used to reconstruct extended fire histories.

3. Individual fire events are identifiable in the charcoal record, and *in situ* burns can be reliably distinguished from nearby burns.

23.1 Introduction

The heather (*Calluna vulgaris*)-dominated moorland of upland Britain is a very important component of the nation's natural and cultural heritage. However, an increasing number of studies report considerable nation wide losses of heather cover (Miller *et al.*, 1984; Sydes and Miller, 1988; National Countryside Monitoring Scheme, 1988; Nature Conservancy Council, 1990), a phenomenon which, according to Stevenson and Thompson (1993), generally commenced during the 17th to 19th centuries.

Fire has been used extensively to manage heather-dominated moorland throughout this period (Muirburn Working Party, 1977), with management practices changing little since the early 20th century (Pearsall, 1950). Accurate long-term fire histories are needed to help assess the impact of prolonged muirburn management on moorland vegetation.

While aerial photographs can be used to estimate ages of individual heather stands burned within the past 50 years (Hester and Sydes, 1992), the detection and reconstruction of muirburns beyond the limit of aerial photographic analyses can be facilitated by microscopic charcoal analyses of moorland soils. Even the most conscientiously kept estate records cannot provide stand-specific burning histories on a time scale of several centuries.

Charcoal analyses of sediments as a proxy measure of fire have been used widely within the fields of palaeoecology and archaeology (e.g. Patterson *et al.*, 1987; Smart and Hoffman, 1988). However, the majority of studies focus on lacustrine sediments (e.g. Swain, 1973, 1978; Odgaard, 1992) and peats (e.g. Simmons and Innes, 1981; Robinson, 1984); charcoal studies on soils, especially mor-humus soils, are rare (Iversen, 1964, 1969; Dodson and Bradshaw, 1987; Bradshaw and Zackrisson, 1990).

In this chapter charcoal analyses of mor-humus soil cores are presented to highlight the potential quality and resolution of moorland soils for the reconstruction of extended, local fire records.

23.2 Site Description

The study site, an SSSI (Grade 1), lies on the eastern flank of Tulach Hill (altitude 300–460 m) approximately 4 km to the ESE of Blair Atholl, Perthshire (NN8663). The moorland vegetation ranges from dry *Callunetum* to *Calluna-Eriophorum* mire.

23.3 Methods

P.C. ARC/INFO, a desk-top geographical information system (GIS), was used to digitally trace the burns visible on a time-series of eight aerial photographs: 1950; 1959; 1965; 1969; 1976; 1980; 1985 and 1988 (Figure 23.1). Muirburns on dry heather moorland remain visible on aerial photographs for between 8–15 years (Hester and Sydes, 1992); the photographic time series used ensures that all burns during the post-1950 period should have been identified.

Sixteen mor-humus cores (<10 cm) were taken by inserting lengths of sharpened plastic drainpipe into the soil. Muirburn maps, taken from the air photographs, enabled the cores to be taken in locations within, or at a known distance from, burns of a known age, and in locations known not to have been burned post-1950. The core positions were located by triangulation using an EDM, from features on a recent aerial photograph. Apart from the unconsolidated surface litter the cores were sectioned into contiguous 2 mm samples.

Samples for charcoal analysis were prepared by two 48-hour digestions in 6 % hydrogen peroxide, which bleached the dark organic matter and prevented misidentification with charcoal. Charcoal counts were made in petri dishes using a stereoscopic microscope at x40 magnification. A gridded eyepiece graticule was used to tally the charcoal particles into six geometrically progressive size classes (0.016–0.031, 0.031–0.063, 0.063–0.125, 0.125–0.25, 0.25–0.5, >0.5 mm). Particles larger than 0.5 mm were sized individually.

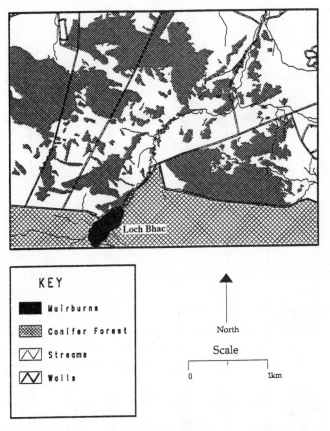

Figure 23.1. The area of Tulach Hill burned during the post-1950 period. Produced by overlaying eight muirburn maps derived from aerial photographs.

Spherical carbonaceous particles (SCPs) were counted with the charcoal. Only particles >10 microns in diameter were discernible.

Linear discriminant function analysis (Klovan and Billings, 1967; Davis, 1986) was performed (using SPSSx) to determine whether *in situ* fires could be differentiated from nearby fires, on the basis of their charcoal assemblage size class signature. Seven *in situ* and 61 non-*in situ* sedimentary charcoal assemblages, dated by aerial photograph analyses, were used to derive the discriminant function. This discriminant function was then used to characterize suspected fire events, outside the range of aerial photograph dating, in the core Tulach 5 (Figure 23.3).

23.4 Results

The three charcoal diagrams presented, Figures 23.2 and 23.3, are typical of those analysed from Tulach Hill. Relative charcoal particle abundance is displayed in individual size classes, as a total sum of particles in all size classes, and as the total area of charcoal in mm². The relative abundance of charcoal particles crudely reflects the proximity of a fire to the core site. *In situ* fires are represented in the sediment

Tulach 1: Charcoal profile.

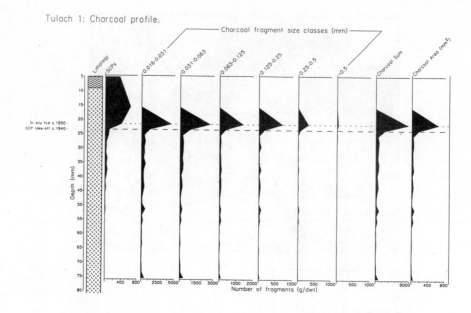

Tulach 4: Charcoal profile

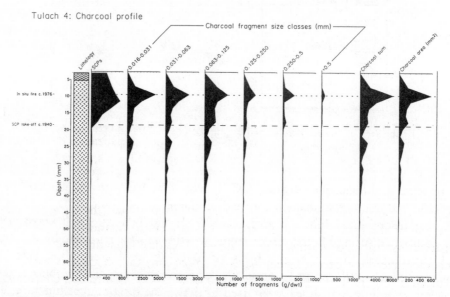

Figure 23.2. Charcoal diagrams from Tulach Hill mor-humus soil cores. Tulach 1 was known to have been last burned *c.* 1950 (from air photographs) and Tulach 4 to have been burned *c.* 1976.

record by prominent peaks across all size classes, nearby fires by less marked peaks, and distant fires by low charcoal levels.

Spherical carbonaceous particles (SCPs) are produced during the high temperature combustion of fossil fuels and are released into the atmosphere along with other atmospheric pollutants (Griffin and Goldberg, 1979, 1981; Renberg and Wik, 1984). Many Scottish lacustrine sediments have very similar SCP profiles for the

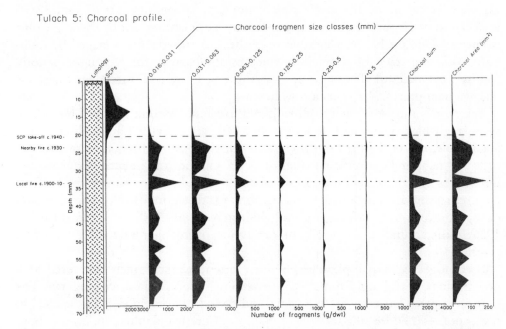

Figure 23.3. Charcoal diagram from a Tulach Hill mor-humus soil core, taken from a location known not to have been burned post-1950. Note the lack of charcoal in the upper 20 mm of the profile and the inferred *in situ* fire *c.* 1900–1910.

last 100–200 years (Wik and Natkanski, 1990; Rose, 1991). The most prominent feature, clearly seen in Figures 23.2 and 23.3, is the marked increase in SCP abundance in the 1940s–1960s, the result of post-war re-industrialization of Europe. A date of about 1940 is assigned to the event in Tulach Hill soils, because in a number of profiles the SCP expansion marginally predates known 1950 fire events, e.g. Tulach 1 (Figure 23.2).

The linear discriminant function effectively differentiated the charcoal assemblages; all of the *in situ* assemblages formed a distinct group, and all but one of the non-*in situ* assemblages another distinct group. This discriminant function was used to characterize the charcoal assemblages at 23–24 mm and 33–34 mm respectively in Tulach 5 (Figure 23.3). The more marked event at 33–34 mm was characterized as an *in situ* fire and the event at 23–24 mm as a non-*in situ*, or nearby, fire. Tulach 5 appears to have been last burnt about 1900–1910.

23.5 Discussion and Conclusions

The use of aerial photographs to map muirburns is not new (Hester and Sydes, 1992), however, the utilization of GIS technology allows much more accurate and effective data-capture and management than was previously possible. The aerial photograph analyses at Tulach Hill indicate that approximately 56 % of the heathland area has not been burned in the post-1950 period (Figure 23.1). Whether Tulach Hill has been particularly poorly burned, perhaps due to the fire risk associated with the nearby forestry plantations; or falling numbers of estate staff available to carry out the burning; or a shift toward management by sheep grazing, is unclear. One might speculate that many heather moorlands, managed by muirburn, have vast tracts of vegetation which escape burning for prolonged periods, and further studies of this nature are warranted to assess recent trends in muirburn management practices on a nation wide scale.

The mor-humus soils on Tulach Hill hold fossil microscopic charcoal records of surprisingly high quality and resolution. Not only are individual burns discrete and identifiable, but *in situ* fires can be differentiated from nearby fires, allowing spatially and temporally specific histories of *in situ* muirburn to be reconstructed over time scales of several centuries. In the absence of radiometric dating, the SCP record represents a readily obtainable isochrone for recent moorland soils. If greater dating control were available, e.g. 'wiggle-matching' of AMS ^{14}C dates (Pearson, 1986), more accurate chronologies of fire events, over longer time scales, would be possible.

Used together, aerial photograph and palaeoecological analyses represent a potentially powerful tool for the reconstruction of moorland burning regimes. The long-term perspective of fire frequency and periodicity provided could be used to test hypotheses addressing the role of fire in: (1) heathland initiation, (2) the long-term decline of *Calluna vulgaris*, (3) the dynamics of *Callunetum* development cycles, and (4) the succession of heather moorland to scrub-woodland.

References

Bradshaw, R. H. W. and Zackrisson, O. (1990). A two thousand-year history of a northern Swedish boreal forest stand. *Journal of Vegetation Science*, **1**, 519–28.

Davis, J. C. (1986). *Statistics and data analysis in Geology.* (2nd ed). John Wiley and Sons, New York, 478–91.

Dodson, J. R. and Bradshaw, R. H. W. (1987). A history of vegetation and fire, 6600 BP to present, County Sligo, western Ireland. *Boreas*, **16**, 113–23.

Griffin, J. J. and Goldberg, E. D. (1979). Morphologies and origin of elemental carbon in the environment. *Science*, **206**, 563–5.

Griffin, J. J. and Goldberg, E. D. (1981). Sphericity as a characteristic of solids from fossil fuel burning in a Lake Michigan sediment. *Geochimica et Cosmochimica Acta*, **45**, 763–9.

Hester, A. J. and Sydes, C. (1992). Changes in burning of Scottish heather moorland since the 1940s from aerial photographs. *Biological Conservation*, **60**, 25–30.

Iversen, J. (1964). Retrogressive vegetational succession in the post-glacial. *Journal of Ecology Supplement*, **52**, 59–70.

Iversen, J. (1969). Retrogressive development of a forest ecosystem demonstrated by pollen diagrams from fossil mor. *Oikos Supplement*, **12**, 35–49.

Klovan, J. E. and Billings, G. K. (1967). Classification of geological samples by discriminant-function analysis. *Bulletin of Canadian Petroleum Geology*, **15** (3), 313–30.

Miller, G. R., Miles, J. and Heal, O. W. (1984). *Moorland Management: A Study of Exmoor.* Institute of Terrestrial Ecology, Cambridge.

Muirburn Working Party (1977). *A Guide to Good Muirburn Practice.* HMSO, Edinburgh.

National Countryside Monitoring Scheme (1988). *Scotland: Grampian.* Nature Conservancy Council and Countryside Commission for Scotland, Perth.

Nature Conservancy Council (1990). *The Heather Regeneration Scheme: a feasibility study for the Department of Environment.* Nature Conservancy Council, Peterborough.

Odgaard, B. V. (1992). The fire history of Danish heathland areas as reflected by pollen and charred particles in lake sediments. *The Holocene*, **2**, 218–27.

Patterson, W. A., Edwards, K. J. and Maguire, D. J. (1987). Microscopic charcoal as a fossil indicator of fire. *Quaternary Science Reviews*, **6**, 3–23.

Pearsall, W. H. (1950). *Mountains and Moorlands*. Collins, London.

Pearson, G. W. (1986). Precision calendrical dating of known growth-period samples using a 'curve fitting' technique. *Radiocarbon*, **28**, 839–62.

Renberg, I. and Wik, M. (1984). Dating recent lake sediments by soot particle counting. *Verhandlungen Internationalen Vereinigung fur Limnologie*, **22**, 712–18.

Robinson, D. (1984). The estimation of the charcoal content of sediments: a comparison of methods on peat sections from the Island of Arran. *Circaea*, **2** (3), 121–8.

Rose, N. L. (1991). *Fly-ash Particles in Lake Sediments: Extraction, Characterisation and Distribution*. (Unpublished PhD thesis, University College London.)

Simmons, I. G. and Innes, J. B. (1981). Tree remains in a North York Moors peat profile. *Nature*, **294**, 76–8.

Smart, T. L. and Hoffman, E. S. (1988). Environmental interpretation of archaeological charcoal. In Hastorf, C. A. and Popper, V. (Eds), *Current Paleoethnobotany*. University of Chicago Press, Chicago, 167–205.

Stevenson, A. C. and Thompson, D. B. A. (1993). Long-term changes in the extent of heather moorland in upland Britain and Ireland: palaeoecological evidence for the importance of grazing. *The Holocene*, **3** (1), 70–6.

Swain, A. M. (1973). A history of fire and vegetation in north-eastern Minnesota as recorded in lake sediments. *Quaternary Research*, **3**, 383–96.

Swain, A. M. (1978). Environmental changes during the past 2000 years in North-central Wisconsin: analysis of pollen, charcoal, and seeds from varved lake sediments. *Quaternary Research*, **10**, 55–68.

Sydes, C. and Miller, G. R. (1988). Range management and nature conservation in the British Uplands. In M. B. Usher, and D. B. A. Thompson, (Eds), *Ecological Change in the Uplands*. Blackwell Scientific Publications, Oxford, 323–37.

Wik, M. and Natkanski, J. (1990). British and Scandinavian lake sediment records of carbonaceous particles from fossil-fuel combustion. *Philosophical Transactions Royal Society London B*, **327**, 319–23.

24 HEATHLAND PATCH DYNAMICS AND CONSEQUENCES FOR WILDLIFE

M. B. Usher

Summary

1. Heathlands may appear as a monotonous expanse of a virtual monoculture of *Calluna vulgaris*, but they have an intricate small-scale patchliness. One's perception of a heathland depends on the scale at which it is observed and measured.

2. As well as the succession induced by heather burning, heathland patch dynamics are influenced by factors such as the nature of the soil, hydrology, grazing, and colonisation by invasive species, such as the moss *Campylopus introflexus*.

3. Composition of the invertebrate fauna relates to the successional trends in the plant community and demonstrates strong seasonal variation in species occurrence.

4. Birds range over a wide area, and have the ability to use different kinds of patch for different functions – feeding, nesting etc.

5. Patch structure, which varies both in space and time, is speculated to contribute to the maintenance of the natural biotic diversity of the heathland habitat. Circumstantial evidence suggests that the patch structure can be modified so as to favour target species.

24.1 Introduction

Under a system of burning and grazing management, heather (*Calluna vulgaris* (L.) Hull) has come to dominate large upland areas of the east of Scotland and the north of England. In the wetter western areas *Calluna* tends to be less dominant, though it is still an abundant species in the blanket bogs (Gimingham, 1972). Gimingham (1972, 1975) described the plant communities with which *Calluna* is associated, as well as the management practices adopted to maintain heaths with vigorously growing *Calluna*, a food for grouse, deer and sheep. Gimingham's (1960) pioneering account of *Calluna*

Muirburn in practice

(Left)
Lighting the fire (D B A Thompson)

(Below)
A well controlled fire, under the supervision of John Phillips,
The Heather Trust (D B A Thompson)

People as part of the moorland environment

(Right)
*Above Loch Skeen,
Moffat* (D B A Thompson)

*(Left) British Ecological
Society Party, led by Professor
David H N Spence, at Brouster,
Shetland, amongst a prehistoric
field system, 16th July 1984*
(M B Usher)

*(Left)
Abandoned but and ben
(two-roomed cottage) in a
young forestry plantation,
above Culrain, Sutherland*
(D B A Thompson)

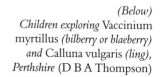

*(Below)
Children exploring Vaccinium
myrtillus (bilberry or blaeberry)
and Calluna vulgaris (ling),
Perthshire* (D B A Thompson)

sparked an interest amongst researchers into the ecology not only of the developmental processes in *Calluna*-dominated communities, but of heaths and moorlands in general.

Ecological thinking had been strongly influenced by Watt's (1947) presidential address to the British Ecological Society on pattern and process in plant communities. Developing Watt's ideas, Gimingham (1972) described the development process in dry *Calluna* heath after fires, with a pioneer phase of scattered plants growing steadily to post-mature plants that are degenerating. Death of the *Calluna* leads to the opening of the canopy, followed by colonisation by other angiosperms or a variety of bryophytes and lichens. The building and mature phases of the development of a Callunetum are marked by a dense growth of *Calluna*, tightly packed together, with little light penetrating to ground level. These phases appear as heathland monocultures, with the earlier and later phases of the post-fire development of *Calluna* being richer in their associated plant species. Under a system of burning management, there is therefore temporal variation in plant species composition, depending upon the length of time since fire last occurred.

An element of spatial variation is imposed by the size of the burns and their distribution across a heath. This introduces the concept of 'scale' to those of 'pattern' and 'process'. There may be a pattern of different ages of *Calluna* juxtaposed across a heath, but what effect does the scale of that pattern have on the community of plants and animals on the heath? There is increasing interest in the ecological implications of scale (e.g. Levin's (1992) Robert H. MacArthur Award Lecture), of the factors influencing scale, and of the effects of scale on populations dispersed amongst patches of suitable habitat.

The aim of this chapter is to review aspects of the patch structure of heathlands, exploring some of the effects of management on the patch structure of the plants and on the invertebrate and vertebrate animal assemblages, with particular reference to data from the North York Moors. As a scale is often imposed by the burning regimes, how does this affect natural biodiversity, and could heathlands be managed for greater biodiversity?

24.2 The Plant Assemblage

There are at least four processes that determine the patch characteristics of a plant community. These are

- the physical environment, especially soil conditions and microtopography;

- the development phase of *Calluna*, and the effects of ecological processes such as succession, herbivory and parasitism;

- the pattern caused by methods of heath and moorland management; and

- interactions with non-native species (for example, the moss *Campylopus introflexus*).

24.2.1 Physical Processes

Heathlands frequently have an undulating topography, with local exposure of bed-rock, ridges of glacial material, or small depressions. On the drier areas associated with rocks and ridges, *Erica cinerea* (bell heather) may become commoner, though still generally with abundant *Calluna* (Gimingham 1972). In the wetter depressions *Calluna* may be totally displaced as species of *Sphagnum* become dominant. The data in Table 24.1 indicate that there can be considerable changes in vegetation composition even over distances of 20 m, the approximate separation distance of the two pairs of transects. Transect B is on dryer ground, with abundant *Calluna* and *Erica cinerea*, whilst the nearby transect A is virtually dominated by *Polytrichum* and *Sphagnum* mosses. Similarly transect D is *Calluna* dominated, though there is a considerable frequency of *Sphagnum* and *Erica tetralix* (cross-leaved heath). On the other hand, transect C is in wetter ground with abundant *Eriophorum* (cotton grass), *Erica tetralix* and *Sphagnum* moss.

Table 24.1   The vegetation on four 12 m transects on Lealholm Moor, North York Moors. Each pair of transects were parallel and separated by a distance of 20–25 m. The data indicate, for selected species, frequency of occurrence (%) in 200 10 cm x 10 cm quadrats.

| | National grid reference and transect letters | | | |
| | NZ2750100 | | NZ755095 | |
Species	A	B	C	D
Calluna vulgaris	12	96	22	58
Erica cinerea	0	48	0	0
Erica tetralix	0	0	60	20
Eriophorum angustifolium	6	0	100	0
No. of vascular plant species	10	3	10	9
Campylopus introflexus	0	10	0	0
Pohlia nutans	0	8	0	1
Polytrichum commune	70	2	14	0
Sphagnum (4 species)	46	0	69	49
No. of bryophyte species	2	6	6	4

These differences occur with only minor changes in topography, perhaps only of the order of a few centimetres between the surface of the wet, *Sphagnum*-dominated area and the surrounding Callunetum (see Figure 24.1). These small wet areas do, however, provide a considerable increase to the biological diversity of a heath, as well as being important feeding areas for young grouse (Hudson, 1986). The data in Table 24.1 indicate the increase in the number of vascular plant species in the wetter areas, whereas the number of bryophyte species is often similar in wet and dry areas.

24.2.2 Biological Processes

Calluna, after a fire, generally develops a closed stand and finally degenerates, as outlined by Gimingham (1972). In a regularly burnt heathland, the Callunetum is generally

Figure 24.1. A view of a small flush set in a very shallow depression within a Callunetum on Danby High Moor, North York Moors. This flush contains open water, a small area where *Eriophorum* is dominant, and a surrounding zone with *Sphagnum* mosses.

re-burnt before the plants start to degenerate so that the full range of the developmental process is not observed (Hobbs and Gimingham, 1987). The speed of regeneration is also dependent on the age of the stand that was burnt (cf. Gardner *et al.*, 1993); the growth of heather shoots is slower from old (mature) stands than from young (building phase) stands of *Calluna*, though there is usually some regeneration from seedlings unless the fire has been particularly severe (Gimingham, 1972).

Miles (1988) outlined aspects of this succession that could lead to different types of plant community. If the degenerate heather is colonised by the seedlings of woody or shrubby species, these could grow, overtop the *Calluna* and eventually lead to a scrub or mixed species forest (see Hester and Miller, this volume). If *Calluna* is grazed, the intensity of grazing is important in determining the type of change (see Armstrong and Milne, this volume). Under heavy grazing pressure, i.e. with the order of 2–3 sheep ha^{-1} or more, then the heather is likely to be eaten and trampled, die and be replaced with grasses, especially an *Agrostis-Festuca* community (Miles, 1988; Hudson, 1992). These successional and developmental processes are therefore dependent upon the land use and the management practices being employed.

Besides the processes that can give rise to heterogeneity in the Callunetum, it is also possible that invertebrate herbivores or pathogens can cause local death of the *Calluna*. The heather beetle, *Lochmaea suturalis*, has caused widespread death of heather in the Netherlands, for example (Diemont and Heil, 1984), and has caused more local death of heather patches in this country (MacDonald, 1990). It is possible that fungal pathogens may also be responsible for heather die-back, as for example the death of

Figure 24.2. A patch of heather die-back on Ronas Hill, Shetland. Although doubt still surrounds the cause of such patches of dead heather, the fungus *Marasmius androsaceus* was associated with the dead and dying heather plants.

patches of *Calluna* on Ronas Hill in Shetland (Fig. 24.2) where *Marasmius androsaceus* is thought to have been the possible pathogenic organism.

These biological processes contribute to heterogeneity in the age and vigour of stands of *Calluna*. The processes of development in the *Calluna* itself are reasonably well known, as are the effects of grazing by large mammals (Gimingham, 1972; Armstrong and Milne, this volume). However, little is known about the effects of invertebrate herbivores, and even less appears to be known about the role of parasitism or disease in the structuring of a Callunetum.

24.2.3 *Management-induced Processes*

The scale of heather burning varies from small-scale intervention (strips of 30 m width or less) for the management of grouse moors to large-scale burning of patches of

Figure 24.3. A patterned hillside caused by burning large strips (Creag Chean, Perthshire).

several hectares if the area is subsequently to be grazed by sheep (Gimingham, 1972; Usher and Gardner, 1988; MacDonald, 1990). The pattern of burns tends to be more regular than the patterns of microtopography, and it can form an obvious landscape feature even from considerable distances (Figure 24.3). From the point of view of the plants, burning provides a flush of nutrients and re-commences the development cycle or successional process (Gimingham 1972; MacDonald 1990). However, for the animals, it does pose difficulties of colonisation, transitory feeding areas, margins of heather of different heights, etc. These are explored in subsequent sections of this chapter.

24.2.4 Colonisation Processes

Heaths and moorlands, below the tree-line, are generally viewed as semi-natural habitats (e.g. Ratcliffe and Thompson, 1988), altered by land management practices and domesticated herbivores, but with communities of native species. This image seems largely true, but during the 21st century heaths and moorlands have been invaded by a number of non-native species, perhaps the most important of which is *Campylopus introflexus*, a southern hemisphere moss that was first discovered in the northern hemisphere – in the south of England – in 1941 (Figure 24.4). The species is now abundant throughout the British Isles (Equihua Zamora, 1991).

Observational evidence indicates that *C. introflexus* could increase the heterogeneity of *Calluna* stands under certain circumstances. After a burn, some of the *Calluna* regeneration is from seeds that have been stimulated to germinate; after a burn, *C. introflexus* can also rapidly colonise the bare substrate (e.g. Equihua and Usher, 1992). Evidence from observations on the North York Moors indicated that some patches after a burn were dominated by *C. introflexus* whilst neighbouring

Figure 24.4. *Campylopus introflexus*, an invasive moss from the southern hemisphere, first found in the British Isles in 1941.

patches had not been colonised to the same extent and were developing a pioneer phase Callunetum. Detailed studies to determine whether there was competition between *C. introflexus* and *Calluna* (Equihua and Usher, 1993) have indicated that it is the dynamics of the moss carpet itself that may have a particular effect on either inhibiting or facilitating the development of *Calluna* seedlings.

There are likely to be complex interactions between *Calluna*, invasive species such as *Campylopus introflexus* or the scarcer *Orthodontium lineare* (also a moss), the effects of grazing and the physical conditions of the site. At the moment there are few potentially invasive species of the heaths and moorlands in north west Europe, but before 1941 there were probably none that were known!

24.3 The Invertebrate Assemblage

Heather burning takes place through the winter and spring months, from November but mostly during March and early April. Most invertebrates will be in diapause – those that are above ground are likely to be killed, whilst those that are in the litter or deeper in the soil may survive a fire. The fires do, however, impose a patch structure on the invertebrate assemblages; this leads to questions of colonisation of patches, movement between patches, extinctions from patches as the *Calluna* develops, etc.

In sampling 55 areas on 10 grouse moors on the North York Moors, Gardner (1991) demonstrated that the ground beetles (family Carabidae) segregated on two ordination axes: one related to the development of the heather (i.e. time since the last burn) and the other related to the wetness of the site. Gardner's study indicated that there was a number of species that were only found in the wet flushes and never in the dryer heath, even within 5–10 m of the flush. Species in this category were the ground beetles *Agonum fulginosum* and *Pterostichus nigrita* and the spiders *Antistea elegans, Pirata* spp. and *Silometopus* elegans. As with the higher plants, there was a distinct assemblage of wet flush species that appeared to play no part in the rest of the heathland.

Gardner's (1991) study also indicated that there were some ground beetles associated only with the open conditions following fire, for example *Calathus erratus, Cicindela campestris* and *Nebria salina*, whilst there was another group associated with tall heather stands, including *Calathus micropterus, Trechus obtusus* and *Trechus quadristriatus*. In addition there were many species of ground beetles that occupied intermediate positions or occurred widely throughout the gradient from open to closed stands of *Calluna*, for example *Carabus problematicus*. Similar analyses of the spider species indicated that some favoured different ends of the gradient from open to closed *Calluna* stands, with perhaps rather fewer intermediate than with the ground beetles.

In order to investigate how quickly burnt patches were colonised by invertebrates, Usher and Smart (1988) established transects of pitfall traps across an area burnt only a few months previously (burnt in mid-April, pitfall trapping mid-July to mid-August). The spiders of open areas, for example *Gnaphosa leporina* and *Xysticus sabulosus*, were abundant, even although the trapping was only 3–4 months after burning. *G. leporina* was only rarely collected in pitfall traps under closed heather canopies, but formed 29 % of all spiders collected in these newly open areas. *X. sabulosus* was never collected in traps under closed heather canopies, but formed 3 % of the catch in the open areas. Gardner and Usher (1989) analysed the insects which were collected in the same series of transect samples. The ground beetles yielded the expected results with *Calathus erratus, Cicindela campestris* and *Nebria salina* all occurring in traps in the open areas. The conclusion from this work is that the species of invertebrates characteristic of open patches are able to find these patches rapidly in the spring following a fire. It is not known from this study whether this colonisation is a random dispersal process or if the invertebrates can detect and hence orientate themselves to the burnt patches.

Perhaps the more interesting finding was the large numbers of Cicadellidae that occurred in traps in these recently burnt patches, with the highest densities in the centre of the patch (Gardner and Usher, 1989). As there was no heather regeneration at the time of trapping, and as the Cicadellidae are exclusively herbivorous, this result was unexpected. Their abundance in the traps does, however, indicate that these herbivorous insects were moving across the heath (where there were no physical barriers to dispersal related to vegetation structure), and hence would be able to colonise any unoccupied areas. The small scale of burns on a grouse moor would therefore appear to offer no barrier to rapid colonisation by many of the invertebrates associated with open conditions.

Arthropod abundance and activity are strongly seasonal. For the ground dwelling species previously mentioned, *G. leporina* is abundant in pitfall traps in June and July, but scarce at other times of the year; *X. sabulosus* was absent from pitfall traps until June, and was particularly abundant in August and September. Although most species occurred most plentifully in traps during the summer months, *Leptothrix hardyi* was abundant during the winter months, when it often formed more than 50 % of the catch, but scarce or absent during the summer months. This seasonality of abundance makes it more difficult to compare diversity estimates (Table 24.2), but it does appear that the control (heather that has neither been burnt nor cut within the previous 12 years) has a more diverse spider fauna than the areas that have been either burnt or cut within the last year.

Table 24.2 The diversity (Simpson's Index) of the spider assemblage in relation to heathland management and season. Simpson's Index is 0 for an assemblage that is infinitely diverse and 1 for a monoculture.

Month	Area burnt during previous year	Area cut during previous year	Control (neither burnt nor cut for previous 12+ years)
May	0.09	0.15	0.07
June	0.10	0.12	0.07
July	0.31	0.18	0.07
August	0.30	0.20	0.09
September	0.53	0.35	0.12

The species richness of these heathland arthropods is remarkable since on the grouse moors of the North York Moors there are at least 20 % of the British spider species and 15 % of the British ground beetle species, but only about 2 % of the British vascular flora (Usher and Thompson, 1993). The patch structure relates largely to the different development stages of *Calluna*, but these stages are related to structurally different environments for the invertebrates. Usher (1992) speculated that it is the structural diversity of the developmental stages of *Calluna* that leads to the large arthropod diversity of these heaths.

24.4 The Vertebrate Assemblage

The vertebrate community of heaths is not particularly rich in species; there are few mammals but more birds characteristic of the heathland habitat (Ratcliffe and Thompson, 1988; Usher and Thompson, 1993). Because of their greater mobility it is often inappropriate to analyse the distribution of vertebrates at the same scale as for the invertebrates – it is perhaps the patches of bracken (*Pteridium aquilinum*), the semi-improved fields, etc., that are more meaningful in terms of the mosaic affecting the distribution of these species. However, Hudson's (1986) study on the feeding behaviour of grouse (*Lagopus lagopus*) chicks in the wet flushes, or D. Allen's (pers. comm.) observation on the nesting sites of meadow pipits (*Anthus pratensis*) within about 2 m of the margin between tall and short heather (Figure 24.5), indicate that the smaller scale effects can be important determinants for heathland birds.

Figure 24.5. Burning on Danby Low Moor, North York Moors. In the foreground there is heather about 20 cm high, forming a straight edge with the area in the middle distance, burnt 4 months previously. In the far distance edges between different ages of heather can be seen; it is just within these edges that meadow pipits are likely to locate their nests (D. Allen, pers. comm.).

In the survey of the occurrence of the whinchat (*Saxicola rubetra*) on the North York Moors, D. Allen (pers. comm.) recorded presence/absence of the species in sample plots of 4 ha (200 m square). At this scale five of his eight variables showed significance; these related to the minimum altitude of the plot (lower favoured by whinchat), the gradient (steeper favoured), the presence of both a length of stream and of bracken (whinchats did not occur if either was absent) and the presence of *Calluna* heath (more favoured). The variables relating to the height of the heather proved non-significant. Such a study starts to give an indication of the requirements of this one bird – the mosaic of heather, bracken and water, possibly with altitude and gradient being factors that determine suitable proportions of these basic habitats (e.g. on steeper slopes there will generally be less improvement of the heath for rough grazings).

Using similar analyses for the other passerine species, D. Allen (pers. comm.) was able to build up a more comprehensive view of the factors affecting the whinchat, skylark (*Alauda arvensis*) and meadow pipit on the North York Moors (Table 24.3). In general, the whinchat favoured areas with bracken, the meadow pipit areas of tall dwarf shrub and the skylark the wetter areas. These results then pose the question 'can heaths and moorlands be managed to favour one bird species at the expense of others, or could the number and diversity of bird species be enhanced by different management practices?'. In order to explore such questions Usher and Thompson (1993) noted that management practices could alter three factors – the size of the burnt areas, the frequency with which these areas are burnt, and the ratio between pasture and heath. Once again scale has an important influence. The ratio of pasture to heath can only be defined in relation to the area over which it is measured; for example, although the lapwing is favoured by a greater proportion of pasture, it is possible that it may benefit from the two habitat types being more heterogeneously mixed rather than there being just one or two large patches of each (Usher and Thompson 1993). Scale seems to be important in determining the effects of burning, with a relatively small number of species apparently favoured by large patches and relatively more by small patches (Figure 24.6). Whether more complex burning cycles – for example, one short rotation and one long rotation – is a feasible method of managing a heath is as yet uncertain, but this could provide an environment that is richer in species of birds.

Table 24.3   Factors affecting the distribution of three passerine species on 4 ha plots on the North York Moors (from D. Allen, pers. comm.). In the table '+' implies a significant positive association, '−' a significant negative association, and '•' no significant association. Significance of association is measured with $P < 0.05$.

Factor	Winchat	Skylark	Meadow Pipit
Altitude	−	−	•
Gradient	+	•	+
Aspect	•	•	−
Dry heath	•	−	•
Wet heath	•	+	•
Tall dwarf shrubs	•	−	+
Bracken	+	•	•

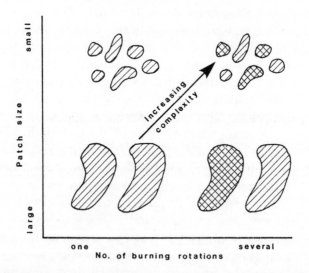

Figure 24.6. Hypotheses about the size and rotation of burns on the bird species likely to be favoured (adapted from Usher and Thompson, 1993). Hatching represents patches burnt on one fire cycle (say 15 years); cross hatching represents patches burnt on a different fire cycle (say 30 years).

24.5 Discussion: Patterns, Patches and Scales

Patchiness and biodiversity of heathland fauna and flora can lead to many management questions. But first, it has to be understood that heathlands are not naturally a widespread type of habitat, though in general they are composed of assemblages of native species. It is the use of fire and grazing, to prevent their succession to scrub and woodland communities, that has resulted in the current dominance of large areas by *Calluna vulgaris*. Such repeated disturbance (cf. Walker, 1989) may be related to the observed diversity of arthropods.

The scales at which patches can be observed vary greatly. The wet flushes, as shown in Figure 24.1, have a scale that is often of the order of 5–20 m. The burns have various scales depending upon the herbivore that is being favoured, but may be 25–50 m for grouse, or up to 200 m for sheep or deer (compare Figure 24.5, for example, with Figure 24.3). The mosaic of different land cover types, especially of heather moorland and rough grassland, which influenced the bird distribution recorded by D. Allen (Table 24.3), may have scales of 1–2 km. In terms of managing for biodiversity, it is important to remember Levin's (1992) comment that 'applied challenges, such as the prediction of the ecological causes and consequences of global climate change, require the interfacing of phenomena that occur on very different scales of space, time, and ecological organisation. Furthermore, there is no single scale at which ecological phenomena should be studied; . . .'. This encapsulates an important concept; managing a heath for biodiversity may affect the biodiversity at other scales. Is the scale of interst 10^0, 10^1, 10^2, 10^3 or 10^4 m? How does one find a method of heathland management that maximises the biodiversity at all of these scales, or is there some algorithm that allows for optimisation? As there is no single scale to study a community, it remains a challenge to find some way of operating across a range of scales.

The challenge of managing vertebrate diversity across multiple land use landscapes has been addressed by Hansen *et al.* (1993). They suggest that there are five key steps, namely

- to set clear objectives,

- to associate target species with specific habitat configurations,

- to assess species life histories and sensitivity to habitat,

- to use simulation models to evaluate alternative management practices, and

- to implement preferred strategies and monitor the response of species and habitats.

Such a scheme is idealistic, though the first step is possible. However, the second step moves away from the diverse community to one (or a few) target species. The remainder of steps require a very strong input of research, though some of this is available for the plants (e.g. Hobbs and Gimingham, 1987) and passerines (e.g. D. Allen, pers. comm.) of heaths and moorlands. The research requirements to develop a similar approach for the invertebrates could be massive, and there may well not be target species that could easily be identified. Such studies all relate to the spatial dynamics of species and communities, though there is increasing interest in how this can be measured (Borchard *et al.*, 1992) and how studies at different scales can reflect our understanding of food webs (Martinez, 1993) or of processes such as predation (Hanski, 1991a).

However, spatial heterogeneity is only one factor that affects the dynamics of heathland species; there is also a temporal component (Gloaguen, 1993). It is this complex spatio-temporal structure that may form the basis of the observed arthropod diversity of the heathland environment. Each patch, isolated from similar habitat patches in space or in time, can be conceived as a metapopulation (Hanski, 1991b). This conceptual framework for a heathland leads to questions of colonisation, persistence and extinction within the patches. The information about plants (e.g. Hobbs and Gimingham, 1987) indicates that patch colonisation can be rapid, particularly by various moss species. The studies of Gimingham (1960) indicated that persistence and extinction of plants are related to the *Calluna* development cycle as well as to the intensity of herbivore grazing. The studies of invertebrates discussed in this paper also tend to indicate that patch colonisation can be rapid, but because trapping or sampling methods all depend upon the habitat structure there is very limited data on patch persistence or extinction. Vertebrates, on the other hand, appear to be less affected by the temporal component because their greater mobility implies that they are more likely to use a variety of patches rather than a single patch (e.g. Usher and Thompson 1993). In terms of Hanski's (1991b) analysis of the extinction of metapopulations, it seems probable that there are no positive equilibrium points for the majority of heathland species, and hence that their continued existence depends upon repeated disturbance by management practices which induce a strong spatio-temporal patch structure.

In terms of biodiversity, this presents strong challenges to the manager. The extensive heaths that have been created during the last two centuries or so are a result of a truncated succession, fire maintaining a habitat without trees or shrubs. A range of species is adapted to live in this ever-changing environment, but the question is one of changing the management practice and the possibility of changing the components of biodiversity. Usher and Thompson's (1993) suggestion (see Figure 24.6) is that a more heterogeneous mixture of burn sizes and burn ages could lead to a richer bird community, especially if patches of scrub and woodland were permitted to develop. Is it true that increasing the spatial and temporal heterogeneity, i.e. with management aiming to create more variable patches, will lead to greater diversity? It is a hypothesis worth testing in a habitat type that is natural, if assessed in terms of its species complement, but unnatural if assessed on the basis of whether the habitat could persist without the intervention of people. Heaths and moorlands provide excellent experimental subjects for investigating such pure and applied ecological hypotheses.

Acknowledgements

I am grateful to Drs Alison Hester and Peter Hudson, and two anonymous referees, for comments on the manuscript.

References

Borchard, D., Legendre, P. and Drapeau, P. (1992). Partitioning out the spatial component of ecological variation. *Ecology*, **73**, 1045–1055.

Diemont, W. H. and Heil, G. W. (1984). Some long-term observations on cyclical and seral processes in Dutch heathlands. *Biological Conservation*, **30**, 283–291.

Equihua, M. and Usher, M. (1992). The invasive moss *Campylopus introflexus* in the North York Moors National Park. *Annual Report of the Joseph Nickerson Reconciliation Project*, 1992, 35–37.

Equihua, M. and Usher, M. B. (1993). Impact of carpets of the invasive moss *Campylopus introflexus* on *Calluna vulgaris* regeneration. *Journal of Ecology*, **81**, 359–365.

Equihua Zamora, M. E. (1991). *The Ecology of the Invasive Moss* Campylopus introflexus *in the North York Moors National Park*. D. Phil. Thesis, University of York.

Gardner, S. M. (1991). Ground beetle (Coleoptera: Carbidae) communities on upland heath and their association with heathland flora. *Journal of Biogeography*, **18**, 281–289.

Gardner, S. M., Liepert, C. and Rees, S. (1993). Managing heather moorland; impacts of burning and cutting on *Calluna* regeneration. *Journal of Environmental Planning and Management*, **36**, 283–293.

Gardner, S. M. and Usher, M. B. (1989). Insect abundance on burned and cut upland *Calluna* heath. *The Entomologist*, **108**, 147–157.

Gimingham, C. H. (1960). Biological flora of the British Isles: *Calluna vulgaris* (L.) Hull. *Journal of Ecology*, **49**, 455–483.

Gimingham, C. H. (1972). *Ecology of Heathlands*. Chapman and Hall, London.

Gimingham, C. H. 1975. *An Introduction to Heathland Ecology*. Oliver and Boyd, Edinburgh.

Gloaguen, J. C. (1993). Spatio-temporal patterns in post-burn succession on Brittany heathlands. *Journal of Vegetation Science*, **4**, 561–566.

Hansen, A. J., Garman, S. L., Marks, B. and Urban, D. L. (1993). An approach for managing vertebrate diversity across multiple-use landscapes. *Ecological Applications*, **3**, 481–496.

Hanski, I. (1991a). The functional response of predators: worries about scale. *Trends in Ecology and Evolution*, **6**, 141–142.

Hanski, I. (1991b). Single-species metapopulation dynamics: concepts, models and observations. *Biological Journal of the Linnean Society*, **42**, 17–38.

Hobbs, R. J. and Gimingham, C. H. (1987). Vegetation, fire and herbivore interactions in heathland. *Advances in Ecological Research*, **16**, 87–171.

Hudson, P. (1986). *Red Grouse: the Biology and Management of a Wild Gamebird*. Game Conservancy Trust, Fordingbridge.

Hudson, P. (1992). *Grouse in Space and Time*. Game Conservancy Ltd, Fordingbridge.

Levin, S. A. (1992). The problem of pattern and scale in ecology. *Ecology*, **73**, 1943–1967.

MacDonald, A. J. (1990) Heather damage: a guide to types of damage and their causes. *Research and Survey in Nature Conservation*, **28**, 1–41.

Martinez, N. D. (1993). Effect of scale on food web structure. *Science*, **260**, 242–243.

Miles, J. (1988). Vegetation and soil change in the uplands. In M. B. Usher and D. B. A. Thompson (Eds.). *Ecological Change in the Uplands*. Blackwell Scientific Publications, Oxford, pp. 57–70.

Ratcliffe, D. A. and Thompson, D. B. A. (1988). The British uplands: their ecological character and international significance. In M. B. Usher and D. B. A. Thompson (Eds.). *Ecological Change in the Uplands*. Blackwell Scientific Publications, Oxford, pp. 9–36.

Usher, M. B. (1992). Management and diversity of arthropods in *Calluna* heathlands. *Biodiversity and Conservation*, **1**, 63–79.

Usher, M. B. and Gardner, S. M. (1988). Animal communities in the uplands: how is naturalness influenced by management? In M. B. Usher and D. B. A. Thompson (Eds.). *Ecological Change in the Uplands*. Blackwell Scientific Publications, Oxford, pp. 75–92.

Usher, M. B. and Smart, L. M. (1988). Recolonization of burnt and cut heathland in the North York Moors by arachnids. *The Naturalist*, **113**, 103–111.

Usher, M. B. and Thompson, D. B. A. (1993). Variation in the upland heathlands of Great Britain: conservation importance. *Biological Conservation*, **66**, 69–81.

Walker, D. (1989). Diversity and stability. In J. M. Cherrett (Ed.) *Ecological Change*. Blackwell Scientific Publications, Oxford, pp. 115–145.

Watt, A. S. (1947). Pattern and process in the plant community. *Journal of Ecology*, **35**, 1–22.

PART THREE
MANAGEMENT FOR THE FUTURE

Experimental demonstration of change

Experimentally fertilised plot at Hoorneboeg, Netherlands, 1981 (application of between 0, 100, 200, 400 and 800kg NPK ha^{-1} yr^{-1}, ratio of 14%N: 16%P: 18%K) (J T de Smidt)

The same areas as above, photographed in 1989, indicating that Deschampsia *spp (hair grasses) have become more dominant at the expense of* Calluna *(ling)* (J T de Smidt)

Options for change

a) An intensively grazed hill landscape
b) A more carefully grazed hill landscape
c) A hill landscape dominated by heather
d) A hill landscape with woodland regeneration

(all produced by H. Insh; refer to C. Bullock's Chapter 25)

a)

b)

c)

d)

PART THREE

MANAGEMENT FOR THE FUTURE

Just as management of change seems to be so important for our society these days, so it is for heaths and moorland. That these landscapes are predominantly the product of management is not in doubt, but how should management continue into the future?

It is perhaps surprising that these managed lands, so revered for their beauty and rich crop of red grouse, have not had their management processes studied at all extensively. Instead, there has been a wealth of work undertaken in just a few parts of upland Britain, notably in NE Scotland by Charles Gimingham and his students. Indeed, there have been decades of research on red grouse populations (e.g. Leslie, 1911; Lawton, 1990), but the actual importance of land management has not featured prominently in the most recent work. At the broader landscape level, there have been many discussions on the likely impacts of agricultural change on hill land, but specific debate on how the shape and tapestry of the hill is likely to change has been lacking.

In Part III of the book there are nine papers that transcend work on management of moorland landscapes and ecological change. Bullock details research that is examining the benefits to the public of changes arising from new, emerging land-use policies. Whilst he is attempting to visualise how vegetation, and therefore landscapes, will alter under different grazing regimes, the novelty is that he has employed Contingent Valuation to explore the willingness of the public to pay for particular features of the landscape. Many questions spring to mind, not least how one should marry up the public's desire to see more woodland in the uplands against the costs of actually establishing it. This pilot study points importantly to how some of these issues might be resolved. Hudson reports on changes in grouse management, and factors influencing these. This builds on his book (Hudson, 1992), pointing to the effects of large herbivores (notably sheep and red deer) and predators (notably crows and foxes) on red grouse populations. Again, it is heartening to hear about new research, supported by several key countryside bodies, seeking to understand which factors actually influence moorland bird populations. There are also many unknowns about the management and impacts of red deer on moorland (Staines *et al.*), though we seem to understand rather more about the suppressive effects of grazing and browsing by deer on woodland regeneration. Here, yet again, we clearly need research tailored towards addressing practitioners' questions about how red deer and their habitats should be managed (SNH, 1994).

Whilst one readily thinks of cropping grouse or sheep when managing the uplands, one easily overlooks some other key land-uses. There are two papers on the extent of domestic peat cutting on Orkney (Kirkpatrick *et al.*) and in the wet heath and blanket bogs of Northern Ireland (Todd *et al.*). In both parts of the United Kingdom it seems that successive cutting has an adverse effect on habitats and wildlife. The latter study indicates that cut-over areas have fewer key invertebrates, with mechanised peat extraction having a rapid effect on plant and invertebrate communities. The Orkney study points to the importance of replacing the top layer of turves when a peat bank has been exhausted.

Ward *et al.* review how conservation of heaths and moorland should be taken forward. Building on the experience and outputs of previous workers, they advocate that the most pragmatic approach to nature conservation should be based on managing habitats specifically for high profile 'flagship' and 'keystone' species. They conclude that, at least in Scotland, only about one third of heath and moorland is likely to be under some form of protection or positive management, with conservation being taken forward effectively only through the implementation of major environmental and/or agricultural schemes. Experiences of people working on two of Britain's Environmentally Sensitive Areas (ESAs) reinforces this last view. The Loch Lomond ESA was one of the first to be designated in Scotland, primarily for the maintenance and enhancement of heather moorland. Monitoring, since 1989, indicates that heather is generally being maintained under present management (Henderson *et al.*). In Northern Ireland, ESAs have had a comprehensive monitoring programme set up more recently (1993), and here it may well be that the ground beetle fauna proves to be particularly useful for revealing changes (McFerran *et al.*).

Part III is concluded with an overview of key requirements for the management of heather moorland (Phillips and Watson). This stresses the importance of sound, traditional, integrated land management. The problems of past mismanagement are spelled out clearly, and far reaching remedial action is proposed.

Three general conclusions emerge from these papers. First, much more work is needed to inform landscape management for public enjoyment, with a particular challenge being to combine this with socio-economic gains. Second, at least two approaches have been adopted towards understanding red grouse management – the empirical habitat management approach and the modelling approach. No wonder that Ratcliffe (1990) ended his review of red grouse research in the British Isles with the words: 'The only general conclusion to be drawn here is that truth has many sides.' Third, there are clearly many opportunities for further work addressing how existing subsidies for hill farming, forestry and other land-use practices might be targeted towards bringing more benefits for wildlife. Here, however, we still have some way to go in defining precisely what society wants and needs from heaths and moorlands. Several of these issues are pursued in more detail in the Finale.

References

Hudson, P. J. (1992). *Grouse in Space and Time. The Population Biology of a Managed Game Bird.* The Game Conservancy Trust, Fordingbridge.

Lawton, J. H. (Editor) (1990). *Red Grouse: Population Processes.* British Ecological Society, London.

Leslie, A. S. (Editor) (1911). *The Grouse in Health and in Disease, being the Final Report of the Committee of Inquiry on Grouse Disease,* Vol I. Smith, Elder, London.

Ratcliffe, D. A. (1990). *Birdlife of Mountain and Upland.* Cambridge University Press, Cambridge.

Scottish Natural Heritage (1994). *Red Deer and the Natural Heritage. SNH Policy Paper.* Scottish Natural Heritage, Battleby.

25 MEASURING THE PUBLIC BENEFITS OF LANDSCAPE AND ENVIRONMENTAL CHANGE: A CASE OF UPLAND GRAZING EXTENSIFICATION

C. Bullock

Summary

1. The research attempts to quantify the public benefits of landscape and environmental change that may arise from new land-use policies.

2. The case of upland grazing extensification is examined for which the associated vegetation change could be diffuse and complex. These problems will require carefully designed environmental valuation methods to communicate the change anticipated.

25.1 Introduction

The new agri-environmental measures that have accompanied the recent reform of the Common Agricultural Policy (CAP) offer an opportunity to decelerate the intensification of agricultural production, to protect the landscape and to restore habitats for wildlife. The resources available for these policies are likely to be restricted for the time being and to remain dwarfed by payments to farmers that are linked to production. Nevertheless, environmental considerations are certain to have more influence on agricultural policies in the future and the measures should be considered as part of this gradual process.

As resources are limited, it is important that policymakers have adequate information on what types of habitats and countryside the public would like to see and use. Here, environmental economics has a role as it can provide valuation techniques which can be used to quantify preferences for public goods. Some goods, for example, attractive landscapes, do not enter a market process and, as such, are unpriced, but are nevertheless *valued* by society.

There is a limited choice of suitable valuation techniques where goods such as landscape or countryside are concerned. For these types of goods, many of the benefits people derive arise from simply knowing that such goods *exist*, irrespective of current or planned use. In this case, contingent valuation (CV) is often the preferred valuation technique as it can estimate much of the satisfaction (or utility) an individual gains from both use and non-use benefits, such as existence. Aggregated over the population, the valuation of these benefits can be compared with the costs of implementing the policy to supply them.

CV relies upon sample surveys to elicit from people an expressed preference for some change in the quantity or quality of a good. It does this by asking how much utility an individual would be prepared to forfeit, expressed as their maximum willingness to pay, to bring about the equivalent increase in utility supplied by an increase in a desirable good. (They could also be asked for their willingness to pay to prevent a *loss* of some desirable good. Or their minimum willingness to *accept* a loss of a desirable good to which they have perceived property rights.) The technique is particularly useful for comparing the value of a current situation with one that would follow from hypothetical future changes.

In this project, the intention is to estimate individuals' willingness to pay to preserve a current situation compared with their willingness to pay for changes that might result from different levels of agri-environmental policy implementation. One agri-environmental measure, upland sheep grazing extensification, is addressed. If an area is subjected to reductions in grazing pressure, environmental changes could affect the whole landscape but would vary from the diffuse, e.g. changes in sward type, to the more overtly visual, e.g. expansion of heather and scrub, depending upon the level of extensification and local conditions. The challenge is how to represent these changes in a public survey, to explain the processes that brought them about and to detach a valuation of their effects from other unrelated environmental attributes.

25.2   The Case of Grazing Extensification

Agri-environmental measures are still being considered by the European Commission, but an indication of the types of extensification policies that might be implemented in the UK is provided by the grazing prescriptions available to farmers in some environmentally sensitive areas such as the new Southern Uplands environmentally sensitive area. Here, payments of up to £45 per hectare are available to farmers who volunteer for reductions in sheep numbers above the hill-dyke. An improvement in the condition and geographical extent of heather is the main objective behind this policy. Although sheep farming in the southern uplands is not particularly intensive, it has had a long history during which grazing has been a factor in reducing the area of native scrub and heather. This process has been hastened in recent years due to less attentive management and muirburn. The countryside retains its attractions, but the uplands themselves are often very open and grassy and, away from the sporting estates, any heather is limited in extent.

25.3   The Method

The survey will concentrate on residents in southern Scotland who will be presented with scenarios that describe the effect of current ESA policy impacts, and the effect of policies which encourage successive stages of natural regeneration:

- An intensively grazed landscape with litle heather or trees/scrub.

- The landscape as it appears now with some remaining heather and trees/scrub.

- A landscape in which heather is dominant and a few gullies have been invaded by more scrub.

- A landscape in which there is some heather but where trees/scrub are dominant.

The first of these represents a landscape that is already familiar in some parts of the uplands and one that could become more common if current sheep numbers and practices are maintained. The second is the type of landscape that current ESA grazing and fencing prescriptions will be seeking to preserve. The third and the fourth are examples of vegetation succession that may follow from, respectively, a radical reduction or elimination of grazing. These last two imply the introduction of some habitat management or habitat creation. Pictorial images similar to those in Plate X(a–d) will help to focus the questions in the survey and to elicit a preferred option.

Landscape scenarios have been used before in environmental valuation surveys (e.g. Willis and Garrod, 1991) and, if well designed, are an effective medium through which to express visual change and stimulate respondent participation. However, *landscape* and *environment* are not synonymous. Therefore, the survey will first attempt to elicit preferences for landscape change, but will go on to ask for individuals' willingness to pay for environmental change once the pictorial scenarios have been supplemented by valid environmental information.

However, the vegetation succession depicted in two of the scenarios has all the qualifications of a so-called 'complex good' (Hutchinson and Chilton, unpublished), that is a good which is not easily described. In particular, problems to be overcome include the representation of: time scale, uncertainty, scale and preservation vs. enhancement.

1. Time scale. Time is an important factor. Unaided, heather, and especially scrub and trees, could regenerate only slowly or near to existing seed sources. There may also be less aesthetically appealing stages.

2. **Uncertainty.** Although vegetation succession is featured rather than extensification *per se*, respondents may doubt that the changes will ever occur.

3. **Scale.** While all the Southern Uplands hills could potentially be protected by an ESA, not all this area could be given over to heather or woodland. Indeed, such lack of diversity would not be desirable to most people.

4. **Preservation.** Psychological studies show the importance people attach to the status-quo (e.g. Samuelson and Zeckhauser, 1988). This survey is asking people to decide between simple preservation and options they may (or may not) regard as 'enhancement'.

Figure 25.1. Scenarios of environmental change due to extensification (1) An intensively grazed landscape (2) A carefully grazed landscape (3) A landscape dominated by heather (4) A landscape with tree regeneration. See final plate

Unless the CV survey is carefully designed so that respondents fully understand what it is they are being asked to value, biases can arise that cause expressed willingness to pay to deviate from its true value. In particular, there is the risk that respondents will be suspicious that the scenarios will never materialise, or of bids motivated less by a rational appraisal of the good in question than by the moral satisfaction of donating to a good cause (Kahneman and Knetch, 1992). This reinforces the fact that

> 'the principle challenge facing the designer of a CV study is to make the scenario sufficiently understandable, plausible and meaningful to respondents so that they can and will give valid and reliable values despite their lack of experience with one or more of the scenario's dimensions.' (Mitchell and Carson, 1986)

The survey must therefore describe the full context and marketplace such as to ensure that respondents understand as equally and exactly as possible what it is they are being asked to value. A procedure of in-depth trial questioning and discussion groups will be used to select appropriate language and question order while eliminating superfluous information. This will help to reduce the length of the final questionnaire.

If these problems can be overcome, it should be possible to arrive at reliable estimates of the aggregate public benefits associated with some new land use policies. This is not to argue that these estimates can be precise or all inclusive, but they can be used in conjunction with other data in the selection of policy and the formulation of environmental priorities. The new agri-environmental measures being considered in Brussels are a case in point. Without environmental valuation and appraisal, political expediency could triumph at the expense of more worthy projects.

References

Hutchinson, W. G. and Chilton, S.M. (unpublished). Topical issues in the use of the contingent valuation method for valuing environmental resources, paper presented to the Agricultural Economics Society Conference, Oxford, April 1993. (Copies available from Queens University, Belfast).

Kahneman, D. and Knetch, J. L. (1992). Valuing public goods: the purchase of moral satisfaction, *Journal of Environmental Economics and Management*, 22, 57–70.

Mitchell, R. C. and Carson, R. T. (1986). *Using Surveys to Value Public Goods – The Contingent Valuation Method*. Resources for the Future, Washington D.C,

Samuelson, W. and Zeckhauser, R. (1988). Status-quo bias in decision making, *Journal of Risk and Uncertainty*, 1, 7–59.

Willis, K. and Garrod, G. (1991). Landscape values: a contingent valuation approach and case study of the Yorkshire Dales National Park *Working Paper*, 21, Countryside Change Unit, University of Newcastle upon Tyne, 1–37.

26 ECOLOGICAL TRENDS AND GROUSE MANAGEMENT IN UPLAND BRITAIN

P. J. Hudson

Summary

1. This chapter reviews trends in grazing intensity and predation pressure and the possible impacts these will have on the abundance of grouse species and sustainability of grouse management over the next 20 years.

2. On average, managed grouse moors make a financial loss although some of this loss may be set against sporting benefits taken by the land owner. Revenue from driven grouse shooting exceeds that of walked up shooting but requires a higher density of grouse (about 60 km^{-2}), and hence greater inputs into grouse management. At the current time, driven shooting is necessary if grouse shooting is to be sustained as a viable land use practice.

3. Overutilization of heaths by large herbivores has directly reduced the extent of suitable gamebird habitat. Overgrazing may also have an indirect impact on the productivity of gamebird populations by reducing cover from predators, the abundance and availability of invertebrates eaten by young grouse, and by increasing the abundance of ticks that transmit diseases.

4. There is evidence to suppose that predators on grouse, particularly foxes and crows, have increased in Scotland. There is evidence that predation may be inversely density-dependent, and effectively form a predation trap where predators may suppress grouse numbers to low density.

26.1 Introduction

Gamebird management has been a major form of land use in the British uplands over the past 100 years and consequently has made a serious impact on the distribution and abundance of moorland habitat and the animal communities associated with this habitat. In Britain there are estimated to be some 47,300 km^2 of pasture and moorland (Ratcliffe and Thompson, 1988) in which there are 746 estates where red grouse shooting is conducted. They occupy 37,900 km^2 or 80 % of the total upland land area (Hudson, 1992). Most of these estates (62 %) have grouse management and the production of a sustainable yield of red grouse (*Lagopus lagopus scoticus*) as their major objective although upland areas generally support a multiple land use system including sheep farming, deer stalking, water catchment, recreational attractions as well as conservation interests. Other game birds may be harvested on these estates but this review will concentrate principally on red grouse and make reference to the other grouse species: capercaillie (Tetrao urogallus), black grouse (*Tetrao tetrix*) and ptarmigan (*Lagopus mutus*).

Grouse shooting became a fashionable sport at the turn of the century when Queen Victoria bought the Balmoral Estate and shotguns became simpler and lighter to use with the development of breech loading. Grouse management intensified and grouse numbers increased as keepers became responsible both for the burning of heather moorland and for the control of predators. Over the following 40 years, numbers of red grouse harvested remained relatively high until the second world war when the number of keepers decreased and grouse numbers fell (Hudson, 1992). In Scotland, the bag records showed a second decline during the 1980s although this was associated not with a decrease in the number of keepers employed but with an apparent increase in fox numbers (Figure 26.1).

This chapter reviews trends in upland management which may have an impact on the number of grouse over the next 20 years. In particular the chapter concentrates on the effects of increased grazing intensity and predation pressure but ignores changes in burning practices, principally because no quantified trend in this practice has been published. Game production is financially expensive so to consider the future of grouse management we must first examine certain economic aspects of upland estate management.

26.2 Economics of Red Grouse Management

At the national level, grouse shooting attracts significant funds to upland areas when visiting sportsmen come to Britain to shoot grouse. An economic research study conducted by McGilvray and Perman (1992) in Scotland found that only 10 % of sportsmen who shot grouse were from Scotland, 50 % came from other parts of the UK, 11 % from The US and the remaining 19 % from the rest of the world. In 1989, these sportsmen paid on average £60 per brace shot and attracted a revenue of £5.8 million to Scotland. Added to this was their expenditure of an estimated £9.5 million on additional services such as accommodation, equipment and gifts; generating a total revenue to Scotland of £15.3 million. The revenue in England is probably of the same order or even greater because of the much higher bags recorded.

Turning now to the balance sheet of the average grouse shooting estate during 1989, the annual income from grouse shooting was £12 000, the total expenditure, balanced between goods, wages and services was £20 000 producing a net loss of £8,000 per estate (McGilvray and Perman, 1992). This loss was usually funded by the private estate owner who principally owns a grouse moor for the enjoyment of

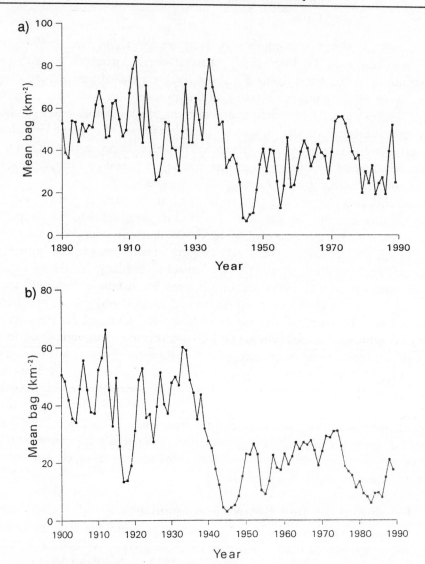

Figure 26.1. Changes in numbers of red grouse shot in (a) Britain, and (b) Scotland. Note the decline in numbers not only associated with the Second World War but also with the 1980s (after Hudson, 1992).

managing an area of Scottish hill but also so he can retain a certain amount of private shooting. Since 1989 was a reasonable year for grouse shooting in Scotland (Figure 26.1) we can expect losses to be generally greater in other years and the scale of this annual loss can become significant with respect to the landowners' other investments. When this cost is too large, the private estate owner is forced to sell, and this often leads to a change in land use.

The income generated by grouse shooting depends first on the density of grouse available to harvest and second on the type of shooting undertaken. Driven grouse shooting in 1992 attracted fees of £60–£90 per brace while walked up shooting attracted fees of £20–£40 per brace. However, driven grouse shooting can only effectively be undertaken when densities of grouse are sufficiently high, usually in excess of 60 birds km^{-2}, while walked-up shooting, with or without pointing dogs, is usually undertaken at densities of less than 60 birds km^{-2}.

The fixed and variable costs of an average grouse shoot in 1992 are summarized in Table 26.1; in Scotland an average estate usually employed one keeper to every 20–40 km^2 while in northern England a keeper is employed to every 10–20 km^2. When the net income is examined in relation to the density of grouse available for shooting it becomes apparent that it is only when there is a sufficient density of grouse for driven shooting that grouse shooting becomes financially viable (Figure 26.2). Of course, costs could be reduced by removing the keeper and the small income from walked up shooting could result in a net profit. In this scenario, only a few grouse could be harvested but this is not the objective of most grouse moor owners who wish to develop a grouse shoot with a reasonable number of birds to harvest.

Table 26.1   A summary of average fixed and variable costs of grouse management during 1992.

	Amount (in £)	Quantity
Fixed costs		
Keepers wages etc.	13 000	annum^{-1}
Additional costs	2000	annum^{-1}
Variable costs		
Beaters wages	15	persons day^{-1}
Beaters employed	20	persons
Driven bag of grouse	150	birds day^{-1}
Shooting rates	5	grouse^{-1}
Income		
Driven grouse shooting	35	grouse^{-1}
Walked up shooting	12	grouse^{-1}
Sale of young grouse	0.50	grouse^{-1}
Sale of old grouse	1.75	grouse^{-1}

In summary it is important to note that factor that could reduce red grouse density to less than 60 birds km^{-2} would result in grouse moors no longer being financially viable and make it difficult for owners to manage these areas.

26.3   Factors influencing Grouse Numbers

A number of ecological trends have decreased the abundance and distribution of grouse species. These include the loss of habitat through overgrazing and a general increase in the abundance of some of the birds natural enemies. There may also be

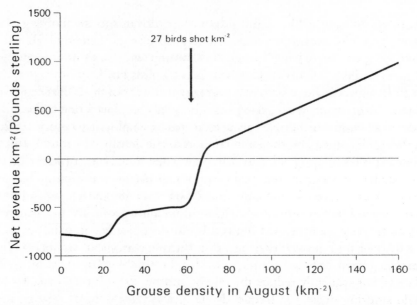

Figure 26.2. Estimated net revenue km^{-2} from grouse shooting in relation to grouse density estimated according to the figures presented in Table 26.2 and assuming a keeper is employed to every 20 km^2. When grouse densities are greater than 60 grouse km^{-2} then driven grouse shooting is undertaken and when less than 60 grouse km^{-2} walked up shooting is undertaken.

a number of anthropogenic effects such as man-induced destruction of habitat, overharvesting and disturbance, but these will not be included within this chapter.

26.3.1 *Increased grazing intensity*
Within the last 40 years, there has been an increase in the grazing intensity of some upland habitats by a range of upland herbivores including sheep and deer that has made a significant impact on the distribution and perhaps quality of gamebird habitat. Grazing may result in the loss of key plant species, such as heather (*Calluna vulgaris*), but there is a need to understand the indirect effects of moderate grazing pressure on vegetation structure which may lead to reduced cover and the availability of arthropods as a good source for young grouse.

26.3.2 *Overgrazing and effects on distribution of gamebirds*
A number of chapters in this volume describe how grazing intensity can result in a change in vegetation composition which can then have consequences for the distribution and abundance of a number of animal species. For upland grouse species, high grazing intensity can lead to a change in vegetation composition and a direct impact on the birds' distribution. Loss of heather dominant vegetation leads to a reduction in the distribution of red grouse (Anderson and Yalden, 1981; Hudson, 1992); loss of blaeberry (*Vaccinium myrtilus*) could lead to a reduction in capercaillie (Storch, 1994) and a loss of dwarf shrubs on the mountain plateaux to a loss of

ptarmigan (Thompson *et al.*, 1987). Each of these impacts can result from heavy grazing intensity by herbivores.

While it is clear that changes in grazing intensity can result in a change in vegetation composition, it is useful to understand the elements that determine the level of grazing intensity. Grazing intensity is frequently expressed as density of the predominant herbivore, usually sheep or deer, but this parameter alone fails to consider the seasonal diet of the herbivore, the distribution of the herbivores throughout the habitat and the interaction between species. The introduction of an additional species into a grazing system, where the introduced species has a different damaging impact on the plant species could act synergistically with the indigenous herbivores and increase the rate of vegetation change at a faster than expected level. On the other hand, when a second grazing animal selectively removes an invading species then the combination of the two grazing species could reduce the rate of vegetation change. For example, cattle introduced onto a sward of heather grazed heavily by sheep could reduce the rate of invasion by *Molinia caerulea* and consequently reduce the rate of heather loss (Torvell *et al.*, 1988).

While stocking density is frequently the primary measure of grazing intensity, there are still many areas of upland Britain where stocking density is below the level where overgrazing is expected to occur but vegetation loss still occurs because herbivore distribution is aggregated within the habitat (Hudson, 1992). A clear example of this is the concentration of sheep at winter feeding sites (a practice known as fothering in northern England), in areas where the sheep are not shepherded after feeding. In this instance, sheep concentrate around the feeding area for several hours before and after feeding and this results in the localized damage of heather vegetation through both grazing and trampling (Figure 26.3). Similar impacts also occur on deer forests when deer are artificially fed but their distribution may also be influenced by weather, disturbance and the siting of fence lines.

26.3.3 Overgrazing and effects on the abundance of gamebirds

While heavy grazing can result in the direct loss of suitable habitat (e.g. Grant *et al.*, 1982) and a reduction in gamebird distribution, a more moderate grazing intensity can have more subtle indirect effects resulting in a reduction in gamebird density. Such effects include reduced cover from predators, increased parasite transmission and reduced availability of arthropods taken by young gamebirds.

Moderate grazing will reduce vegetation biomass and may well result in reduced cover from predators. Good cover is known to reduce nest losses in some gamebird species including grey partridge, *Perdix perdix* (Rands, 1986), willow ptarmigan *Lagopus lagopus lagopus* (Erikstad *et al.*, 1982), black grouse (Baines, 1993) and capercaillie (Storaas, 1988). However this may vary between areas since nest cover was not found to be important in some willow ptarmigan populations (Myrberget, 1985; O'Reilly and Hannon, 1989) or in black grouse (Brittas and Willebrand, 1991).

Since grazing animals reduce the biomass of vegetation it seems likely that they will have a direct impact on the herbivorous arthropods associated with the

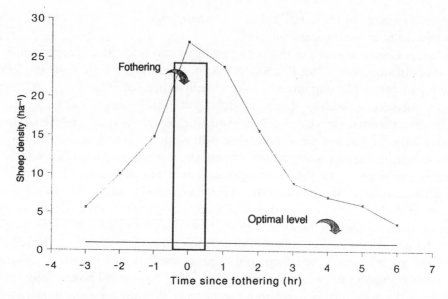

Figure 26.3. Average sheep density within 200 m of sheep winter feeding sites in relation to time since artificial feeding (fothering) commenced. Note that sheep density remained well above the optimum grazing level necessary to sustain heather throughout this period and rapidly resulted in over utilisation of the heather within one area even though overall density of sheep was relatively low.

vegetation and thus may reduce the availability of food for grouse chicks. Extensive sampling of blaeberry has shown that heavily grazed plots had only 28 % of the number of lepidopteran larvae that were found on ungrazed sites although the biomass of the blaeberry was only reduced to 43 % by the heavy grazing (Baines *et al.*, 1993). In other words, the grazing animals appear to have had a greater than expected impact on the lepidopteran larvae which may have consequences for the availability of food for woodland grouse.

A number of parasites are known to have a direct impact on the breeding production and survival of red grouse including the flavivirus that causes the disease louping ill. Infected grouse suffer an 80 % mortality from the disease which is transmitted between viraemic hosts (principally sheep and grouse) by the sheep tick *Ixodes ricinus* (Duncan *et al.*, 1979; Hudson, 1992). The abundance of ticks and consequently the likelihood of hosts being infected is a function of the frequency with which ticks bite their hosts. In areas where ticks occur, abundance is greatest where the vegetation has a thick mat layer, such as in bracken beds (Hudson, 1985) or areas of unpalatable grass. Heavy grazing can result in the replacement of palatable vegetation by unpalatable vegetation which develops a thick mat layer leading to more ticks and consequently increased transmission of the virus and reduced grouse densities.

In summary, heavy grazing intensity will decrease the extent of suitable game-bird habitat. However, moderate grazing intensity can lead to a reduction in cover, a reduction in invertebrate food for chicks and possibly an increase in the abundance of ticks and associated diseases which may lead to reduced grouse densities.

26.4 Increased Predation Pressure

Grouse species are prey to a range of predators, numbers of which have generally increased since 1940. Greater numbers of predators may lead to increased predation pressure and mortality of grouse which will have an impact on the size of the grouse population and the potential harvest. Even so, the extent to which predation reduces the size of the grouse population will depend on when the predation operates, the pattern of predation (density dependent or not) and on compensation from other causes of mortality.

26.4.1 Changes in grouse predators

The predators of grouse include two groups, those that can be legally controlled and those that can not be legally controlled. In the former category, the principal predator is the fox (*Vulpes vulpes*), a generalist predator that takes grouse when available. Anecdotal or, at best, 'natural experiments' provide evidence that these predators are important in reducing the breeding production and harvest of red grouse. Grouse moors which have a high density of keepers controlling predators tend to have more grouse. When keepering ceases, grouse numbers fall and when predator control is initiated, irrespective of heather management, numbers of grouse increase (Hudson, 1992).

In Scotland, the numer of foxes killed by keepers has increased since 1960 (Hewson, 1984; Hudson, 1992), probably for two reasons. First, the number of keepers employed on upland estates decreased over the War years (Hudson, 1992) so the levels of fox control were reduced. Second, the number of foxes killed by keepers was associated with the number of rabbits (*Oryctolagus cuniculus*) killed in the same area and when rabbit numbers recovered from myxomatosis in the early seventies there was an increase in the number of foxes taken by keepers (Figure 26.4). While this is not a demonstration of an increase in fox predation pressure it is interesting to note that comparisons between moors indicate that in areas where keepers kill many foxes the majority of grouse found dead have died through predation whereas in areas where there are few foxes, the grouse tend to die from other factors such as heavy levels of parasitism from the caecal nematode *Trichostrongylus tenuis* (Hudson *et al.*, 1992).

Crow (*Corvus corone*) numbers killed by keepers have also increased and in both eastern Scotland and southern Scotland this has been associated with an increase in the extent of afforestation (Hudson, 1992). Forestry ground provides a refuge for crows from keepering activities but it also provides an abundance of suitable nesting sites compared with the relatively treeless moorland areas.

In the past, keepers have probably made a significant impact on the distribution and abundance of some predatory birds. At the turn of the century hen harriers (*Circus cyaneus*) were restricted to parts of northern Scotland (Watson, 1977), probably as a consequence of persecution. With protection, numbers and distribution

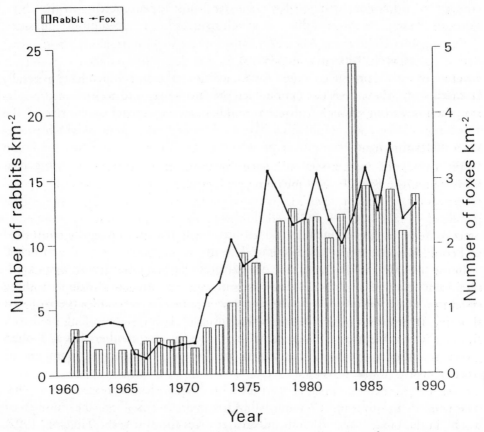

Figure 26.4. The change in the number of foxes and rabbits killed per km^2 on grouse moors in eastern and southern Scotland in relation to the number of rabbits shot. The close association between rabbit and fox numbers suggest the rabbits may have provided a food source which allowed numbers to increase although at the same time the density of keepers was lower than it had been prior to myxomatosis.

have increased although the extent of the current distribution still remains much less than the potential distribution within suitable habitat both on moorland and lowland habitats (Etheridge, 1993).

26.4.2 Dynamics of predation

The relative importance of predation to changes in the population depend on the pattern and processes of the predation. Recent studies provide evidence to suppose that winter predation on grouse is inversely density dependent (Hudson, 1992, unpublished). Comparisons of mortality to predators both within and between study areas shows that the mortality was lower at high grouse densities than at low grouse densities. Such an effect can be destabilizing and lead to a 'predation trap' where predators suppress grouse numbers to very low densities although the relative importance of this to equilibrium grouse density will depend on the timing and strength of other density dependent processes such as density dependent dispersal (Hudson, 1992).

One problem with managing a population where inverse density dependent predation occurs is that density independent factors that act to reduce the population severely, or even density dependent losses acting with a time delay, can cause populations to fall to low densities from which the inverse density dependent predation may then be strong enough to prevent numbers increasing.

26.5 Discussion

While a range of factors may influence the abundance and distribution of game birds within the next 20 years including ecological, anthropogenic as well as political pressures, this chapter has concentrated on the two specific ecological trends of increased grazing intensity and predation pressure. Not that these two factors can be considered independent since a change in grazing intensity may influence cover and could influence vulnerability of game birds to predators.

In the uplands, and in particular in the Scottish Highlands, red grouse shooting is a significant form of land use. To be sustained and to maintain a multiple land use system on these estates, moorland managers will attempt to produce driven grouse shooting. If pressures reduce density of red grouse below a level where driven grouse shooting is possible, then the majority of land owners and their clients lose interest in grouse shooting as a form of land use. This in effect reduces the capital value of the piece of land and may then be sold to an alternative form of singular land use which are less sympathetic to a multiple land use system that incorporates the objectives of conservation and tourism. Commercial afforestation and large areas of sheep walk would, in the broad sense, fall into this category since they would effectively result in the loss of heather, associated upland animal communities and a range of land use practices. Even so, in their early stages, young plantations may prove beneficial for species such as black grouse and hen harriers.

Heather moorland managed for red grouse produces a relatively homogenous habitat in which the diversity of plants and animals could be increased through the regeneration of scrub alongside streams. In pragmatic terms, this could be achieved through selective burning and reduced grazing. If driven grouse shooting could still be sustained in this habitat, and this has yet to be tested, then numbers of black grouse could be increased and the overall sporting value maintained through a greater diversity of sporting opportunities. Indeed, an important aspect of the economics of many estates is to attract paying guests who stay in accommodation supplied by the estate. Thus slightly reduced revenue from red grouse shooting, still harvested through driving, could be balanced against an increase in sporting diversity and income generated from the letting of accommodation.

While gross changes in habitat through over grazing are obvious, it is apparent that this is not merely related to stocking density. Distribution of herbivores and the interaction between herbivore species will also play a significant role. Moreover, moderate levels of grazing intensity could reduce densities of some species of game bird by reducing abundance (or possibly quality) of food or increasing vulnerability to natural enemies such as parasites and predators. In this respect, the practices of game management will need to change in the future as causes of mortality change. In the past, birds of prey were killed by keepers in the name of game production but few practical steps were taken against the impacts of grazing animals or the mortality induced by parasites. In the future, grouse managers must accept greater levels of mortality from birds of prey and may have to compensate these losses by reducing mortality from other causes such as parasitism or the loss of food abundance indirectly caused by grazing animals. Techniques for the control of parasitic worms have been developed and proved highly successful in preventing populations of grouse from falling to low densities (Hudson, 1992; Newborn *et al.*, 1994) although there is evidence that there is still a need to control foxes and crows if driven grouse shooting is to be sustained.

Ultimately a greater understanding of the dynamics of predation, the interaction between predators and the range of prey species needs to be understood on moorland. Inverse density dependent predation suggests that management should concentrate on the inimical factors that cause the large scale fall in numbers, such as parasitism, rather than controlling other causes of mortality when these are not significant. Control of predation in the past has tended to concentrate on lethal means but non lethal means (e.g. habitat alteration, management of alternative food supplies, taste aversion and predator exclusion) may provide a more acceptable approach. Moreover there is a need to understand how the timing of predator control influences the future impacts of predators. These studies should be considered against the requirement of maintaining driven grouse shooting. In this respect, studies such as The Joint Raptor Study, undertaken by the Game Conservancy Trust and Institute of Terrestrial Ecology and supported by the leading conservation bodies, which is studying the functional and numerical response of raptors to moorland prey will provide important guidelines for the future management and maintenance of a multiple land use system in the uplands.

Acknowledgements

I would like to thank Dave Newborn, John Drysdale, Ian McCall, Des Thompson, Lord Peel, David Baines, Simon Thirgood, Steve Redpath, David Laird and Nicola Crockford for a discussion on the points presented in this paper. David Baines, John Coulson, Simon Thirgood and two referees made constructive comments on the manuscript.

References

Anderson, P. and Yalden D. W. (1981). Increased sheep numbers and loss of heather moorland in the Peak District, England. *Biological Conservation*, **20**, 195–213.

Baines, D. (1993). *The Black Grouse Report*, Game Conservancy Trust. Fordingbridge.

Baines, D., Baines, M. M. and Sage, R. (1993). The importance of large herbivore management to woodland grouse and their habitats. In *Proceedings of the International Grouse Symposium*, Italy.

Brittas, R. and Willebrand, T. (1991). Nesting habitats and egg predation in Swedish black grouse. *Ornis Scandinavica* **22**, 261–3.

Duncan, J. S., Reid, H. W., Moss, R., Phillips, J. D. and Watson, A. (1979). Ticks, louping ill and red grouse on moors in Speyside, Scotland (*Lagopus lagopus scoticus*). *Journal of Wildlife Management* **43**, 500–505.

Erikstad, K. E., Blom., R. and Myrberget, S. (1982). Territorial hooded crows as predators on willow ptarmigan nests. *Journal of Wildlife Management* **46**, 109–14.

Etheridge, B. (1993). The hen harrier. In D. W. Gibbons, J. B. Reid, and R. A. Chapman, (Comp.), *The New Atlas of Breeding Birds in Britain and Ireland: 1988–1991. T and AD Poyser, London.*

Grant, S. A., Milne, J. A., Barthram, G. T. and Souter, W. G. (1982). Effects of season and level of grazing on the utilization of heather by sheep. III. Longer-term responses and sward recovery. *Grass Forage Science* **37**, 311–20.

Hewson, R. (1984). Changes in the number of foxes (*Vulpes vulpes*) in Scotland. *Journal of Zoology London.* **204**, 561–9.

Hudson, P. J. (1985). Bracken and ticks on grouse moors in northern England. In R. T. Smith and J. A. Taylor, (Eds.) *Bracken, Ecology land use and control technology.* Parthenon Publishing, Carnforth. 161–170.

Hudson, P. J. (1992). *Grouse in Space and Time.* The Game Conservancy Trust. Fordingbridge,

Hudons, P. J., Dobson, A. P. and Newborn, D. (1992). Do parasites make prey vulnerable to predation? red grouse and parasites. *Journal of Animal Ecology*, **61**, 681–92.

McGilvray, J. and Perman, R. (1992). Grouse shooting in Scotland: analysis of its importance to the economy and environment. Appendix 3 in P. J. Hudson, *Grouse in Space and Time*, Game Conservancy Trust, Fordingbridge.

Myrberget S. (1985). Egg predation in an island population of willow ptarmigan *Lagopus lagopus. Fauna norv. Ser. C, Cinculus.* **8**, 82–7.

Newborn, D., Hudson, P. J., Booth, F. and Howarth, D. (1994). Parasite control during 1993. *Game Conservancy Annual Review for 1993,* **25**, 117–9.

O'Reilly, P. and Hannon, S. J. (1989). Predation of simulated willow ptarmigan nests: the influence of density and cover on spatial and temporal patterns of predation. *Canadian Journal of Zoology* **67**, 1263–7.

Rands, M. R. W. (1986). The effects of hedgerow characteristics on partridge breeding densities. *Journal of Applied Ecology* **23**, 479–87.

Ratcliffe, D. A. and Thompson, D. B. A. (1988). The British Uplands: their ecological character and international; significance. In M. B. Usher, and D. B. A. Thompson, (Eds.) *Ecological Change in the Uplands* Blackwell Scientific Publications, Oxford. 9–36.

Storass, T. (1988). A comparison of nest losses of artificial and naturally occurring capercaillie nests. *Journal of Wildlife Management* **51**, 123–6.

Storch, I. (1994). The relationship between capercaillie and bilberry (Vaccinium myrtilus). *Proceedings of the International Symposium on Grouse VI.* In press.

Thompson, D. B. A., Galbraith, H. and Horsfield, D. (1987). Ecology and resources of Britain's mountain plateaux: land conflicts and impacts. In M. Bell, and R. G. H. Bunce, (Eds) *Agriculture and Conservation in the Hills and Uplands.* ITE Symposium no. 23, ITE, Grange-over-Sands, 22–31.

Torvell, L., Common, T. G. and Grant, S. A. (1988). Seasonal patterns of tissue flow and responses of *Molinia* to defoliation. In M. B. Usher, and D. B. A. Thompson, (Eds.) *Ecological Change in the Uplands.* Blackwell Scientific Publications, Oxford, 219–222.

Watson, D. (1977). *The Hen Harrier.* T. and A. D. Poyser, Berkhamstead.

27 THE IMPACT OF RED DEER AND THEIR MANAGEMENT ON THE NATURAL HERITAGE IN THE UPLANDS

B. W. Staines, R. Balharry and D. Welch

Summary

1. Interactions between the management of red deer and the natural heritage are discussed.

2. Red deer populations in Scotland living on the open hill ground and in forestry plantations have increased considerably over the last 20 years, to a total population of around 300 000 in 1990.

3. The main impacts of red deer involve overgrazing, which especially affects the regeneration of native woodlands.

4. Reductions in deer densities are considered to be the best ecological means of allowing woodland regeneration. Fencing is a complementary tool, not a substitute.

5. The merits of lower deer densities for deer population dynamics are discussed. It is argued that the 'crop' from red deer would be affected less than is currently considered likely because lower densities should improve deer performance.

27.1 Introduction

This chapter discusses the problems associated with the management of red deer (*Cervus elaphus*) and how this management affects the natural heritage in upland Britain. We suggest ways to integrate red deer management with nature conservation.

Red deer are Britain's largest native land herbivore. They are a valuable sporting resource but also can cause considerable damage to other land use interests (Mitchell *et al.*, 1977; Callander and MacKenzie, 1991). Moreover, red deer have great public appeal, and the management of red deer is an important factor in helping to shape the attractive open landscapes over some 3 million ha of Highland Scotland (Scottish Natural Heritage, 1994).

Red deer have long been regarded as damaging to forestry and agriculture and the issues are well documented (Darling, 1937; Lowe, 1961; Mitchell *et al.*, 1977; Clutton-Brock and Albon, 1989; Staines and Welch, 1989; Callander and MacKenzie, 1991). Indeed, a major part of the Deer (Scotland) Act 1959 is concerned with protecting these other land uses. Nature conservation had little influence in the thinking behind the 1959 Act except with regard to the deer themselves. However, in recent years there has been a more general awareness of the problems associated with red deer and the natural heritage, especially those resulting from overgrazing (e.g. Clutton-Brock, 1991; McKelvie, 1991; Staines, 1991).

The adverse impacts of overgrazing by red deer and hill sheep have been recognized for decades by ecologists (Gordon, 1925; Darling, 1937, 1955; Mitchell *et al.*, 1977). The main areas of concern with respect to the natural heritage are the regeneration of native woodlands, loss of dwarf shrub and tall herb communities, effects on rare plant species (especially alpines) and, in some districts, soil erosion.

Concomitant with this awareness of the damaging effects by red deer on nature conservation interests has been a reaction from some people who fear that those concerned with wildlife will propose a massive reduction in deer numbers for the benefit of the natural heritage but to the detriment of those people mainly interested in deer (McKelvie, 1991; Wigan, 1991).

While accepting that red deer share much of their range with some 2 million hill sheep, and it is difficult to quantify the relative impacts of either herbivore, we here focus on red deer and their management.

27.2 Background

Red deer were originally animals of open woodland and have been present in Britain since the last Ice Age some 11 000 years ago. However, over the last 5000 years there has been a progressive loss of forest due to climate and to man, so that by 1900 only 3 % of the land surface had woodland cover.

Red deer were able to adapt to the loss of woodland habitat in Scotland by occupying the remoter, open moorlands where some topographic shelter was available and where they were relatively free from persecution (Ritchie, 1920; Mitchell *et al.*, 1977; Lister, 1984). The extent of heather (*Calluna vulgaris*) on the moors provided an abundant winter food, albeit of low quality (Kay and Staines, 1981). As a consequence of occupying this relatively infertile habitat, red deer have adapted in several ways. Body size is greatly reduced, puberty in females is delayed, and fertility is low. For example, puberty in females does not generally occur until 2 years 4 months or 3 years 4 months in most hill areas and 30–40 % of females giving birth in one year fail to breed in the next. In many woodlands (Ratcliffe, 1984a) and in some low-density hill populations (Staines, 1978a) fertile yearlings are common. Indeed, in some plantation forests in western and southwestern Scotland, fertile calves have been found (Ratcliffe, personal communication). Being relatively large ruminants, red deer are able to adapt to a low-quality diet in winter (e.g. heather) provided sufficient higher quality grasses are available to maintain the rumen microflora necessary for the digestion of forage (Kay and Staines, 1981). Shelter-seeking is an important facet in the behaviour of deer on open moors, and shelter may be the most limiting factor affecting winter distribution (Staines 1977, 1978b; Grace and Easterbee, 1979.

27.3 Red Deer Populations

27.3.1 Pre-1900

Red deer numbers in Scotland probably reached their lowest during the mid- to late-18th century (Cameron, 1923). During the 19th century, sport shooting became fashionable and there was a large increase in the number of estates devoted to deer stalking ('Deer forests') where deer were actively encouraged (Mitchell *et al.*, 1977; Callander and MacKenzie, 1991). The number of deer forests increased from 9 in 1790 to 99 in 1883 and 213 in 1912 (Lowe, 1961).

There are no good estimates of numbers at these times, but an example of possible trends comes from Evans (1890) who counted red deer on the Island of Jura, Western Scotland. His counts indicated an increase from 1394 to 1965 between 1878 and 1890.

27.3.2 Post-1900

Because of the long-standing conflict between red deer management and other land uses (see Mitchell *et al.*, 1977; Callander and MacKenzie, 1991), there has been a continual interest in estimating the total population of red deer in Scotland. From a management viewpoint such global figures have limited value, and local densities related to local problems are much more important (Staines and Ratcliffe, 1987). Nevertheless, attempts at estimating total populations have been made (Table 27.1), but until recently they have been little more than intelligent guesses. Since 1959 the Red Deer Commission (RDC) has systematically counted large areas of Scotland annually (see Stewart, 1985) (Table 27.1). Analyses of the Scottish red deer population can be found in Mitchell *et al.*, (1977), Stewart (1985), Staines and Ratcliffe (1987) and particularly Clutton-Brock and Albon (1989), who used a more sophisticated modelling approach on the RDC data. Numbers of red deer on hill land appeared to decline in the early 1960s before rising sharply in the late 1960s and early 1970s; they reached about 300 000 in 1989. The main increase appears to be in the hind stock with stags remaining relatively constant (Clutton-Brock and Albon, 1989).

The increases in red deer numbers appear to be greater in the eastern and central Highlands than in the west (Stewart, 1985) (Tables 27.2 and 27.3). There has also been an extension of range, especially in areas previously managed for other land uses such as red grouse (*Lagopus lagopus scoticus*) and hill sheep (Staines and Ratcliffe,

1987). Probably a variety of interacting factors such as underculling of hinds, reduced competition with hill sheep and less severe winters have caused the population increase, and afforestation of low ground has led to a change in distribution in some places (Staines and Ratcliffe, 1987; Clutton-Brock and Albon, 1989).

Table 27.1   Estimates of the Scottish red deer population.

Year	Numbers (thousands)	Source
1900+	150	Cameron (1923)
1930	250	Parnell (1932)
1959	150–160	Lowe (1961)
1965	180	Stewart (1979)
1970	185	Stewart (1985)
1975	270	Stewart (1985)
1979	255	Red Deer Commission (1980)
1986	290	Stewart (1990)
1989	300	Stewart (1990)

Note: Population figures after 1970 include an estimate for the numbers of red deer thought to be living in forestry plantations; before this date, estimates related to open hill ground only (from Staines and Ratcliffe, 1987).

Table 27.2   Increase in red deer numbers in different areas of Scotland. Data from Staines and Ratcliffe (1987).

Area	Red deer numbers (date of count)			% increase
North Ross	7550 (1968)	10 850 (1984)	—	44
Monadhliaths	12 000 (1968)	20 350 (1977)	—	70
West Grampians	23 850 (1968)	33 100 (1983)	—	39
East Grampians	10 050 (1966)	19 300 (1975)	25 520 (1986)	154
Corrour/Ben Alder	7350 (1968)	9750 (1978)	—	33

Since the 1950s, red deer have colonized, many forestry plantations in Scotland, and have become resident. The total population living in plantations is believed to be between 27–50k (see Staines and Ratcliffe, 1987) with estimated densities as high as 1/2.2 ha in some areas (Ratcliffe, 1984a, b).

27.4 Conflicts between Deer and the Natural Heritage

27.4.1. *Woodland regeneration*

The lack of regeneration in many native woodlands brought about by high densities of red deer is probably the main concern of conservationists. This is not a new phenomenon (Ritchie, 1920; Darling, 1937, 1955). In 1925, Seton Gordon pointed out that the failure of the native pinewoods to regenerate in Upper Deeside was due to the large numbers of red deer found there in winter. Watson (1983) traced the history of woodland regeneration on the Mar Lodge estate back to the late 18th century when the Duke of Fife began to encourage the red deer stock for sport-shooting. Since that time, there has been little tree regeneration except in enclosures or in inaccessible places.

Table 27.3   Range of red deer densities found on open hill land in Scotland. From Staines and Ratcliffe (1987).

Count area	Area (ha)	Density (deer/100 ha)
Rovie/Skibo	20 500	0.5
Skye	60 750	1.6
North Sutherland	196 350	4.3
North Ross	160 750	4.8
South Ross	177 750	13.1
West Grampians	237 650	13.9
East Grampians	118 600	14.1
Glenartney	14 150	26.9
Scalpay	1 600	31.3

Because of the number of factors affecting woodland regeneration (Chapter 12), and the variety of situations where regeneration is required, it is not possible to give an overall deer density at which trees will regenerate. Nevertheless, from empirical studies, guideline figures can be proposed, which at least give an order of magnitude for deer reductions. These deer densities refer to the occupance of particular areas of ground and not to the overall stocking of the ground within which the deer range.

Holloway (1967) monitored Scots pine regeneration in three study areas on Deeside with different deer densities. At an estimated winter density of 1 deer/4 ha, few saplings of pine or birch lived beyond 10 years. At 1 deer/25 ha, saplings survived longer and some at least were likely to develop into trees; at 1 deer/60 ha there was little effect of deer on regeneration. Although sheep were present seasonally on these study sites, most damage occurred at times when they were absent. However, Holloway did not have sites in the forests of Upper Deeside with very high deer densities.

At Inshriach National Nature Reserve, Central Highlands, around 300 deer were estimated to be using the 3085 ha Reserve regularly (1/14 ha) before an increase in cull and live capture were introduced. Numbers have now been reduced to c. 80

(1/39 ha). This has allowed existing small saplings, especially of Scots pine, previously held in check, to get away (Table 27.4).

Table 27.4 Total number of Scots pine trees taller than the surrounding vegetation on 1000 m transects on the Inshriach and Invereshie NNRs. ( ) = % damage.

| Transect | No. of trees taller than the surrounding vegetation | | | |
	1983	1987	1991	1993
10	23 (62)	65 (51)	90 (57)	98 (18)
11	1 (100)	7 (29)	11 (27)	70 (16)
12	4 (100)	47 (9)	42 (36)	77 (29)
13	—	—	84 (7)	105 (46)

A reduction of deer numbers has also occurred at Creag Meagaidh NNR to c. 1/19 ha, apparently allowing regeneration of birch and rowan. Although the situation at Creag Meagaidh was complicated by a high sheep stock until 1983, the amount of tree regeneration seemed to accelerate only after the heavy deer 'culls' (Figure 27.1). Watson and Hinge (1989) surveyed moorlands throughout Deeside and Donside and found much regeneration of pine and birch in the middle and lower parts of the valleys where red deer were absent or at low density; sheep grazed many of these moors, but their occupance rates were low.

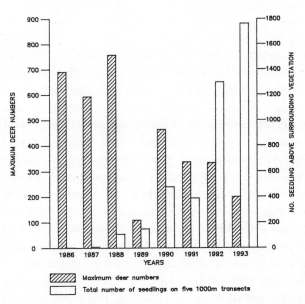

Figure 27.1. Relationship between maximum deer numbers and tree seedling growth at the Creag Meagaidh NNR. (Scottish Natural Heritage, unpublished data).

Current information, therefore, although crude, suggests that regeneration may occur on open ground where deer are approximately 1/15 ha or less. Darling (1955) intuitively suggested a density of 1/16 ha to allow woodland regeneration.

Other native trees such as rowan, willow (*Salix* spp.) and aspen (*Populus tremula*) are more affected than pine and birch because they are preferentially browsed by herbivores (Mitchell *et al.*, 1977; Chapter 12). Therefore, in order to have a full complement of tree and shrub species within a wood there would need to be a lower grazing pressure than if pine or birch alone were required.

27.4.2 Heather moorland

Many plant successions are affected by grazing by red deer and other herbivores (Miles, 1987). Dwarf shrub communities are replaced by monocotyledonous ones as grazing pressure increases and heather moorland in particular has declined throughout Scotland in the last 50 years, in part due to grazing or grazing management. There has been recent concern by various landowners, especially in north-east Scotland, that increased red deer numbers are adversely affecting heather moorland and consequently the viability of the grouse moor economy. However, because red deer and hill sheep frequently share the same range and since there are eight times as many sheep as deer in Scotland, it is difficult to quantify the relative effects of red deer and sheep on the decline in heather.

Mitchell *et al.*, (1977) believed that red deer would rarely cause succession from dwarf shrub heath to graminoid vegetation in open situations whereas hill sheep are frequently responsible. Red deer and sheep both graze grassy *Callunetum* in preference to pure *Callunetum*, but in one experiment red deer exerted less pressure on the peripheral heather in the 0–5 m zone next to large grass patches than did sheep, less time being spent on these patches by deer than by sheep (Clarke *et al.*, 1995a, 1995b). This suggests that when grazing pressures are heavy, sheep are the more likely species to cause existing grasslands to spread. Ball (1974) argued that, following the removal of the sheep stock on Rum NNR, much species-poor *Agrosto-Festucetum* became dominated by a few tall grass species and diversity declined. The inference was that red deer alone could not maintain the swards in a short and species-rich condition.

Changes in vegetation composition have been inferred in mixed-grazing situations where one herbivore only has changed in density. Thus, at Glen Clunie, Aberdeenshire, the glen floor supports about 1000 hill sheep in spring and autumn and large numbers of deer from November–April, but in summer both species mostly graze the higher ground. The botanical composition and state of the heather has been monitored at 7 sites since 1969 (Welch, 1984; Welch and Scott, 1995). Height is assessed in Autumn by 10 spot measures in each of 16 1 metre square quadrats at each site, and Figure 27.2 shows the trend in the mean yearly changes in height since 1970. This method of calculation was adopted since not all sites were assessed every year e.g. one site burnt in 1983 was not recorded again until 1991. It is clear from Figure 27.2 that heather steadily increased in height during the 1970s but in recent years has changed little. We believe that this has resulted

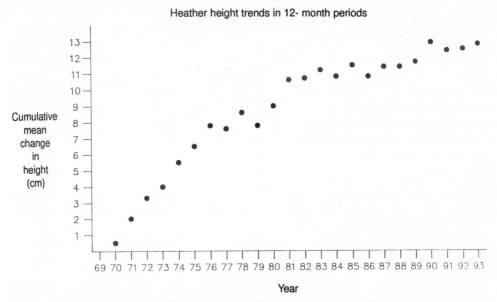

Figure 27.2. The effect of increasing stocking by red deer and sheep on trends in heather height in Glen Clunie (means are calculated from differences between successive years at up to seven monitoring sites).

from the build-up in deer numbers (an estimated 60 % increase in dung deposition from 1970–1973 to 1986–1989). The size of the sheep flock has been fairly constant over the last 30 years. Watson (1989) also, but subjectively, believed there was a shift from dwarf shrubs to graminoids in the same glen. However, at the study sites heather cover either showed a gradual increase or has remained in balance with grasses over the last 20 years. These cover trends, like the height trends, were calculated for sites not burnt during the observation periods; if losses in cover and height due to burning are taken into account it is probable that an overall decline in heather cover is now occurring in Glen Clunie.

In Glen Feshie, Inverness-shire, changes in the composition of vegetation since 1970 can be largely attributed to red deer although around 30 cattle were summered in the main glen from 1967–1972; sheep were here absent and grazing by hares and rabbits was light. All the vegetation along an 8 km length of the glen floor was classified according to the relative extent of heather and graminoids (5 classes) and heather height (5 classes) in ground surveys in 1970 and 1992 (Welch *et al.*, 1993), aerial photographs being used to delimit homogenous stands. It was found that 'pure' *Callunetum* with graminoid cover less than 10 % considerably declined and that 'pure' grassland considerably increased (Table 27.5), stands of grassy *Callunetum* replacing pure *Callunetum*. The extent of stands with heather taller than 20 cm also declined sharply between 1970 and 1992 in the north and middle lengths of the glen (Welch *et al.*, 1993). Here some ground was limed and fertilized to improve forage quality for the deer, and deer were given supplementary food in winter; heather declined most in these areas. At some sites away from the main concentrations of wintering red deer, heather cover increased.

Table 27.5   Change in percentage extent of heather-grass vegetation classes in a c. 500 ha area along the Glen Feshie glen floor.

	1970	1970*	1992
Pure *Callunetum*	38	29	22
Grassy *Callunetum* (*Calluna* >50 %)	14	14	15
Grassy *Callunetum* (*Calluna* 10–50 %)	15	14	14
Wet grassy *Callunetum* (*Calluna* >10 %)	5	5	5
Grassland with *Calluna* 1–10 %)	6	6	4
Pure grassland	22	21	29[+]
Ground fenced off 1970–1992	—	11	11

* Recalculated to show extent in the ground not later fenced off, and hence is comparable to 1992.
[+] Includes 1% of ground *Juncus*-dominated.
Graminoid cover is <10 % in pure *Callunetum*, 10–50 % in grassy *Callunetum*, and >50 % in grassland.

Deer management, therefore, is probably more important than the direct effects of deer grazing naturally. Fertilizing or providing supplementary winter food concentrates deer locally at very high densities: it is in these situations where heather loss is most apparent. Other sites in the Grampians have also shown marked changes in heather cover. On Mar Lodge estate at Glen Lui, where fertilizing has taken place and deer have been given additional feed, heather has declined dramatically from 65 % cover in 1946 to 61 % in 1966 and 40 % in 1989. At a higher site, in the contiguous Glen Derry where there was no feeding or fertilizing, no such effect was measured (66 % cover in 1946, 62 % in 1989).

27.4.3   Other plant communities

Although most attention has been given to woodland and dwarf shrub regeneration, other plant species are susceptible to damage by deer. On one Scottish NNR, 50 % of flowers of the rare purple coltsfoot (*Homogyne alpina*) were eaten by deer in 1989 and 1991 which seems high enough to warrant concern (Francis *et al.*, 1991). Many other species are restricted to ledges or other inaccessible places because of grazing (e.g. *Cicerbita alpina*, Raven and Walters, 1956).

In a long-term study on the Island of Rum NNR, Ball (personal communication) has shown that, after the removal of the sheep stock, 12 out of the 80 species present showed a decline with a change to more tussocky vegetation. Species diversity was maintained under moderate deer densities and where cattle were present. However, in part of the Island where the deer population had trebled, he reported a loss of 14 species.

27.5   Remedies

It is clear that high densities of deer can effect natural heritage interests, especially woodland regeneration. The obvious solutions are, therefore, to reduce numbers or where this is not feasible to protect important areas by fencing.

27.5.1 Fencing

Enclosures in several areas of Scotland clearly show the value of fencing in allowing woodland regeneration to occur (Mardon, 1990; Marrs and Welch, 1991; Sykes, 1992). However, there are many arguments against fences as the only acceptable remedy to the problem of excessive deer numbers (e.g. Watson, 1993; Chapter 12), including cost, access and visual impact. The direct effects of fencing on the deer are also not always desirable, for example:

- Large exclosures only move deer and the problem elsewhere. When fencing is necessary, concomitant reductions in deer numbers are generally advocated, but in practice they have seldom been sufficient to stop increased, local damage nearby;

- Exclosures may restrict access by deer to lower ground and sheltered grazings, and as a result the carrying capacity of the whole area is reduced more than would be expected from the amount of grazing land enclosed.

Nevertheless, in some areas, other land-use objectives may dictate that fencing is the only practical solution.

27.5.2 Reduction in deer numbers

This is the ideal ecological solution to allow woodland and moorland habitats to regenerate in the presence of a major herbivore. This is the most controversial method because many deer managers believe that there will be a subsequent loss of revenue to the estates – both directly because of reduced stalking and also in terms of loss of capital value of the estates (this is judged on the number of stags culled). In addition, there is the fear that heavy culling on one estate will lead to mass immigration from neighbouring ground (the so-called 'vacuum effect'). We now consider these issues.

While revenue is likely to fall somewhat because of lower deer numbers, the loss will not be so marked as supposed because of density-dependent effects. It has been long recognized that density affects growth rates and fertility in red deer (Staines, 1970; Mitchell *et al.*, 1977). When animals are at lower densities, females may become fertile as yearlings leading to increased recruitment rates (Staines, 1978a). In addition growth rates are faster, adult body size greater and natural mortality lower. Clutton-Brock and his colleagues (see Clutton-Brock and Albon, 1989) showed the reverse on Rum when densities increased. In their classic study, they allowed a local sub-population to increase more than 2.5 times. As density increased:

- fertility in milk hinds decreased;

- calves were lighter;

- overwinter mortality in calves was greater (especially in males);

- growth rates of stags were lower;

- emigration of young stags was greater;

- antler weight declined.

They produced a model to show how both the yield of venison and the number of animals shot was highest at half the final density. We therefore argue that lower densities will in part be compensated by higher body weights and better recruitment and survival. Quantification of the effects of density on deer populations in different areas of Scotland is badly needed.

For stags, the number stalked (the main source of revenue and the *raison d'être* for the estates) need not be lower. This is because the number stalked is not necessarily related to stag density. The stag cull is affected and set by:

- other estate duties (i.e. conflict for time with grouse shooting or salmon fishing);

- the number of keepers and beats;

- the number of guests that can be accommodated;

- the number of days with suitable weather;

- tradition.

In addition, high numbers of hinds adversely affect the stag stock partly through competition for food (Clutton-Brock and Albon, 1992). As they state, 'many ungulate populations that are subject to little or no culling or predation show a strongly female-biased adult sex ratio and poor growth in males'. They indicate that, in areas where less than 6 % of females are culled each year, the offtake of adult stags could be increased by 30 % simply by increasing the hind cull to 16–18 %.

27.5.3 *Vacuum effect*

The 'vacuum effect' is another controversial issue. There is no good scientific evidence that deer leave their hefts to fill unoccupied areas, but there are pointers to the contrary. Although no experiments have been done to test whether deer will move into vacant areas, other studies indicate that this is unlikely, at least in the short term. Much would depend on the local topography; animals would be less likely to move over high ridges than in less formidable country. The strong hefting of red and other deer, particularly females but also mature males, is well known (e.g. Lowe, 1966; Craighead *et al.*, 1973; Franklin *et al.*, 1975; Clutton-Brock and Albon, 1989) and evidence from animals marked by the RDC shows that most deer are shot close to their natal areas, hinds more so than stags.

Clutton-Brock and his colleagues (see Clutton-Brock and Albon, 1989) in their long-term studies of red deer on Rum, allowed the population in one part of the island to increase to 2.5–3 times its original figure (already high by conservation standards). Hinds were strongly hefted to their home ranges and there was no marked emigration despite the big increase in density. Over a 16 year period only 9 hinds over 1 year old emigrated from the area. Young stags, however, were affected, with more moving out and few immigrating into the area.

At Glen Dye, a different situation arose. Deer numbers were greatly reduced by shooting (from about 10/100 ha to 3.4/100 ha over 7 years), but evidence from regular counts and from marked animals suggested that there was no great influx of deer from adjacent areas (Staines, 1977; 1978a).

However, there are problems in interpretation from both the Rum and Glen Dye studies. On Rum, the study area was surrounded by glens with reasonably high densities of deer. Would emigration have taken place if the deer there were at low densities? At Glen Dye, low deer densities surrounded the estate. Would there have been immigration if there were high deer numbers on neighbouring ground? Current studies on Rum may help answer some of these questions.

In addition, there has been no evidence so far from the National Nature Reserves of Inshriach and Creag Meagaidh of movements on to the Reserves following heavy 'culling' there.

Despite the reservations in interpreting these studies, we feel that there is no reason for much alarm among neighbours. First, in most places, there are already too many deer, and most estates accept this. Second, by the simple expedient of the neighbouring estates culling hard on their boundaries, they will create their own 'vacuum'. This would act as a buffer zone, and should give the estates more control over their stock and stop any possible emigration.

27.5.4   Capital values

The capital value of estates attributable to the number of stags shot increased dramatically from £5–£8k per stag shot in 1985 to £20–£40k in 1990 (Callander and MacKenzie, 1991). This then declined to about £10–£20k in 1994. Because of the reasons given in the preceding sections, estates could still cull the same number of stags (not density-dependent) with fewer hinds. For three estates in the Central Cairngorms, the cull of stalked stags has remained virtually the same between 1966 and 1992 yet the deer stock doubled in that period. The same stalking could be achieved, therefore, with at least half the current population.

27.6   Conclusions

It is clear that high densities of red deer adversely affect many aspects of the natural heritage, but especially woodland regeneration.

We argue that the value of stalking could be maintained with a much reduced deer stock, to the benefit of the natural heritage. However we recognize that in order to get woodland regeneration without fencing, densities will probably have to be much lower than the levels required to sustain current sporting levels. We suggest that reduced densities would lead to better 'quality' animals and higher recruitment and survival, thus in part compensating for the loss in overall numbers.

Finally we recommend that a number of demonstration projects are devised, within the main parts of red deer range in Scotland, to quantify the economic and social effects of reduced deer populations and the benefits to the natural heritage. We believe that this is the best way to convince deer managers of the merits of reduced deer density.

Acknowledgements

We thank David Scott for his help with the data analyses and figures. We also acknowledge the assistance of Scottish Natural Heritage, NE Region.

References

Ball, M. E. (1974). Floristic changes on grasslands and heaths on the Isle of Rum after a reduction or exclusion of grazing, *Journal of Environmental Management*, **2**, 299–318.

Callander, R. F. and MacKenzie, N. A. (1991). The management of wild red deer in Scotland, *Rural Forum, Scotland*.

Cameron, A.G. (1923). *The Wild Red Deer of Scotland*, Blackwood and Sons, Edinburgh and London,

Clarke, J. L., Welch, D. and Gordon, I. J. (1995a). The influence of vegetation pattern on the grazing of heather moorland by sheep and deer. I. The location of animals on grass/heather mosaics, *Journal of Applied Ecology*, **32**.

Clarke, J. L., Welch, D. and Gordon, I. J. (1995b). The influence of vegetation pattern on the grazing of heather moorland by sheep and deer. II. The impact on heather, *Journal of Applied Ecology*, **32**.

Clutton-Brock, T. H. (1991). Red deer and sacred cows, *Deer*, **8**, 301–3.

Clutton-Brock, T. H. and Albon, S. D. (1989). *Red Deer in the Highlands*, Blackwell Scientific Publications, Oxford.

Clutton-Brock, T. H. and Albon, S. D. (1992). Trial and error in the Highlands, *Nature*, **358**, 11–12.

Craighead, J. J., Craighead, F. C. Jnr., Ruff, R. L. and O'Gara, B. W. (1973). Home ranges and activity patterns of non-migratory elk of the Madison Drainage herd as determined by biotelemetry, *Wildlife Monographs*, **33**, 50 pp.

Darling, F. F. (1937). *A Herd of Red Deer*, Oxford University Press, London.

Darling, F. F. (1955). *West Highland Survey*, Oxford University Press, London.

Evans, H. (1890). *Some Account of Jura Red Deer*, Carter, Derby.

Francis, J. M., Balharry, R. and Thompson, D. B. (1991). The implications for upland management: A summary paper. In Rose, H. (Ed), *Deer, Mountains and Man*, British Deer Society and Red Deer Commission.

Franklin, W. L., Mossman, A. S. and Dole, M. (1975). Social organization and home range of Roosevelt elk, *Journal of Mammalogy*, **56**, 102–18.

Gordon, S. (1925). *The Cairngorm Hills of Scotland*, Cassell, London.

Grace, J. and Easterbee, N. (1979). The natural shelter for red deer (*Cervus elaphus*) in a Scottish glen, *Journal of Applied Ecology*, **16**, 37–48.

Holloway, C. W. (1967). The effects of red deer and other animals on naturally regenerated Scots pine, PhD thesis, University of Aberdeen.

Kay, R. N. B. and Staines, B. W. (1981). The nutrition of the red deer (*Cervus elaphus*), *Nutrition Abstracts and Reviews*, **51**, 601–22.

Lister, A. M. (1984). Evolutionary and ecological origins of British deer, *Proceedings of the Royal Society of Edinburgh*, **82B**, 205–29.

Lowe, V. P. W. (1961). A discussion on the history, present status and future conservation of red deer (*Cervus elaphus* L.) in Scotland, *Terre et la Vie*, **1**, 9–40.

Lowe, V. P. W. (1966). Observations on the dispersal of red deer on Rhum. In Jewell, P. A. and Loizos, C. (Eds), *Play, territory and exploration in mammals*, Academic Press, London, 211–28.

Mardon, D. (1990). Conservation of montane willow scrub in Scotland, *Transactions of the Botanical Society of Edinburgh*, **45**, 427–36.

Marrs, R. H. and Welch, D. (1991). Moorland wilderness: the potential effects of removing domestic livestock, particularly sheep, Department of the Environment, 88pp.

McKelvie, C. (1991). The battle for Scotland, *Shooting Times*, **May**, 9–15.

Miles, J. (1987). Vegetation succession: past and present perceptions. In Gray, A. J., Crawley, M. J. and Edwards, P.J. (Eds), *Colonization, succession and stability*, Blackwell Scientific Publications, Oxford, 1–29.

Mitchell, B., Staines, B. W. and Welch, D. (1977). The ecology of red deer: a research review relevant to their management in Scotland, Institute of Terrestrial Ecology, Cambridge, 74 pp.

Parnell, I. W. (1932). Some notes on the natural history of red deer, *Proceedings of the Royal Philosophical Society, Edinburgh*, **22**, 75–80.

Ratcliffe, P. R. (1984a). Population density and reproduction of red deer in Scottish commercial forests, *Acta Zoologica Fennica*, **172**, 191–92.

Ratcliffe, P. R. (1984b). Population dynamics of red deer (*Cervus elaphus* L.) in Scottish commercial forests, *Proceedings of the Royal Society of Edinburgh*, **82B**, 291–302.

Raven, J. and Walters, M. (1956). *Mountain Flowers*, Collins, London.

Red Deer Commission. (1980). Annual Report for 1979, HMSO, Edinburgh.

Ritchie, J. (1920). *The Influence of Man on Animal Life in Scotland*, University Press, Cambridge.

Scottish Natural Heritage (1994). *Red Deer and the Natural Heritage*, SNH Policy Paper. Scottish Natural Heritage, Battleby.

Staines, B. W. (1970). The management and dispersion of a red deer population in Glen Dye, Kincardineshire, Unpublished PhD thesis, University of Aberdeen.

Staines, B. W. (1977). Factors affecting the seasonal distribution of red deer (*Cervus elaphus*) at Glen Dye, north-east Scotland, *Annals of Applied Biology*, **87**, 495–512.

Staines, B. W. (1978a). The dynamics and performance of declining populations of red deer (*Cervus elaphus*), *Journal of Zoology, London*, **184**, 403–19.

Staines, B. W. (1978b). The use of natural shelter by Red deer (*Cervus elaphus*) in relation to weather in North-east Scotland, *Journal of Zoology, London*, **180**, 1–8.

Staines, B. W. (1991). Factors affecting the distribution and abundance of red and roe deer in Great Britain, *Atti del II Convegno Nazionale dei Biologi della Selvaggina, Bologna 7–9 March 1991*, **Vol. XIX**, 237–51.

Staines, B. W. and Ratcliffe, P. R. (1987). Estimating the abundance of red deer and roe deer and their current status in Great Britain. In S. Harris, (Ed), *Mammal Population Studies, Symposium of the Zoological Society of London*, **58**, 131–152.

Staines, B. W. and Welch, D. (1989). An appraisal of deer damage in conifer plantations. In McIntosh, R. (Ed), Deer and Forestry, *Institute of Chartered Foresters, Edinburgh*, 61–76.

Stewart, L. K. (1979). The present position. The red deer population. In *The next twenty years*, Red Deer Commission, Inverness, 4–5.

Stewart, L. K. (1985). *Vegetation management in Northern Britain*, BCPC Publication, No. 30, 45–50.

Stewart, L. K. (1990). In Deer in Scotland. *The changing scene*, Red Deer Commission, Inverness.

Sykes, J. M. (1992). Caledonian pinewood regeneration: progress after sixteen years of enclosure at Coille Coire Chuilc, Perthshire, *Arboricultural Journal*, **16**, 61–7.

Watson, A. (1983). Eighteenth century deer numbers and pine regeneration near Braemar, Scotland, *Biological Conservation*, **25**, 289–305.

Watson, A. (1989). Land use, reduction of heather, and natural tree regeneration on open upland, ITE Annual Report, HMSO, London.

Watson, A. (1993). Defects of fencing for native woodlands, *Native Woodlands Discussion Group Newsletter*, **No. 18**, 53–5.

Watson, A. and Hinge, M. D. C. (1989). Natural tree regeneration on open upland in Deeside and Donside, Report to Nature Conservancy Council, Institute of Terrestrial Ecology, Banchory.

Welch, D. (1984). Studies in the grazing of heather moorland in north-east Scotland. III. Floristics, *Journal of Applied Ecology*, **21**, 209–25.

Welch, D. and Scott, D. (1995). Studies in the grazing of heather moorland in north-east Scotland. VI. 20–year trends in botanical composition, *Journal of Applied Ecology,* **32.**

Welch, D., Scott, D. and Staines, B. W. (1993). Study on Effects of Wintering Red Deer on Heather Moorland, Progress Report, 2, Scottish Natural Heritage, 52 pp.

Wigan, M. (1991). *The Scottish Highland Estate: Preserving an Environment,* Swan Hill Press, Shrewsbury.

28 MOORLANDS OF ORKNEY — CULTURAL LANDSCAPES

A. H. Kirkpatrick, L. Scott and A. J. MacDonald

Summary

1. With increased access to other fuel sources peat cutting has declined on Orkney's moorlands. On 1987/88 aerial photographs the extent of visible peat cutting on Mainland was 18 km^2 compared with 24 km^2 on 1969/70.

2. The traditional practice of replacing the top layer of turves should be encouraged. Results from a site at West Mainland indicate good recovery of the vegetation.

28.1 Introduction

The historic role of Orkney's moorlands has been to provide grazing and as a source of fuel through traditional peat cutting. Extensive areas of peat were cut by Viking settlers and Fenton (1970) notes that most of the technical terms associated with peat cutting in Orkney are of Norse origin. When peat was the only fuel available the identification and protection of turbary rights was of immense importance to families and small communities (Fenton, 1978). With increasing access to other fuel sources the extent of peat cutting is likely to have declined.

Traditionally the top layer of turves was stripped off and laid in the base of the bank leaving a surface well below the level of the original. A man would cut the peat and his assistant (usually a female relative) took the peats as they were cut and flung them up to dry. Orkney peats were broader than Shetland peats because of the greater length of the wing on the 'tusker' or peat spade (Fenton, 1970). This work aims to assess changes in the overall extent of peat cutting on Mainland by using aerial photographs. At a site on West Mainland (HY 335 243) the ability of the vegetation to recover from such disturbance was investigated. At this site two rows of turves had been replaced this year and each turf was around 0.5 x 0.5 m

28.2 Methods

In an area with active peat cutting a series of 0.5 x 0.5 m quadrats were placed end to end in a transect from the most recently laid down turves to the remains of an old bank. The percentage cover of all species present was estimated and the height of *Calluna vulgaris* in the centre of each quadrat was measured.

Changes in the overall extent of peat cutting were examined using the 1969/70 and 1987/88 aerial photograph coverage for Mainland. All visible areas of peat cutting were digitised and the information stored in a Geographical Information System (GIS).

28.3 Results

The area of visible peat cutting on Mainland declined from 24 km^2 in 1969/70 to 18 km^2 in 1987/88. Data from the field site showed that *Empetrum nigrum* is abundant in the area of replaced turves while *Eriophorum angustifolium* and *Hypnum cupressiforme* attained highest cover in the disturbed areas (Figure 28.1). Although the cover of *Calluna* on the most recently replaced turves was low it had higher cover values on older turves (Figure 28.1). In the most recently replaced turves *Calluna* had a height of 5–8 cm while in turves replaced earlier heights ranged from 16–46 cm (Figure 28.2).

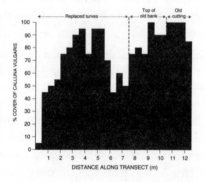
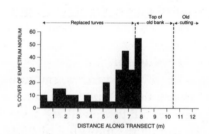
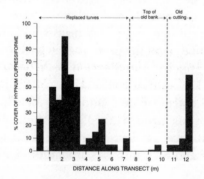
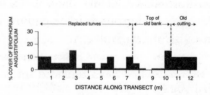

Figure 28.1. The percentage cover of *Calluna vulgaris, Empetrum nigrum, Eriophorum angustifolium* and *Hypnum cupressiforme* along a transect from recently replaced turves to an old peat cutting at West Mainland.

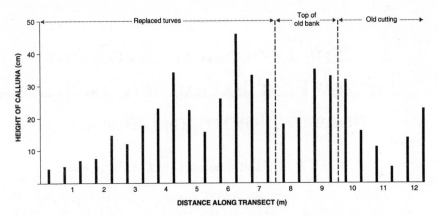

Figure 28.2. Height of *Calluna vulgaris* along a transect from recently replaced turves to an old peat cutting at West Mainland.

28.4 Discussion

Observations at this site indicate a rapid recover of *Calluna* cover providing the top layer of turves is carefully replaced. The first metre of the transect represents the two rows of turves replaced this season. Assuming a regular supply of fuel will require a similar amount of peats cut each year there are about seven years of replaced turves in this transect. These results give an indication that there is good recovery of the vegetation after about three years. The effect on the hydrology of the site is as yet unknown. However, in at least one area near the Burn of Lushan (HY 342 238) the top layer of turves has been dumped in heaps 3–4 m high. This effectively prevents revegetation of the worked out area and large cracks have begun to appear on the uncut bog surface. Thus where active peat cutting still occurs people should be encouraged to retain the traditional practice of replacing the top layer as the most effective means of revegetating a site.

Acknowledgements

This study was funded by Scottish Natural Heritage and forms part of the SNH/Stirling University project *'Moorland Audit and Management in the Northern Isles'*. The authors would like to thank the SNH staff on Orkney and Eric Meek, RSPB, for helpful background information as well as John McArthur, Chief GIS Technician, Stirling University.

References

Fenton, A. (1970) Paring and Burning and the Cutting of Turf and Peat in Scotland in Gailey, A. and Fenton, A. (eds.) *The Spade in Northern and Atlantic Europe*. Ulster Folk Museum and the Institute of Irish Studies, Queen's University of Belfast.

Fenton, A. (1978) *The Northern Isles: Orkney and Shetland*. John Donald, Edinburgh.

29 THE ECOLOGICAL EFFECTS OF MECHANIZED PEAT EXTRACTION ON BLANKET BOGS IN NORTHERN IRELAND

P. A. Todd, J. H. McAdam and W. I. Montgomery

Summary

1. The effect of mechanized peat extraction on the flora and fauna of blanket bogs was studied at three sites.

2. Peat cutting reduced herbage biomass and vegetation surface height. There was an increase in the proportion of dead plant material on cutover areas. These effects increased with successive cutting.

3. Spiders and beetles were trapped on two sites. There were significant differences between intact and cutover plots. For example, more *Pardosa pullata* and fewer *Antistea elegans* were recorded on cutover plots than intact plots.

4. Mechanized peat extraction appears to have a rapid effect on plant and invertebrate communities of blanket bog in Northern Ireland.

29.1 Introduction

Northern Ireland's peatlands are important culturally, aesthetically and ecologically (Goodwillie, 1980; Council for Nature Conservation and the Countryside, CNCC, 1992; Pryce, 1991). They cover 167 580 ha, of which 142 384 ha are blanket bog (Cruickshank and Tomlinson, 1991). Mechanized peat extraction for fuel peat was introduced to mid-Tyrone in 1981; the industry expanded rapidly, with a further increase after 1986 and the introduction of field press machines alongside chain and disc cutters (compact harvesters). Six hand cut peat turves may be cut per minute compared to 240 turves per minute through mechanization. The Local Enterprise Development Unit (1986), in keeping with their remit to create jobs in areas of high unemployment, promoted the activity — their motto being 'creating wealth out of wasteland by developing Northern Ireland's peat resources'.

Cruickshank and Tomlinson (1991) surveyed the scale, extent and socio-economics of peat extraction in Northern Ireland using field surveys and satellite imagery. Little research, however, has been carried out to examine the effects of mechanized peat cutting on blanket bog flora and fauna. Preliminary field surveys by Meharg (1988) and Cooper *et al.*, (1991) highlighted the need for a more detailed examination of the ecological effects of mechanized peat extraction on blanket bog.

This chapter is a preliminary report of a replicated, controlled experiment on the effects of mechanized peat cutting on flora and associated invertebrate communities of blanket bog.

29.2 Methods

Three sites where mechanized peat extraction is actively occurring were selected in Co. Antrim (sites 1 and 2 NR J327404) and Co. Fermanagh (site 3 NR G203352). On site 1 *Calluna vulgaris* was dominant, *Molinia caerulea* was dominant on site 2, *Trichophorum cespitosum*/*Calluna vulgaris* — co-dominant on site 3. Plots (10 x 10 m each) were assigned to treatments independently and randomly within an area which was relatively homogeneous with respect to vegetation cover. There were two replicates for each treatment on each of sites 1 and 2. Comparisons were made between intact (uncut) plots and those mechanically cutover either once or in successive years.

Data were collected on vegetation height and canopy structure, biomass and botanical composition. Height measurements were made using a 'sward height stick' (modified Hill Farming Research Organization pattern) and, where necessary, a meter ruler. Forty randomly selected records were taken per plot. An inclined point quadrat (Grant, 1981) with a penetration angle of 32.5° was used to determine sward canopy structure. The point quadrat frame was positioned randomly five times per plot. Base level, (0 cms), was taken as ground level or where a dense, impenetrable tussock was encountered.

Botanical composition and herbage biomass were estimated on three randomly selected 1.0 x 0.2 m quadrats per plot, cut to ground level with hand held battery operated shears (Gardena–Accu 6). Detailed botanical separations of a subsample of the harvested material were made to determine the botanical composition. These subsamples were oven dried at 90 °C for 24 h and the dry matter percentage of each species determined. A further subsample was oven dried at 90 °C to determine the DM content of the vegetation and calculate the biomass (tonnes/ha).

Pitfall trapping was employed to collect ground fauna. These were predominantly beetles (Coleoptera) and spiders (Araneae). Three plastic beakers, (10 cm diameter, 11 cm deep) were placed randomly away from the margins of each plot. Each was filled with 5 % formalin solution plus detergent. Traps were emptied fortnightly from August to October. The three samples from each plot were bulked. Collections were frozen, and, at a later date, identified to species level.

Plant and animal data were analysed using two-way analysis of variance carried out on $\log_{10}$ (numbers + 1) or arcsin (%), with habitat and intact/cutover treatments as the factors. Community data were also analysed using TWINSPAN (Hill, 1979) conducted on numbers (invertebrates) and percentage composition (plants).

These analyses were also carried out on presence and absence data to evaluate the robustness of the results.

29.3 Results

29.3.1 Effects on the vegetation

Mean vegetation height was less significant in cutover plots compared with intact plots at sites 1 and 2 in both July (F=161.22, df 1,2, p<0.001) and October (F=52.75, df 1,2, p<0.001). At site 3 the vegetation height of the area cutover five times was 72 % lower than that of the intact area (Figure 29.1). Cutting reduced the frequency of hits in the upper horizons. For example sites 1 and 2 showed a significant difference between cutover and intact plots for both total number of hits and for *Calluna vulgaris* (Figure 29.2). Biomass was reduced by cutting at each site. At site 3 biomass was 9.78, 1.98, and 1.02 t ha^{-1} for intact areas, cutover twice areas and areas cutover five times respectively. The result was not significant for sites 1 and 2 in July, but by October, after grazing in August subsequent to peat cutting in June, biomass was significantly less in cutover plots; 6.65 t ha^{-1} and 3.83 t ha^{-1} (F=8.63 df 1,2, p<0.01) in intact and cutover treatments, respectively.

The percentage composition of six plant species showed significant differences between intact and cutover areas at sites 1 and 2 (Table 29.1). The total amount of dead material was found to be significantly greater on cutover plots (F=36.10, df 1,2, p<0.001). TWINSPAN classification of percentage species composition at sites 1 and 2 revealed a strong habitat effect. Despite only one year of peat cutting, however, a treatment effect was also evident although this was less than the habitat effect (Figure 29.3).

Table 29.1 The effect of peat cutting in June 1992 on the percentage composition of plant species in October 1992 at sites 1 and 2.

Species	F(df 1,2)	Probability	Intact mean s.d.	Cutover mean s.d.
Dead *Calluna vulgaris*	5.23	<0.05	8	20
			10.7	26.2
Erica tetralix	4.16	<0.05	4	1
			6.0	1.5
Eriophorum angustifolium	6.71	<0.05	3	1
			2.2	1.1
Eriophorum vaginatum	4.47	<0.05	1	0
			1.2	0.1
Molinia caerulea	4.23	<0.05	1	0
			2.5	0.2
Juncus articulatus	5.32	<0.05	1	0
			2.2	0

Table 29.2 The effect of peat cutting on numbers of Araneae and Coleoptera captured in pitfall traps from July to October 1992.

Species	F(df 1,2)	Probability	Intact mean	Cutover mean
Spiders				
Agroeca proxima	5.22	<0.05	0.6	0.4
Xysticus cristatus	13.60	<0.001	0.2	0.5
Pardosa pullata	26.23	<0.001	1.2	1.7
Antistea elegans	10.69	<0.01	1.1	0.7
Pachygnatha clerki	6.22	<0.05	0.2	0.1
Bolyphantes luteolus	4.77	<0.05	0.1	0.0
Lepthyphantes zimmermanni	9.15	<0.01	0.5	0.2
Beetles				
Nebria salina	8.45	<0.01	5.3	13.6
Loricera pilicornis	6.18	<0.05	0.8	3.1
Pterostichus diligens	5.91	<0.05	0.8	2.3
Pterostichus niger	8.17	<0.05	1.4	0.6

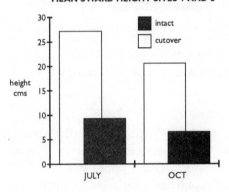

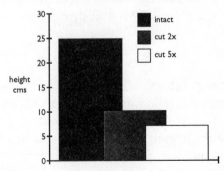

Figure 29.1. The effect of peat cutting on sward height at sites 1, 2 and 3.

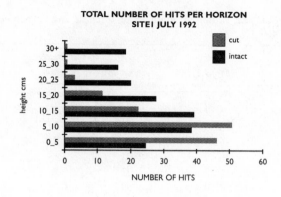

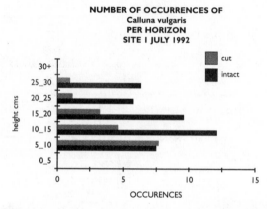

Figure 29.2. The effect of peat cutting on sward canopy structure on site 1.

29.3.2 Effects on the fauna

Forty-four species of spiders and 49 species of beetles were trapped on sites 1 and 2 from August–October 1992. Numbers of seven spider and four ground beetle (Carabidae) species significantly differed between cut and intact areas (Table 29.2). Classification of the arthropod data separated habitats on the basis of species composition. The cutting effect was less clear (Figure 29.4) but there was some indication that plots subject to cutting were associated with different beetle and spider communities than intact areas. This is likely to be more marked after further peat extraction.

29.4 Discussion

One year of mechanized peat extraction has significant effects on blanket bog flora and fauna. Mechanized peat extraction was associated with sward canopy structure and appeared to reduce the vegetation surface, accounting for the greater number of hits in the lower horizons (Figure 29.2), as was found by Meharg (1988). Breakdown of the sward canopy was pronounced following the first harvest and appeared to be progressive with more damage occurring after the subsequent removal of peat. Sward height and biomass were reduced on cutover areas of all

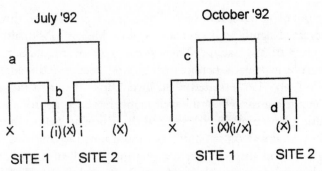

Figure 29.3. TWINSPAN analysis — Botanical dendrograms for sites 1 and 2 using data collected in both July and October on percentage species composition (biomass), after peat cutting had occurred in June. For example indicator species see positions (a) *Calluna vulgaris*, (b) *Erica tetralix*, (c) Dead *Calluna vulgaris*, (d) *Carex* spp. (*x* = cutover, *i* = intact, () = mainly, site 1 = *Calluna* dominated, site 2 = *Molinia* dominated).

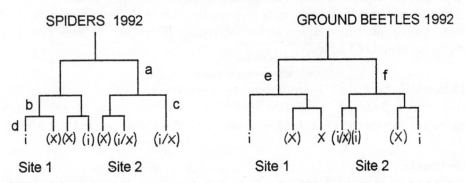

Figure 29.4. TWINSPAN analysis — Araneae and Coleoptera dendrograms using pitfall trap data collected after peat cutting (July–October 1992) from each plot from sites 1 and 2. For example indicator species see positions — (a) *Xysticus cristatus*, (b) *Erigone atra*, (c) *Centromerita bicolor*, (d) *Micrargus herbigradus*, (e) *Carabus problematius*, (f) *Loricera pilicornis*. (*x* = cutover, *i* = intact, () = mainly, site 1 = *Calluna* dominated, site 2 = *Molinia* dominated).

sites. They were progressively lower with successive peat harvests on the *Trichophorum/Calluna* heath.

Cutting increased the proportion of dead herbage material. This is likely to affect the *Calluna* cycle as heather plants evidently underwent premature ageing towards the degenerate stage. Heather, unlike many grass species, has an apical meristem (Armstrong and Milne, this volume). Peat cutting, therefore, removes the annual shoot production, subsequently increasing the chance of a decline in heather cover.

Until recently, so little has been known of the invertebrates on peat bogs in Britain that there is little evidence of anthropogenic activities reducing their numbers. Human impact has been indirect as a result of action taken for other reasons, e.g. drainage (Coulson, 1992). Many beetle species are markedly stenibiotic, with very special ecological requirements for their continued existence. Such species may be sensitive indicators of ecological conditions and of the effect of human activities on ecosystems (Crowson, 1981). This study has shown that even after one peat harvest, five out of seven spider species affected, decreased and three out of four beetle species increased significantly on cutover plots. Meharg (1988) also found an increase in the numbers of the Carabid *Nebria salina* on cutover plots but, in general, he found little difference in species richness of ground beetles and spiders trapped on cutover plots. Coulson (1992) stated that invertebrate fauna is little affected by drainage except in a few areas where the water table has been appreciably lowered. To facilitate peat cutting, land must be drained and the action of peat cutting itself opens the ground further. Drainage on uplands has been claimed to improve the vegetation cover for both grouse and sheep by encouraging the growth of *Calluna vulgaris*. However, this also reduced the water table and removes the habitat of many invertebrates. Kirby (1992) stated that varied vegetation structure is important to invertebrates of every aspect and at every scale. Maintenance of invertebrate diversity, therefore, requires habitat continuity and structural variation. Peat cutting alters the vegetation canopy and subsequently affects the habitat for invertebrate communities.

The present study ultimately aims to provide scientific information to help formulate management techniques which will reduce the impact of peat cutting on indigenous plants and animals.

Acknowledgements

The project is financially supported by DENI and Environment Service DoENI. Thanks are also due to Dr R Anderson who helped with the beetle identification.

References

Armstrong, H. M. and Milne, J. A. (this volume) The effects of grazing on vegetation species composition.

CNCC, (1992). *Peatland Conservation Strategy*. Department of the Environment for Northern Ireland, Belfast.

Cooper, A., Murray, R. and McCann, T. (1991). The environmental effects of blanket peat exploitation. UUC Report to Countryside and Wildlife Branch, DoENI, Belfast, 48–58.

Coulson, J. C. (1992). Fauna. In O.M. Bragg, P. D. Hulme, H. A. P. Ingram and R. A. Robertson (Eds) *Peatland Ecosystems and Man: An Impact Assessment*, Dundee University Press, 297–307.

Crowson, R. A. (1981). *Biology of the Coleoptera*. Academic Press, London, 802.

Cruickshank, M. M. and Tomlinson, R. W. (1991). *Survey of the Scale, Extent and Rate of Peat Extraction from Blanket Bogs in N. Ireland. Part 1 Survey*. Department of the Environment for Northern Ireland, Belfast, 9–20.

Goodwillie (1980). *European Peatlands. Nature and Environment Series No. 19*. Council of Europe, Strasbourg.

Grant, S. A. (1981). Sward components. In J. Hodgson, R. D. Baker, A. Davies, A. S. Laidlaw and J. D. Leaver (Eds). *Sward Measurement Handbook*, The British Grassland Society, Hurley, 71–92.

Hill, M. O. (1979). TWINSPAN: a FORTRAN Program for Arranging Multivariate Data in an Ordered Two-way Table by Classification of the Individuals and Attributes. Cornell University, Ithaca, New York.

Kirby, P. (1992). *Habitat Management for Invertebrates: a Practical Handbook*. JNCC. RSPB. Joint Nature Conservation Committee, Peterborough, 7–9.

Local Enterprise Development Unit. (1986). *Peats Progress —— Creating Wealth out of Wastelands by Developing Northern Ireland's Peat Resources*. Local Enterprise Development Unit, Belfast; 12–14.

Meharg, M. (1988). *Changing Management and the Ecology of Uplands in Northern Ireland*. PhD Thesis, Queen's University Belfast.

Pryce, S. (1991). *The Peat Alternatives Manual*. A guide for the professional horticulturalist and landscape. Friends of the Earth, London, 1–3.

30 SCOTTISH HEATHS AND MOORLAND: HOW SHOULD CONSERVATION BE TAKEN FORWARD?

S. D. Ward, A. J. MacDonald and E. M. Matthew

Summary

1. Scottish heaths and moorlands are reviewed in relation to their general natural heritage features and statutory designations.

2. Open moorland and its characteristic fauna and flora are a distinctive feature of Scottish landscapes.

3. Heaths and moorlands are largely the product of management, or of management and changing climate, in some locations over more than 5000 years. Large-scale changes between moorland and forest plantation, and between heath- and graminoid-dominated vegetation types, have occurred in the last 50 years.

4. The most immediately practical approach to nature conservation is likely to be based on habitat management for high profile 'flagship' and 'keystone' species.

5. Practical management problems are considered, principally the management of grazing and burning. Habitat fragmentation effects in relation to both loss of habitat and the targetting and design of restoration cannot yet be fully addressed.

6. Taking account of all existing mechanisms we estimate that, at most, only a third of heath and moorland is likely to be under some form of protection or positive management.

7. Natural heritage conservation needs to be integrated with other heath and moorland uses. Conservation effectiveness could be increased further by more integration in the implementation of schemes and designations. Natural Heritage Areas may offer an opportunity to achieve this.

30.1 Introduction

This chapter reviews the general features of Scottish moorland which may affect its conservation for natural heritage and assesses some of the mechanisms which are being or could be employed, to take forward its conservation. The definition of moorland we work to is very similar to that given in *The Chambers Dictionary* (1993), 'a wide expanse of uncultivated ground, *esp.* upland, often covered with heath, and having a poor, peaty soil'. Heath can also exist in situations where the description 'moorland' may not be appropriate e.g. when it occurs as relatively small fragments in the lowlands.

We do not intend to provide a comprehensive review of the detailed natural heritage characteristics of heath and moorland. Nor do we intend to become em-broiled in this chapter in the continuing debate about the relative value of moorland compared with other land cover types, particularly naturally regenerated scrub and woodland, and the determination of the optimum mix of these land types. This requires much more detailed discussion than we can undertake here.

In this context we attempt to briefly consider the following questions:

1. What is the extent of heath and moorland?

2. What does heath and moorland contribute to landscape and habitat diversity?

3. How do we approach conservation of the dependent species?

4. Which management problems need to be addressed?

5. What conservation measures are available and how effective have they been?

In considering these questions we attempt to answer the question posed by the title.

30.2 What is the extent of Heath and Moorland?

Above the treeline there are natural heathlands; where conditions are too wet to sustain tree growth there are mires. But on drier areas below the treeline the occur-rence of heath and moorland is a product of management, or a combination of management and climate changes, dating back over not just 200 years of grouse moor management, but over perhaps 5 000 years of hunter-gatherer and pastoral management activity (e.g. Simmons, 1990; Hirons and Edwards, 1990; Bennet *et al.*, 1992). One has only to look at the ericaceous dwarf shrubs which comprise the ground flora of the remnant Caledonian pinewoods to realize the ease with which heath and moorland can be created by forest clearance.

The fate of such areas is determined by management. Management for red grouse (*Lagopus lagopus scoticus*) maximizes the importance of heather (*Calluna vul-garis*); but management of heather for red deer (*Cervus elaphus*) or sheep (*Ovis aries*) is likely to be a much more hit and miss affair. The findings of the National Coun-tryside Monitoring Scheme (Tudor and Mackey, this volume), illustrate the dynamic, large-scale interchange which has taken place between heather-dominated moorland and grassland, as well as conversion of extensive areas of both to coniferous plantation. This, combined with recent afforestation, makes it difficult to know with any certainty the likely extent of heath and moorland at any one time. Even using satellite observation, which promises more or less instantaneous measurements across wide areas, significant errors can occur due to spectral confusion between established heather and coniferous woodland, recently burned heather and bare soil, and the occurrence of ground masked by shadow in areas of strong topography (National Remote Sensing Centre, 1989).

Published estimates of the likely extent of heather moorland and related land types in Scotland vary according to whether they are considering the drier, more distinctive end of the spectrum or broader land use categories (Table 30.1).

Table 30.1 Published estimates of the extent of moorland or related land-use types in Scotland.

Area (Million ha)	Land-use type	Source and year
1.20	Dry heather moorland	Tivy, 1976
1.70	Heather moorland	SDD, 1990
1.87	Grouse moor	McGilvray and Perman, 1991
3.25	Red deer range	Red Deer Commission quoted in Callander and Mackenzie, 1991
4.03	Rough grazing	The Scottish Office, 1992
4.80	Free range grazing	Miller, 1979
6.82	Less favoured areas	Williams and Green, 1993

Heather is one of the most abundant and widespread of moorland plant species, and its extent as a dominant part of the vegetation can be reliably mapped from aerial photographs. The most recent estimate of the likely extent of heather-dominated communities comes from the Land Cover of Scotland Project, commissioned from the Macaulay Land Use Research Institute by the Scottish Office Environment Department (Table 30.2). The figures given here are believed to provide a reliable indicative estimate of heather ground but the large number of mosaic categories, and their significant total area, provide scope for different interpretations.

Table 30.2 The most recent estimates of heather cover for Scotland, taken from the Land Cover of Scotland dataset (Macaulay Land Use Research Institute, 1993).

Habitat type	Uniform areas	Area (million ha) Mosaics	Total
Dry heather dominated moor	0.245M	0.094M	0.339M
Wet heather dominated moor and blanket bog	0.725M	0.760M	1.485M
Undifferentiated heather moor	0.378M	0.881M	1.260M
Totals	1.348M	1.735M	3.084M ha

These figures suggest that about 1.35 million ha, equivalent to about 17 % of Scotland, is dominated by heather. This in turn comprises part of an overall area of some 3 million ha, equivalent to about 38 % of Scotland, which has heather present in significant quantities. For comparison, estimates of 0.46 million ha and 0.125 million ha have been made for areas in England and Wales (respectively) with more than 25 % heather cover (Institute of Terrestrial Ecology, 1989), though more recent estimates (Bardgett and Marsden, 1992) which include *Vaccinium myrtillus*-dominated vegetation suggest rather larger areas, particularly in Wales (0.298 million ha). The scale of the challenge for heath and moorland conservation is evident from these estimates.

Some of these estimates include heather-dominated vegetation in the lowlands. The occurrence of continental European species, near the northwestern edge of their range, in the fragmentary heaths of the lowlands of south and east England contribute to their distinctive character (e.g. Webb, 1986). They also have distinctive management problems due to cessation of traditional land uses, resulting in vegetation succession, and fragmentation within an otherwise intensively used landscape. However, the distinction between upland and lowland heathland is less clear as one moves north as 'upland' climatic conditions occur at progressively lower altitudes (Webb, 1986; Gimingham, 1992).

30.3 What does Heather Moorland contribute to Landscape and Habitat Diversity?

The extensive, open moorlands of the Scottish uplands contribute to the distinctive character of the Scottish landscape. However, this very extensiveness is sometimes taken to imply uniformity and lack of diversity. Species diversity is indeed often low compared with vegetation on less acid soils or in more equable climatic conditions, but there is considerable diversity of distinct vegetation types. For example, in the British uplands, most of which could be considered moorland, there are 82 distinct, principal vegetation communities (Rodwell, 1991; 1992). In Scotland, 5 heath communities, 3 blanket mire and 2 wet heath communities, and 4 associated acid grassland communities comprise most of the area of heath and moorland vegetation. This can be compared with totals of, for example, 25 woodland communities and 13 mesotrophic grasslands, for British vegetation as a whole.

30.4 How do we approach Conservation of the Dependent Species?

If there was no limit to the extent of heath and moorland under conservation management, it might be a reasonable assumption that — provided a varied vegetation composition and structure was maintained — the requirements of the full range of dependent flora and fauna would be met. Coulson *et al.*, (1992) state that this basic assumption has not been tested. It becomes crucial in an approach to conservation based on land-type selection to check that the specialist requirements of individual species are considered. A practical advantage of the species-based approach is that, on the whole, species are much better defined than their habitats (or the vegetation types used as surrogates). That the full range of dependent species, particularly invertebrates, and their habitat requirements are not known remains a major challenge. However, it is unlikely that we will ever have complete species information even for some functionally important groups of organisms e.g. the soil microflora and microfauna. One has therefore to be selective and focus initially on the higher profile dependent species, recognizing that even for many of these, their habitat requirements or their importance as habitat providers or shapers for other species are imprecisely known.

Disturbance, for example by fire, is an important and natural component of many natural and semi-natural systems (see Hobbs and Huenneke, 1992, for a recent review). This is particularly true of Boreal and Atlantic moorlands. Appropriate regimes of disturbance are often critical to distinctiveness and diversity (e.g. Hobbs and Gimingham, 1987). Some species will be more disturbance sensitive and may suffer as increased human use imposes a more rigorous disturbance regime. Some species are key indicators of undisturbed habitat for example, the leafy liverwort *Herbertus borealis* in upland heaths, the bog moss *Sphagnum imbricatum* (in conjunction with appropriate microtopography) in peatlands. Their occurrence and abundance would be a criterion in selecting the least disturbed examples of their respective habitats. Other dependent species are very localized and the added diversity their presence brings is again likely to feature in habitat selection for nature conservation purposes e.g. marsh saxifrage (*Saxifraga hirculus*), blue mountain heath (*Phyllodoce caerulea*), or the bryophyte *Drepanocladus vernicosus*.

When, however, one comes to the conservation of common, or once common, heath and moorland species such as the large heath butterfly (*Coenonympha tullia*), common frog (*Rana temporaria*), adder (*Vipera berus*) and curlew (*Numenius arquata*), the need for a more comprehensive approach than one based solely on the selection of less disturbed habitat becomes immediately apparent. Monitoring such populations is in itself a major challenge. When, for example, The Scottish Office stated that it would seek Scottish Natural Heritage's advice on the status of the adder at the 1996 quinquennial review of the Wildlife and Countryside Act schedules, it was evident that special steps would be required to ascertain its population and the Institute of Terrestrial Ecology was contracted to conduct a survey (Reading *et al.*, 1993).

The biggest current challenge posed by a species conservation strategy is the implementation of the EC Wild Birds Directive. Several species listed in its Annexes frequent heath and moorland (Usher and Thompson, 1993; Coulson *et al.*, 1992; Thompson *et al.*, 1995). To conserve some of these species requires conservation of extensive areas of hunting range beyond that which can be safeguarded solely by a site-based approach, e.g. a golden eagle (*Aquila chrysaetos*) breeding pair may require a home range of 45–70 km^2 (Cramp, 1980). How the UK should meet this challenge is under active consideration.

30.5 Which Management Problems need to be Addressed?

It is evident from the National Countryside Monitoring Scheme that there is a continuing need to monitor, and where necessary control, the reclamation of heath and moorland for agriculture and forestry. These impacts and their consequences for natural heritage conservation have been reviewed by Thompson *et al.*, (1995). Successful management requires skilful control and integration of the two main tools of management, grazing and burning, especially as they affect the dwarf-shrub component of heath and moorland. Without this, most heaths and moorland below the natural treeline would either revert to woodland and scrub or would be converted to acid grasslands.

30.5.1 Grazing

Retention of a varied moorland resource requires a balance between low-grazing pressure, permitting invasion of trees and shrubs, and high-grazing pressure, which can lead to the spread of grasses and to the loss of dwarf shrubs. Sheep are the dominant herbivores on heaths and moorlands, together with red deer over most of the Scottish Highlands. Optimum stocking rates depend on a number of factors including the underlying geology and derived soils, local climate, the amount of grassland present, the age and condition of the heather, the seasonal grazing pattern, whether there is any supplementary feeding and on the purposes of management. It is not simply a question of setting a preferred stocking rate for the unit as a whole, but of influencing local grazing intensities to suit local conditions by stock management. Thus, young vigorous heather on well drained ground in eastern Scotland may support 2.5 ewes/ha/yr without damage while less than 0.5 ewes/ha/yr would be more appropriate on blanket bog (MacDonald, 1993). This range of sensitivity may be present even within a single management unit. Knowledge of critical grazing rates for other species and vegetation types is much less precise.

30.5.2 Burning

Grouse moor managers burn on a rotation of 10–25 years to rejuvenate the heather and achieve a mixture of small patches of different ages, suited to the various stages of the grouse's life cycle. On moors managed chiefly for sheep and deer, fires tend to be larger and more frequent. This is often for logistic reasons, since it is well known that the range would be better utilized with a more dispersed burning pattern. Burning tends to be carried out more frequently on the drier, lower altitude, and more accessible moors. Striking a balance between different interests in order to decide on the optimum burning frequency and pattern can be difficult. Conservation interests have long considered that western areas of Scotland suffer from 'overburning' (e.g. Darling, 1955). However, the problem is perhaps not the use of fire *per se*, although there are extensive peatland areas in the west where burning would not be desirable, but lack of understanding of the effects of fire, used as a management tool, and of the need for careful fire control.

30.5.3 Cutting

Injudicious use of fire when vegetation or weather conditions are not suitable can jeopardize the regeneration of vegetation it is meant to encourage, and may risk

expensive damage to other land uses if fires run out of control. Cutting is a potential solution to a number of these problems. However, machinery can damage
fragile peaty ground. Cutting is also often restricted to smaller areas of suitable
topography than burning, and it is more expensive. It is probably best regarded as
a back-up to burning, being useful for creating firebreaks to improve fire control
and for treating problem areas, e.g. next to forestry plantations, which may be
difficult or dangerous to attempt to burn. On Cairnsmore of Fleet National
Nature Reserve, Scottish Natural Heritage has found cutting to be very effective,
both to create firebreaks and as a substitute for burning, particularly in vegetation
containing a high proportion of *Molinia caerulea*.

30.5.4   Drainage

Moorland drainage was subsidized and widespread in the past but is now discouraged, Agricultural Department grant aid being reduced to 30 % in 1984 then
ceasing altogether in 1985 (although 65 % grant is still available under the Crofting
Counties Agricultural Grants [Scotland] Scheme). The beneficial effects were negligible, and open drains could cause serious erosion and act as traps for lambs and
young birds (Coulson *et al.*, 1990; Stewart and Lance, 1983).

30.5.5   Bracken control

Bracken has invaded heaths and moorland extensively, particularly at lower altitudes
and in the south and west, with local and regional rates of spread in excess of
1 % per year having been estimated (Miller *et al.*, 1990). It is generally of low
nature conservation value and brings little or no economic benefit (Pakeman and
Marrs, 1992), although it can make a significant and arguably attractive contribution
to landscape character. It can be controlled by repeated cutting or careful spraying
but success requires persistent effort.

30.5.6   Other factors

Heather may also be damaged locally by other factors including trampling, various
fungal pathogens, desiccation and herbivorous insects (particularly heather beetle,
Lochmaea suturalis, and a number of polyphagous Lepidoptera species). These normally only affect limited areas, although outbreaks of defoliation by the larvae of
a number of Lepidoptera species, particularly the winter moth (*Operophtera brumata*), may have become more frequent and extensive in recent decades (Hartley,
1993; Watson and Phillips, 1991).

30.5.7   Restoration

The problems of restoring heather to former heaths and moorland which have lost
all heather cover are naturally greater than repairing damage to existing heather
areas. However the soil under a heather canopy contains a seedbank of heathland
species which remains viable long after the living heather above has disappeared.
There may be up to 800 000 seeds/m^2 in the top 5 cms of soil (Legg *et al.*, 1992),
but germination normally requires disturbance of the soil. Heather seed

production declines rapidly with altitude but there is a much less marked effect on the viable seedbank due to greater seed longevity at higher altitudes (Miller and Cummins, 1987). Where viable heather seed is absent it can be reintroduced by collecting litter and surface soil from recently burned areas of vigorous heather, or by cutting and collecting seed-capsule bearing heather shoots between October and January. Areas under treatment may need to be protected from grazing for up to 5 years and may need a nurse grass crop and light fertilizer dressing.

30.5.8 *Habitat fragmentation and restoration*

How can amounts, patch sizes and locations of heather to be restored (relative to existing blocks of heather) be prioritized to provide conservation benefits in the most cost-effective way? This is a question which could be asked at a number of spatial scales of design, from the regional down to individual management units. The information needed to answer this question is largely lacking but undoubtedly lessons could be drawn from other areas of landscape ecology (Selman, 1993).

30.6 What Natural Heritage Conservation Measures are available and how Effective have they been?

We will begin by looking at those measures restricted to localized areas.

30.6.1 *Sites of Special Scientific Interest and related measures*

In all, 435 of Scotland's 1039 biological Sites of Special Scientific Interest (SSSI) contain significant areas of heath or moorland. This amounts to over 500 000 ha, or more than half the total extent of biological SSSI.

A total of 43 of these have been declared as *National Nature Reserves*, two of which, Muir of Dinnet and Forvie, have been further designated by the Council of Europe as heathland *Biogenetic Reserves* to conserve representative examples of European flora, fauna and natural areas.

SSSI is the designation which also serves as the basis for areas of conservation importance under European Directives. To date 10 *Special Protection Areas* containing heath or moorland have been designated by the Secretary of State and at least 40 candidate sites await consultation. It is still too early to say how many areas may similarly be designated by the Secretary of State as *Special Areas of Conservation* under the Habitats and Species Directive, but the habitats listed on Annex I of that Directive include northern Atlantic wet heath, dry heath, alpine and subalpine heaths, and actively forming blanket bog.

A total of 200 *Management Agreements* for heath or moorland management in whole or part have been reached covering approximately 21 000 ha of SSSI. Negotiating individual management agreements is a time-consuming process and may only ever cover a small proportion of SSSIs. Of particular interest, therefore, is the *Peatland Management Scheme* on trial by Scotland Natural Heritage in Caithness and Sutherland. Like the Environmentally Sensitive Area schemes discussed below, participants opt-in. Eligibility is limited in this instance to owners and occupiers of peatland SSSIs. Agreements are for 5 years and cover such matters as muirburn and grazing control. The scheme commenced in 1992 and in its first year some 30 % of eligible land has been entered. These areas amount to 33 000 ha giving a total area, when combined with the individually negotiated Management Agreements, of 54 000 ha.

30.6.2   National Scenic Areas (NSAs)
Heath and moorland forms a substantial component of the landscape in all but 7 of the 40 NSAs, which in area cover about 13 % of Scotland and comprise one of SNH's suite of protected areas. Protection from this designation operates primarily through planning mechanisms and as such is not designed to control major land use change such as afforestation.

30.6.3   Natural Heritage Areas (NHAs)
The way in which NHAs will be selected and operated is still under discussion but, as a land use coordinating mechanism NHAs can be expected to contribute to the conservation of heath and moorland.

Turning now to measures which can be applied more widely in influencing agricultural and forestry land use and the way they impinge upon heath and moorland, we find a number of schemes in operation or planned.

30.6.4   Farm and Conservation Grant Scheme
Instituted in 1989, this scheme includes provision for muirburn, regeneration of heather by cutting, and exclusion of stock to encourage heather regeneration. A higher rate of grant (50 %) is provided within the Less Favoured Area (designated under European Community Directives 75/268/EEC and 84/169/EEC) than elsewhere (40 %). These rates of grant were reduced as from 1 December 1993 to 30 % and 25 % respectively (Scottish Office News Release of 30 November/1827/93). However, grant is limited to capital work and for most farmers without grouse shooting rights, heathland regeneration is unlikely to be very attractive given the low grazing value of such areas, but for estates with in-hand farms where shooting is also an enterprise it is more likely to be of interest. To date, grants for regeneration of heath and moorland amounts to about £25 000 (Scottish Office Agriculture and Fisheries Department, personal communication), which probably covers less than 1 000 ha.

30.6.5   Livestock support: Annual Premiums and Hill Livestock Compensatory Allowance
Livestock farming is supported through two main mechanisms financed by a mixture of UK and EC funding. One is the Sheep Annual Premium, the other (part of the Less Favoured Areas package) is the Hill Livestock Compensatory Allowance. Both operate as headage payments and since for many farmers they form a significant proportion of income, farmers have tended to respond by increasing stocking rates. In its discussion document 'This Common Inheritance', the Government undertook to examine whether environmental safeguards could be introduced to

the HLCA. Reform has been postponed, although rates of payment have been reduced. The Sheep Annual Premium has also been revised by the introduction of quotas but it is too early to say whether any environmental benefits will ensue.

However, some reform proposals are going ahead, including extensification measures to reduce overgrazing on heath and moorland, the promulgation of a Code of Good Upland Management (issued in 1992) and the introduction of further Environmentally Sensitive Areas.

30.6.6 Environmentally Sensitive Areas (ESAs)

The ESA schemes apply to designated areas covering about 15 % of Scotland (amounting to some 1.7 million ha) with heath and moorland extensively represented in many, although its actual extent is unknown. Farmers opt to enter based on a whole farm plan and receive payment for undertaking, among other things, to avoid damage to rough grazings (which include heath and moorland) by either improvement or overgrazing, and to observe the Muirburn Code (Phillips *et al.*, 1993). The advantage of the whole farm approach is that payment to promote conservation on one part of the farm is unlikely to be used for inappropriate intensification on another. In addition, most ESAs have an option to introduce a grazing plan specifically for the regeneration and retention of heather. In the two southern upland ESAs this is mandatory.

Uptake rates (SOAFD, February 1993 review) reveal that between 42 % and 60 % of eligible land has been entered in some ESA scheme areas. The perceived benefits of being within an ESA and being paid to farm in an environmentally friendly manner are now such that farmers in Orkney and Caithness are lobbying for their areas to be included within an ESA. Monitoring heath and moorland in ESA's has been undertaken by the Macaulay Land Use Research Institute, but it is still too soon to judge success.

30.6.7 Islands Agricultural Development Programme

In the northern and western islands (excluding the 'Western Isles' — the Outer Hebrides — which had their own scheme), an agricultural development programme operated in the 5 years to March 1993, funded in part by the EC. Within the context of a farm development plan, farmers and crofters could apply for payments to cover positive management of areas of particular importance for the natural environment, including heather suppressed by overgrazing.

Uptake rates in some areas (e.g. Orkney) were high and up to 60 % of farms entering took up some of the environmental options. For the scheme as a whole 491 plans involved environmental measures on hill land, covering just over 15 000 ha of land (SOAFD, provisional figures).

30.6.8 Extensification

Pilot schemes commenced in Scotland in 1990 in Borders Region and parts of Highland and Strathclyde. Participating farmers entered for 5 years and received payments to reduce stocking by between 20 % and 70 % and undertaking to maintain such features as unimproved heath and moor.

In response to the Agri-Environment Council Regulation, agreed as part of the Common Agricultural Policy reform package in May 1992, SOAFD submitted proposals to the EC in July 1993. For heaths and moorlands, apart from proposals for further ESAs, the most important proposal is the *Heather Moorland Scheme* under which payments will be made to farmers and crofters to reduce the number of sheep grazing on their moorland and to follow a basic programme of moorland management covering matters such as muirburn and supplementary feeding. There will also be a *Habitat Creation Scheme* which will include options for upland scrub regeneration and the protection of coastal heathland. Both schemes would only apply in areas outside ESAs. Participants will be required to enter a five year agreement. Budgets are limited, however, with about £3 million projected to be available for the Heather Moorland Extensification Scheme in 1995/96.

30.6.9 *Indicative Forestry Strategies and Environmental Assessment for Afforestation*

As shown by Tudor and Mackey (this volume), afforestation is one of the major agents of loss of heath and moorland in the uplands. A strategic approach to land use is required to guide land use change to the most appropriate areas. To this end the Indicative Forestry Strategies now in operation over much of Scotland, together with the application of the Environmental Assessments (Afforestation) Regulations 1988 can be seen as a contribution to this process, though their effectiveness has been questioned (e.g. Adger and Whitby, 1991). The removal of tax incentives for afforestation in 1988 has been followed by a substantial reduction (approximately 50 %) in new private planting. However, in the absence of statutory controls, combined with the Government policy target of afforesting 33 000 ha per annum, could clearly result in further areas of heath and moorland being planted, especially if new financial incentives were to be offered.

30.6.10 *Extent of heath and moorland under conservation management*

Taking the foregoing schemes into consideration how much of the resource is already, or may shortly be, under some form of conservation management? Even with quite optimistic estimates of uptake rates it is seems unlikely that more than a third will be protected or positively managed.

30.7 How Should Natural Heritage Conservation be taken Forward?

30.7.1 *Resource inventory*

The Land Cover of Scotland dataset provides an excellent basis from which to take conservation forward and to measure future change. (Compare the requirement under the Wildlife and Countryside Act 1981 (Section 43 as amended) for National Park Authorities in England and Wales to map areas of moorland and heath they consider important to conserve, to publish the results and review them every five years.) There is, however, a need for much more work on the characterization and inventory of heath and moorland landscapes.

30.7.2 Monitoring resource change

There is a continuing need to monitor land use changes. Refinement of satellite monitoring techniques to ensure they can produce reliable results would be a useful contribution to taking conservation forward. There is also scope to develop satellite image analysis as a tool for monitoring muirburn.

30.7.3 Integration of species and habitat requirements

There is a need to ensure that habitat- and species-based approaches to conservation are integrated. Implementation of the EC Wild Birds Directive and Habitat and Species Directive, together with the quinquennial review of Schedules 5 and 8 of the Wildlife and Countryside Act, already provide a useful basis from which to take conservation forward.

A review of the conservation needs of heath and moorland species would be timely. Such a review must inevitably be selective but should cover a wide taxonomic range and could usefully develop some of the approaches outlined by Coulson *et al.*, 1992; Usher and Thompson, 1993; Thompson *et al.*, (1995). It will be important to monitor the species selected (some already are monitored), and to try to identify any management which should ideally be undertaken to maintain these populations.

30.7.4 Natural heritage conservation measures

Looking at conservation measures and their effectiveness in Scotland it is evident, from the huge disparity between the likely total extent of heath and moorland compared with that arguably under some form of conservation management, that an approach based solely on conservation objectives in a narrow sense is not capable of safeguarding more than a limited proportion of the resource. For conservation to be taken forward the term 'conservation' in the title must be interpreted in its widest sense as 'wise land use'. That is, conservation of heath and moorland (below the treeline) can succeed only if it is an integral part of the working countryside.

This approach is already being developed, but must be maintained and extended. In recent years, several wider countryside measures have been introduced, targeted on agriculture. Many of these have the considerable attraction for the Government of eligibility for partial refunds from the European Community. These have been supplemented by the Code of Good Upland Management and the Muirburn Code. Fiscal measures have discouraged afforestation, but if these were to be relaxed it might prove necessary to take steps to safeguard key areas of heath and moorland.

Conspicuous by their absence are any measures specifically targeted on the retention of grouse moors. Thompson *et al.*, (1995) identify grouse moor management, compared with hill-sheep farming and forestry, as closest to complying with nature conservation objectives and of providing the greatest sustainable income from heather moorland. Perhaps a relaxation of the sporting rates applied to Scottish moors compared with their English and Welsh counterparts would further the conservation of heath and moorland. But a condition of such relaxation should be a more sustainable approach to the nature conservation interest of grouse moors as specified in Thompson *et al.*, (1995), e.g. less emphasis on bags of grouse and a total cessation of illegal persecution of birds of prey.

Lastly, we should keep an eye on developments elsewhere. MAFF will be introducing similar extensification measures to the SOAFD measures, already described, in England and Wales. In Wales, *Tir Cymen* is an experimental whole-farm scheme, administered by the Countryside Council for Wales, with some similarities to Environmentally Sensitive Area schemes. In two of the three pilot areas (Meirionnydd and Dinefwr) there are significant areas of heath and moorland. The scheme is voluntary, and involves 10-year agreements which provide annual payments in return for adherence to a basic protection code and positive management for conservation, including options for grazing management of heathland and moorland and capital payments for fencing, scrub and bracken control, and establishing regular muirburn.

In England the *Countryside Stewardship Scheme*, a voluntary scheme administerd by the Countryside Commission, has options which include the management and recreation of lowland heath and the regeneration of suppressed heather on moorland. Both schemes are sufficiently flexible to take advantage of local requirements and opportunities. This approach is likely to maximize conservation benefits but it does require substantial investment in local advisory staff (the Countryside Commission recruited 36 staff to their regional offices). Another feature of these schemes is that payments have not been based on 'profits foregone', a principle which has been much criticised in respect of SSSI management agreements. Instead, the philosophy is to provide incentives which will encourage positive management for conservation, with standardized payments based on research commissioned to establish the market price that would attract a predetermined target number of entrants.

English Nature's National Lowland Heathland Programme, initiated in 1992, is intended to raise the profile of lowland heath and its associated wildlife and in particular to develop new proposals for its sustainable management. The lesson from this and from the lowland heathland part of Countryside Stewardship is that once the economic use of such areas for livestock grazing has lapsed it can be extremely expensive (£1000–£2000 per ha) to maintain these areas as open heath of conservation value.

An interesting feature of these schemes is convergence in their principles and prescriptions towards voluntary entry, payments in return for basic protection measures with enhancement payments for positive management, and the flexibility to tailor precise prescriptions to local requirements and opportunities within fairly simple, standardised guidelines. This convergence, perhaps, is a hopeful sign. Nevertheless, if the range of schemes on offer is not carefully integrated delivery of heath and moorland conservation is not likely to achieve maximum effectiveness.

Within Scotland, perhaps the Natural Heritage Area mechanism presents an opportunity to develop a more integrated approach.

References

Adger, W. N. and Whitby, M. C. (1991). Environmental assessment in forestry: the initial experience. *Journal of Rural Studies*, **7**, 385–95.

Bardgett, R. D. and Marsden, J. H. (1992). *Heather Condition and Management in England and Wales*. English Nature Science Directorate, Peterborough.

Bennet, K. D., Boreham, S., Sharp, M. J. and Switsur, V. R. (1992). Holocene history of environment, vegetation and human settlement on Catta Ness, Lunnasting, Shetland. *Journal of Ecology*, **80**, 241–72.

Callander, R. F. and Mackenzie, N. A. (1991). *The Management of Wild Red Deer in Scotland*. Rural Forum Scotland, Perth, 5–8.

Chambers Dictionary (1993). Edinburgh, Chambers Harrap Publishers Ltd,

Coulson, J. C., Butterfield, J. E. L. and Henderson, E. (1990). The effect of open drainage ditches on the plant and invertebrate communities of moorland and on the decomposition of peat. *Journal of Applied Ecology*, **27**, 549–61.

Coulson, J. C., Fielding, C. A., Goodyer S. A. (1992). *The management of moorland areas to enhance their nature conservation interest*. JNCC Report 134, Joint Nature Conservation Committee, Peterborough.

Cramp, S. (1980) (Ed). *Handbook of the Birds of Europe, the Middle East and North Africa. The Birds of the Western Paleartic. Volume II Hawks to Bustards*. Oxford University Press, London, 234–244

Darling, F. F. (1955). *West Highland Survey. An Essay in Human Ecology*. Oxford University Press, Oxford, 170–1.

Gimingham, C. H. (1992). *The Lowland Heathland Management Handbook*. English Nature Science No. 8, English Nature, Peterborough, 15–18

The Scottish Office (1992) Scottish Abstract of Statistics 1991, Edinburgh. p.349

Hartley, S. 1993. Insect pests on heather moorland. In *The Joseph Nickerson Reconciliation Project Ninth Annual Report*, May 1993, 46–7.

Hirons, K. R. and Edwards, K. J. (1990). Pollen and related studies at Kinloch, Isle of Rum, Scotland, with particular reference to possible early human impacts on vegetation. *New Phytologist*, **116**, 715–27.

Hobbs, R. J. and Gimingham, C. H. (1987). Vegetation, fire and herbivore interactions in heathland. *Advances in Ecological Research*, **16**, 87–173.

Hobbs, R. J. and Huenneke, L. F. (1992). Disturbance, diversity, and invasion: implications for conservation. *Conservation Biology*, **6**, 324–37.

Institute of Terrestrial Ecology (1989). *Heather in England and Wales*. HMSO, London, 13.

Legg, C. J., Maltby, E., and Proctor, M. C. F. 1992. The ecology of severe moorland fire on the North York Moors. II. The seed distribution and seedling establishment of *Calluna vulgaris* (L.) Hull. *Journal of Ecology*, **80**, 737–52.

Macaulay Land Use Research Institute (1993). *The Land Cover of Scotland 1988. Final Report*. Aberdeen.

MacDonald, A. (1993). *Heather Damage: A Guide to Types of Damage and their Causes*. 2nd Edition. Research and Survey in Nature Conservation No. 28, Joint Nature Conservation Committee, Peterborough.

McGilvray, J. and Perman, R. (1991). *Grouse Shooting in Scotland: An Analysis of its Importance to the Economy and Environment*. Report by the Department of Economics, University of Strathclyde, to the Brouse Research Project, Game Conservancy Trust, 17–20.

Miller, D. R., Morrice, J. G. and Whitworth, P. L. (1990). Bracken distribution and spread in upland Scotland: an assessment using digital mapping techniques. In *Bracken Biology and Management*, Thomson, J. A. and Smith, R. T. (Eds), Australian Institute of Agricultural Science Occasional Publications No. **40**. 121–32.

Miller, G. R. (1979). Quantity and quality of the annual production of shoots and flowers by *Calluna vulgaris* in north-east Scotland. *Journal of Ecology*, **67**, 109–30.

Miller, G. R. (1987). Role of buried viable seeds in the recolonization of disturbed ground by heather (*Calluna vulgaris* [L.] Hull) in the Cairngorm Mountains, Scotland, UK. *Arctic and Alpine Research*, **19**, 396–401.

National Remote Sensing Centre (1989). *The Use of Satellite Data for Mapping and Monitoring Heather.* SP1 Division Working Paper, SP(89)WP22, Report to the Department of the Environment,

Pakeman, R. J. and Marrs, R. H. (1992). The conservation value of bracken *Pteridium aquilinum* (L.) Kuhn-dominated communities in the UK, and an assessment of the ecological impact of bracken expansion or its removal. *Biological Conservation*, **62**, 101–14.

Phillips, J., Watson, A. and MacDonald, A. (1993) *A Muirburn Code.* Scottish Natural Heritage,

Reading, C. J., Buckland, S., Gorzula, S., McGowan, G. M., Staines, B. W. (1993). *Status of the Adder in Scotland.* Unpublished interim ITE report to SNH.

Rodwell, J. S. (1991). *British Plant Communities. Volume 1 Woodlands and Scrub, Volume 2 Mires and Heaths.* Cambridge University Press, Cambridge.

Rodwell, J. S. (1992). *British Plant Communities. Volume 3 Grassland and Montane Communities.* Cambridge University Press.

Scottish Development Department (1990). *The Scottish Environment — Statistics No. 2.*

Selman, P. (1993). Landscape ecology and countryside planning: visions theory and practice. *Journal of Rural Studies*, **9**, 1–22.

Simmons, I. G. (1990). The mid-Holocene ecological history of the moorlands of England and Wales and its relevance to conservation. *Environmental Conservation*, **17**, 61–69.

Stewart, A. J. A. and Lance, A. N. (1983). Moor drainage: a review of impacts on land use. *Journal of Environmental Management*, **4**, 251–74.

Thompson, D. B. A., MacDonald, A. J. and Hudson, P. J. (1994) 'Upland moors and heaths'. In W. J. Sutherland, and D. Hill (Eds.), *Habitat Management*, Cambridge University Press, Cambridge, 292-326.

Thompson, D. B. A., MacDonald, A. J., Marsden, J. H., Galbraith, C. A., (1995). Upland heather moorland in Great Britain: a review of international importance, vegetation change and some objectives for nature conservation. *Biological Conservation.* **71**, in press.

Tivy, J. (1976). *Organic Resources of Scotland.* Oliver and Boyd.

Tudor, G. and Mackey, E. C. (this volume) Upland land cover change in post-war Scotland.

Usher, M. B., and Thompson, D. B. A. (1993). Variation in the upland heathland of Great Britain: conservation importance. *Biological Conservation*, **66**, 69–81.

Watson, A. and Phillips, J. (1991). Vapourers and beetles. *Shooting Times and Country Magazine*, **46**, 33.

Webb, N. (1986). *Heathlands.* New Naturalist Series, Collins.

Williams, G. and Green, R. (1993). Towards an upland habitat action plan. *Royal Society for the Protection of Birds Conservation Review 1993* RSPB, No. **7**, 5–11.

31 HEATHER MOORLAND MONITORING IN THE LOCH LOMOND ENVIRONMENTALLY SENSITIVE AREA, SCOTLAND

D. J. Henderson, A. Lilly, S. Madden and M. J. Still

Summary

1. The Loch Lomond ESA was one of the first two ESAs designated in Scotland, and a principal objective of this voluntary scheme was the maintenance and enhancement of heather moorlands.

2. In 1989, botanical monitoring commenced on a sample of heather moorlands from both within and outwith the ESA.

3. Preliminary results indicate that, apart from some localised overgrazing, heather moorlands are being maintained in both areas, though utilization levels outwith the ESA are generally greater.

31.1 Introduction

The Agriculture Act 1986 empowered the Secretary of State to designate areas as being 'environmentally sensitive'. Within such Environmentally Sensitive Areas (ESAs), landowners and farmers could voluntarily enter the scheme and would then receive grants to follow codes of management practice and implement conservation plans on their land. Under the terms of the Act, the Scottish Office Agriculture and Fisheries Department (SOAFD) has a statutory obligation to review the effects of the Scheme, and has commissioned the Macaulay Land Use Research Institute to conduct systematic botanical monitoring. The effectiveness of ESA management prescriptions on aspects of nature conservation, principally maintenance of heather (*Calluna vulgaris* (L.) Hull) moorland, broadleaved woodland regeneration and the preservation of botanical diversity, is being assessed. This chapter focuses on the monitoring of heather moorlands in the Loch Lomond ESA. As well as describing the trends on farms entered into the scheme, information is also being gathered from similar 'control' sites situated on heather moorlands outwith the designated area.

The principal heather moorland ESA management guidelines stipulate that in general there should be no overgrazing, and that in particular, a maximum stocking rate of 0.5 livestock units per hectare, approximately 3 ewes/ha^{-1} should not be exceeded; it is also necessary to maintain good muirburn practice. However, even below the maximum permissible stocking rate the impact of any specified grazing level on heather moorland vegetation will vary from site to site, depending on management inputs and the nature of the remaining grazing resource. A summary of the SOAFD objectives and requirements is given in Appendix 31.

31.2 Methods

Since plant communities with heather as a dominant or co-dominant species covered over 10 km^2 of the farms sampled, and soil and topographic conditions varied widely, it was decided to sample within broad ecological types of moorland easily distinguishable in the field. These were:

- steep slopes immediately above the in-bye land where heather under severe grazing pressure forms a mosaic with bracken and grassland on humus-iron podzols;

- mid-slopes with peaty soils (peat <50 cm depth) and heather under moderate grazing pressure;

- mid-hill gentle slopes with peat (>1 m depth) and blanket bog vegetation under light to moderate grazing pressure and

- upper slopes with peaty soils (peat <50 cm depth) under light grazing pressure.

Within most of these categories, paired recently burned (heather in pioneer or building phase) and unburned (mature heather) areas were chosen for investigation, as sheep foraging behaviour is known to be influenced by stand type. On each patch of burned or mature heather, 20 permanent 1 m x 1 m quadrats were set up along transects at 10 m spacing. Transects were also laid out on similar moors outwith the ESA, around Stronachlachar near Loch Katrine. In addition, at one farm within the ESA, five pairs of quadrats were established within/outside a small exclosure erected to protect overgrazed heather.

Site information collected includes slope, aspect, soil type and management. Estimates of the percentage cover and utilization rate of *C. vulgaris* were made as described in Grant *et al.*, (1981), based on the number of current shoots grazed and the amount of offtake from each shoot. Records of height, growth phase and morphology were made annually, in September, for all sites in 1989, 1991 and 1993, and for a subsample of sites in the intervening years. Data are reported for 1989 and 1991 from two farms within the ESA and from the control area.

31.3 Results and Discussion

Figure 31.1 illustrates heather height trends, and Figure 31.2 heather cover trends between 1989 and 1991 for a range of moorland types. Results from two farms

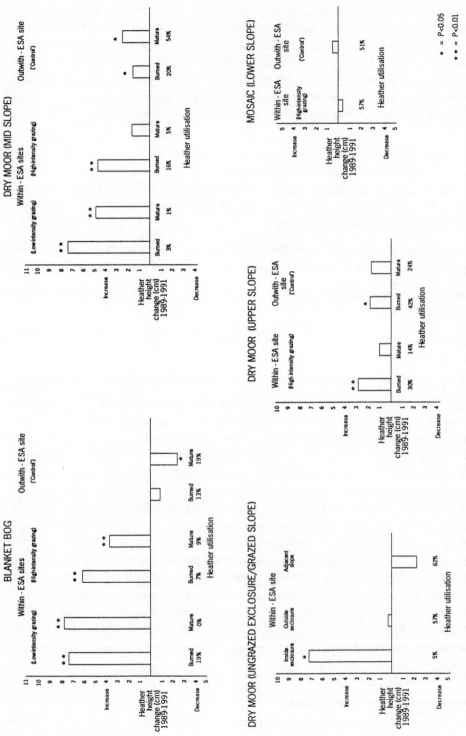

Figure 31.1. Heather height trends between 1989 and 1991, for a range of ecological situations within and outwith the Loch Lomond ESA.

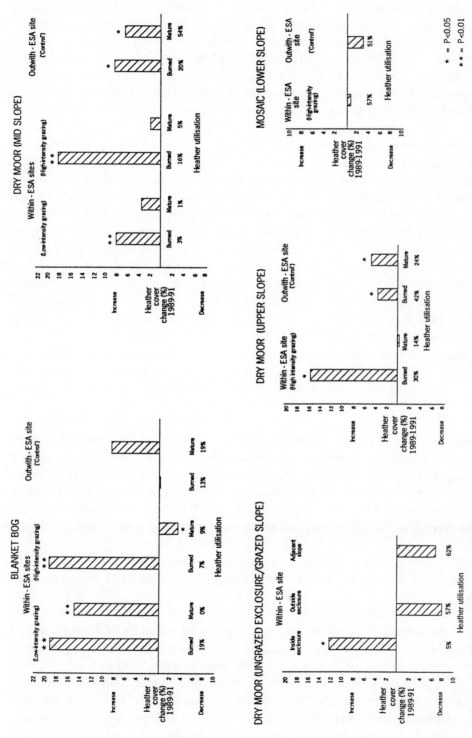

Figure 31.2. Heather cover trends between 1989 and 1991, for a range of ecological situations within and outwith the Loch Lomond ESA.

have been included, one having, relatively speaking, 'low-intensity grazing' and the other 'high-intensity grazing', which correspond to approximately 0.5 ewe/ha^{-1} and 1.0 ewe/ha^{-1} respectively, well below the ceiling prescribed. However, the actual grazing pressure on individual species and communities will not necessarily reflect this difference, as utilization rates depend more on the quality of the overall grazing resource, the foraging behaviour of sheep and shepherding inputs, rather than stocking rates *per se*. On sites outwith the ESA, though stocking rates are generally higher, they are nevertheless below the mandatory maximum applicable within the designated area, ranging from 1 to 3 ewes/ha^{-1}.

Annual increments of ungrazed heather show a wide variation depending on the site and soil conditions and the age of the heather. On the basis of height data from similar areas of heather where stock have been excluded, increases of about 5 to 10 cm per year would be expected in the Loch Lomond ESA. Most of the heather at sites within the ESA showed significant increments in height between 1989 and 1991 (Figure 31.1), the main exceptions being in the mosaic area and on the 'preferred' slope (where sheep tend to congregate and graze) adjacent to the exclosure, as decreases in height occurred and heather utilization rates were particularly high at around 60 %. In contrast to a significant increase of 7 cm within the exclosure, heather height outside was virtually unchanged over the two years. On sites outwith the ESA, increments in height (and in one instance a significant decrease) were generally smaller and associated with higher utilization rates than those found within the ESA. Heather height within the mosaic area showed little change from 1989.

Similar trends are apparent for percentage cover (Figure 31.2), as most sites within the ESA displayed significant increases, particularly on recently burned stands. By contrast, percentage cover changed little on areas with mature heather, although initial values were generally high and in the 60–90 % range. The heather of the low-intensity grazed blanket bog site and that inside the exclosure, however, had increments of 8 % and 6 % respectively, which were associated with low utilization rates. The heather in the mosaic area, on the preferred slope and outside the exclosure, showed non-significant decreases in percentage cover over the two-year period. Although still significant, increases are less on sites outwith the ESA, reflecting the greater utilization rates which occur in association with higher stocking rates.

Overall, the results indicate that most of the heather moorland monitored can sustain the current levels of utilization, as significant increases of height and percentage cover of heather were generally evident. However, heather patches in mosaics and on other 'preferred' areas were heavily utilized and showed decreases of height and cover; such trends could eventually lead to reduction in the extent of heather-dominated vegetation, both within and outwith the ESA. The localized areas of heavy grazing were concentrated on sheltered slopes with good drainage, usually where better-quality grazings, such as *Agrostis/Festuca* grassland, were in close proximity.

Appendix 31.1   SOAFD Summary of Objectives and Requirements of the Scheme in the Loch Lomond ESA

The Loch Lomond area has worldwide fame as an area of outstanding natural beauty. It contains a mixture of mountain, loch and island scenery, spanning the Highland Boundary Fault, which has been enhanced over the years by traditional farming practices.

Objectives

1. To protect the heather moor and species rich grassland within the uplands.

2. To protect and enhance broadleaved and semi-natural farm woodland to encourage natural regeneration.

3. To rectify the neglect of traditional farm dykes and hedges.

4. To protect the landscape from damaging agricultural improvements such as badly constructed or designed hill tracks and unsympathetic farm buildings.

Requirements

1. For open hill rough grazings the farmer shall restrict stocking to less than 0.5 livestock units per ha, shall not carry out any land reclamation works or apply herbicides or pesticides (except in certain limited circumstances using approved techniques), and shall undertake traditional heather management through muirburn.

2. For enclosed land, the farmer shall maintain stockproof dykes and hedges.

3. For both categories of land, the farmer shall agree to follow a code of practice on agricultural developments and works, to get approval for the construction of vehicular tracks and to take advice on new farm buildings. Farmers shall also protect any archaeological remains from damage and ensure that there is no pollution of watercourses.

4. Farmers shall draw up a farm conservation plan which will include details of farming operations necessary as positive conservation measures to restore badly neglected hedges and dykes and to protect farm woodlands and encourage natural regeneration.

Reference

Grant, S. A., Hamilton, W. J. and Souter, C (1981). The responses of heather-dominated vegetation in north-east Scotland to grazing by red deer, *Journal of Ecology*, **69**, 189–204.

32 MONITORING OF HEATHER MOORLAND WITHIN ENVIRONMENTALLY SENSITIVE AREAS IN NORTHERN IRELAND

D. M. McFerran, C. A. Hegarty, A. Cameron, F. P. Mulholland and J. H. McAdam

Summary

1. Within Environmentally Sensitive Areas (ESAs), heather moorland provides a useful grazing resource and a valuable wildlife habitat.

2. In April 1993 a comprehensive monitoring programme was initiated in the newly designated Erne Lakeland and West Fermanagh ESA to determine the impact of ESA management prescriptions on flora and fauna associated with several habitats. Preliminary ordination of ground beetle species suggested that heather moorland sites formed a distinct grouping.

32.1 Introduction

Environmentally Sensitive Areas (ESAs) are designated in locations that are highly valued for their scenic beauty, wildlife habitats or distinctive heritage. The Mournes and Slieve Croob ESA was designated in May 1988 and extended in 1993; the Glens of Antrim was designated in July 1989, extended and renamed in 1993 (Antrim Coast, Glens and Rathlin ESA); and the West Fermanagh and Erne Lakeland ESA was designated in 1993. Participation within the scheme is entirely voluntary. Uptake within the initial two ESA's has been more than 65%

Heather moorland is important in the uplands of Northern Ireland as a grazing resource and a valuable wildlife habitat. As a consequence of poor management, particularly overgrazing and uncontrolled burning, large expanses of heather moorland have disappeared. Within the three current ESAs in Northern Ireland habitat-specific management prescriptions have been incorporated to prevent future loss and encourage regeneration of the heather moorland.

Considerable funding has been invested in establishing Environmentally Sensitive Areas within the British Isles. To evaluate the impact of the scheme, monitoring specific target habitats is necessary. This chapter deals with the monitoring of heather moorland and reports on preliminary results obtained from the invertebrate monitoring exercise.

32.2 Methods

In April 1993 a detailed monitoring programme to determine the impact of the ESA management prescriptions on flora and fauna (avifauna, spiders, ground beetles and water beetles) was initiated. The programme concentrates on several habitats within the newly designated West Fermanagh and Erne Lakeland ESA, including heather moorland. Areas of heather moorland within other designated and proposed ESAs are also subject to biological monitoring.

Time efficiency and ease of relocation have been major considerations in determining monitoring methods. Flora monitoring of heather moorland was carried out in August 1993. The centre of each site was marked by a wooden stake and four equidistant 2 x 2 m quadrats permanently marked out. Plant species and percentage cover was recorded for a 1 x 1 m nested quadrat. Additional species were recorded in the outer part of the 2 x 2 m quadrat. Aspect, slope, soil depth and canopy height were also recorded. Avifauna monitoring was carried out in early February and late May/early June. A standardized viewing time of 20 minutes was allocated. Sites were then walked to disturb any birds hidden in the vegetation. Spiders and ground beetles are being used to monitor change and are trapped and collected from pitfall traps and D-vac samples. Five pitfall traps, with ethylene-glycol as the preservative, were positioned in each study site (Figure 32.1) and sampling was carried out in three, four week periods between April and October 1993. All adult ground beetles (Coleoptera: Carabidae) were separated and stored in 70 % alcohol and later identified to species level. Nomenclature follows Lindroth (1974). Identifications were confirmed by Dr. R. Anderson (Agricultural Chemistry Research Division, DANI)

To facilitate comparison of species lists with other surveys the data from this monitoring programme will be stored on the Recorder database. The data were analysed using multivariate statistical techniques and together with individual species frequency and cover abundance data will provide the baseline to evaluate the success of the ESA scheme in 1996.

32.3 Results

A total of 4281 ground beetles of 45 species were collected from pitfall traps between 19 April and 17 June 1993. Detrended correspondence analysis (DCA) was carried out on collated adult ground beetles on the basis of presence and absence of each species. Following ordination each habitat was located in two-dimensions of ordination space. Heather moorland sites have low axis 1 scores (Figure 32.2) and formed a distinct grouping.

32.4 Discussion

Ground beetles are an important group ecologically, reflecting the soil and disturbance conditions, and have proved useful in assessing environmental quality in

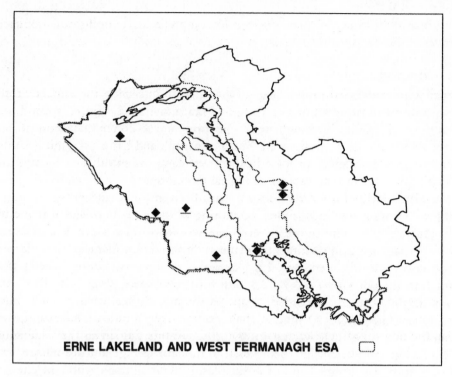

Figure 32.1. Location of sites used in invertebrate monitoring of heather moorland.

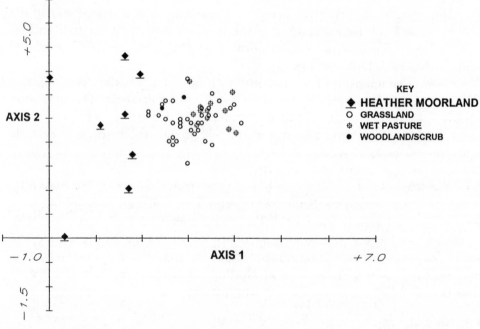

Figure 32.2. Detrended correspondence analysis (DCA) ordination of sites used in invertebrate monitoring.

Britain (Rushton *et al.*, 1989a; 1989b). Despite the methodological problems (Greenslade, 1964), pitfall trapping has been used to assess the ground beetles of upland sites in northern Britain (Butterfield and Coulson, 1983) and across a range of habitats in Northern Ireland (Day, 1987; Meharg, 1988; McFerran, 1991). Although spiders have not proved as useful as ground beetles in assessing environmental quality the two groups together, collected from pitfall traps, give a good indication of a site's conservation value (M. Eyre, personal communication). Preliminary investigation of the ground beetles trapped during the initial monitoring period suggests that in the West Fermanagh and Erne Lakeland ESA species assemblages differed between habitats. There was a distinct ground beetle grouping associated with heather dominated vegetation.

A detailed discussion of the status of individual species is beyond the scope of this chapter. What is noteworthy, for both its apparent rarity in recent decades and its very hygrophilous affinities, is the distribution of *Carabus clatratus* L., a species previously thought to be rare in Co. Fermanagh (R. Anderson, personal communication). Hyman and Parsons (1992) describe *C. clatratus* as being predatory and typical of wetland, bogs and lake margins, particularly on heather moorland. This species was recorded from a variety of habitats types; hay meadows, heathland, wet grassland, unimproved grassland and woodland. Despite this diversity of habitats, this species was only trapped on sites close to water or where natural drainage was poor.

Acknowledgements
This study was funded by the Department of Agriculture (NI). We thank Dr R. Anderson for his help with the identification of the ground beetle species.

References
Butterfield, J. E. L. and Coulson, J. C. (1983). The carabid communities on peat and upland grasslands in northern England, *Holarctic Ecology*, **6**, 63–74.

Day, K. R. (1987). The species and community characteristics of the ground beetles (Coleoptera: Carabidae) in some Northern Ireland Nature Reserves, *Proceedings of the Royal Irish Academy*, **87b**, 65–82.

Greenslade, P. J. M. (1964). Pitfall trapping as a method for studying the populations of Carabidae (Coleoptera), *Journal of Animal Ecology*, **33**, 301–10.

Hyman, P. S. and Parsons, M. S. (1992). *A Review of the Scarce and Threatened Coleoptera of Great Britain*. (UK Nature Conservation No 3). JNCC, Peterborough.

Lindroth, C. H. (1974). *Handbooks for the Identification of British Insects. Coleoptera, Carabidae*, **IV Part 2**. Royal Entomological Society, London.

McFerran, D. M. (1991). *The Impact of Burning and Grazing on Upland Vegetation Types and Invertebrate Communities in Co. Antrim*. (PhD. Thesis. Queen's University Belfast).

Meharg, M. J. (1988). *Changing Management and the Ecology of Uplands in Northern Ireland*. (PhD. Thesis. Queen's University Belfast).

Rushton, S. P., Eyre, M. D. and Luff, M. L. (1989a). The effects of management on the occurrence of some carabid species in grassland, In N. Stork (Ed), *Ground Beetles: Their Role in Ecological and Environmental Studies*, Intercept, Andover, 209–16.

Rushton, S. P., Luff, M. L. and Eyre, M. D. (1989b). Effects of pasture improvement and management on the ground beetle and spider communities of upland grassland, *Journal of Applied Ecology*, **26**, 489–503.

33 KEY REQUIREMENTS FOR MANAGEMENT OF HEATHER MOORLAND: NOW AND FOR THE FUTURE

J. Phillips and A. Watson

Summary

1. British moorland dominated by heather *Calluna vulgaris* — 'heather moorland' — is managed primarily for gamebird shooting, and also supports sheep, and in Scotland, red deer (*Cervus elaphus*).

2. The red grouse (*Lagopus lagopus scoticus*) is the only species primarily dependent on, and attaching direct economic benefit to, heather moorland. Scottish moors yield a mean annual bag of about 300 000 birds.

3. Standards of management of British heather moorland have declined due to: fewer gamekeepers; sheep, cattle and red deer browsing the heather heavily; afforestation; and more carrion crows (*Corvus corone*) and foxes (*Vulpes vulpes*).

4. Sound sward management for red grouse benefits domestic stock, and control of carrion crows and foxes benefits large moorland birds. Examples are given where changes in management have resulted in increased grouse bags.

5. Proposals for rectifying key problems include lower [or no] subsidies for moorland sheep, more cattle, and tree planting so that moorland management for grouse is not at a financial disadvantage.

33.1 Introduction

This chapter assesses the most pressing problems facing moorland managers, and outlines proven methods to overcome some of these problems. Other problems caused or accentuated by government policies will be solved only with reforms of those policies.

The area of British heather moorland is very large but is imprecisely known, partly because of difficulties in agreeing its definition. There have been major losses of heather moorland as a result of changes in land use and inadequate management. In the north Ayrshire–Renfrewshire area, which has been known intimately for decades by one of us (JP), 43% of the 135 km² of heather moorland in 1950 has been lost, and Grampian Region lost over 25% of its heather moorland between the 1940s and 1970s (Sydes, 1988). More than half of the total Scottish losses in Sydes' study were due to afforestation. A quarter of the losses resulted from expansion of grass-dominated vegetation due to heavy grazing and inadequate burning, and 8% from cultivation to agricultural grassland plus conversion to grassland without cultivation. Losses to afforestation and expansion of grass-dominated vegetation are continuing. Further large areas will continue to be lost at a fast rate unless there is a widespread improvement in moorland management.

Heather moorland provides some large crops of animals. Scottish red deer number about 300 000; most live on the open hill and largely on heather moorland, but some exclusively in woodland (Red Deer Commission, 1989). There are 2.4 million hill sheep in Scotland (Scottish Natural Heritage, 1993), many living wholly on heather moorland. Heather moorland yields a highly variable bag of red grouse, estimated at a mean of about 300 000 shot per annum (McGilvray *et al.*, 1990; McGilvray and Perman, 1991). Many other species of animals and plants of conservation value depend on heather moorland in Britain (Usher and Thompson, 1993) and Ireland, though of little or no direct commercial value.

The red grouse is the only species primarily dependent on heather which attaches a direct cash value to heather moorland. Although such moorland provides valuable grazing for sheep and deer, they are not solely dependent on it. Grouse provide an economic reason to maintain it as well as the money to do so. Only because of this can the large indirect economic benefits of it [*e.g.* through its appreciation by tourists] continue to be realized now and in the future.

In the late 1960s, many Scottish moors yielded a regular bag of 500–2000 brace of grouse each year. Today, few moors produce 1000 brace even in the best years, so over the last 30 years there has been a large drop in output. Long-term declines have occurred in different regions (Barnes, 1987; Hudson, 1992).

Picozzi (1968) showed that grouse bags in Scotland were related to the base-status of underlying bedrock. English moors tend to support more grouse per unit area than Scottish ones; limestone and other base-rich rocks occur widely and support more nutrient-rich food plants for grouse to feed on. Many produce large bags of grouse from a sward management regime that would yield few grouse from the average Scottish moor over poorer rocks. Moreover, nitrogen compounds from precipitation and fog have increased greatly in parts of northern England (Lee *et al.*, 1987; 1992), and the fertilizing effect of this on heather may have helped maintain high grouse stocks there.

In recent decades many Scottish grouse moors have been burned less well than formerly. The main defect is that major declines in the numbers of fires burned each year have lengthened the rotation. The practice on heather moorland on deer forests is different as stalkers usually burn large, wide fires (Watson, 1990). Although this leads to much young heather, it tends to result subsequently in high local densities of deer which browse heather and blaeberry (*Vaccinium myrtillus*) heavily. In turn this can encourage the spread of unpalatable grasses, sedges and rushes such as mat grass (*Nardus stricta*), tufted hair grass (*Deschampsia caespitosa*), purple moor grass (*Molinia caerulea*), deer sedge (*Scirpus cespitosus*), and soft rush (*Juncus effusus*) and also bracken (*Pteridium aquilinum*). These vegetation changes on deer wintering grounds at low altitude reduce habitat quality for several bird species that depend on heather moorland. Browsing by red deer also depresses habitat quality for red grouse and some other moorland birds by reducing the heather's height and ground coverage (Watson, 1989).

The ideal of many narrow fires creates a fine-grained mosaic of different age-classes of heather and other vegetation, and results in a more even utilisation of vegetation by grazing animals. It is also beneficial for invertebrate diversity on well-drained moorland (Usher and Thompson, 1993).

Most hill farmers with moorland and rough grazing want more grass for their animals and practise a 'two-pasture' method originally developed by the Hill Farming Research Organization to increase sheep and cattle productivity. Many farmers have applied this method on heather areas in Scotland as well as on grass-dominated moorland. Ploughing heather ground to create moorland pasture by this method destroys heather. Associated heavy browsing of adjacent unploughed land damages the heather there.

On infertile wet soils, heavy browsing replaces heather swards with indigestible and unpalatable highly acid grasslands dominated by mat grass and purple moor grass (Miles, 1988; Moss and Hudson, 1990). On more fertile soils, heavy browsing of heather leads to *Agrostis-Festuca* grassland, which offers stock more nutritious food than heather, but the result is again damage to it, and frequently its elimination.

33.2 Benefits of sound grouse management for other species

In terms of plants and animals, the conservation value of heather moorland is higher than that of the highly acidic grassland which often replaces it as a result of inadequate management. Heather moorland supports a wide variety of plants, vertebrates and invertebrates (Usher and Thompson, 1993), many of them uncommon nationally and internationally.

Grouse moor management aims to maintain high stocks by practising vegetation management favourable to red grouse. Whether this benefits other birds has been questioned (e.g. Usher and Thompson, 1993). Brown and Stillman (1993) concluded that although red grouse numbers were associated with heather in several Scottish regions, golden plover (*Pluvialis apricaria*) numbers were not; a number of moorland bird species favour habitats other than the well-burned heather swards managed for red grouse. However, this is not the crucial issue. What is crucial is that without vegetation management for grouse, sheep and deer, all habitats on most British moorland (except perhaps for the very wettest blanket bogs) would disappear, to be replaced either by tree-planting or natural woodland.

Management for red grouse benefits other birds such as curlew (*Numenius arquata*), redshank (*Tringa totanus*) and golden plover, in secondary manner (mentioned briefly by Usher and Thompson, 1993). Control in late winter and spring of the two main grouse predators — crow and fox — reduces predation on eggs and chicks of other birds as well as of red grouse.

For example, a flourishing population of 80–120 golden plover on Kerloch moor in Kincardineshire became extinct over some years, following increased nest-robbing by foxes after keepering ceased (Parr, 1992), and despite the experimental removal of crows and common gulls (*Larus canus*) (Parr, 1993). Breeding success was very low and recruitment insufficient to replace losses which took place away from the area in winter.

In Crick's (1992) survey of UK nest-record cards for golden plover, nest failure rates were high on grassy moorland in 1982–1989. In contrast, failure rates have remained low and stable over the years on heather moorland and bog. In our view, the latter would be where good grouse management has maintained heather-domi-nated habitat and has reduced fox and crow numbers from artificially high levels.

A further example is at Misty Law Muir, Renfrewshire, where many fires have been burned and crow and fox numbers controlled. Since 1985, when a competent keeper was appointed, lekking black grouse (*Tetrao tetrix*) increased from 2 cocks in 1985 to 24 in 1990 and then 46 in 1993, with a large increase of nesting greyhens and successful broods. Nesting curlews increased from 4 to 28 pairs over the same period.

33.3 Adverse Changes

33.3.1 Introduction

The five main reasons why so few moors yield top bags of red grouse are inade-quate muirburn, heavy browsing, increases of sheep ticks (*Ixodes ricinus*) and tick-borne virus disease, insufficient control of crows and foxes, and haphazard grouse cropping policies. These are discussed in Sections 33.3.2–33.3.9.

33.3.2 Inadequate muirburn

In Britain and Ireland generally, standards of burning on heather moorland have declined greatly since 1950.

Not one of the 77 managed Scottish moorland study areas that one of us [AW] used from the late 1950s to the early 1970s is still as well burned and well managed for grazing stock as it was. The numbers of grouse have declined generally and on one area grouse are extinct. A revealing contrast is that grouse on the unmanaged Cairnwell, just below the arctic-alpine zone on the Aberdeenshire/Perthshire bor-der, are as abundant today as in the 1950s. That area is not rotationally burned or heavily browsed, and without any burning the fairly severe climate at this altitude prevents vegetation from becoming too tall.

Furthermore, thousands of hectares of land traditionally regarded as grouse moor have had no fires for 30 years or more. Much of this can hardly now be classed as grouse moor, as it contains uninterrupted tracts of rank heather, no short heather for nutritious feeding, and in some parts enough self-sown trees to be regarded as semi-woodland. Hester and Sydes (1992) pointed out that the percentage burnt was generally far less than that considered optimal (every 10–15 years). Infrequent burning reduces the worth of moorland for browsing mammals and grouse, and in consequence their performance declines.

Many moors with little or no burning have become little used by farm stock because the tall heather is less accessible and palatable, and because self-sown trees have spread in some parts. Such areas, and also some burnt, browsed moorland without self-sown trees, are increasingly becoming potential subjects for the New Native Pinewood Scheme and Birchwood Scheme. There are specific sites where subsidies for such a change of use can be justified on conservation grounds. However, in many areas there is no such justification.

33.3.3 Muirburn and conservation

In general, conservationists have neither the management control nor the money necessary to burn heather properly, usually lack the expertise to do the work to high standards, and frequently do not appreciate many of the practical difficulties faced by managers. When the paper on which this chapter was presented, those in the audience who had controlled a narrow fire running for many hundreds of metres were asked to raise their hands. No one in the large audience, which consisted of people with many different interests in moorland, did so. This confirmed the lack of first hand experience.

This lack is often associated with negative attitudes to heather burning such as 'do not burn too much, or too hot, or too high a percentage'. Some have recommended that to increase biodiversity, certain areas of moorland should not be burned or should be burned less often than is normal on grouse and sheep ground. If such recommendations were implemented widely there would be forage of lower nutritive value for grazing animals, higher risks of runaway fires, lower grouse bags, and thus an increased likelihood of part or all of the moor being totally lost to afforestation. Certainly moorland could be managed solely for its wildlife and landscape importance rather than for gamebird shooting, using public funds or funds of voluntary conservation organizations to do so. However, we know of no large moorland area which has been managed successfully in this way.

Blanket bogs pose different problems. Burning such areas in the same manner as dry heaths can reduce their conservation value (Usher and Thompson, 1993). Frequent burning of blanket bog with hot fires reduces grouse numbers also, but the adverse effects of fire in those circumstances are mostly due to shepherds and deer stalkers, not grouse keepers. For grouse, blanket bog should be burned fairly infrequently, but not too infrequently; a 20-year frequency favours cotton sedge *Eriophorum vaginatum* at the expense of heather (Hobbs, 1984).

33.3.4 Heavy browsing of heather

Nationwide, a widespread adverse change is that the off-take of moorland vegetation by grazing animals has increased greatly. Red deer on Scottish moorland approximately doubled in number between 1963 and 1989 (Red Deer Commission,

1989), and on some eastern moors increased even more. Sheep numbers have also increased markedly overall, though not in all areas. On some farms, sheep management differs little today from that of the mid-1960s and numbers there have changed little, but on others there have been large increases.

The moorland range available to red deer and sheep has contracted because of major losses of moorland to tree plantations. The range available to red deer has also contracted because of smaller conversions to deer-fenced pastures for sheep and cattle. Poor siting of many plantations has increased browsing damage to the remaining moorland. Some heavy browsing by sheep and/or deer at low altitudes is almost universal, and locally severe on most moors where sheep are kept, as well as being widespread at high altitudes. Cattle can do much damage, but it is localized compared with that caused by sheep and deer.

Heavy browsing of heather can result in less food for grouse because large mammals eat it first. Furthermore, heavy browsing coupled with burning of large wide fires leads to shortage of cover, and in turn to higher winter losses of grouse due to emigration. Shortage of cover is also likely to increase the vulnerability of grouse to predation. It is common to see many pairs of grouse in autumn on ground where sheep, cattle or deer browse heavily in winter, but by April, only an odd pair or unmated cock remains, and none in the most severely browsed areas (Watson and O'Hare, 1979a; Watson and Moss, 1990).

33.3.5 Increase of ticks and tick-borne disease

Higher numbers of sheep and deer provide more hosts for sheep ticks. Many red deer summering on Highland heather moorland have been associated with an increase of ticks and tick-borne virus disease on ground below 500 m.

33.3.6 Increases in carrion availability

When standards of husbandry of farm stock fall, mortality tends to increase, resulting in more carrion food throughout the winter for scavengers, particularly crows and foxes. The large increase in the number of red deer also results in more dead deer, and on estates where increased numbers are shot, there is an equal increase in discarded viscera (grallochs). The combined effect of these factors is to support populations of scavengers at artificially high levels.

If there were a mechanism in place to enforce the Dogs Act (1906) and SI No. 3303 Animal Byproducts Order (1992), there would be fewer carcases of sheep and deer left to rot and populations of scavengers would fall to lower and more natural levels.

33.3.7 Afforestation

By far the main single cause of loss of Scottish heather moorland is tree planting (Sydes, 1988). Grant-aided afforestation was an easy option to many owners when grouse stocks declined due to their own inadequate moorland management. Tree planting is seen by many people — including politicians — as being the only credible land use for these places. However, it requires large grants for an enterprise which is at root uneconomic. In contrast, a grouse enterprise neither gets nor needs grants or other public funds and integrates easily with well-managed extensive sheep farming. The single best step to reducing further rapid losses of heather moorland to tree planting would be to make taxpayers' money unavailable for moorland tree planting.

33.3.8 Open draining
A farm operation still being carried out, although less commonly than in past decades, is open draining of wet moorland using a heavy plough pulled by a crawler tractor. This increases run-off, soil erosion and the incidence of flooding (Stewart and Lance, 1983). It also damages and sometimes destroys the insect-rich mires and flushes which provide high-protein invertebrate food for grouse chicks in their first 2–3 weeks and for chicks of other species in early summer.

33.3.9 Gamekeepers, owners and managers
The number of keepers employed has decreased on many estates (Hudson, 1992). With fewer men on the ground, control of crow and fox numbers tends to be less thorough. This can seriously reduce grouse breeding success and hence the subsequent bag. An example from a Wester Ross deer forest illustrates the point. Grouse keepering ceased in 1988 and moorland which had consistently yielded fairly large grouse bags over pointing dogs for over 25 years, and never fell below 70 brace in a season, now carries so few birds that shooting is not worthwhile (Table 33.1). Another useful example (Figure 33.1) shows how grouse bags can be improved by a competent keeper.

Table 33.1 Numbers of red grouse shot on two deer forests in Wester Ross in 1984–1993. Estate A keepered, the adjacent estate B unkeepered. Both estates have similar sized areas of grouse ground.

Year	Estate A	Estate B
1984	450	7
1985	502	5
1986	559	6
1987	460	29
1988	498	14
1989	96*	2
1990	62	0
1991	8	12
1992	7	22
1993	3	2

*Grouse keepering ceased in March

Secondly, burning requires the maximum number of people who understand the work and know the ground well. Some committed managers using modern techniques have maintained or even increased standards of burning, despite fewer

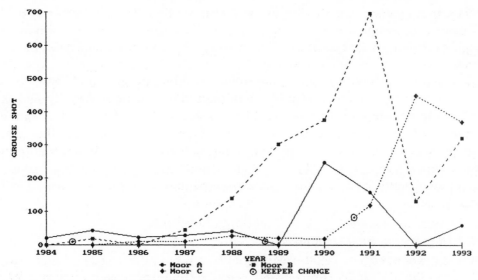

Figure 33.1. How grouse bags follow a competent keeper.

keepers and hence an increase in the beat or area looked after by each man. However, on all too many moors the reverse is the case.

In Scotland there are now very few really dedicated and technically well-informed grouse keepers who are doing a first-class job of managing vegetation for grouse. Many owners and factors either do not know this or if they do, accept it too readily. This clearly indicates that their attitude is less positive towards grouse management than that of their forebears.

Moreover, on many moors the keeper's job specification has altered with the spread and increase of red deer on moorland. Many moor owners and their financial managers regard the arrival of deer as a bonus. Revenue can be obtained from stalking lets and venison sales regularly each year, unlike the fluctuating and more unpredictable income from grouse shooting. They fail to appreciate that this policy is likely to carry a penalty, which is a further decline in heather quality and grouse numbers due to deer browsing the heather heavily and spreading ticks. It is also worth noting that revenue from venison, like that from grouse lets, can fluctuate markedly. For instance, an average price of only 66p per kilo was paid in 1991 but about 176p per kilo in 1993.

Many keepers, owners and factors are pessimistic because they perceive that too much is against them. They blame the government, farm tenants, red deer, ticks, afforestation, crows and foxes, bracken, raptor increases, public access and various other issues (Anon, 1993). They fail to consider the quality of management, which is generally the key issue and is usually in their own hands.

In 1993, many owners decided that there should be no grouse shooting, or proposed to start only in September. These decisions followed gloomy press publicity in previous weeks and seldom rested upon reliable population assessments. One such affected area was the Lammermuirs. Although grouse bred less well there in

1993 than for some years, breeding was still adequate enough for one moor to yield 73 brace shot in one day in the first week of the season. Meanwhile, owners of neighbouring moors had cancelled their shooting or postponed it until well into the autumn.

In years of low breeding success and late-hatched broods, such as 1993, it is better to shoot early, and then stop shooting by the end of August or early September. This results in removing many single old cocks and unsuccessful hens, leaving the way clearer for more juveniles to take territories later in the autumn. It is likely that this also serves to reduce the amplitude of fluctuations in breeding numbers from year to year (Watson *et al.*, 1988). Cancellations and postponements indicate an unprofessional approach to the management of the grouse crop by proprietors and their staffs.

33.3.10 Examples of improvement

On a few moors, adverse changes have been held at bay or reversed by better management (Table 33.2). These increases in grouse bags have taken place not in a contiguous moorland block but in widely different districts in Scotland. The lack of material bag change on nearby 'control' moors where such changes in management did not occur offers a striking contrast. These examples indicate that present grouse bags are much lower than they could be if the best management were applied more widely. The best Scottish moors under top management yield a mean annual bag of about one bird per hectare on a 10-year average. This high yield is based on numerous fires burned in strips and patches, adequate controls on stock browsing, limitation of crow and fox numbers, careful counts to assess grouse stocks and shooting policies closely geared to these counts.

Table 33.2 Bags of red grouse over the period 1985–1992 on five pairs of moors in South Scotland. The first moor in each pair had greatly improved management over the years stated and the second was a control without this.

Moor	District	Size (ha)	Numbers of grouse shot per 100 ha† at start	at end
1	Ayrshire N	2225	1 [1985]	31 [1991]
1a	Renfrewshire	1300	0 [1985]	0 [1991]
2	Ayrshire S	1400	0 [1989]	18 [1990]
2a	Ayrshire S	1400	1 [1989]	2 [1990]
3	Stirlingshire	1215	0 [1989]	20 [1992]
3a	Perthshire SW	741	3 [1989]	0 [1992]
4	Peebleshire	1820	1 [1990]	25 [1992]
4a	Peebleshire	1800	0 [1990]	0 [1992]
5	East Lothian	1380	39 [1987]	126 [1992]
5a	East Lothian	1215	165 [1987]*	160 [1992]

* Already well-managed.

† Expressed to the nearest whole number.

As an example of competent fire management, on the 1400 ha Priestlaw farm in the Lammermuirs, 1053 fires have been burned in the last four years, covering 23 % of the moor area. In the 1992/3 burning season alone, 419 fires averaging 0.3 ha were burned, representing 9 % of the moor. On the 3500 ha Misty Law Muir in Renfrewshire, 648 fires varying in size from 0.05 — 4 ha were burned in October 1993. When added to the 859 burned at Misty Law since 1990/91, this amounted to ca 20 % of the heather moorland area. What distinguishes moors such as these is that the managers hardly ever miss a day's burning. They have a short chain of command from the person who draws up the plans to those who do the work on the ground. They 'live' grouse 365 days a year — spending [in the eyes of some of their family and friends] an excessive amount of time on the topic with an enthusiasm amounting to an obsession. In our view this obsession is both commendable and necessary for such standard-bearers, and needs to be copied more widely.

Such managers practise grazing management which reduces the incidence of 'grey' moorland dominated largely by mat grass and purple moor grass. Some have fenced vulnerable areas of heather to protect them from excessive winter grazing. Others use new farm-scale techniques of scarifying and heather seeding along with grazing control, so as to recreate heather/grass mixtures on areas of highly acidic grassland. In winter, much of the grass is dead and hence of very low nutritional value to stock, so the new advances in heather management benefit sheep as well. The Joseph Nickerson Reconciliation Project (Phillips, 1993) has pioneered the techniques for this work, which is the first successful attempt to recreate heather moorland on a scale of tens and hundreds of hectares.

33.4 Recommendations for Change

33.4.1 Muirburn

Where fires have been infrequent, the large areas of tall heather should be broken up initially with a lattice pattern of long fire-breaks (Figure 33.2). The aim is to achieve an interspersion of young heather over the whole moor as soon as possible. This can be done with normally available manpower if cutters and water sprayers are used. If 20–30 % of the moor can be burned in the first two or three years of a revised programme, stock have a wide choice of forage and subsequent local severe browsing is much less likely to occur.

With fire-breaks in place, it becomes progressively easier to burn many small patches and strips with the same labour force, because fires cannot run far before encountering either a previous burnt patch or a natural break. In the Misty Law example [see section 33.3.10], burning began on a Monday when two keepers burned 17 fires in a short afternoon. Next day, conditions were drier and 19 fires were burned. Two days later, four men completed 51 fires, and on a fourth day that week, seven people burned 159 fires. This very large total was mainly due to the head keeper's awareness that conditions were becoming ideal for burning.

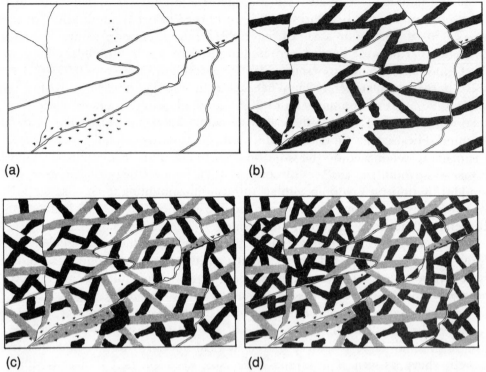

Figure 33.2. The creation of a good burning pattern over time: (a) typical area of unburned moorland; (b) first year's burning programme, 20 % covered in 50 m-wide fires; (c) years 4–12; a further 40 % is burned — making about 60 % total by year 12; (d) year 12; two-thirds of the way through the rotation and two-thirds burned, after Lovat (1911). (After Phillips, 1991).

Good, competent organization enabled him to move on a wide front with as many people as he could manage properly.

33.4.2 *Browsing*

Heavy browsing of heather by farm stock is encouraged by large subsidies. Until quotas were made obligatory recently, a farmer received a headage payment for as many breeding ewes as he cared to put on the hill. Although eligibility for subsidy was subject to an upper limit based on ewes/ha, this was set so high that the sanction had little effect on capping sheep numbers on hill farms. Under Statutory Instrument 1992/269 — the Hill Livestock (Compensatory Allowances) Regulations 1992 — overgrazing has been redefined as 'grazing land with livestock in such numbers as adversely to affect growth, quality or species composition ... to a significant degree'. Highly imprecise definitions of this kind cloud the issue of heavy grazing further, where one man's 'good' utilization is perceived as damage by another. It is unlikely that heavy browsing will be reduced by this vague new statute.

Sheep quotas go with the farmer and not the farm. Presently even 'bound' flocks are included, which is particularly damaging (a bound flock is one which goes with the land; sheep which are acclimatized to a particular hill farm, or even a section of it, know it in all weathers, which benefits their performance, and the stock also has a substantial immunity to the diseases endemic on that farm). So far, quotas have been damaging to grazing quality, as they discourage the traditional use of hill land on a sustainable basis. On the other hand, a quota 'market' might result in fewer sheep on moorland; farmers with less profitable hill sheep might sell them off the farm altogether, and the quota might go to lowland farmers. This would further jeopardize traditional sustainable grazing, because it would completely clear stock from some moorland areas.

This indicates a common drawback of centrally planned schemes, that side-effects are difficult to foresee and so the schemes become more complex and bureaucratic. Major long-term reform of the Common Agricultural Policy [CAP] as it affects moorland would be beneficial, and not simply a short-term attempted 'fix' such as quotas. With the conclusion of the General Agreement on Tariffs and Trade (GATT) in December 1993, further reform of the CAP will become more urgent.

Estimating a precise and meaningful sheep and cattle density that would be compatible with long-term maintenance of Scottish heather moorland as a whole is impossible because of variations between regions, between farms, and within farms. However, a useful rule of thumb for stocking heather moorland with sheep in winter, normally considered as the six months from 1 October, is that stocking should not exceed 175 ewe days per hectare of heather, or roughly 1 ewe per hectare. Obviously a precise estimate for any given area will depend on the percentage of heather present, its condition and its interspersion with other vegetation. An appropriate, sustainable density for blackfaced ewes in the southern uplands differs greatly from that for the much larger north country Cheviot ewes in Sutherland. Moreover, this takes no account of the amount and quality of shepherding, the depth and duration of snow in winter, the amount of supplementary food and other relevant issues. Generalizations are danger-ous, and for heather conservation, farm prescriptions need to be both specific and detailed.

33.4.3 Change of use to forestry

There is increasing acceptance that procedures for allowing grant aid for change of use to forestry on Scottish moorland should be tightened (mechanisms in England are now better, since the government introduced a presumption against allowing grant aid for new planting — predominantly of conifers — in the English uplands in March 1988). Two obvious recent examples of heavily criticized schemes in Scotland have been at Glen Dye (Jones, 1991; Watson, 1993) and Croick (Clarke, 1993). The advent of Regional Indicative Forestry Strategies has not prevented serious conflict, for example, at Croick.

A good case can be made for zoning discrete areas of moorland where tree planting in areas exceeding say 10 ha would not be grant-aided and indeed would not be permitted on heather moorland. This would reduce or prevent further damage from moorland fragmentation, which has been so adverse to farmers, grouse managers and moorland wildlife generally. Examples of suitable areas for such zoning would be the Pentlands, the Lammermuirs, the North Ayrshire/Renfrewshire heights, the Lowthers, the Ochils, the Sidlaws, east Sutherland/Caithness and the whole of the North/Central Highlands east of the A9 road and north of the great valley running northeast from Perth to Aberdeen.

33.4.4 Grouse-manager groups

A strong case can be made for "Grouse Groups", like the deer groups which have long been a feature of the Red Deer Commission's policy. Many individual moor owners and their managers are isolated and have little opportunity to discuss issues with others before making decisions. Groups might also engender a more professional approach to moorland management regionally and to the marketing and cropping of the grouse product.

33.4.5 Environmentally sensitive areas (ESAs)

Many agree that it would be useful to extend the Environmentally Sensitive Areas (ESAs). However, the present ESA schemes will achieve little for heather moorland, and may well be damaging to it. This is because the ESA criteria (Scottish Office Agriculture and Fisheries Department, 1993) were not developed to conserve existing vigorous heather or enhance relict heather. Despite some optimistic comments (Henderson, this volume; McFerran *et al.*, this volume), it would be helpful if ESA grants were made conditional on much tighter management prescriptions being followed for stock on heather, as well as for heather burning.

It is already apparent that ineffective stock reductions in ESA schemes are insufficient to achieve heather improvement and that there are no conditions or limitations on seasonal use, which is widely accepted as critical for heather survival.

33.4.6 Sporting rates

For many years, owners and others called for the removal of all sporting rates levied on bags of moor game in Scotland. In October 1993, the Secretary of State for Scotland announced that sporting rates would end with effect from April 1995. The cessation of rates may help engender a change to more optimistic attitudes among managers.

33.4.7 Changes of attitudes

Some changes of attitude by managers and others are beginning to take place. Heather moorland is a landscape and wildlife habitat unique to western Europe (Gimingham, 1972) and of great value to a wide public as well as to grouse shooting. It is being more widely recognized that the management of grouse for shooting and the conservation of moorland and its other wildlife are closely linked.

There is a clear international responsibility as well as requirements under EC directives to conserve heather moorland. Despite this, many traditional schemes for farm subsidies and grants are adverse to moorland conservation, and new support schemes with conservation in mind have not been well enough thought out. For instance, the Department of Agriculture and Fisheries for Scotland's Farm and Conservation Grant Scheme (1989) was a first step towards providing financial assistance for heather conservation. It included a provision to pay grants of 50 % for this, but the farmer has to find the other 50 %. As most farmers traditionally put little value on heather, few are interested and so the rate of grant uptake has been very low. Sound heather management will be undertaken by most farmers and landowners only when it is perceived as profitable or at least likely to produce a considerable income. Currently this can come in unsubsidized form only from a grouse enterprise.

The numbers of red grouse generally in Scotland and Wales are now lower than for well over a century — in fact probably since the great population crash of 1873. However, within the past few years, changes in attitude such as we have outlined leading to radical improvements in management on some Scottish moors have been followed by major increases in grouse bags (Table 33.2). They have occurred despite these years being marked by many alarmist and gloomy statements in the popular press about the performance of grouse, the future of grouse shooting and the need for more money for more applied research on grouse.

For those who hold pessimistic views, success or failure lies in their own hands. If sheep stocks are too high, they could negotiate reductions. If deer numbers are excessive, they could shoot more. If crows are robbing many grouse nests, they could set out Larsen traps — not two or three but 20 or 30 — and keep moving them. If tree plantations locally harbour many foxes, they could set many snares around carrion bait (Kerr, 1986), and so on.

The moor managers who have moved against continual decline and maintained or increased their bags in the past decade are those who were open minded, identified the limiting factors imposed by habitat and fox and crow predation, employed competent people and motivated them well. They were quick to use valuable new techniques such as swiping fire-breaks to improve safety when burning, and using water-sprayers to improve their control of fire. Most of them did not take up the idea of giving grouse access to 'medicated' grit with the object of reducing infestations of *Trichostrongylus tenuis* (Game Conservancy, 1994) — an idea promoted without published documentation of rigorous tests (Delahay and Moss, 1992). They measured their potential crop by accurate grouse counts in spring and late summer. They applied a shooting policy which cropped the surplus in years of high numbers, thus reducing or avoiding population crashes. They sold their product in advance, priced it realistically and were quick to offer financial redress on the few occasions when bags failed to come up to expectations.

Competent moor managers have much to be proud of. However, the reputation of managers and shooters in general is adversely affected by widespread publicity about the controversial attitude of the very few — particularly on the specific issues of the killing of protected raptors and public access — while these same few individuals make scant attempt on their own ground to tackle the more general key problems of decline in habitat quality and increases in crow and fox numbers.

The priority is to implement traditional sound practice more widely. It has been so for some time. Phillips (1983) stated this 10 years ago at a conference organized by the Scottish Landowners' Federation and Game Conservancy, and from this the Reconciliation Project was born, which led later to what is now the Heather Trust.

Lovat (1911) described a burning pattern which worked, and which delivered – year after year – grouse in large numbers (Figure 33.2). In Scotland today, probably not more than five moors are burned to levels which even approach Lovat's standards. Moreover, their bag yields are often affected adversely because as 'islands' of optimal managed habitat, they tend to lose grouse by emigration to the extensive 'sea' of marginal habitat nearby (Watson and O'Hare, 1979b; Watson and Moss, 1993).

33.4.8   Co-operation with other interests

It is becoming increasingly important for all concerned with moorland to be more conciliatory. Although there are obvious overlaps of interest, the five main interest groups are first, ramblers, other recreationists and specialist birdwatchers; second, statutory agencies and conservation bodies dealing with designated sites and wild-life reserves; third, farmers; fourth, foresters; and fifth, shooters and managers. The first two groups seldom have a direct immediate economic interest in moor-land, unlike the other three groups. This sometimes results in conflict, particularly over protected birds of prey and public access.

The Royal Society for the Protection of Birds has a very large membership of 840 000 and the Ramblers Association 94 000. Many other wildlife conservation and outdoor recreational bodies, such as the Scottish Wildlife Trust, Worldwide Fund for Nature and British Mountaineering Council, have big membership or supporters' groups. Such organizations have increasing political influence. In contrast, the British Association for Shooting and Conservation has only 110 000 members and the Game Conservancy 25 000. However, all these groups, except foresters, have a common interest in maintaining heather moorland.

Progress and unity would follow if shooters and moor managers made greater efforts to ally themselves more closely with those who share some common interests with them, and *vice versa*. If not, strife will continue and further declines in the quality of moor management and thus eventually in the area of moorland will be likely.

33.4.9   Demonstration moors

It would be useful to develop several demonstration moors in different regions of Scotland and North England where well-tried practices would be put in place and the results measured carefully and written up for others to follow. This would help encourage optimism among managers in each region.

For the grouse crop to increase and maintain an important role in the economy of remote upland areas, there has to be a new attitude in owners, factors and keepers. Money may have to be spent on capital equipment and more people of ability may have to be employed. Education and training at all levels of management may have to be increased. Positive decisions based upon what others have recently achieved and are achieving will have to be made.

Given the one-sided competition for moorland conversion from subsidised forestry and farming, either an increase in financial support for maintaining the land use of heather moorland is essential, or a removal of all upland subsidies. The heather manager needs a level playing-field. He need not fear an end to subsidy; this would entail a cessation of the large-scale moorland tree planting that has done so much harm to landscape and wildlife. It would result also in a reversion to levels of hill sheep farming which would be sustainable in the long term without damage to the interests of grouse and other heather moorland wildlife.

Only by better management can the grouse productivity of heather moorland be increased and thus help maintain and enhance these habitats for the future.

Acknowledgements

We thank Peter Straker-Smith and two referees for comments, and several moor owners and keepers for providing data.

References

Anon. (1993). Late snow shoots down hopes of a Glorious XII. *The Scotsman*, 19 July 1993.

Barnes, R. F. W. (1987). Long-term declines of red grouse in Scotland. *Journal of Applied Ecology*, **24**, 735–41.

Brown, A. F. and Stillman, R. A. (1993). Bird-habitat associations in the eastern Highlands of Scotland. *Journal of Applied Ecology*, **30**, 31–42.

Clarke, R. (1993). Strath Cuileannach in 1992. *Scottish Wild Land News*, Winter 1993, 11–13.

Crick, H. Q. P. (1992). Trends in the Breeding Performance of Golden Plover in Britain. British Trust for Ornithology. *Research Report*, **76**.

Delahay, R. and Moss, R. (1992). Grouse disease: counts of hypobiotic larvae. *Joseph Nickerson Reconciliation Project Annual Report*, **9**, 51–2.

Department of Agriculture and Fisheries for Scotland (1989). *Farm and Conservation Grant Scheme*. DAFS, Edinburgh.

Game Conservancy (1994). *Review of 1993*, 117–119. Game Conservancy Trust, Fordingbridge, Hampshire.

Gimingham, C. H. (1972). *Ecology of Heathlands*. Chapman and Hall, London.

Henderson, D. J. (this volume). Heather moorlands in the Loch Lomond Environmentally Sensitive Area.

Hester, A. and Sydes, C. (1992). Changes in burning of Scottish heather moorland since the 1940s from aerial photographs. *Biological Conservation*, **60**, 25–30.

Hobbs, R. J. (1984). Length of burning rotation and community composition in high-level *Calluna-Eriophorum* bog in N. England. *Vegetatio*, **57**, 129–36.

Hudson, P. J. (1992). *Grouse in Space and Time*. The Game Conservancy Trust. Fordingbridge, Hampshire.

Jones, K. (1991). The battle for Glen Dye. *Tree News*, September 1991, 10–2.

Kerr, R. (1986). Fox control methods. *Reconciliation Project Annual Report*, **2**, 37.

Lee, J. A., Caporn, S. J. M., and Read, D. J. (1992). Effects of increasing nitrogen deposition and acidification on heathlands. In T. Schneider (Ed), *Acidification Research. Evaluation and Policy Applications*, Elsevier, Colchester, 97–106.

Lee, J. A., Press, M. C., Woodin, S. J. and Ferguson, P. (1987). Responses to acidic deposition in ombrotrophic mires in the UK. In T. C. Hutchison and K. M. Meema (Eds), *Effects of Atmospheric Pollutants on Forests, Wetlands and Agricultural Ecosystems*, Springer Verlag, Berlin, 549–60.

Lovat, Lord (1911). Moor Management [Chapter 17] and Heather Burning [Chapter 18]. In A. S. Leslie (Ed), *The Grouse in Health and in Disease*, Smith Elder and Co, London, 372–413.

McFerran, D. M., Hegarty, C. A., Mulholland, F. P. and McAdam, J. H. (this volume). The monitoring of heather moorland within Environmentally Sensitive Areas [ESAs] in Northern Ireland.

McGilvray, J. and Perman, R. (1991). *Grouse Shooting in Scotland: an Analysis of its Importance to the Economy and Environment*. Department of Economics, University of Strathclyde.

McGilvray, J., McRory, E., Perman, R. and Stewart, W. J. (1990). *The Economic Impact of Sporting Shooting in Scotland*. Fraser of Allander Institute, University of Strathclyde.

Miles, J. (1988). Vegetation and soil change in the uplands. In M. B. Usher and D. B. A. Thompson (Eds), *Ecological Change in the Uplands*. Blackwell Scientific Publications, Oxford, 57–70.

Moss, R. and Hudson, P. (1990). Changes in numbers of red grouse In M. Whitby and S. Grant (Eds), *Modelling Heather Management*, University of Newcastle upon Tyne, 9–19.

Parr, R. (1992). The decline to extinction of a population of Golden Plover in north-east Scotland. *Ornis Scandinavica*, **23**, 152–58.

Parr, R. (1993). Nest predation and numbers of Golden Plovers *Pluvialis apricaria* and other moorland waders. *Bird Study*, **40**, 223–31.

Phillips, J. (1983). *John Phillips' submission*. Scottish Landowners Federation/Game Conservancy Conference, Edinburgh. 30th March 1983.

Phillips, J. (1991). Heather burning and management 1911–1991. *Joseph Nickerson Reconciliation Project Annual Report*, **7**, 41–4.

Phillips, J. (1993). The white moorland programme. *Joseph Nickerson Reconciliation Project Annual Report*, **9**, 23–6.

Picozzi, N. (1968). Grouse bags in relation to the management and geology of heather moors. *Journal of Applied Ecology*, **5**, 483–8.

Red Deer Commission (1989). *Annual Report for 1989*. RDC, Inverness.

Scottish Natural Heritage (1993). *Scotland's Natural Heritage*, 1.

Scottish Office Agriculture and Fisheries Department (1993). *Cairngorms Straths Environmentally Sensitive Area*. CS/ESA 1 — 1993. SOAFD, Inverurie.

Stewart, A. J. A. and Lance, A. N. (1983). Moor-draining: a review of impacts on land use. *Journal of Environmental Management*, **17**, 81–99.

Sydes, C. (1988). Recent assessments of moorland losses in Scotland. *Unpublished Chief Scientist's Directorate Notes*, **43**, Nature Conservancy Council, Edinburgh.

Usher, M. B. and Thompson, D. B. A. (1993). Variation in the upland heathlands of Great Britain: conservation importance. *Biological Conservation*, **66**, 69–81.

Watson, A. (1989). Land use, reduction of heather, and natural tree regeneration on open upland. *Report of the Institute of Terrestrial Ecology for 1988/89*, 25–26.

Watson, A. (1990a). Human impact on the Cairngorms environment above timber line. In J. W. H. Conroy, A. Watson and A. R. Gunson, (Eds), *Caring for the High Mountains — Conservation of the Cairngorms*. Centre for Scottish Studies, University of Aberdeen, and Natural Environment Research Council, Swindon, 61–82.

Watson, A. (1993). The Glen Dye story — a reply. *Scottish Forestry*, **47**, 30–1.

Watson, A. and Moss, R. (1993). Red grouse in marginal areas. *Joseph Nickerson Reconciliation Project Annual Report*, **9**, 39–41.

Watson, A. and Moss, R. (1990). Spacing behaviour and winter loss in red grouse. In A. N. Lance and J. H. Lawton (Eds), *Red Grouse Population Processes*, Royal Society for the Protection of Birds, Sandy, Bedfordshire, 35–52.

Watson, A., Moss, R., Parr, R., Trenholm, I. B. and Robertson, A. (1988). Preventing a population decline of red grouse [*Lagopus lagopus scoticus*] by manipulating density. Experientia, **44**, 274–75.

Watson, A. and O'Hare, P. J. (1979a). Spacing behaviour of Red Grouse at low density on Irish bog. *Ornis Scandinavica*, **10**, 252–61.

Watson, A. and O'Hare, P. J. (1979b). Red grouse populations on experimentally treated and untreated Irish bog. *Journal of Applied Ecology*, **16**, 433–52.

34. HEATHS AND MOORLAND: SOME CONCLUSIONS AND QUESTIONS ABOUT ENVIRONMENTAL CHANGE

D B A Thompson and John Miles

Summary

1. This chapter reaches general conclusions on moorland research and management, and raises some key questions about environmental change in the uplands.

2. The broad regional representation of plant communities of upland heaths and moorland in Great Britain is summarised. Distinctions are made between dry *Calluna vulgaris*-dominated heaths in the eastern uplands, and wet heaths of the north and west characteristically dominated by mosaics of *Calluna vulgaris, Eriophorum vaginatum, Scirpus cespitosus, Erica tetralix* and *Sphagnum* spp.

3. Vegetation succession has been well studied in dry heaths but not in western heaths. Palaeoecological studies are sparse.

4. Many of the wet heaths possibly date back to the early Holocene, and some may have natural rather than anthropogenic origins.

5. We question the assumption that moorlands have predominantly arisen from burning and/or felling of ancient woodland rather than from grazing.

6. We explore the importance of fire as a management tool for dry and wet heaths. Watt's (1955) model of the 'heather cycle' via seedling establishment probably applies differently to wet heaths and the more productive eastern and southern dry heaths, and may not apply at all to many moorland areas in Scotland.

7. Ornithological work should embrace agricultural and forested habitats to determine the habitat requirements of moorland birds.

8. Simple, linear bird foodchains for grassland, moorland and scrub-woodland are compared. More species seem to experience major increases in abundance

with an expansion of woodland than of grassland from moorland. Numbers of intermediate predators are greater in rough grasslands.

9. More research is needed to determine the condition of dry and wet heaths in Scotland, and for subsequent audits of condition.

10. There are concluding questions about some potential key areas for further work, notably on productivity of moorland, regional variation and environmental history.

34.1 Introduction

"Two centuries of misuse have changed the composition of the vegetation on Scottish hill land."

(D.N. McVean and J.D. Lockie, *Ecology and Land Use in Upland Scotland*, 1969).

Of any wild landscape found in Europe, heather moorland is arguably the single most intensively researched, discussed and utilised. The preceding chapters focus on the resource, the dynamic processes shaping the landscape, and management for the future. This chapter summarises some of the key conclusions, and raises some fundamental questions regarding the origins, management and persistence of sub-montane heaths and moorlands.

34.2 Geographical variation: where do moorland communities begin and end?

There is considerable variation in the occurrence and relative extent of dry and wet heaths and blanket bog throughout the British Isles. Furthermore, different regions are characterised by different assemblages of vegetation types, with the main gradients being with latitude and longitude, and from drier to wetter areas (McVean and Ratcliffe, 1962; Ratcliffe, 1977; Rodwell, 1991; Brown *et al.*, 1993; Usher and Thompson, 1993; Thompson *et al.*, 1994, 1995). The foregoing chapters have added much substance to this. Table 34.1 provides a geographical overview of the principal moorland communities, indicating that in any region there may be a complex of drier and wetter heaths as well as bogs. The principal regional differences are shown more clearly in Figure 34.1, giving a synoptic topographical overview across nine biogeographical areas of Great Britain.

There are major differences and distinctions between the dry heaths of the eastern Highlands, the uplands of northern England and Wales, and the wetter heaths of northern and western Scotland, the Isles and Ireland. In the introduction to Part I of this volume, geographical differences and affinities between the extent of these two key CORINE (Co-ordination of information on the environment) moorland communities are illustrated (Figures I.1 and I.2). Other workers have

Table 34.1   The broad regional representation of plant communities (classified after Rodwell, 1991, 1992) making up moorland.

NVC code	NVC type name	International importance	South west England	Mid and south Wales	North Wales	South Pennines	North Pennines	North York Moors	Lake District	South west Scotland	South east Scotland	North east Scotland	North west Scotland
Dry heaths													
H4	*Ulex gallii-Agrostis curtisii* heath	GB	3	2	0	0	0	0	0	0	0	0	0
H8	*Calluna vulgaris-Ulex gallii* heath	GB	2	2	2	1	0	0	2	0	0	0	0
H9	*Calluna vulgaris-Deschampsia flexuosa* heath	I	0	0	2	3	2	3	0	0	0	0	0
H10	*Calluna vulgaris-Erica cinerea* heath	I	1	2	2	0	1	1	2	2	2	2	3
H12	*Calluna vulgaris-Vaccinium myrtillus* heath	I	2	3	3	2	3	2	3	2	3	3	3
H16	*Calluna vulgaris-Arctostaphylos uva-ursi* heath	W	0	0	0	0	0	0	1	0	2	3	1
H18	*Vaccinium myrtillus-Deschampsia flexuosa* heath	W	1	3	3	2	2	1	2	3	3	3	2
H21	*Calluna vulgaris-Vaccinium myrtillus-Sphagnum capillifolium* heath	GB	0	2	2	0	1	0	2	2	2	0	3
Wet heath													
M15	*Scirpus cespitosus-Erica tetralix* wet heath	I	2	2	2	0	1	2	2	3	2	2	3
M16	*Erica tetralix-Sphagnum compactum* wet heath	GB	1	2	2	1	1	2	1	1	1	2	2
Blanket mire/bog													
M1	*Sphagnum auriculatum* bog-pool community	W	2	2	1	0	0	0	1	2	2	0	3
M2	*Sphagnum cuspidatum/recurvum* bog-pool community	W	1	2	1	1	2	0	1	2	2	1	2
M17	*Scirpus cespitosus-Eriophorum vaginatum* blanket mire	GB	2	2	2	0	0	0	1	3	2	2	3
M18	*Erica tetralix-Sphagnum papillosum* raised and blanket mire	I	0	3	3	0	2	0	2	3	2	1	1
M19	*Calluna vulgaris-Eriophorum vaginatum* blanket mire	I	0	3	3	1	3	0	3	3	3	3	3
M20	*Eriophorum vaginatum* blanket and raised mire	I	0	3	2	3	3	2	2	0	1	1	0
Acid grasslands													
U2	*Deschampsia flexuosa* grassland	W	2	2	2	2	2	1	0	1	2	1	0
U4	*Festuca ovina-Agrostis capillaris-Galium saxatile* grassland	W	3	3	3	3	3	2	3	3	3	2	2
U5	*Nardus stricta-Galium saxatile* grassland	W	2	3	3	2	3	2	3	3	3	2	3
U6	*Juncus squarrosus-Festuca ovina* grassland	GB	1	3	3	1	2	1	3	3	2	2	2

Regional representation: 1=rare/very local; 2=locally frequent/locally extensive; 3=widespread/extensive; 0=not known to occur.
International importance: GB=communities with no, or rare, close equivalents outside Britain; I=communities with local equivalents internationally; W=communities with well-developed equivalents internationally.

emphasised distinctions between Atlantic and boreal heather moor (Nolan & Robertson, 1987), whilst Rodwell (1991, 1992) gives great detail on climatic and altitudinal elements of community occurrences.

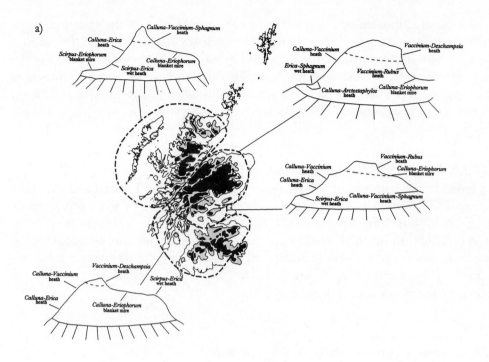

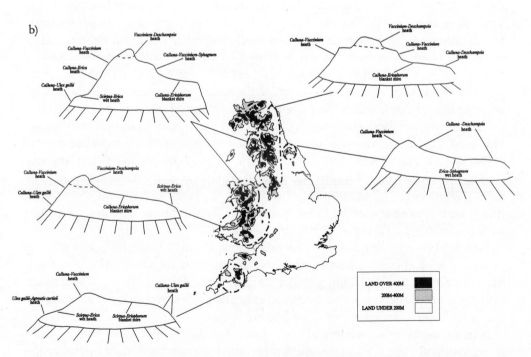

Figure 34.1. Schematic representation (with slopes exaggerated) of the general British altitudinal occurrence of upland heaths and moorlands, across key biogeographical areas of a) Scotland, and b) England and Wales

We question to what extent moorland managers take note of the variety of vegetation types on their land. Are managers sufficiently aware of the differences in productivity and sensitivity to burning and grazing of these communities? Foresters, for example, usually take into account drier and wetter areas in designing planting schemes; do moorland managers do likewise before designing burning, cutting or grazing regimes? We think not (see Thompson, *et al.*, 1994)!

34.2.1 Land cover of Scotland assessment

A broad-brush portrayal of the range of Scottish moorland habitats and land-uses is provided by the Land Cover of Scotland, interpreted from aerial photographs taken in 1988 (see Frontispiece). The vegetation is, however, much more complex and variable than this. The descriptions below summarise the main biogeographical variation in wet and dry upland heath communities (using the syntaxonomy and details of floristics given by Rodwell, 1991, 1992); these provide an overview on some of the earlier accounts on moorlands.

34.2.2 Some plant community distribution maps

Figure 34.2 gives distribution maps for four key communities (sensu Rodwell, 1991; Thompson *et al.*, 1995). The two predominant blanket bog and dry heath community distributions are shown in Figure 34.2a,b. A western wet heath distribution is given in Figure 34.2c, and the dry eastern *Calluna-Arctostaphylos uva-ursi* heath is shown in Figure 34.2d. These maps, and others in Rodwell (1991), Thompson *et al.* (1995) and Tidswell *et al.* (in press), show the variety of extent in distribution of communities across Great Britain. Data are not yet available, however, on the relative abundance of these communities in different parts of Britain. Furthermore, as Figure 34.2 indicates, many upland areas remain to be surveyed comprehensively.

North-east Highlands. Dry heaths occur extensively on steep and shallow slopes. Three types of tall heather-dominated vegetation characteristically predominate: *Calluna vulgaris-Arctostaphylos uva-ursi* heath, *Calluna vulgaris-Vaccinium myrtillus* heath, and *Vaccinium myrtillus-Rubus chamaemorus* heath. These together constitute Scotland's most boreal types of tall, dry heath.

Calluna-Arctostaphylos heath is developed at low altitudes, often on gently-sloping ground. *Calluna-Vaccinium* heath is the most extensive of the three types occupying broad sweeps across from low ground up to around 800m. *Vaccinium-Rubus* heath occurs on the peatier soils which develop at high altitudes, and at lower altitudes on cooler and more shaded north to east-facing slopes.

Blanket bog is only extensive above about 600m; below that mires are restricted to hollows and valleys. As in most upland areas of Scotland the most extensive upland mire type is *Calluna vulgaris-Eriophorum vaginatum* blanket bog, with *Erica tetralix-Sphagnum papillosum* raised and blanket mire occurring in hollows at the bottom of the main massifs. The main type of wet heath is *Erica tetralix-Sphagnum compactum*, though this is nowhere extensive, being restricted to hollows and around ombrogenous bogs at low to moderately high altitudes.

Central Highlands. The main heath on the low ground is *Calluna vulgaris-Erica cinerea* heath, which becomes even more prominent further west. *Calluna-Vaccinium* heath occurs over cool, north-facing slopes and at higher altitudes, being replaced by *Vaccinium-Rubus* heath on the upper reaches on northerly to easterly aspects. *Scirpus cespitosus-Eriophorum vaginatum* western blanket bog appears on the low ground, though generally not extensively, and *Erica tetralix-Scirpus cespitosus* western wet heath is locally extensive on gentle slopes.

North-west and western Highlands. Towards the north and west, there is extensive *Scirpus-Eriophorum* blanket bog in glens and on the foreland surrounding the massifs, notably in the far west. This grades into extensive *Scirpus-Erica* wet heath, which also occurs on steep slopes that in the central and eastern Highlands would be occupied by dry heath. The main type of tall *Calluna* heath here is of *Calluna-Erica cinerea*, though on more north-easterly aspects this is replaced by *Calluna vulgaris-Vaccinium myrtillus-Sphagnum capillifolium* heath. These together are the best expression of Scotland's Atlantic tall heaths. *Calluna-Vaccinium-Sphagnum* heath attains its most extensive development in the North-west Highlands, where more widespread *Sphagnum* and hypnaceous moss-rich forms are replaced by an Atlantic hepatic- rich form, largely restricted to the north-west Highlands (Averis, 1992).

The Southern Uplands. The assemblage of moorland vegetation here most closely resembles that in the central Highlands. Nevertheless, the range spans a good deal of variation found in the western Highlands (Galloway granite) to the north-east Highlands (Moorfoots and Lammermuirs). Blanket bog occurs only locally, predominantly on the low ground, mainly in the west, or confined to hollows. *Erica-Sphagnum* wet heath is local in the east and is replaced by *Scirpus-Erica tetralix* wet heath in the west which is locally extensive. The extensive dry heaths are *Erica-Calluna* and *Calluna-Vaccinium*, the former mainly in the west and the latter in the east.

North-west England. Here *Calluna vulgaris-Ulex gallii* heaths make a patchy appearance, becoming more extensive in Wales and south-west England. *Calluna-Vaccinium* heath is the most extensive upland heath, replaced by *Vaccinium-Deschampsia* heath on northerly slopes at high altitude or lower down where there has been heavy grazing. *Calluna-Vaccinium-Sphagnum* heath is restricted to shady, north-easterly facing slopes.

Pennines. *Calluna-Vaccinium* is the main heath on steep slopes at moderately high altitude, chiefly on the high hills of the western and more northern parts of the Pennines. In the east, on the low-altitude gentle-dip slopes, *Calluna vulgaris-Deschampsia flexuosa* heath predominates, forming the main vegetation of extensive grouse moors. *Calluna-Eriophorum* blanket mire is developed on the higher parts of these slopes.

North York Moors. The dominant heath is *Calluna-Deschampsia* heath, which covers most of the gently sloping or steep ground except where there is impeded drainage or waterlogging - where wet heath or valley mire develops (*Erica-Sphagnum* wet heath is frequent in such circumstances). At high altitude, especially on northerly-facing slopes, *Calluna-Vaccinium* heath is local.

Wales. The suites of heaths on the moorlands of north Wales are similar to those of north-west England. Mid-south Wales has locally extensive *Calluna-Ulex gallii* heath on the lower slopes giving way to *Calluna-Vaccinium* heath higher up, with *Calluna-Erica* heath very local. *Calluna-Eriophorum* bog occupies the extensive gentle slopes with *Scirpus-Erica* wet heath at the edges of the deeper peat where waterlogging is not so pronounced.

South-west England. South-western heaths of *Ulex gallii-Agrostis curtisii* occupy the lower slopes where drainage is poor or where there have been fires, and these are replaced by *Calluna-Ulex gallii* heath where drainage is better. *Scirpus-Erica* wet heath occupies areas of impeded drainage, commonly fringing the extensive *Scirpus-Eriophorum* blanket bogs of the plateaux. *Calluna-Vaccinium* heath occurs on the high ground.

34.3 What are the origins of heaths and moorland?

34.3.1 Antiquity
The ericaceous and ericoid species characteristic of moorland seem to have evolved in the late Tertiary (Stevenson and Birks, this volume), whilst the palaeoecological evidence in Britain points to the occurrence of *Calluna* and *Empetrum* spp. communities, comparable with those of today, as far back as 10,000 years ago (e.g. Birks, 1986, 1988). The extent of heathlands has changed markedly since the early post-glacial, with extensive heaths of dwarf shrubs present by around 4,000 years ago (Stevenson and Birks, this volume; Edwards *et al.*, this volume; Bennett *et al.*, 1992). As a generality, *Empetrum* heaths tended to precede *Calluna* heaths, though whether or not the former were displaced by *Calluna* in a northward direction is not clear.

Work by Bennett *et al.* (1992) on Shetland shows the complexity of change, with large herbivores (possibly red deer, *Cervus elaphus*) and Mesolithic people apparently reducing the extent of herb- and fern-rich vegetation, and giving rise to heath and bog between 7500 and 5400 years ago. Then there was an apparent gap, until human impacts on the vegetation are detectable again some 4500 years ago, with heath communities expanding considerably, covering areas by 3,000 years ago that have not changed substantially since.

34.3.2 Naturalness and cultural landscapes
There has been much debate about whether or not the ancient heaths can be regarded as 'natural' climax communities (e.g. Marrs, 1986; Odgaard, 1988; Kaland, 1986; Thompson and Brown, 1992; Averis, 1992). As Gimingham (this volume) has shown, at the turn of the century it was suggested that much heath and moorland had been derived from ancient forest. Even in the boreal forests of Fennoscandia, however, much of the vegetation has been influenced by man. But there, as in western and northern Britain, the wet ground/wet heath communities appear more

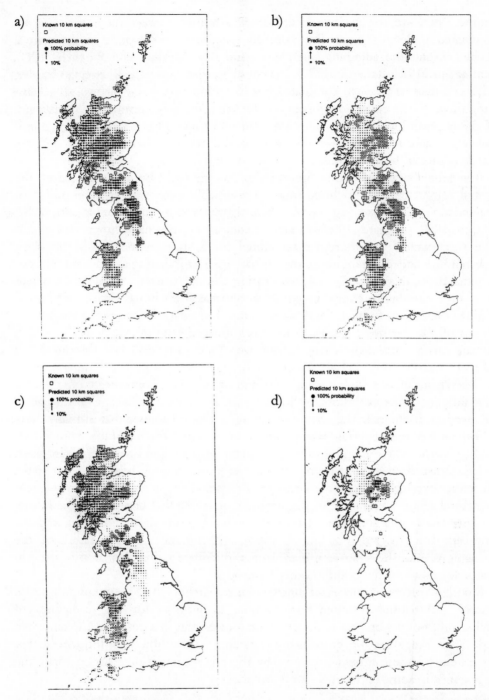

Figure 34.2. GB distribution maps for 4 dry and wet heath communities in Great Britain. Classification of communities follows Rodwell (1991). a) *Calluna vulgaris-Eriophorum vaginatum* blanket bog, b) *Calluna-Vaccinium myrtillus* dry heath, c) *Scirpus cespitosus-Erica tetralix* wet heath, and d) *Calluna-Arctostaphylos uva-ursi* eastern dry heath. These data are taken from Tidswell *et al.* (in press).

natural. There are, for instance, clear floristic affinities between the mossy *Calluna*-dominated understoreys of the so-called Caledonian pinewoods in the central Highlands and the adjoining open moorland (e.g. McVean and Ratcliffe, 1962; Gimingham, 1972; Ratcliffe, 1977). In central Sweden, near the Norwegian border, there are areas of *Calluna* dominated heaths within very open pinewoods resembling those in the eastern Highlands (D.A. Ratcliffe, pers. comm.). In some parts of the Highland woods the glades are large, and *Calluna* has probably been dominant over these for more than 200 years. If the life of individual glades and tree stands is similar, both arguably are equally 'natural'.

It is generally assumed that fire, whether natural or lit by man, has played the central role in creating such clearings. Presumably there was invasion and then domination by *Calluna* (e.g. Gimingham, 1972; Hobbs and Gimingham, 1987; Iversen, 1969; Odgaard, 1992), though grazing alone may have suppressed woodland regeneration and therefore accounted for a shift to moorland. To date, research has tended to emphasise the role of fire in eliminating woodlands (Stevenson and Birks, this volume). But, did grazing, instead, prevent regeneration where herbivores were highly concentrated? In some areas fires should have created good seedbed conditions for woodland regeneration. Indeed, questions remain about the origins of blanket bogs, and there has been much debate on the extent to which human activity caused the changes from woodland to blanket bog (Moore, 1987; Ratcliffe and Thompson, 1988; Birks, 1988).

The various effects of human activity and of wild and domesticated herbivores have influenced the evolution and form of today's upland landscape. Do we actually need to disentangle the effects of the two? Does it matter that in many parts of Britain we are not certain when man first influenced the transition from woodland to heath and moorland, or the subsequent perpetuation of these? There seem to be at least three answers in the affirmative: (i) our wildlife heritage is not static, but rather ever-changing, and it helps to understand the extent of past influences of natural agents and man in managing and conserving that heritage for the future; (ii) both the public and researchers want to learn more about how and why the landscape has changed (e.g. Smout, 1993); and (iii) the complex nature of the changing relationships between man, land and climate is manifest in moorland at scales not now usually found in other biomes.

Moorland offers an important juncture for researchers in ecology, environmental history and natural resource conservation, as well as for the disciplines of philosophy, politics and economics. At the root of this is a desire to explain when today's landscape first began to take on its appearance, how man influenced this, the extent of these influences, and why there is so much diversity in form and appearance in some parts - but not in others.

34.4 What are the historical effects of grazing and burning on the nature of change?

There have been several recent reviews of the effects of grazing (by sheep, cattle and red deer) and burning on the composition and structure of moorland vegetation (Marrs and Welch, 1991; Hester and Sydes, 1992; Cadbury, 1992; Thompson *et al.*, 1994, 1995; Armstrong and Milne, this volume). Much more is known about the effects of sheep than of deer (Scottish Natural Heritage, 1994). Studies of the effects of burning on the soils and plants, and vegetation-environment relationships in relation to large herbivore management, have sometimes given ambiguous conclusions.

Studies such as those by Tudor and Mackey (this volume) and Stevenson and Thompson (1993) have shown reductions in *Calluna* in Scotland this century that are generally associated with agricultural reclamation, forestry or heavy grazing pressure. Three fundamental questions arise here from the literature:

1). How different were the effects of grazing on heaths and moorland in prehistoric times, when range fires were less frequent but possibly more extensive, when domesticated herbivore populations were smaller, and when red deer populations were probably more in balance with their habitat?

2). What would happen if extensive moorland areas were cleared of grazing sheep and red deer and/or left unburned?

3). What level of grazing causes shifts from woodland to moorland, and then to grassland?

In this last case, large 'keyston' predators presumably influenced the distribution if not the size of red deer herds so having an important role in varying their effects on habitat, that today are effected by stock management, burning, culling and fencing.

To address question 1), we need further palaeoecological studies that examine pollen and charcoal relationships. So far as question 2) is concerned, what is attributed to fire may or may not have begun under heavy grazing, competition, changes in soil fertility or some other factor. Marrs and Welch's (1991) survey of 74 exclosures - where sheep grazing had been eliminated for more than 50 years in some plots - reveals the complexity of addressing questions 2) and 3). They found that where heather was originally present (particularly greater than 25% cover), and sheep were removed, heather tended to increase by up to 5% per annum. However, where heather was originally absent invasion and subsequent spread by it were not readily observed or predicted. They also found that the older grazing exclosures had a lower species richness; there was a suggestion that wet heath communities were particularly prone to this decline. An important question here concerns what determines such lags in vegetation change? Certainly, a lack of a seed source, and of niches for establishment, are important factors (Miles, 1973, 1974a,b). Observations suggest that stands with dominance of *Deschampsia flexuosa* or *Festuca* spp. begin to show signs of instability, with gaps appearing in the sward, after 20+ years -a phenomenon commonly seen over only a few years in herbaceous perennials in gardens!

Clearly, it is difficult to reach firm conclusions about the nature of change, not least because the direction and pace of successional shifts seem to depend heavily on the source of plant species (and particularly the seed viability of some). Moorland change shows strong dependence on initial conditions and a range of lag responses to many environmental variables. The 'behaviour' of vegetation change is therefore bound to be highly complex. Nevertheless, researchers have managed to explain a considerable amount of the observed changes. It is our view that more work is now needed to translate past efforts into practical guidance for moorland managers.

34.5 Resumé of heath and moorland succession - what is natural?

Figure 34.3 mainly develops some of our previously published studies and views of heath and moorland succession or change under management (Miles, 1985, 1988; Ratcliffe and Thompson, 1988; Thompson *et al.*, 1995). The figure summarises only shifts between communities under burning, heavy grazing or drainage, excluding natural zonations found with altitude, drainage and aspects (as shown at the broad topographical scale in Figure 34.1). Interestingly, the wet heaths and blanket bog communities appear to have a greater number and range of relatively stable derivatives under management than do the dry heaths.

Those communities which appear to be little modified, floristically and structurally, by current human activities, and which would not change to other communities if that influence was removed, are the most natural. These arguably bear close similarity, in terms of structure and community processes, to those assumed or known to have occured naturally (*sensu* Tansley, 1939; Thompson and Horsfield, 1990). Whilst the successional shifts shown in Figure 34.3 also draw on work by Miles (1985), Welch (1984), Rodwell (1991) and Thompson *et al.* (1995), many of the relationships are based largely on unpublished observations, as well as on inferences from studies by Ratcliffe (1959, 1977), Lindsay *et al.* (1988) and Reid *et al.* (1994). Work is needed to verify the nature of these relationships, the factors involved, and the actual "natural" condition of the different communities.

We suggest that the *Scirpus cespitosus-Eriophorum vaginatum* and *Erica tetralix-Sphagnum papillosum/S.compactum* wet heaths and blanket bogs may, in some north-western parts of Britain, be as natural (or at least as ancient) as the *Betula-Corylus* woodlands found there (e.g. Keatinge *et al.*, this volume). It would be useful to collect data to test this notion, notably from pollen, spores and charcoal in soil/peat cores from grazing-free situations (e.g. cliff ledges, ravines, 'crowns' on enormous boulders). These data could be contrasted with data from grazed situations in order to achieve a better understanding of successional shifts and naturalness in upland vegetation.

34.6 Is fire a good management tool?

Fire management keeps moorland in a state of arrested ecological succession - the extent of the productive, early 'building' phase of ericaceous dwarf shrubs is maintained in excess over what would occur in the absence of such management. Properly controlled burning largely results in vegetative regeneration of *Calluna*, usually with little seed germination. If burning is badly managed (or accidental) and too intense (e.g. when stands are too old, or burning takes place at the wrong time of year), then resprouting may not occur and regeneration has to be from

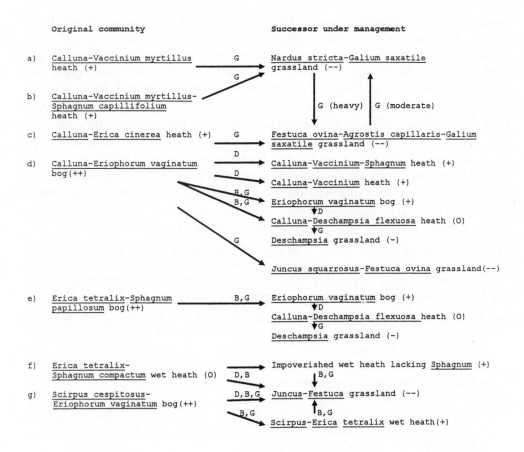

Figure 34.3. Successional shifts in moorland plant communities of Great Britain under human influence. G = heavy grazing, B = burning, D = drainage. Naturalness is indicated along a continuum from ++ (highly natural) through 0 (semi-natural) to – – (highly anthropogenic) (see text for explanation). Part of the figure adapted from Miles (1988), Thompson *et al.* (1995).

seedling establishment. Cutting also coppices *Calluna*, but without creating a favourable seedbed, with the result that few seeds germinate. Several factors influence the consequences of burning (Gimingham, this volume; Phillips and Watson, this volume). Despite considerable research, however, there remains much debate (notably amongst researchers and practitioners) about the effects of burning on moorland - be it frequent or infrequent, light or intense (McVean and Lockie, 1969; Marrs, 1986; Hester and Sydes, 1992; Usher and Thompson, 1993). It seems surprising, therefore, that the more recent literature does not stress adverse effects of burning on moorland vegetation, even though discussions amongst conservationists highlight fire as a "problem", notably in the west (e.g. Lister-Kaye, 1994).

For some time we have questioned the need, on conservation grounds, for burning all moorland regularly (Miles, 1981; Usher and Thompson, 1993; Thompson *et al.*, 1994, 1995). Does moorland need to be burned in order to persist? Since the early part of this century workers have known about heather moorland regeneration by layering (i.e. adventitious rooting of stems). But it has generally been discounted or ignored as an important contributor to heather persistence. Miles (1981), Gimingham (1988) and MacDonald *et al.* (1995), however, found that this phenomenon was widespread, notably in the wetter heaths. Indeed, there is growing evidence of regeneration, particularly in the younger plants, in the absence of burning (Keatinge, 1975; Scandrett and Gimingham, 1989a,b). According to MacDonald *et al.* (1995) layering tends to be associated more with deep peat, a high frequency of *Hypnum* spp. around the stems, and more sheltered situations. Crucial factors for layering were the presence of prostrate *Calluna* stems not eliminated by shading, and conditions that lead to burial of stems so that they remain undisturbed in a shaded, humid environment.

Five questions emerge from the above and allied work:

1). Does burning eliminate, or select against, layering so that muirburn is viewed as the best means of maintaining heather?

2). Under what conditions is layering continuous?

3). What are the characteristics of stands maintained in a dynamic steady state by layering?

4). What densities of red grouse, and indeed of other moorland birds, can occur on unburnt compared with burnt moorland?

5). Given that fire (apart from cutting) is the main factor that will prevent tree invasion while still maintaining a heather cover, are the majority of layering stands liable to change to woodland?

In the western heaths, where *Calluna* associates with a greater variety of plant species (Rodwell, 1991; Thompson *et al.*, 1995), we question the extent to which Watt's (1947, 1955) successional phases in *Calluna* actually apply. Indeed, Miles (1981) has questioned the reality of the *Calluna* cycle through seedling establishment in drier heaths in eastern Scotland. Gimingham (1987) reflects on his and other observations stating "in my view it is a mistake to assume that if *Calluna* is to re-occupy gap sites, thereby initiating a cyclical process, this must necessarily involve seedling establishment." This is a point that Watt (1955) did, however, cover in his classic paper. Here, distinctions need to be made between the inherent cyclical changes observed in the absence of fire with or without gap formation (e.g. Gimingham, 1988, this volume) and the effects of fire on competition and the rate of succession in the more floristically diverse western heaths and blanket bogs.

34.7 Does the fauna respond to moorland habitat change?

34.7.1 Invertebrates

Changes in the invertebrate fauna in relation to plant community succession are not well described, though much is known about the effects of dry-wet conditions and development phases of *Calluna* (e.g. Usher, 1992; Usher and Thompson, 1993; Coulson *et al.*, this volume; Usher, this volume). The structural diversity of moorland probably accounts for its high invertebrate species richness. But again, the wet heaths have been so inadequately studied that community differences or similarities in assemblages are not yet known (though see Coulson *et al.*, this volume). Recent work in the pinewoods of the central Highlands reveals the high importance of *Vaccinium myrtillus* for invertebrate species richness and biomass (and therefore as feeding habitat for capercaillie and black grouse) (D. Baines, pers. comm.). Does the amount of *V. myrtillus* in moorland have an equally important effect on invertebrates? Or is it only in woodlands, where the *Vaccinium*-dominated communities are more natural, that this dwarf-shrub is so important?

Long term research on the *Calluna*-dominated heathlands of the Netherlands (reviewed by Aerts and Heil, 1993; de Smidt, this volume) and of southern England (Webb, 1986) has taken a holistic approach to understanding habitat and faunal change and management. For the western heaths of Great Britain as a whole, we do not even have adequate estimates of invertebrate abundance for each community. Are there likely to be considerable differences between the communities in the complement of herbivores, detritivores and predators (Coulson, 1988)? If we are to understand nutrient cycling, decomposition processes and the importance of these habitats for vertebrates, then we need more information on the invertebrates. Hudson (this volume) has suggested that there is a lower overall biomass of soil invertebrates towards the west, corresponding with what several workers have referred to as the "wet desert" phenomenon: a greater downturn in numbers of red grouse shot and numbers of predators observed in the west than in the east during this century (Hudson, 1988; Lister-Kaye, 1994). Perhaps the invertebrates are sensitive to excessive burning, with standing crop reflecting net effects on vegetation and soil? We suggest that more data are needed to allow us either to support or reject such views.

34.7.2 Birds

There is much debate about how heath and moorland birds will be affected by shifts to grassland or to scrub and woodland (e.g. Usher and Thompson, 1993; Thompson *et al.*, 1995; Brown and Bainbridge, this volume). Indeed, there are even question-marks hanging over the importance of grouse moor for birds (see Haworth and Thompson, 1990; Brown and Bainbridge, this volume; cf. Hudson, this volume; Thompson *et al.*, 1995). In particular, researchers as well as land managers question whether or not an expansion of woodland at the expense of moorland (e.g. Staines *et al.*, this volume) will eliminate characteristic open-moor breeding birds and give rise to high densities of predators harboured by scrub and woodland?

In Figure 34.4a,b we suggest, from our own observations and the literature, simple avian foodchains for moorland, grassland and scrub/woodland derivatives. When there is a major expansion of woodland, more species seem to experience major increases in abundance. Numbers of intermediate predators (crows and

a)

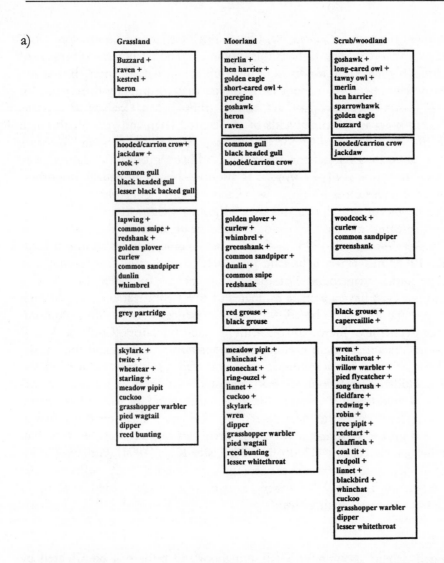

Figure 34.4a. Simple linear avian moorland foodchains that correspond with shifts either to grassland under heavy grazing/burning pressure, or to early successional woodland (scrub) where grazing and burning are prevented or greatly reduced. These successions occur on acid brown earths, humus iron podzols or shallow blanket peat (partly adapted from Sydes and Miller, 1988; Thompson *et al.*, 1988, 1995; Ratcliffe, 1990; Gibbons *et al.*, 1993; Usher and Thompson, 1993). a) gives the full species lists, which are not comprehensive (note that some species such as gulls belong more to wetlands than to grasslands *per se*, and in some districts black grouse are typical of marginal rough grasslands). Appendix 34.1 gives scientific names.

gulls) are greater over grassland-dominated habitats than over the other two. The species richness of small passerine assemblages increases in relation to the structural complexity of the habitat, with highest values for woodland.

The sort of analyses done by Stillman (this volume) and Brown and Stillman (1993) are important in clarifying what we know about bird-habitat associations. A

b)

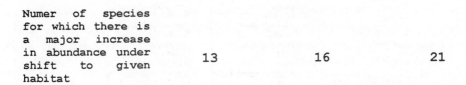

| Numer of species for which there is a major increase in abundance under shift to given habitat | 13 | 16 | 21 |

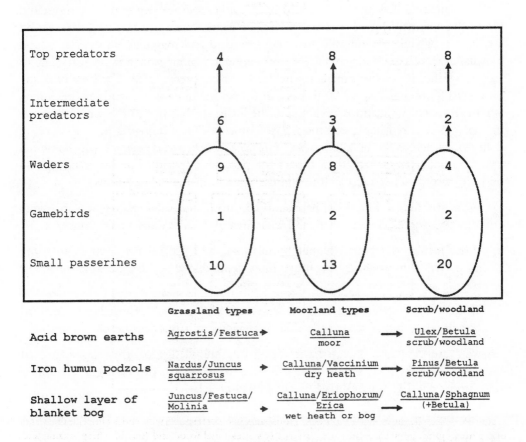

	Grassland types	Moorland types	Scrub/woodland
Acid brown earths	Agrostis/Festuca ➤	Calluna moor	→ Ulex/Betula scrub/woodland
Iron humun podzols	Nardus/Juncus squarrosus ➤	Calluna/Vaccinium dry heath	Pinus/Betula scrub/woodland
Shallow layer of blanket bog	Juncus/Festuca/Molinia ➤	Calluna/Eriophorum/Erica wet heath or bog	→ Calluna/Sphagnum (+Betula)

Figure 34.4b. Schematic linear avian foodchains under three wet or dry heath regimes that shift either to grassland under heavy grazing pressure (or drainage) or through to scrub/woodland where grazing and burning are prevented or greatly reduced. The habitat shifts occur on acid brown earths, humus from iron podzols or shallow blanket peat (partly adapted from Sydes and Miller, 1988; Thompson *et al.*, 1988, 1995; Ratcliffe, 1990; Gibbons *et al.*, 1993; Usher and Thompson, 1993). Note that given species may increase in abundance only in one of the three habitats.

general conclusion is that altitude and topography, and secondly vegetation gradients from grassland to moorland, influence the composition of bird assemblages. No evidence linking bird species diversity with mosaic patterns across habitats, and their invertebrates, is yet available (but see Allen, this volume; Usher and Thompson, 1993). Hudson (1992, this volume) has made a strong case for the presence or absence of predators, particularly foxes (*Vulpes vulpes*) and crows, in determining both red grouse densities and increases in grouse numbers from low densities. However, habitat composition and structure may mediate between these predators/intermediate predators and their prey. Further investigations are needed to disentangle the effects of burning management, grazing by sheep, red deer and cattle, and predators/intermediate predators on moorland birds (Brown and Bainbridge, this volume).

One conclusion reached by us concerns the rather sectoral perception of moorland birds. The majority of bird species breeding on moor, heath and bog now depends on a range of habitats, notably the adjoining farmland and marginal hill grasslands and woodlands/forestry. Management of hill vegetation alone will not be sufficient to have a significant positive impact on hill birds - except red grouse. The new breeding birds atlas (Gibbons *et al.*, 1993) shows that for several birds the uplands are becoming a 'retreat' - with populations declining in the lowlands, but not to the same degree in the uplands (e.g. redshank, common snipe, lapwing). Ornithologists need to develop their studies across the upland-lowland interface in order to determine why some hill areas are better or poorer than others for particular species. For the main upland breeding birds, we need research to address three fundamental questions:

1). What are the key functional habitats used throughout the breeding season - what are they, where do they occur, and what area of habitat does a pair require?

2). What factors determine higher populations, and greater production, in some areas over others - and how much inter-dependency is there between different populations?

3). What are the specific effects of landscape change and of predation on bird populations, and at what scale does management influence these?

Answers are vital not only for furthering our knowledge of the importance of moorland for birds, but for devising effective measures for protecting bird populations under the EC Wild Birds Directive 79/409/EEC.

34.8 What is the condition of moorland?

Gimingham (this volume) mentioned that during nearly 50 years of research on heathland ecology the one major change in perception was that of a growing realisation about the disappearance of heaths throughout western Europe. Tudor and Mackey (this volume) estimate that in Scotland between the 1940s and 1970s there has been an 18% reduction in the extent of moorland and an 8% reduction in the extent of blanket bog. The extent of change in England and Wales is greater, at around 20% (Thompson *et al.*, 1995; Bardgett *et al.*, 1995).

What is the condition of our remaining moor and heath? Thompson *et al.* (1995) estimate that in England and Wales 70% of remaining heather moorland is at risk of change, with at least 50% with its *Calluna* in 'poor' or 'suppressed' condition, liable to further reductions and damage under sheep grazing densities of around 2 ewes or greater per hectare. Bardgett *et al.* (1995, this volume) provide details of these estimates at the region level.

Can an audit of moorland condition be made in Scotland? Approximately one-third of the resource is under some form of protection or positive management (Ward *et al.*, this volume). Should research be done to audit condition and change on 'protected' and 'non-protected' areas? As Henderson *et al.* (this volume) and McFerran *et al.* (this volume) demonstrate, monitoring takes place within environmentally sensitive areas (ESAs) - in Scotland covering some 18% of the land surface. Our own observations suggest that the general condition of western wet heaths and blanket bogs may be poorer than comparable sized areas of moorland in the east. This needs to be examined, with work focusing particularly on the history and current practice of muirburn.

Questions remain over the changing 'condition' of the landscape, and its perception by people. Bullock (this volume) outlines how reliable estimates of public benefits associated with different landscape, and indeed socio-economic, scenarios can be measured. Mackay's (this volume) pilot survey reveals the extent of variation in public valuation of these landscapes. Here there is considerable scope to study the representation and perception of change. Do we really understand the importance attached by many to the cultural landscape in which they were reared, or on which they depend?

34.9 The future - fifty years on?

When Charles Gimingham began his research on moorland, in the mid-1940s, he set out to investigate the autecology of *Calluna* and the ecological consequences of moorland management. Almost 50 years on, we recognise the significant advances made in these areas. Looking ahead, we indeed wonder what will be reported towards the middle of the next century!

34.9.1 Land management and sustainability

There remain many unknowns! Will there be a major study of the fragmentation and local demise of moorland and heaths in the British Isles, comparable with that in the Netherlands (e.g. Aerts and Heil, 1993), to guide site conservation priorities? It is unclear to what extent the wet heaths of the west and north depend on good management (burning and grazing) for their continuance. Will sporting-related management continue to decline to the extent that substantial *Calluna*-dominated tracts of hill country change, perhaps shifting towards large mosaics of heath, grassland and woodland? If so, will less muirburn reduce the extent of building-phase *Calluna*? Would this permit an increase in local biodiversity, of plants and invertebrates in particular? Both Gimingham (this volume) and Usher and Thompson (1993) have urged the adoption of more than one cycle and scale of burning and cutting. Will managers test the putative benefits of these practices?

There are also questions about the practicalities of management. Will there be an "improvement" in land management - as sought by Phillips and Watson (this volume), Hudson (this volume) and Thompson *et al.* (1995). There is a crucial role here for education through training, and the sorts of modelling approaches being developed by the Macaulay Land Use Research Institute (e.g. Armstrong and Milne, this volume) may prove the best means for enabling managers to care for their land sustainably.

But the objectives of management need to be stated clearly. We have the impression that many managers "sign up" to fashionable, omniscient concepts rather than to precise, locally-determined objectives. Why should wet heaths and blanket bog in the Western Isles or in the north of Scotland be managed for red grouse (ideally for large bags) just because some of the very different North Pennine and eastern Highland moors are so productive?

34.9.2 Predators and predation

We hope that there will be significant advances in disentangling the importance of habitat management and predation (or predator control) for moorland bird populations. Targets should be set for the recovery of raptor populations in some parts (e.g. Thompson *et al.*, 1995). Any expansion of native woodland types in place of heath and moor will be crucial here, for questions will arise about what will be gained and lost, and whether or not these woodlands should be managed, and if so, how (e.g. Cairngorms Working Party, 1993).

34.9.3 Regional objectives for conservation and management

Is there any scope for having regional objectives for managing moorland? Several recent key publications on land management in Scotland have set regional rather than just national targets for restoration and management of habitats (e.g. Cairngorms Working Party, 1993; prescriptions for Scotland's ten Environmentally Sensitive Areas; Regional Indicative Forest Strategies). Will the present-day diversity of land management approaches to large-scale countryside change in the uplands remain until regional objectives are devised and then developed towards common acceptance? Interestingly, McVean and Lockie (1969) posed similar sets of questions based on their work some thirty years ago, when regional land capability maps were being produced for some of the uplands.

Moorland requires sustainable management. Much of the Government's recent proposals on putting sustainability into practice (CM 2428, 1994) is relevant to moorland, and there is a particular challenge in striking the right balance between conserving the natural heritage and exploiting its natural resources. The EC Habitats Directive 92/43/EEC will have a significant bearing on moorland conservation. Moorland habitats covered by this are: (i) Northern Atlantic wet heaths with *Erica tetralix*, (ii) dry heaths, (iii) alpine and subalpine heaths, (iv) blanket bog (active and non-active), and occurrences of (v) species-rich *Nardus* grasslands, and (vi) *Molinia* meadows. Under the directive many of the best and most representative areas with these communities will be designated as 'Special Areas of Conservation'. These will be managed to protect the habitat, including the "... specific structure and functions which are necessary for its long-term maintenance ..." (Article 1e).

34.9.4 Scientific understanding on change

How much more do we need to know to be able to manage moorland sustainably? Are we yet clear about whether or not traditional moorland management depletes the nutrient stock, and in turn the productivity of the hill (e.g. Lister-Kaye, 1994)? Muirburn seems to have a significant effect on levels of phosphorus and nitrogen cycling. As Gimingham (this volume) and a few others have pointed out, burning favours *Calluna* which is well adapted to the low nutrient status of the soils. The long-term persistence of *Calluna* under muirburn ought to reduce the inherent productivity of some parts. We should, therefore, not be surprised at the circumstantial evidence for a general decline in the productivity of some upland areas, or the spread of grass at the expense of *Calluna* where there has been an increase in soil nitrogen? Again, the nutrient budgets of wetter and drier heaths may respond in very different ways to management. How critical is the influence of maritime (or oceanic) conditions in the west?

More work on the invertebrates may be vital to understanding variation in the rates of change. Insect pest outbreaks can destroy *Calluna* and *Betula* stands. We have much to learn on why these occur. To what extent does the herbivorous insect fauna influence the relationship between *Calluna*, other shrubs, grasses and sedges, and the nutrient regime of the soils? Some researchers argue that we need a large-scale experiment involving the presence/absence of (i) sheep and deer (and possibly cattle), (ii) burning, and (iii) nutrient additions. We remain sceptical about the need for this given what has already been researched, and difficulties relating to the methodology.

34.9.5 Finale

Almost fifty years after the onset of Charles Gimingham's endeavours on heathlands and moorland we have accumulated a large body of knowledge, and have addressed some key questions. We now regard these habitats in a different light. In the future, the "cultural" importance of sporting management may be replaced by a greater emphasis on native woodland regeneration, agricultural use, and wildlife and amenity conservation. Hopefully there will be more collaborative research on the different, but associated, aspects of moorland change, with more work being done in the west and north of Britain, as well as in Ireland. The research discipline of environmental history seems to offer a particularly promising opportunity for embracing ecological and historical approaches to understanding the nature of change, as well as for promoting the importance of knowledge gained. There may even be a less sectoral approach to managing hill land, and instead the pursuit of more locally appropriate goals for sustaining natural resources and the natural heritage.

Such developments would be a further testimony to the signal work of Charles Gimingham and, of course, would reflect our continuing, abiding fascination in *Calluna vulgaris* and its associates.

Acknowledgements

We are grateful to: Professor Charles Gimingham for his wisdom and guidance; Dr David Horsfield, Angus MacDonald, Dr David Baines, Dr Tony Stevenson, Professor Michael B Usher, Dr Alison Hester, Eliane Reid, Dr Torstein Sølhoy, Dr Derek

Ratcliffe, Patrick Gordon-Duff-Pennington, David Laird, Sir John Lister-Kaye and two anonymous referees for discussions and/or detailed comments on an earlier draft; and the participants of the Heaths and Moorland conference for producing-such stimulating papers. The views expressed in this chapter should not be read as being the policy of either Scottish Natural Heritage or The Scottish Office.

References

Aerts, R. and Heil, G.W. (Ed.). (1993). *Heathlands: patterns and processes in a changing environment. Geobotany* **20**. Klewer Academic Publishers, London.

Allen, D.S. (this volume). Habitat selection by whinchats: a case for bracken in the Uplands?

Armstrong, H.M. and Milne, J.A. (this volume). The effects of grazing on vegetation species composition.

Averis, A. (1992). Where are all the hepatic mat liverworts in Scotland? *Botanical Journal of Scotland*, **46**,191–198.

Bardgett, R.D., Marsden, J.H. & Howard, D.C. (1995). The extent and condition of heather in the uplands of England and Wales. *Biological Conservation*, **71**, in press.

Bardgett, R.D., Marsden, J.H., Howard, D.C. and Hossell, J.E. (this volume). The extent and condition of heather in moorland, and the potential impact of climate change.

Bennett, K.D., Boreham, S., Sharp, M.J. and Switsur, V.R. (1992). Holocene history of environment, vegetation and human settlement on Catta Ness, Lunnasting, Shetland. *Journal of Ecology*, **80**, 241-273.

Birks, H.J.B. (1986). Late-Quaternary biotic changes in terrestrial and lacustrine environments, with particular reference to north-west Europe. In *Handbook of Holocene Palaeoecology and Palaeohydrology*, ed. by B. E. Berglund. John Wylie, Chichester, pp3-65.

Birks, H.J.B. (1988). Long-term ecological change in the British uplands. In *Ecological Change in the Uplands*, ed. by M.B. Usher and D.B.A.Thompson. Blackwell, Oxford, pp37-56.

Brown, A.F. and Bainbridge, I.P. (this volume). Grouse moors and upland breeding birds.

Brown, A., Birks, H.J.B. and Thompson, D.B.A. (1993). A new biogeographical classification of the Scottish uplands. II. Vegetation - Environment relationships. *Journal of Ecology*, **81**, 231-251.

Brown, A.F. and Stillman, R.A. (1993). Bird-habitat associations in the eastern Highlands of Scotland. *Journal of Applied Ecology*, **30**, 31-42.

Bullock, C. (this volume). Measuring the public benefits of landseape and environmental change: a case of upland grazing extensification.

Cadbury, C.J. (1992). *Grazing and other management of upland vegetation: a review with special reference to birds*. Royal Society for the Protection of Birds, Sandy.

Cairngorms Working Party. (1993). *Common sense and sustainability: a partnership for the Cairngorms*. The Scottish Office, Edinburgh.

Coulson, J.C. (1988). The structure and importance of invertebrate communities on peatlands and moorlands, and effects of environmental and management changes. In *Ecological Change in the Uplands*, ed. by M.B. Usher and D.B.A. Thompson. Blackwell, Oxford, pp365-380.

Coulson, J., Bauer, L., Butterfield, J., Downie, I., Cranna, L. and Smith, C. (this volume). The invertebrates of the northern Scottish Flows, and a comparison with other peatland habitats.

CM 2428. (1994). *Sustainable development. The UK strategy*. Command 2428. HMSO, London.

Gibbons, D.W., Reid, J.B. and Chapman, R.A. (comp.) (1993). *The New Atlas of Breeding Birds in Britain and Ireland, 1988-1991*. Poyser, London.

Gimingham, C.H. (1972). *Ecology of Heathlands*. Chapman & Hall, London.

Gimingham, C.H. (1987). Harnessing the winds of change: heathland ecology in retrospect and prospect. Presidential address to the British Ecological Society, December 1986. *Journal of Ecology*, **75**, 895-914.

Gimingham, C.H. (1988). A re-appraisal of cyclical processes in *Calluna* heath. *Vegetatio*, **77**, 61-64.

Gimingham, C.H. (this volume). Heaths and Moorland: an overview of ecological change.

Haworth, P.F. and Thompson, D.B.A. (1990). Factors associated with the breeding distribution of upland birds in the south Pennines, England. *Journal of Applied Ecology*, **271**, 562-577.

Henderson, D.J., Lilly, A., Madden, S. and Still, M.J. (this volume). Heather moorland and monitoring in the Loch Lomond Environmentally Sensitive Area, Scotland.

Hester, A. and Sydes, C. (1992). Changes in burning of Scottish heather moorland since the 1940s from aerial photographs. *Biological Conservation*, **60**, 25-30.

Hobbs, R.J. and Gimingham, C.H. (1987). Vegetation, fire and herbivore interactions in heathland. *Advances in Ecological Research*. **16**, 87-173.

Hudson, P.J. (1988). Spatial variations, patterns and management options in upland bird communities. In *Ecological Change in the Uplands*, ed. by M.B. Usher and D.B.A. Thompson. Blackwell, Oxford, pp381-398.

Hudson, P.J. (1992). *Grouse in Space and Time*. The Game Conservancy, Fordingbridge.

Hudson, P.J. (this volume). Ecological trends and grouse management in upland Britain.

Iversen, J. (1969). Retrogressive development of a forest ecosystem demonstrated by pollen diagrams from fossil mor. *Oikos*, **12** (supplement), 35-49.

Kaland, P.E. (1986). The origin and management of Norwegian coastal heaths as reflected by pollen analysis. In *Anthropogenic indicators in pollen diagrams*, ed. by K E Behre. Balkema, Rotterdam. pp19-36.

Keatinge, T.H. (1975). Plant community dynamics in wet heathland. *Journal of Ecology*. **63**, 163-172.

Keatinge, T.H., Coupar, A.M. and Reid, E. (this volume). Wet heaths in Caithness and Sutherland, Scotland.

Lindsay, R.A., Charman, D.J., Everingham, F., O'Reilly, R.M., Palmer, M.A., Rowell, T.A. and Stroud, D.A. (1988). *The Flow Country - the peatlands of Caithness and Sutherland*. Nature Conservancy Council, Peterborough, U.K.

Lister-Kaye, J. (1994). *Ill Fares the Land. A sustainable land ethic for the sporting estates of the Highlands and Islands of Scotland*. Canan Teangue, Isle of Skye.

MacDonald, A.J., Kirkpatrick, A.H., Hester, A.J. and Sydes, C. (1995). Regeneration by natural layering of heather (*Calluna vulgaris*); frequency and characteristics in upland Britain. *Journal of Ecology* (in press).

Mackay, J.W. (this volume). People, perceptions and moorland.

Marrs, R.H. (1986). The role of catastrophic death of *Calluna* in heathland communities. *Vegetatio*, **51**, 109-115.

Marrs, R.H. and Welch, D. (1991). *Moorland wilderness: the potential effects of a reduced grazing pressure*. Report to Department of the Environment, London.

McFerran, D.M., Hegarty, C.A., Cameron, A., Mulholland, and McAdam, J.H. (this volume). Monitoring of heather moorland within Environmentally Sensitive Areas in Northern Ireland.

McVean, D.N. and Lockie, J.D. (1969). *Ecology and Land Use in Upland Scotland*. Edinburgh University Press, Edinburgh.

McVean, D.N. and Ratcliffe, D.A. (1962). *Plant Communities of the Scottish Highlands*. HMSO, London.

Miles, J. (1973). Natural recolonization of experimentally bared soil in Callunetum in north-east Scotland. *Journal of Ecology*, **61**, 399-412.

Miles, J. (1974a). Experimental establishment of new species from seed in Callunetum in north-east Scotland. *Journal of Ecology*, **62**, 527-551.

Miles, J. (1974b). Effects of experimental interference with stand structure on establishment of seedlings in Callunetum. *Journal of Ecology*, **62**, 675-687.

Miles, J. (1981). Problems in heathland and grassland dynamics. *Vegetatio*, **46**, 61-64.

Miles, J. (1985). The pedogenic effects of different species and vegetation types and the implications of succession. *Journal of Soil Science*, **36**, 571-584.

Miles, J. (1988). Vegetation and soil change in the uplands. In *Ecological Change in the Uplands*, ed. by M.B. Usher and D.B.A. Thompson. Blackwell, Oxford, pp57-70.

Moore, P.D. (1987). A thousand years of death. *New Scientist*, **113**, 46-48.

Nolan, A.J. and Robertson, J.S. (1987). Regional trends in dry and moist Scottish moorland vegetation in relation to climate, soils and other ecological factors. *Journal of Ecology*, **75**, 1145-1157.

Odgaard, B. (1988). Heathland history in western Jutland, Denmark. In *The Cultural Landscape: past, present and future*, ed. by H.H. Birks, H.J.B. Birks, P.E. Kaland and D. Moe. Cambridge University Press, Cambridge, pp311-319.

Odgaard, B. (1992). The fire history of Danish heathland areas as reflected by pollen and charred particles in lake sediments. *The Holocene*, **2**, 218-226.

Phillips, J. and Watson, A. (this volume). Key requirements for management of heather moorland: now and for the future.

Ratcliffe, D.A. (1959). The vegetation of the Carneddau, North Wales, I. Grasslands, heaths and bogs. *Journal of Ecology*, **47**, 371-413.

Ratcliffe, D.A. (Ed.) (1977). *A Nature Conservation Review*. Volume 1, Cambridge University Press, Cambridge.

Ratcliffe, D.A. (1990). *Birdlife of Mountain and Upland*. Cambridge University Press, Cambridge.

Ratcliffe, D.A. and Thompson, D.B.A. (1988). The British uplands: their ecological character and international significance. In *Ecological Change in the Uplands*, ed. by M.B. Usher and D.B.A. Thompson. Blackwell, Oxford, pp9-36.

Reid, E., Mortimer, G.N., Lindsay, R.A. and Thompson, D.B.A. (1994). Blanket bogs in Great Britain: an assessment of large-scale pattern and distribution using remote sensing and GIS. In *Large Scale Pattern in Ecology*, ed. by R.M. May, N. Webb and P.J. Edwards. Blackwell, Oxford, pp. 229–246.

Rodwell, J. (Ed.) (1991). *British Plant Communities. Volume 2. Mires and Heaths*. Cambridge University Press, Cambridge.

Rodwell, J. (Ed.) (1992). *British Plant Communities. Volume 3. Grasslands and montane communities*. Cambridge University Press, Cambridge.

Scandrett, E. and Gimingham, C.H. (1989a). Vegetative regeneration by layering in *Calluna vulgaris* (L.) Hull. *Botanical Society of Edinburgh Transactions*, **45**, 323-334.

Scandrett, E. and Gimingham, C.H. (1989b). A model of *Calluna* population dynamics; the effects of varying seed and vegetative regeneration. *Vegetatio*, **84**,143-152.

Scottish Natural Heritage (1994). *Red Deer and the Natural Heritage. SNH Policy Paper*. Scottish Natural Heritage, Battleby.

Smidt, J.T. de. (this volume). The imminent destruction of north west European heaths due to atmospheric nitrogen deposition.

Smout, T.C. (Ed.) (1993). *Scotland since Pre-history - natural change and human impact*. Scottish Cultural Press, Aberdeen.

Staines, B.W., Balharry, R. and Welch, D. (this volume). Moorland management and impacts of red deer.

Stevenson, A.C. and Birks, H.J.B. (this volume). Heaths and moorland: long-term changes, and interactions with climate and people.

Stevenson, A.C. and Thompson, D.B.A. (1993). Long-term changes in the extent of heather moorland in upland Britain and Ireland: Palaeoecological evidence for the importance of grazing. *The Holocene*, **3**, 70-76.

Stillman, R.A. (this volume). Bird associations with heather moorland in the Scottish and English uplands.

Sydes, C. and Miller, G.R. (1988). Range management and nature conservation in the British uplands. In *Ecological Change in the Uplands*, ed. by M.B. Usher and D.B.A. Thompson. Blackwell, Oxford, pp323-338.

Tansley, A.G. (1939). *The British Islands and their Vegetation*. Cambridge University Press, Cambridge.

Thompson, D.B.A. and Brown, A. (1992). Biodiversity in montane Britain: habitat variation, vegetation diversity and some objectives for conservation. *Biodiversity and Conservation*, **1**,179-208.

Thompson, D.B.A. and Horsfield, D. (1990). Towards an assessment of nature conservation criteria in the British uplands. In *Grazing research and nature conservation in the uplands: proceedings of a seminar*, 1988. ed. by D.B.A. Thompson, and K.J. Kirby. Research and Survey in Nature Conservation, No. 31. Nature Conservancy Council, Peterborough, pp9-18.

Thompson, D.B.A., MacDonald, A.J. and Hudson, P.J. (1994). Upland moors and heaths. In *Habitat Management* ed. by W.J. Sutherland and D.A. Hill. Cambridge University Press, Cambridge, pp292-328.

Thompson, D.B.A., MacDonald, A.J., Marsden, J.H. and Galbraith, C.A. (1995). Upland heather moorland in Great Britain: a review of international importance, vegetation change and some objectives for nature conservation. *Biological Conservation*, **71**, in press.

Thompson, D.B.A., Stroud, D.A. and Pienkowski, M.W. (1988). Afforestation and upland birds: consequences for population ecology. In *Ecological Change in the Uplands*, ed. by M.B. Usher and D.B.A. Thompson. Blackwell, Oxford, pp. 237-259

Tidswell, R., Reid, J.B., Horsfield, D. and Thompson, D.B.A. (in press). The GB distribution of upland and peatland CORINE biotopes. Research Review Report. Scottish Natural Heritage, Battleby.

Tudor, G. and Mackey, E.C. (this volume). Upland land cover change in post-War Scotland.

Usher, M.B. (1992). Management and diversity of arthropods in *Calluna* heathlands. *Biodiversity and Conservation*, **1**, 63-79.

Usher, M.B. (this volume). Heather moorland patch dynamics and consequences for wildlife.

Usher, M.B. and Thompson, D.B.A. (1993). Variation in the upland heathlands of Great Britain: conservation importance. *Biological Conservation*, **66**, 69-81.

Ward, S.D., MacDonald, A.J. and Matthew, E.M. (this volume). Scottish heaths and moorland: how should conservation be taken forward?

Watt, A.S. (1947). Pattern and process in the plant community. *Journal of Ecology*, **35**, 1-22.

Watt, A.S. (1955). Bracken versus heather, a study of plant sociology. *Journal of Ecology*, **43**, 490-506.

Webb, N. (1986). *Heathlands*. Collins, London.

Welch, D. (1984). Studies in the grazing of heather moorland in north-east Scotland. II. Response of heather. *Journal of Applied Ecology*, **21**, 197-201.

Appendix 34.1. Latin names of birds mentioned.

Common name	*Latin Name*
Heron	*Ardea cinerea*
Sparrowhawk	*Accipiter nisus*
Goshawk	*Accipiter gentilis*
Buzzard	*Buteo buteo*
Golden eagle	*Aquila chrysaetos*
Hen harrier	*Circus cyaneus*
Peregrine	*Falco peregrinus*
Merlin	*Falco columbarius*
Kestrel	*Falco tinnunculus*
Red grouse	*Lagopus lagopus scoticus*
Black grouse	*Lagopus tetrix*
Capercaillie	*Tetrao urogallus*
Grey partridge	*Perdix perdix*
Golden plover	*Pluvialis apricaria*
Lapwing	*Vanellus vanellus*
Dunlin	*Calidris alpina*
Redshank	*Tringa totanus*
Greenshank	*Tringa nebularia*
Woodcock	*Scolopax rusticola*
Common sandpiper	*Actitis hypoleucos*
Curlew	*Numenius arquata*
Whimbrel	*Numenius phaeopus*
Common snipe	*Gallinago gallinago*
Black-headed gull	*Larus ridibundus*
Lesser black backed gull	*Larus fuscus*
Common gull	*Larus canus*
Cuckoo	*Cuculus canorus*
Long-eared owl	*Asio otus*
Short-eared owl	*Asio flammeus*
Tawny owl	*Strix aluco*
Skylark	*Alauda arvensis*
Tree pipit	*Anthus trivialis*
Meadow pipit	*Anthus pratensis*
Pied wagtail	*Motacilla alba*
Grasshopper warbler	*Locustella naevia*
Whitethroat	*Sylvia communis*
Lesser whitethroat	*Sylvia curruca*
Willow warbler	*Phylloscopus trochilus*
Pied flycatcher	*Ficedula hypoleuca*
Stonechat	*Saxicola torquata*

Appendix 34.1. Latin names of birds mentioned (continued).

Common name	*Latin Name*
Whinchat	*Saxicola rubetra*
Wheatear	*Oenanthe oenanthe*
Redstart	*Phoenicurus phoenicurus*
Robin	*Erithacus rubecula*
Blackbird	*Turdus merula*
Ring-ouzel	*Turdus torquata*
Fieldfare	*Turdus pilaris*
Redwing	*Turdus iliacus*
Song thrush	*Turdus philomelos*
Coal tit	*Parus ater*
Wren	*Troglodytes troglodytes*
Dipper	*Cinclus cinclus*
Reed bunting	*Emberiza schoeniclus*
Chaffinch	*Fringilla coelebs*
Redpoll	*Acanthis flammea*
Twite	*Acanthis flavirostris*
Linnet	*Acanthis cannabina*
Starling	*Sturnus vulgaris*
Raven	*Corvus corax*
Rook	*Corvus frugilegus*
Carrion crow	*Corvus corone corone*
Hooded crow	*Corvus corone cornix*
Jackdaw	*Corvus monedula*

INDEX

HMSO

HMSO Bookshops
71 Lothian Road, Edinburgh EH3 9AZ
0131-228 4181 Fax 0131-229 2734
49 High Holborn, London WC1V 6HB
(counter service only)
0171-873 0011 Fax 0171-831 1326
68-69 Bull Street, Birmingham B4 6AD
0121-236 9696 Fax 0121-236 9699
33 Wine Street, Bristol BS1 2BQ
0117 9264306 Fax 0117 9294515
9-21 Princess Street, Manchester M60 8AS
0161-834 7201 Fax 0161-833 0634
16 Arthur Street, Belfast BT1 4GD
01232 238451 Fax 01232 235401

HMSO publications are available from:

HMSO Publications Centre
(Mail, fax and telephone orders only)
PO Box 276, London SW8 5DT
Telephone orders 0171-873 9090
General enquiries 0171-873 0011
(queuing system in operation for both numbers)
Fax orders 0171-873 8200

HMSO's Accredited Agents
(see Yellow Pages)

and through good booksellers

Printed for HMSO Scotland by CCN° 20249 8c 3/95